Oh My Goddess!

ああっ女神さまっ

10

STORY AND ART BY
Kosuke Fujishima

TRANSLATION BY
Dana Lewis AND Toren Smith

LETTERING AND TOUCH-UP BY
Susie Lee AND Betty Dong
WITH Tom2K

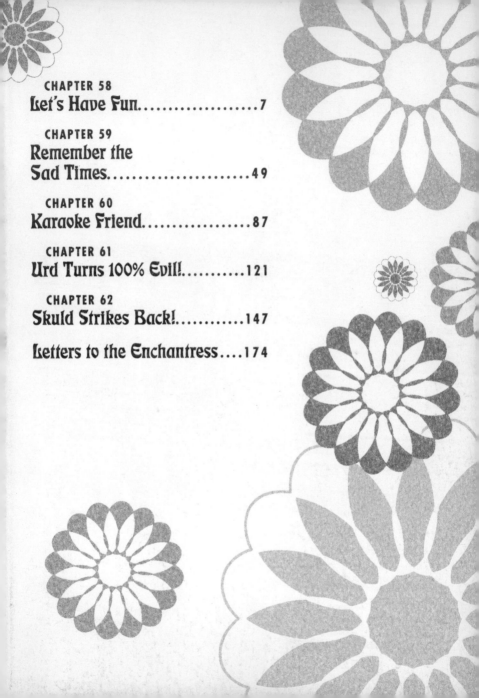

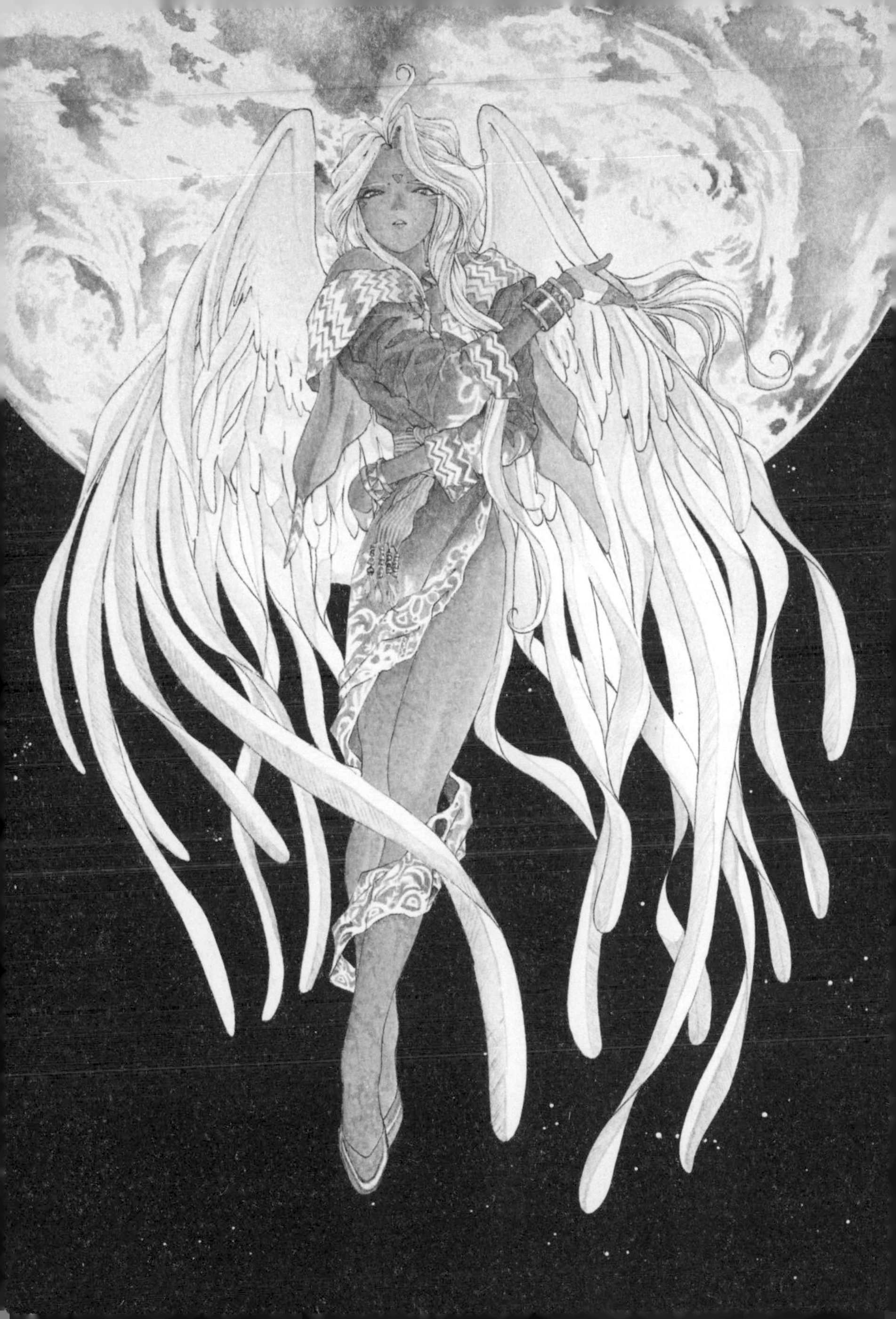

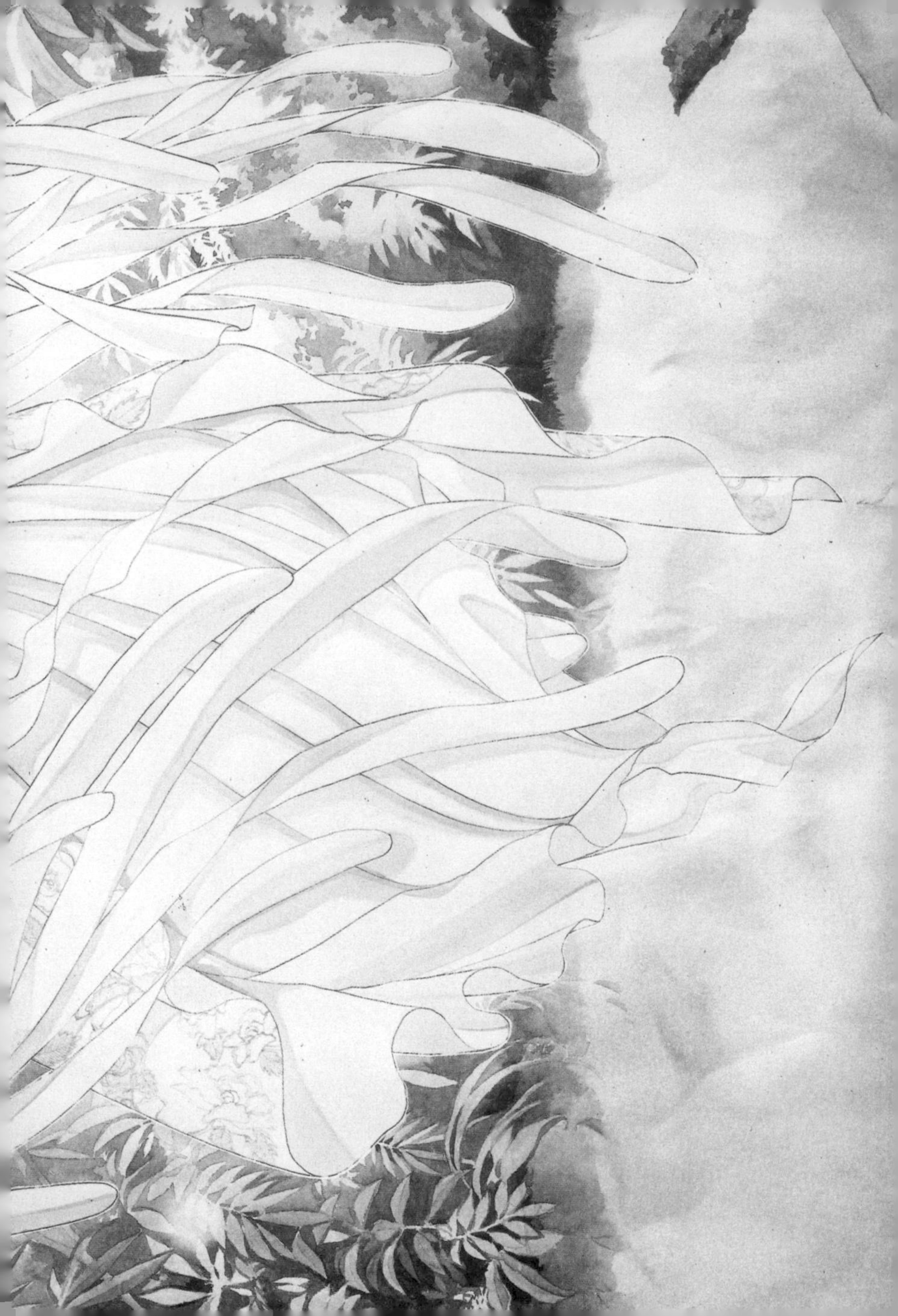

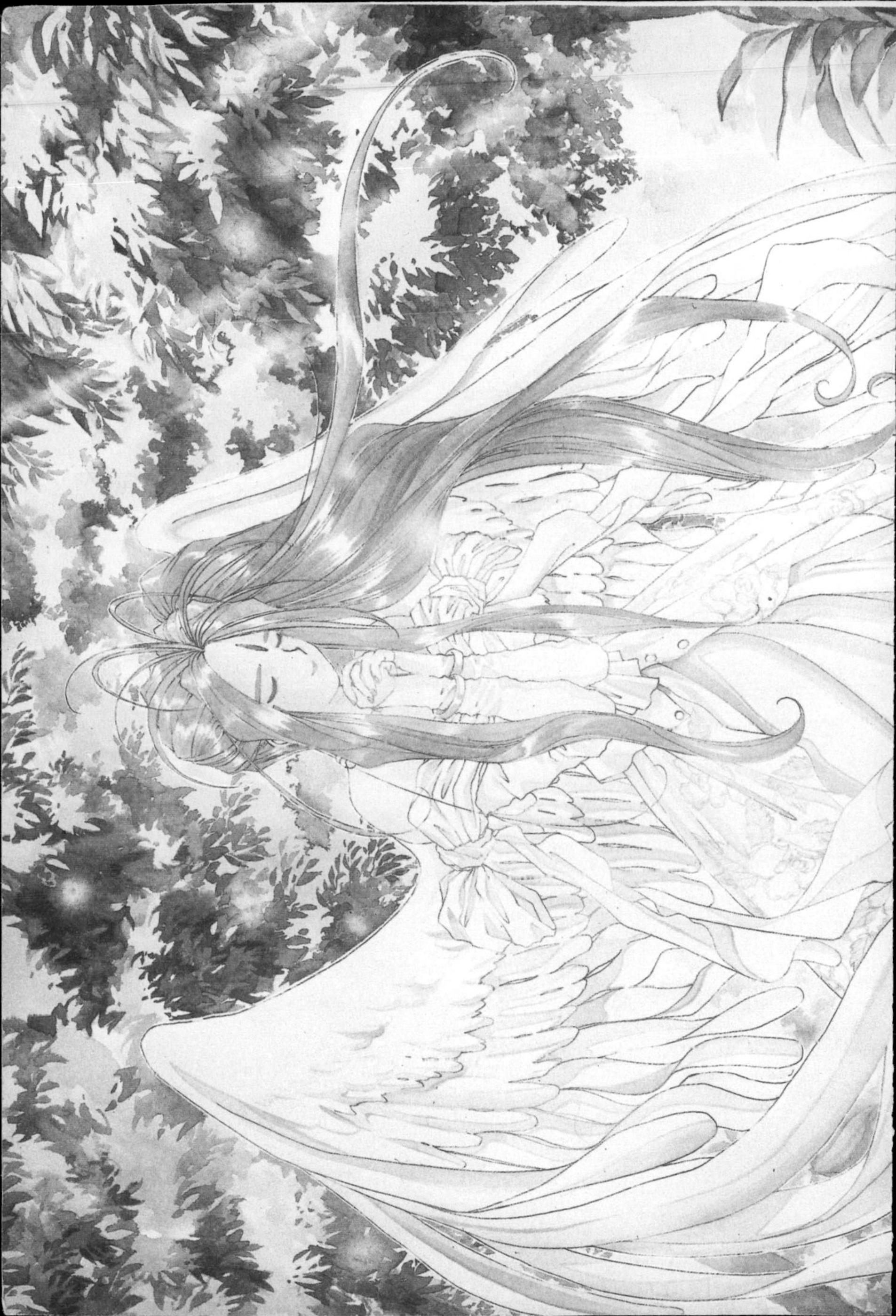

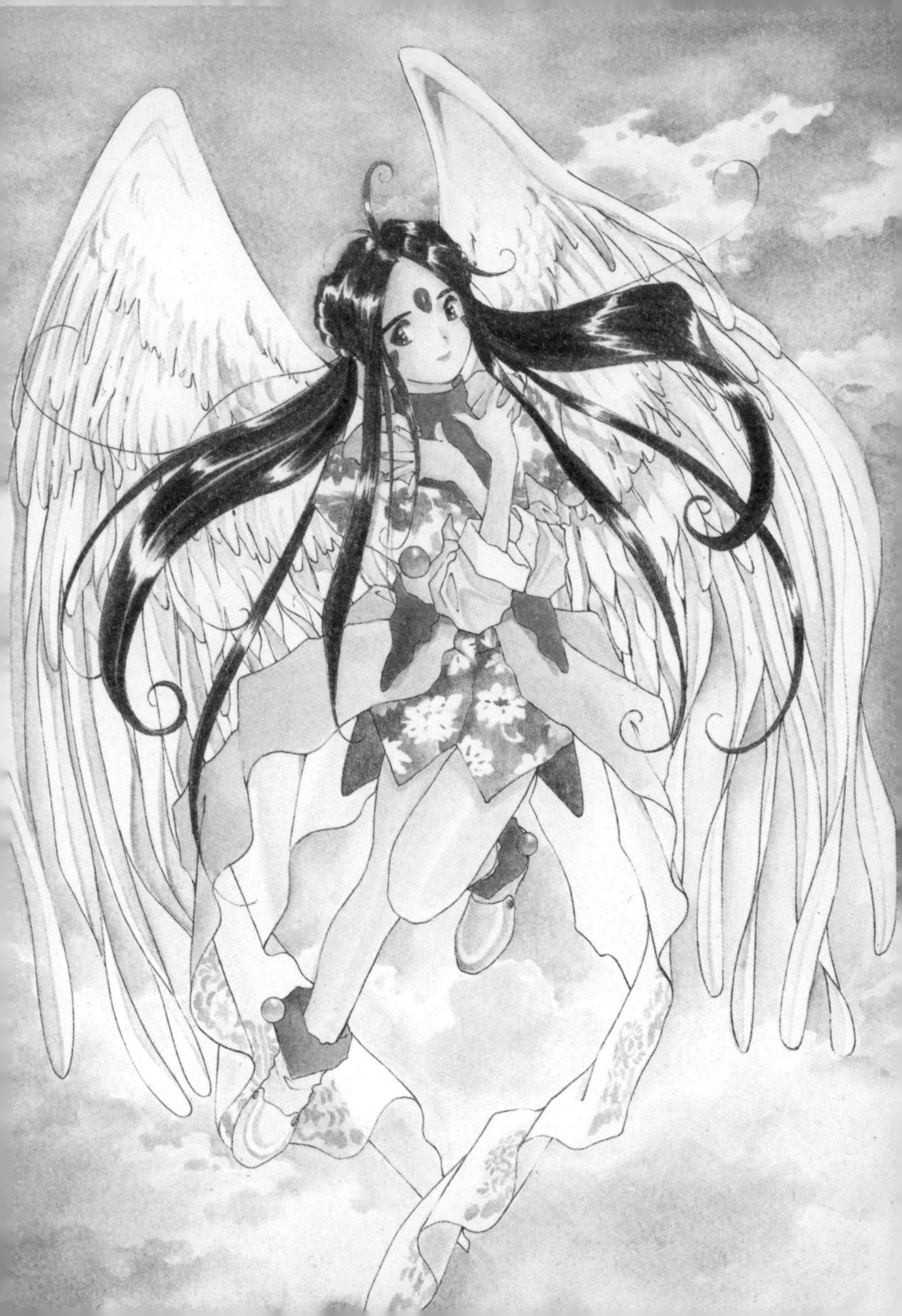

CHAPTER 58

Let's Have Fun

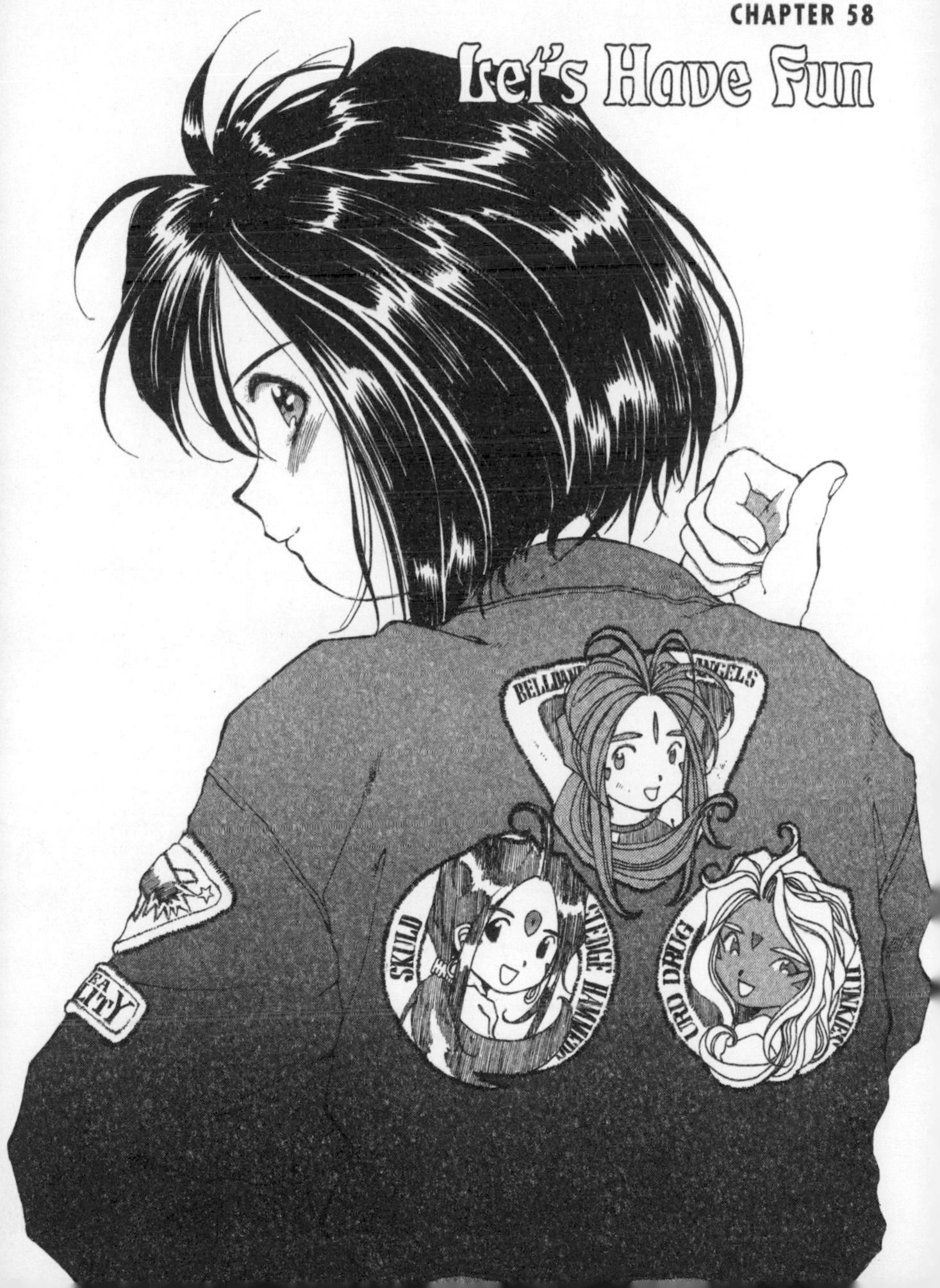
SKULD
URD DRUG

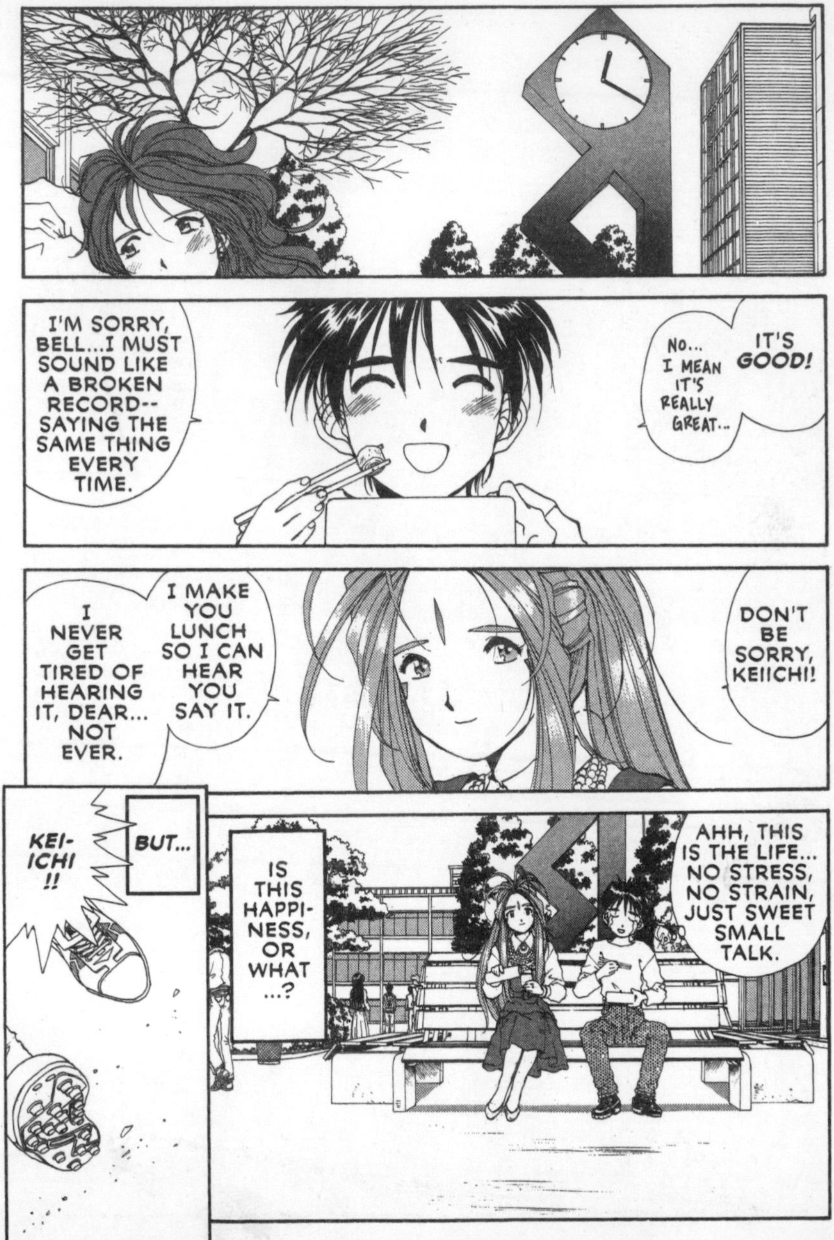
IT'S GOOD!
NO... I MEAN IT'S REALLY GREAT...
I'M SORRY, BELL...I MUST SOUND LIKE A BROKEN RECORD-- SAYING THE SAME THING EVERY TIME.
DON'T BE SORRY, KEIICHI!
I MAKE YOU LUNCH SO I CAN HEAR YOU SAY IT.
I NEVER GET TIRED OF HEARING IT, DEAR... NOT EVER.
AHH, THIS IS THE LIFE... NO STRESS, NO STRAIN, JUST SWEET SMALL TALK.
IS THIS HAPPINESS, OR WHAT ...?
BUT...
KEI-ICHI !!

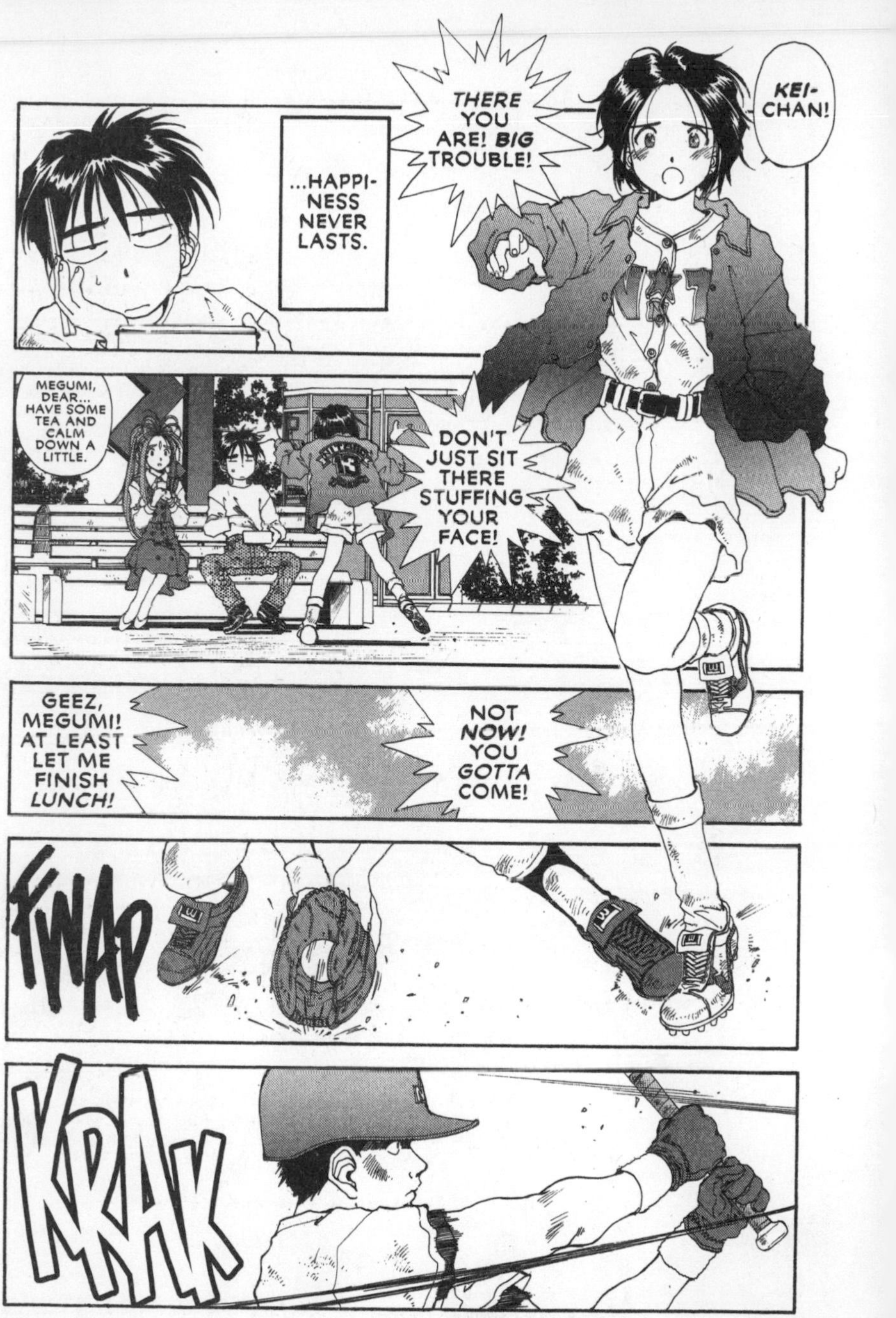
KEI-CHAN!
THERE YOU ARE! BIG TROUBLE!
...HAPPINESS NEVER LASTS.
DON'T JUST SIT THERE STUFFING YOUR FACE!
MEGUMI, DEAR... HAVE SOME TEA AND CALM DOWN A LITTLE.
NOT NOW! YOU GOTTA COME!
GEEZ, MEGUMI! AT LEAST LET ME FINISH LUNCH!
FWAP
KRAK

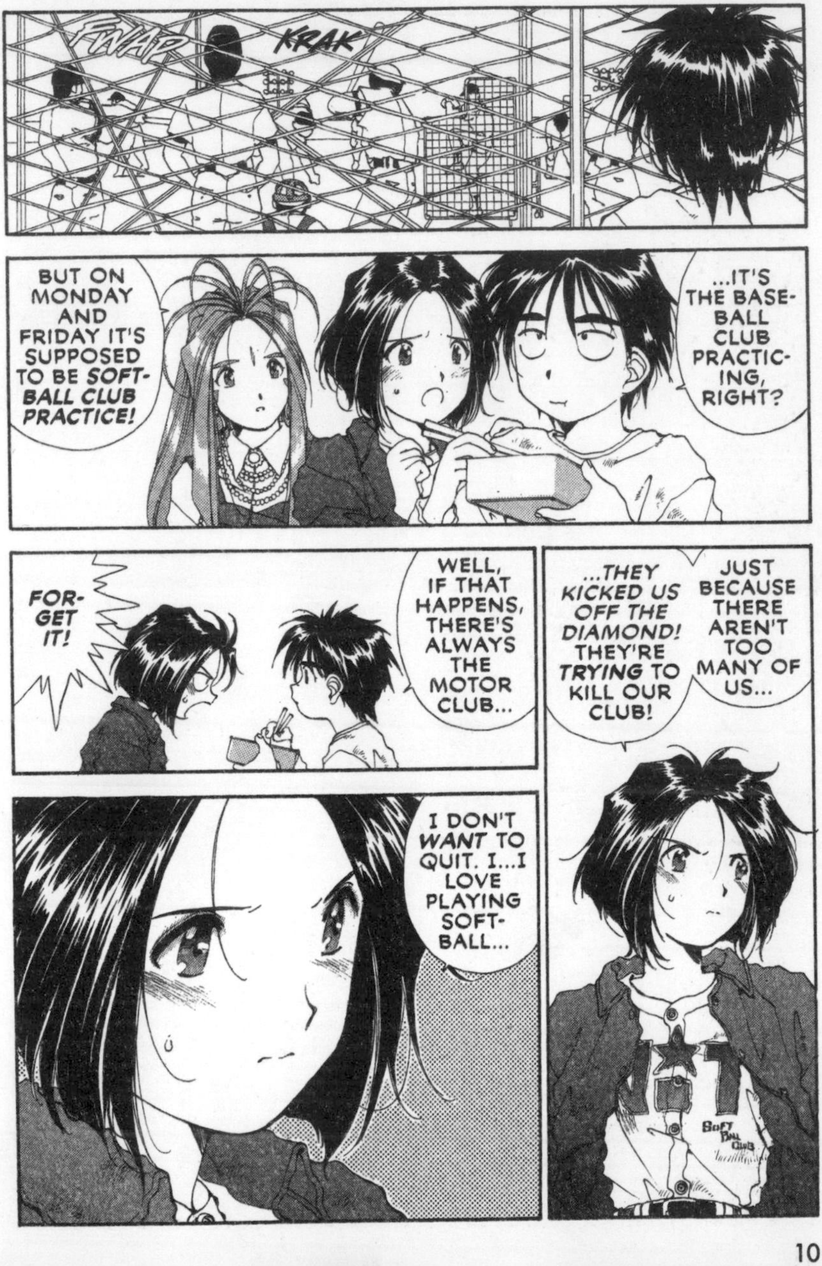
KRAK
FWAP
...IT'S THE BASEBALL CLUB PRACTICING, RIGHT?
BUT ON MONDAY AND FRIDAY IT'S SUPPOSED TO BE *SOFTBALL CLUB PRACTICE!*
JUST BECAUSE THERE AREN'T TOO MANY OF US...
...*THEY KICKED US OFF THE DIAMOND!* THEY'RE *TRYING* TO KILL OUR CLUB!
WELL, IF THAT HAPPENS, THERE'S ALWAYS THE MOTOR CLUB...
FORGET IT!
I DON'T *WANT* TO QUIT. I...I LOVE PLAYING SOFTBALL...

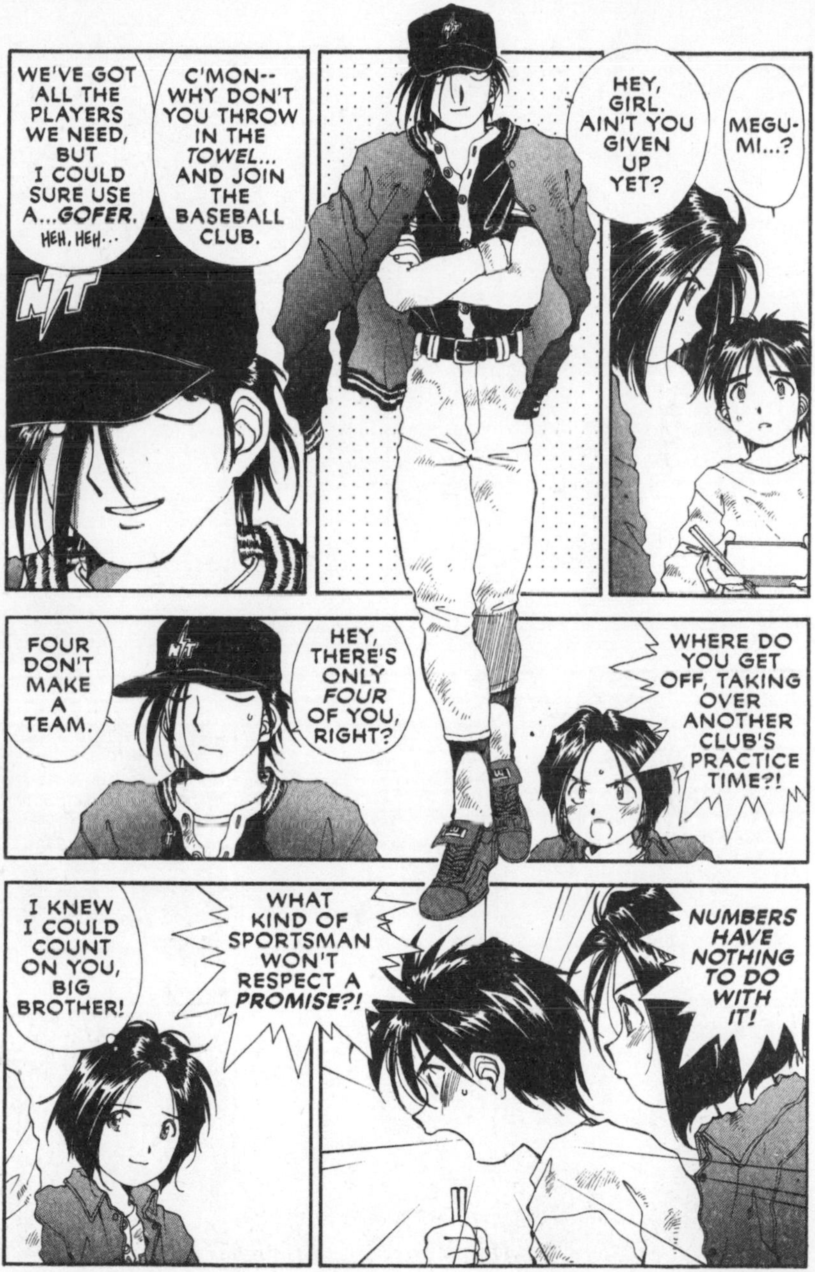
HEY, GIRL. AIN'T YOU GIVEN UP YET?
MEGU-MI...?
C'MON-- WHY DON'T YOU THROW IN THE *TOWEL*... AND JOIN THE BASEBALL CLUB.
WE'VE GOT ALL THE PLAYERS WE NEED, BUT I COULD SURE USE A...*GOFER*.
HEH, HEH...
WHERE DO YOU GET OFF, TAKING OVER ANOTHER CLUB'S PRACTICE TIME?!
HEY, THERE'S ONLY *FOUR* OF YOU, RIGHT?
FOUR DON'T MAKE A TEAM.
NUMBERS HAVE NOTHING TO DO WITH IT!
WHAT KIND OF SPORTSMAN WON'T RESPECT A *PROMISE?!*
I KNEW I COULD COUNT ON YOU, BIG BROTHER!

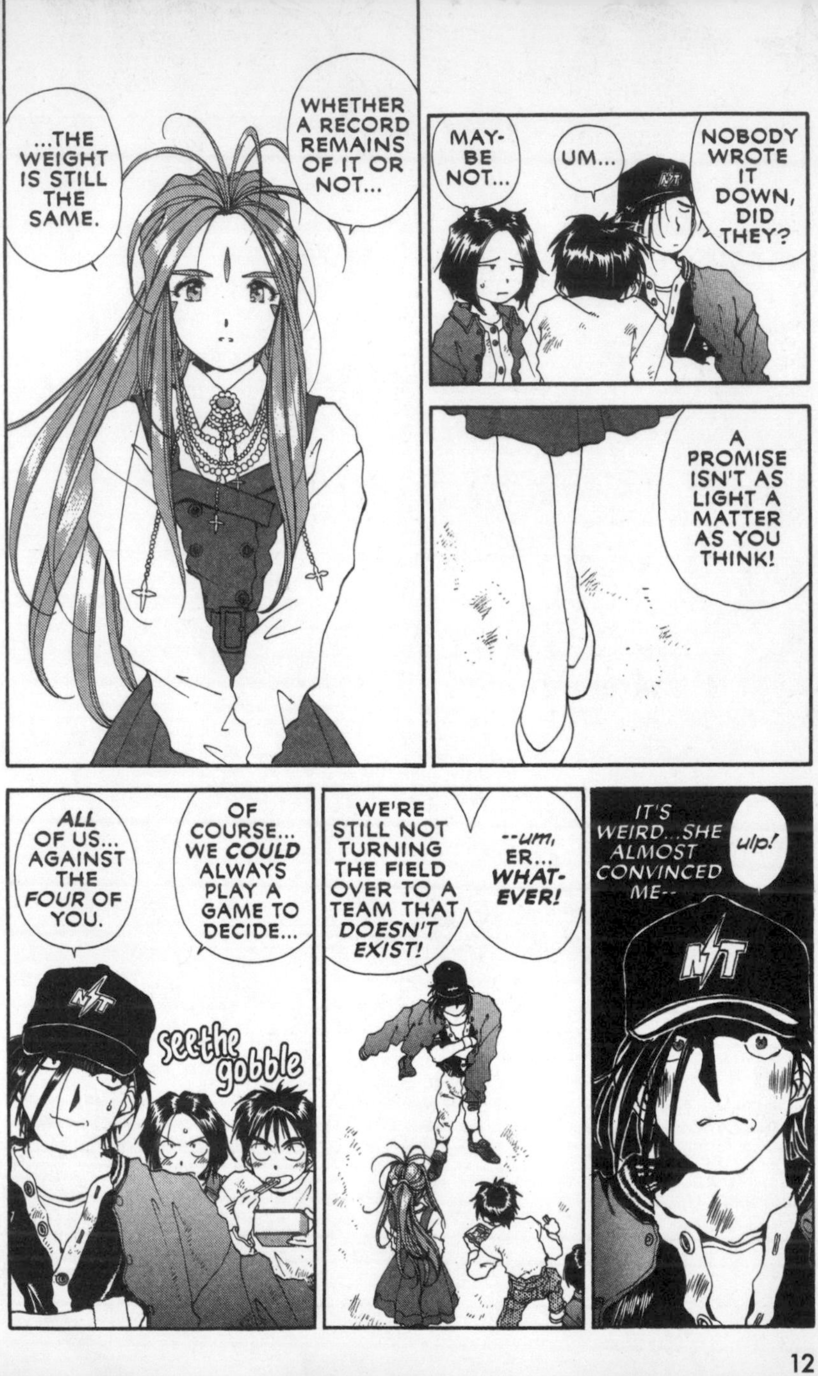
NOBODY WROTE IT DOWN, DID THEY?
UM...
MAY-BE NOT...
A PROMISE ISN'T AS LIGHT A MATTER AS YOU THINK!
WHETHER A RECORD REMAINS OF IT OR NOT...
...THE WEIGHT IS STILL THE SAME.
ulp!
IT'S WEIRD...SHE ALMOST CONVINCED ME--
WE'RE STILL NOT TURNING THE FIELD OVER TO A TEAM THAT DOESN'T EXIST!
--um, ER... WHAT-EVER!
OF COURSE... WE COULD ALWAYS PLAY A GAME TO DECIDE...
ALL OF US... AGAINST THE FOUR OF YOU.
seethe
gobble

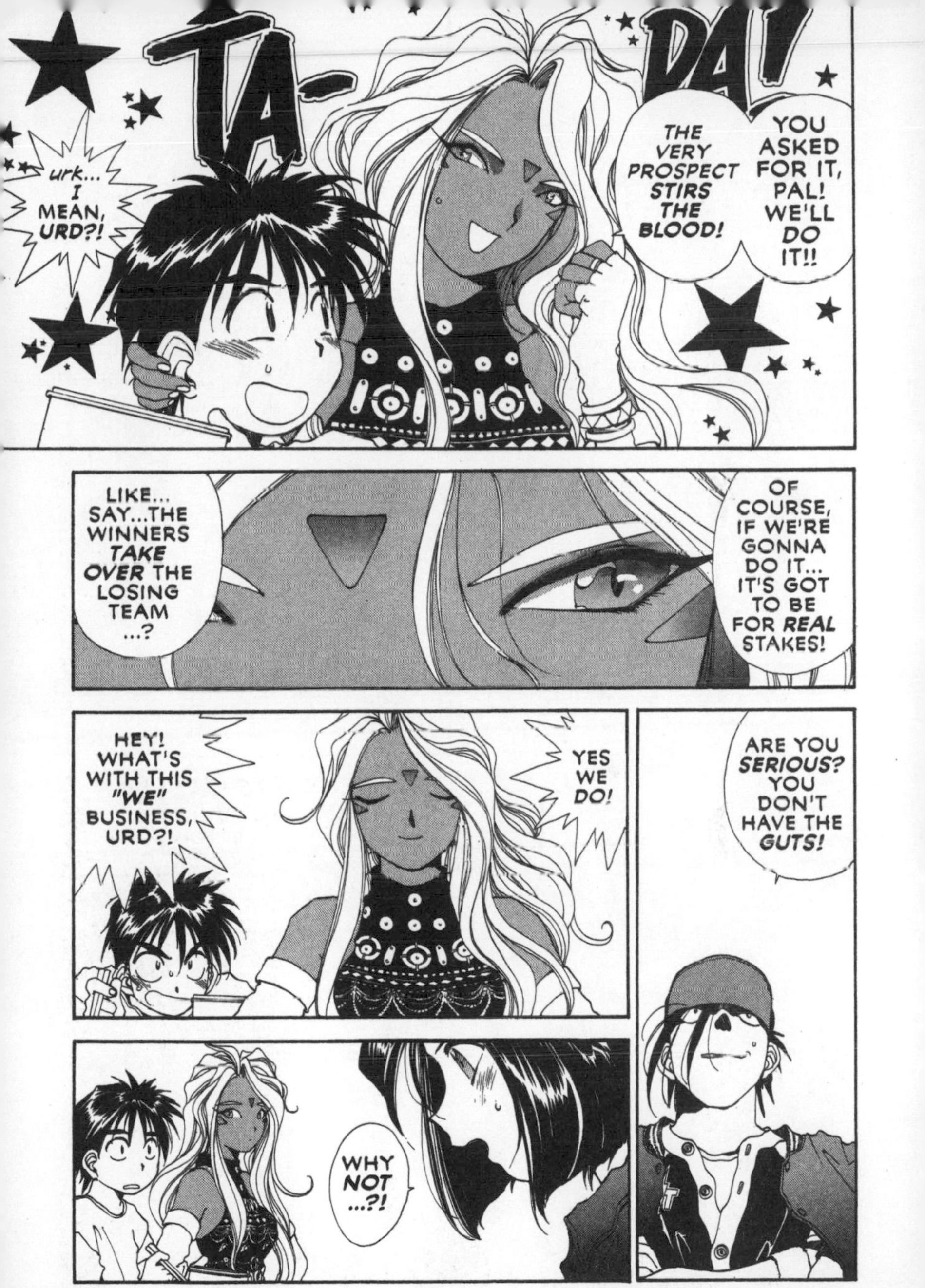
TA-DA!
YOU ASKED FOR IT, PAL! WE'LL DO IT!!
THE VERY PROSPECT STIRS THE BLOOD!
urk... I MEAN, URD?!
OF COURSE, IF WE'RE GONNA DO IT... IT'S GOT TO BE FOR REAL STAKES!
LIKE... SAY...THE WINNERS TAKE OVER THE LOSING TEAM ...?
ARE YOU SERIOUS? YOU DON'T HAVE THE GUTS!
YES WE DO!
HEY! WHAT'S WITH THIS "WE" BUSINESS, URD?!
WHY NOT ...?!

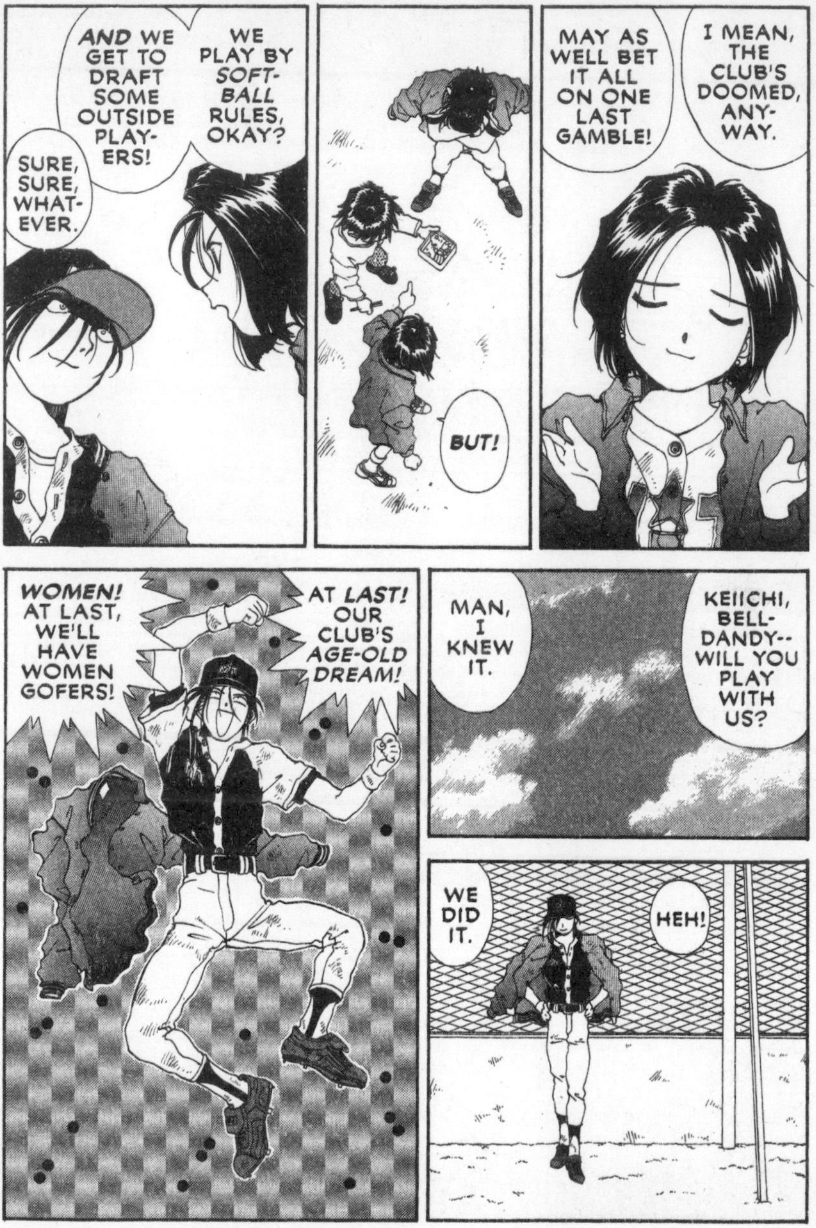
I MEAN, THE CLUB'S DOOMED, ANYWAY.
MAY AS WELL BET IT ALL ON ONE LAST GAMBLE!
BUT!
WE PLAY BY SOFTBALL RULES, OKAY?
AND WE GET TO DRAFT SOME OUTSIDE PLAYERS!
SURE, SURE, WHATEVER.
KEIICHI, BELLDANDY-- WILL YOU PLAY WITH US?
MAN, I KNEW IT.
HEH!
WE DID IT.
AT LAST! OUR CLUB'S AGE-OLD DREAM!
WOMEN! AT LAST, WE'LL HAVE WOMEN GOFERS!

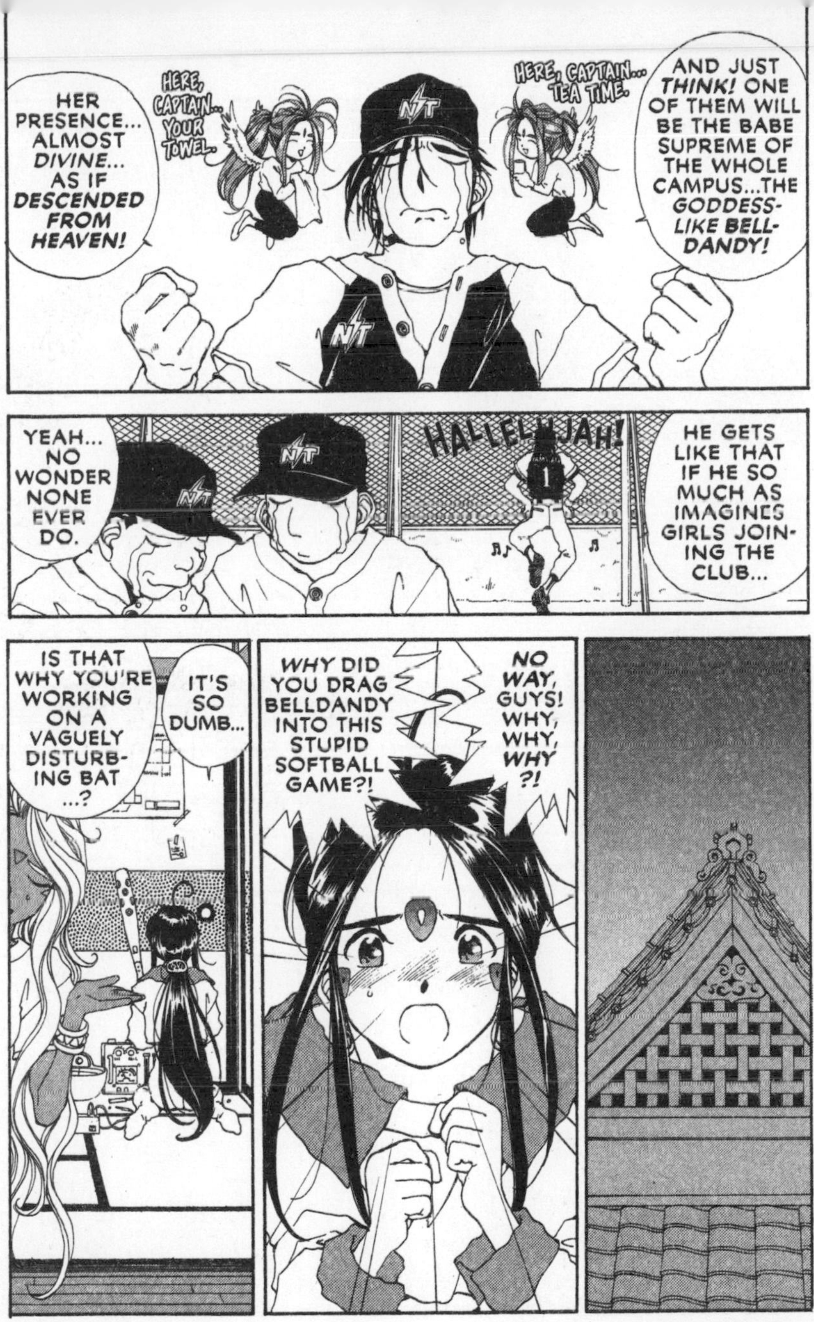
AND JUST THINK! ONE OF THEM WILL BE THE BABE SUPREME OF THE WHOLE CAMPUS...THE GODDESS-LIKE BELL-DANDY!
HERE, CAPTAIN... TEA TIME.
HERE, CAPTAIN... YOUR TOWEL.
HER PRESENCE... ALMOST DIVINE... AS IF DESCENDED FROM HEAVEN!
HE GETS LIKE THAT IF HE SO MUCH AS IMAGINES GIRLS JOIN-ING THE CLUB...
HALLELUJAH!
YEAH... NO WONDER NONE EVER DO.
NO WAY, GUYS! WHY, WHY, WHY?!
WHY DID YOU DRAG BELLDANDY INTO THIS STUPID SOFTBALL GAME?!
IT'S SO DUMB...
IS THAT WHY YOU'RE WORKING ON A VAGUELY DISTURB-ING BAT ...?

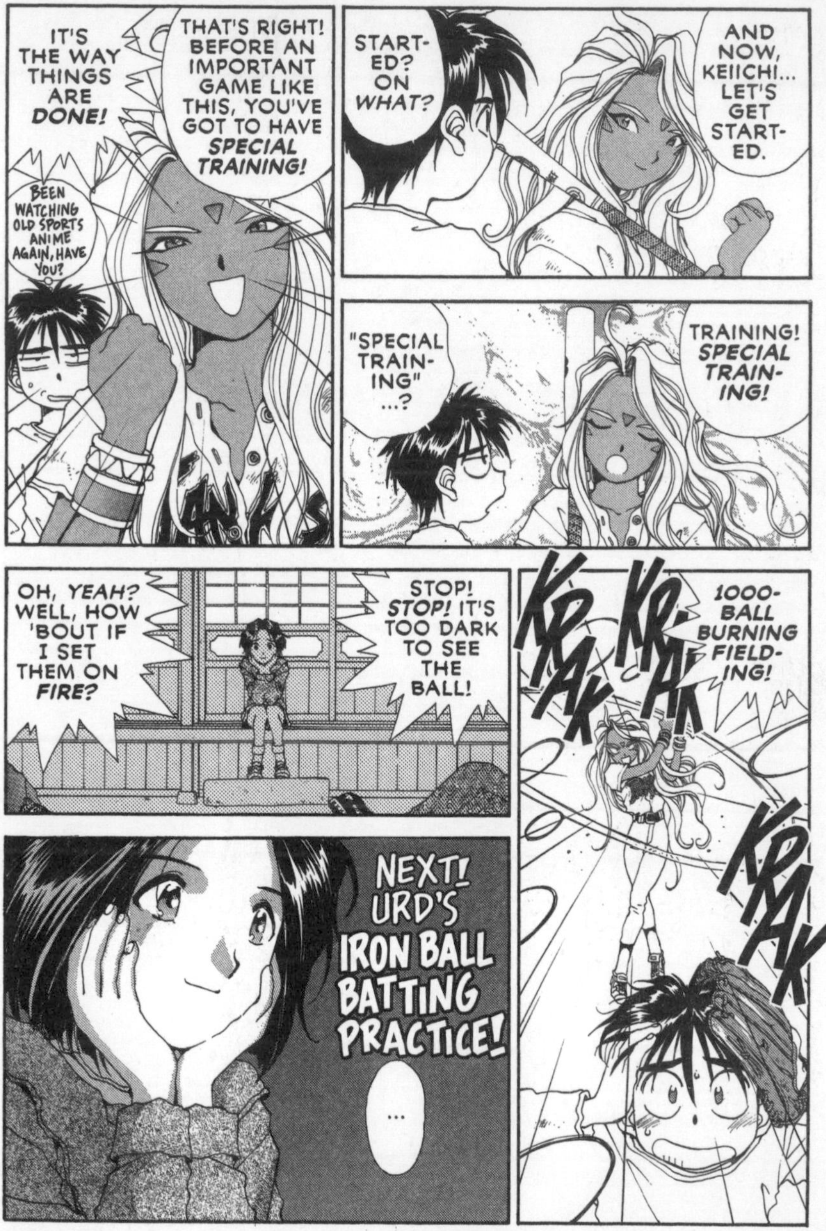
AND NOW, KEIICHI... LET'S GET STARTED.
STARTED? ON WHAT?
TRAINING! SPECIAL TRAINING!
"SPECIAL TRAINING" ...?
THAT'S RIGHT! BEFORE AN IMPORTANT GAME LIKE THIS, YOU'VE GOT TO HAVE SPECIAL TRAINING!
IT'S THE WAY THINGS ARE DONE!
BEEN WATCHING OLD SPORTS ANIME AGAIN, HAVE YOU?
1000-BALL BURNING FIELDING!
KRAK
KRAK
KRAK
STOP! STOP! IT'S TOO DARK TO SEE THE BALL!
OH, YEAH? WELL, HOW 'BOUT IF I SET THEM ON FIRE?
NEXT! URD'S IRON BALL BATTING PRACTICE!
...

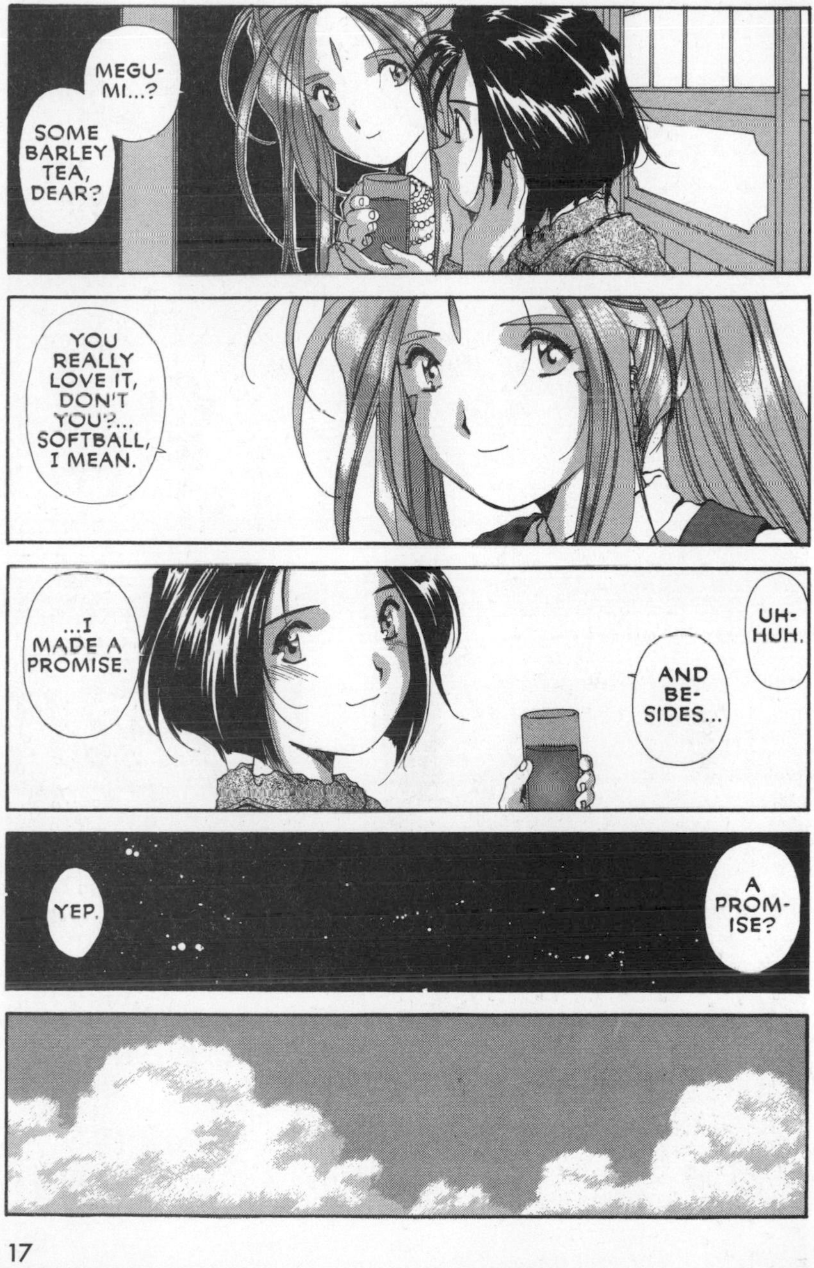
MEGU-MI...?
SOME BARLEY TEA, DEAR?
YOU REALLY LOVE IT, DON'T YOU?... SOFTBALL, I MEAN.
UH-HUH.
AND BE-SIDES...
...I MADE A PROMISE.
A PROM-ISE?
YEP.

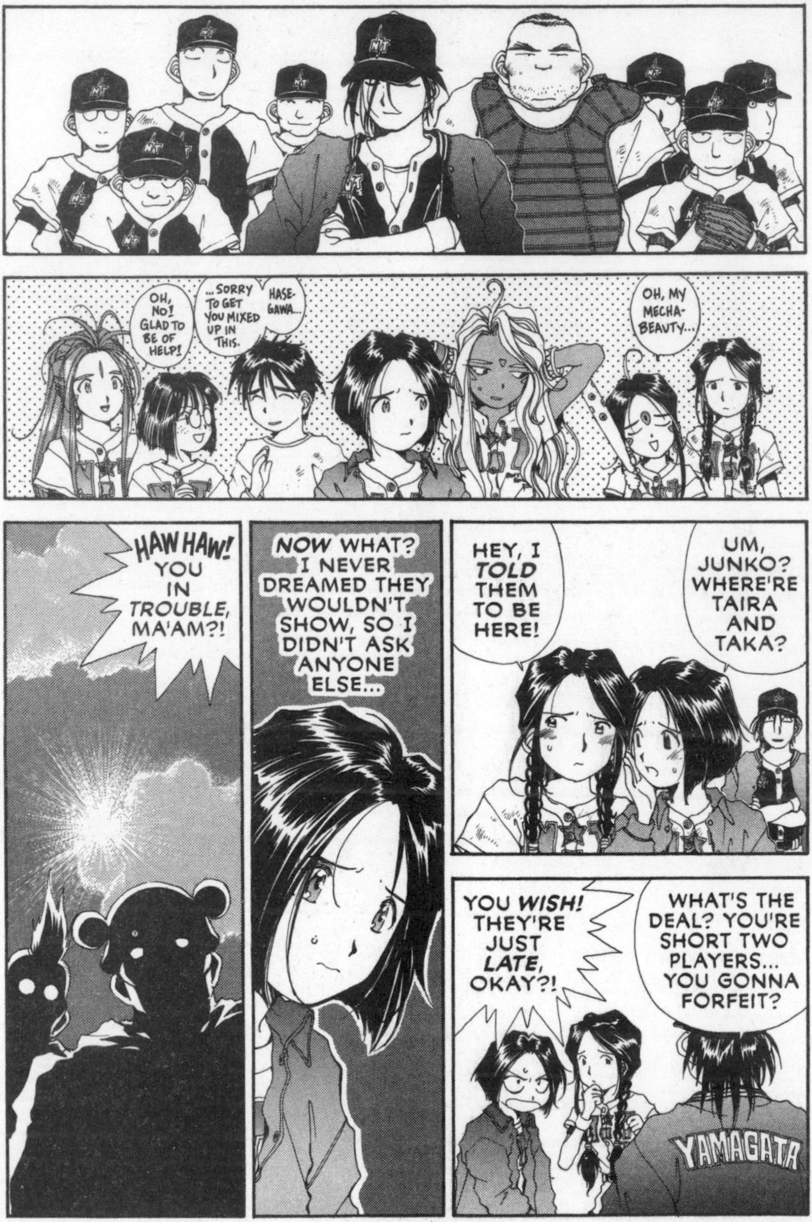
OH, MY MECHA-BEAUTY...
HASE-GAWA...
...SORRY TO GET YOU MIXED UP IN THIS.
OH, NO! GLAD TO BE OF HELP!
UM, JUNKO? WHERE'RE TAIRA AND TAKA?
HEY, I TOLD THEM TO BE HERE!
WHAT'S THE DEAL? YOU'RE SHORT TWO PLAYERS... YOU GONNA FORFEIT?
YOU WISH! THEY'RE JUST LATE, OKAY?!
YAMAGATA
NOW WHAT? I NEVER DREAMED THEY WOULDN'T SHOW, SO I DIDN'T ASK ANYONE ELSE...
HAW HAW! YOU IN TROUBLE, MA'AM?!

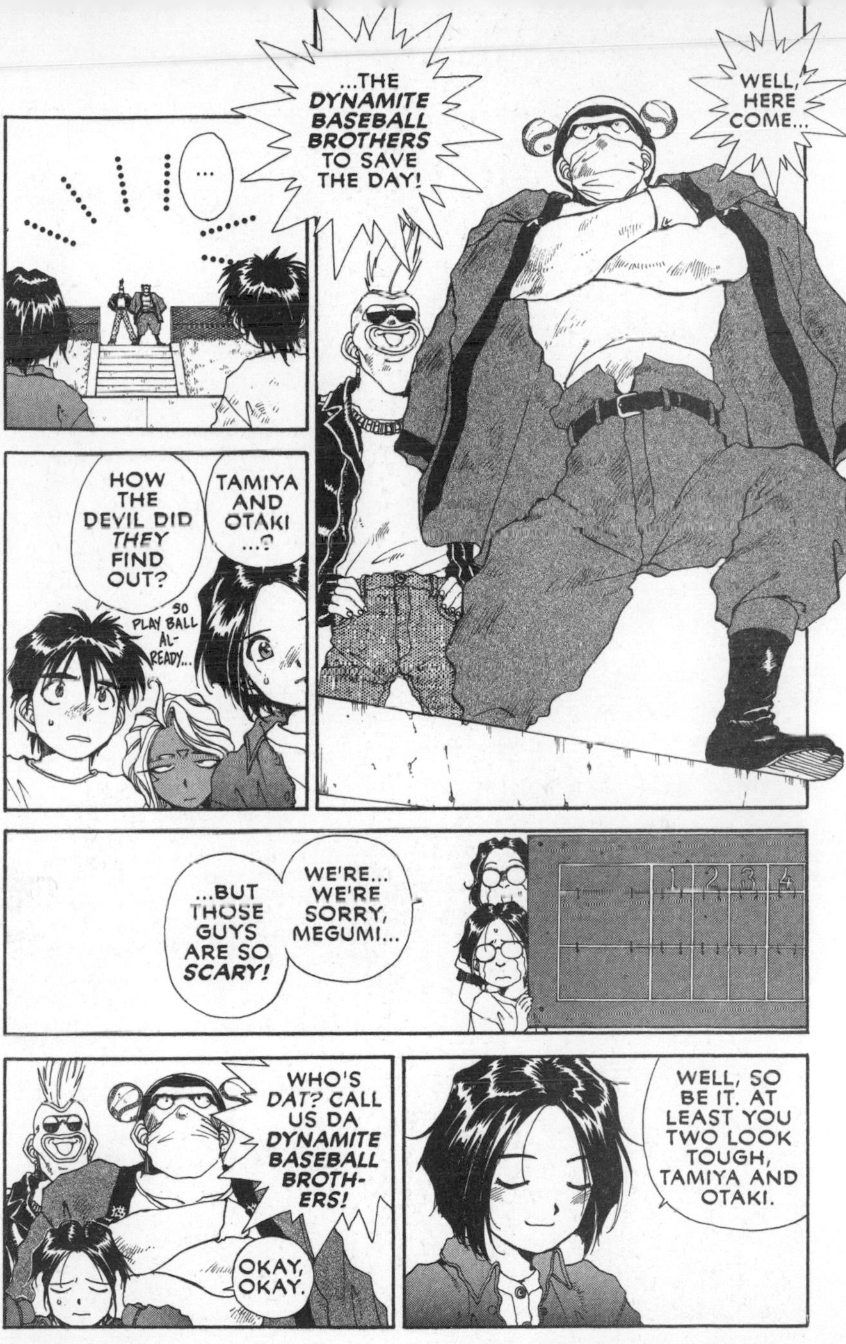
WELL, HERE COME...
...THE *DYNAMITE BASEBALL BROTHERS* TO SAVE THE DAY!
...
TAMIYA AND OTAKI ...?
HOW THE DEVIL DID *THEY* FIND OUT?
SO PLAY BALL AL-READY...
1 2 3 4
WE'RE... WE'RE SORRY, MEGUMI...
...BUT THOSE GUYS ARE SO *SCARY!*
WELL, SO BE IT. AT LEAST YOU TWO LOOK TOUGH, TAMIYA AND OTAKI.
WHO'S *DAT?* CALL US DA *DYNAMITE BASEBALL BROTH-ERS!*
OKAY, OKAY.

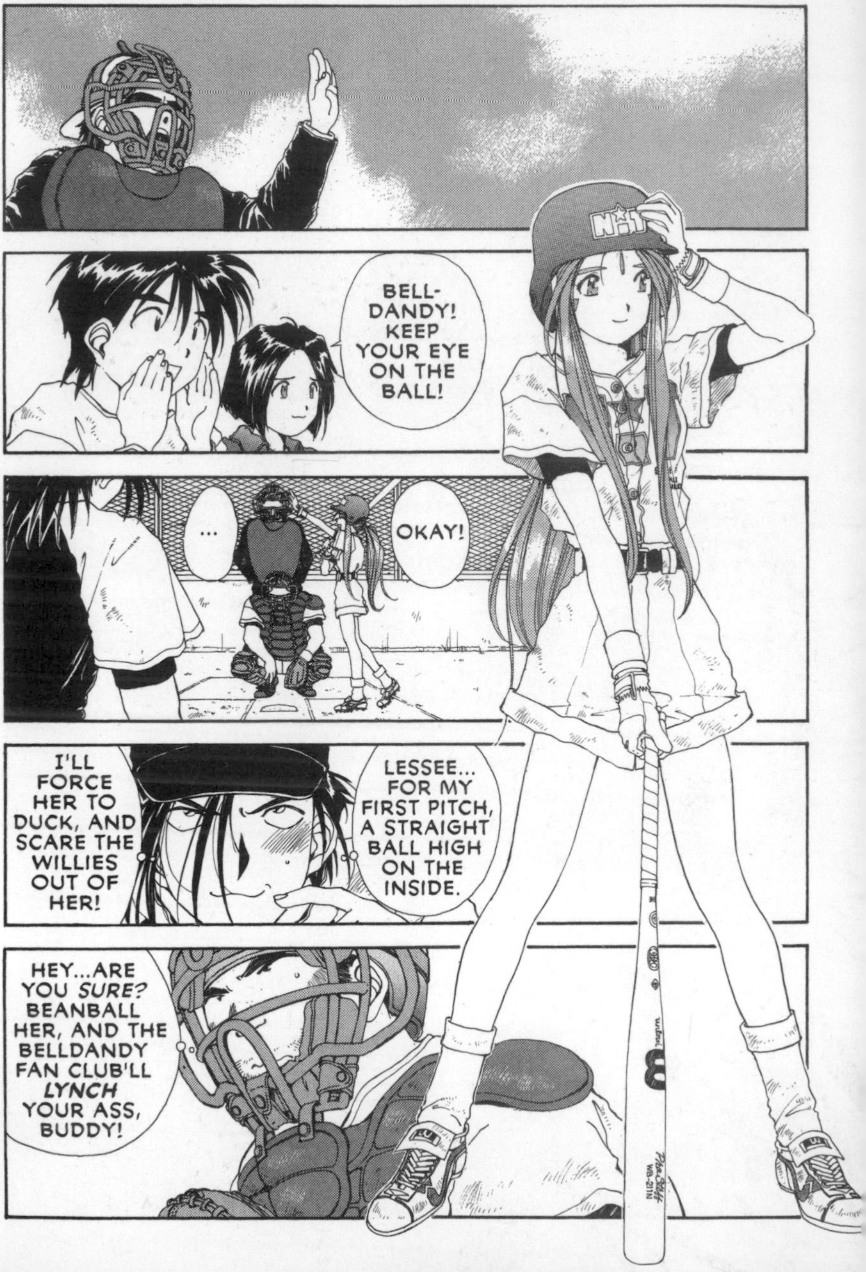
BELL-DANDY! KEEP YOUR EYE ON THE BALL!
OKAY!
...
LESSEE... FOR MY FIRST PITCH, A STRAIGHT BALL HIGH ON THE INSIDE.
I'LL FORCE HER TO DUCK, AND SCARE THE WILLIES OUT OF HER!
HEY...ARE YOU *SURE?* BEANBALL HER, AND THE BELLDANDY FAN CLUB'LL *LYNCH* YOUR ASS, BUDDY!

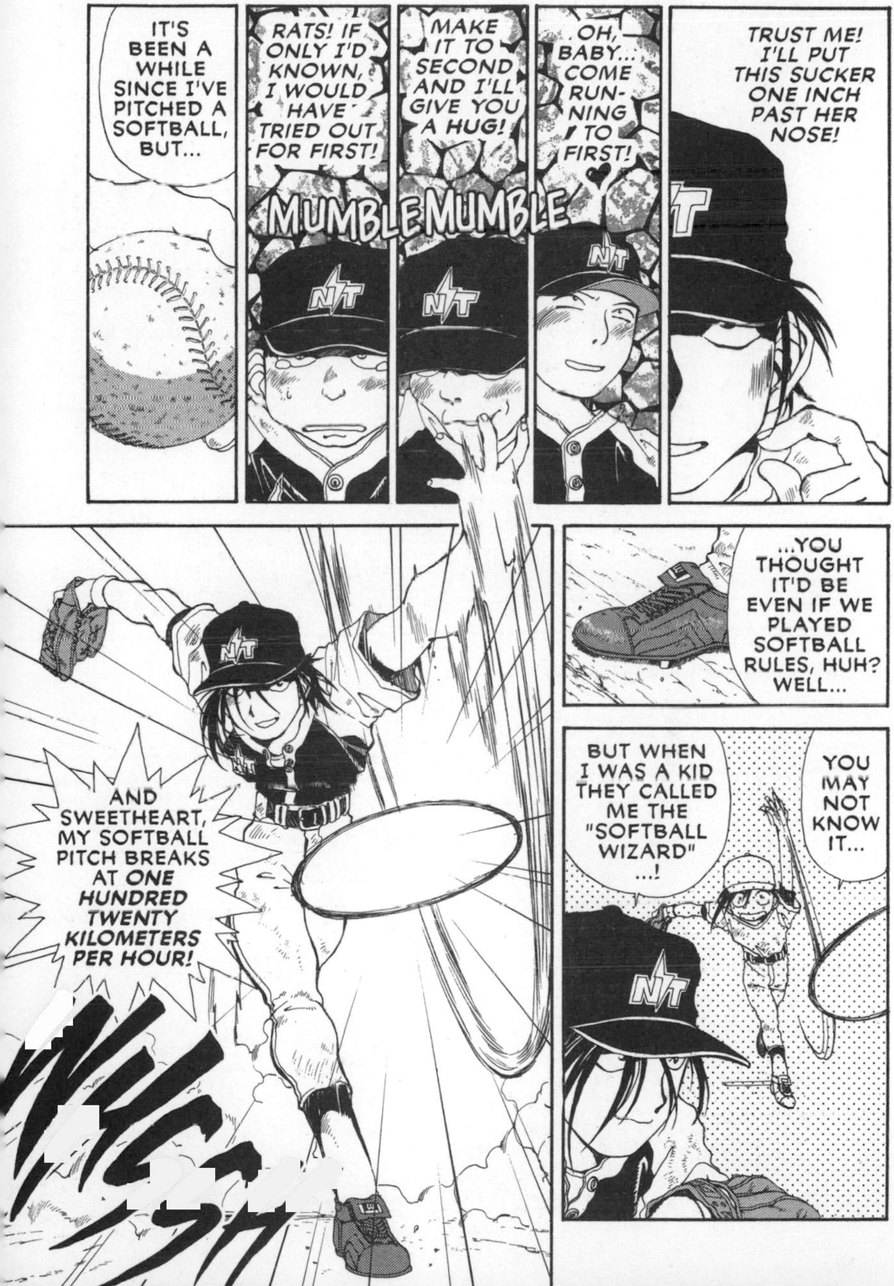
TRUST ME! I'LL PUT THIS SUCKER ONE INCH PAST HER NOSE!
OH, BABY... COME RUN-NING TO FIRST!
MAKE IT TO SECOND AND I'LL GIVE YOU A HUG!
RATS! IF ONLY I'D KNOWN, I WOULD HAVE TRIED OUT FOR FIRST!
MUMBLE MUMBLE
IT'S BEEN A WHILE SINCE I'VE PITCHED A SOFTBALL, BUT...
...YOU THOUGHT IT'D BE EVEN IF WE PLAYED SOFTBALL RULES, HUH? WELL...
YOU MAY NOT KNOW IT...
BUT WHEN I WAS A KID THEY CALLED ME THE "SOFTBALL WIZARD" ...!
AND SWEETHEART, MY SOFTBALL PITCH BREAKS AT ONE HUNDRED TWENTY KILOMETERS PER HOUR!

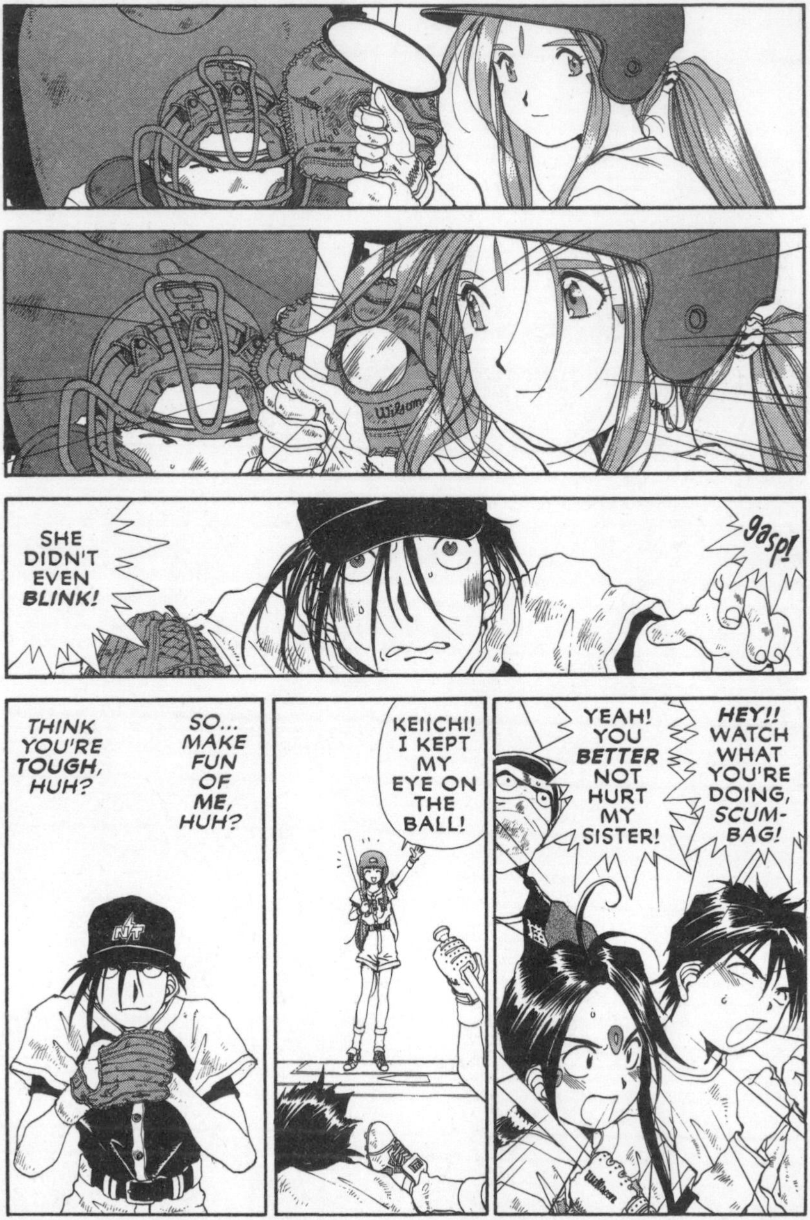
gasp!
SHE DIDN'T EVEN BLINK!
HEY!! WATCH WHAT YOU'RE DOING, SCUM-BAG!
YEAH! YOU BETTER NOT HURT MY SISTER!
KEIICHI! I KEPT MY EYE ON THE BALL!
SO... MAKE FUN OF ME, HUH?
THINK YOU'RE TOUGH, HUH?

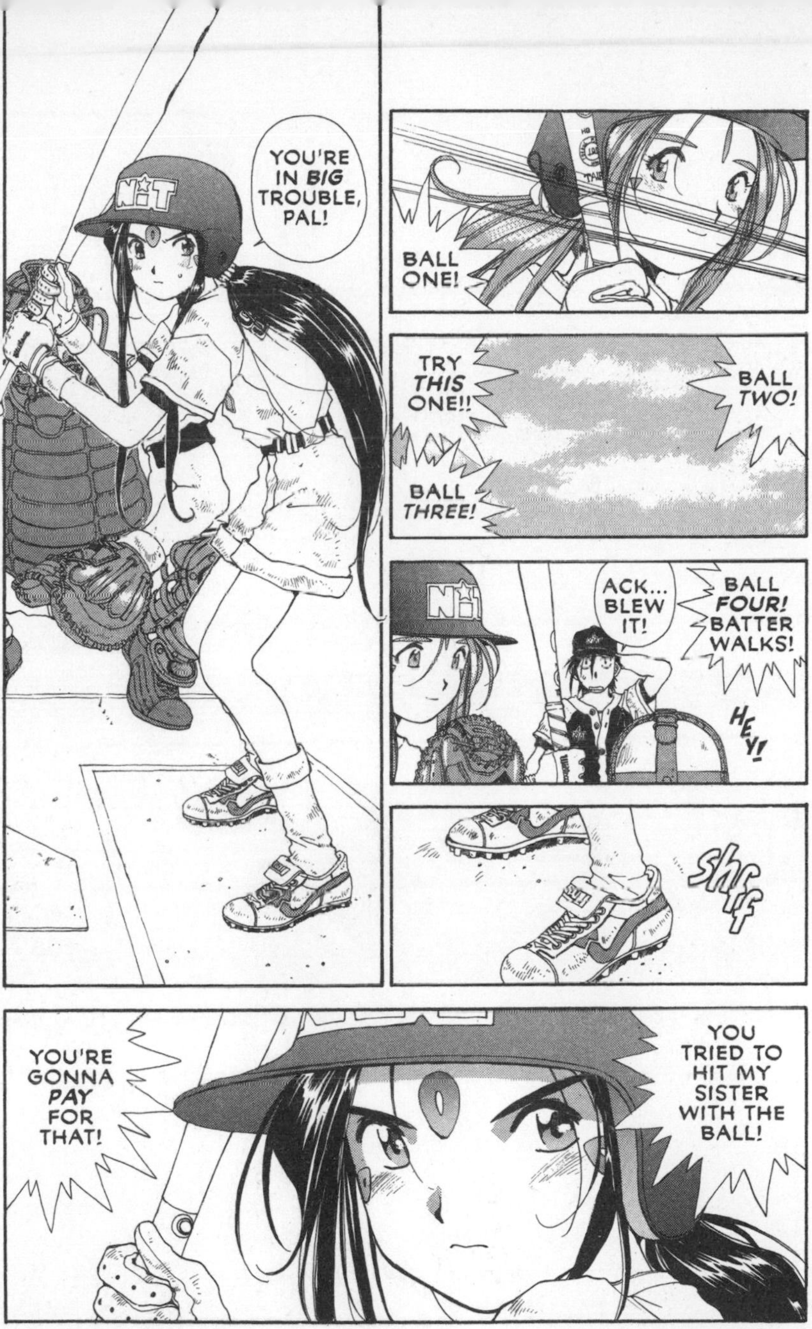
BALL ONE!
BALL TWO!
TRY THIS ONE!!
BALL THREE!
BALL FOUR! BATTER WALKS!
ACK... BLEW IT!
HEY!
SHFF
YOU'RE IN BIG TROUBLE, PAL!
YOU TRIED TO HIT MY SISTER WITH THE BALL!
YOU'RE GONNA PAY FOR THAT!

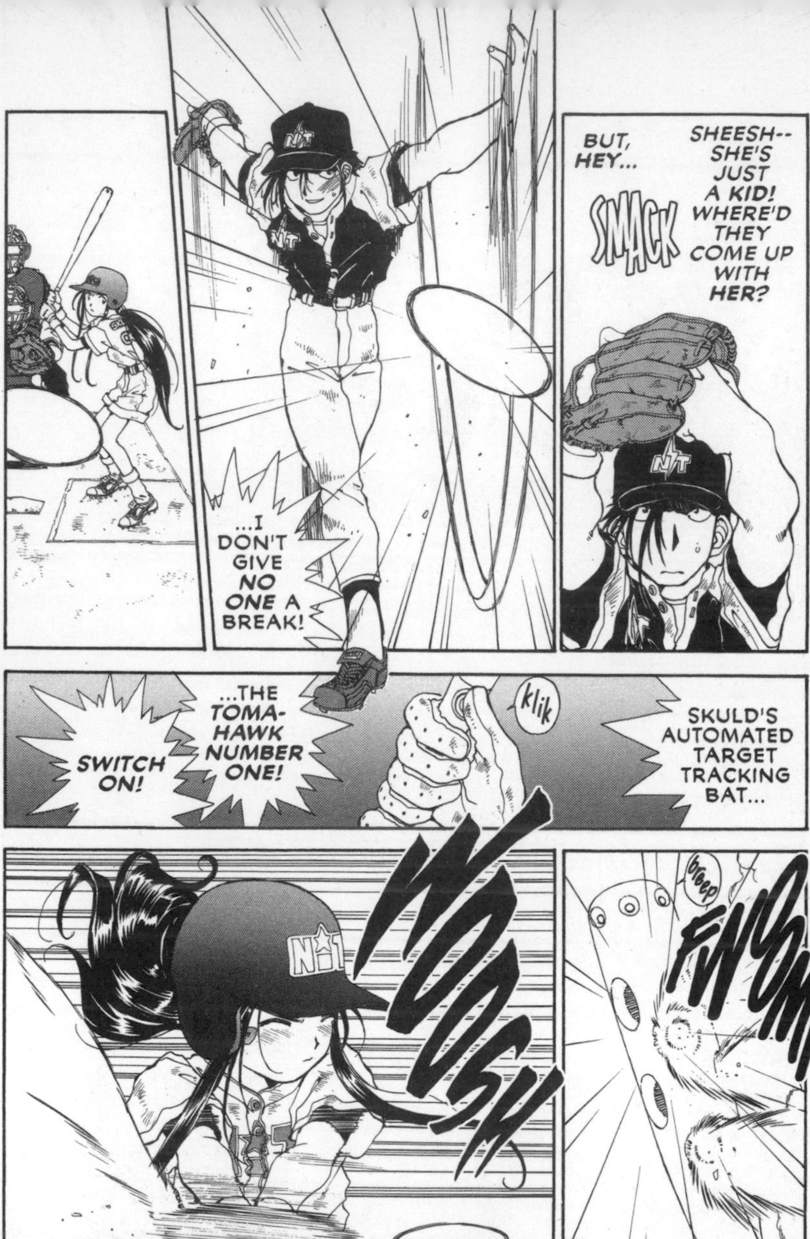
SHEESH-- SHE'S JUST A KID! WHERE'D THEY COME UP WITH HER?
SMACK
BUT, HEY...
...I DON'T GIVE NO ONE A BREAK!
SKULD'S AUTOMATED TARGET TRACKING BAT...
klik
...THE TOMA-HAWK NUMBER ONE!
SWITCH ON!
breep
FWOMP
WOOSH

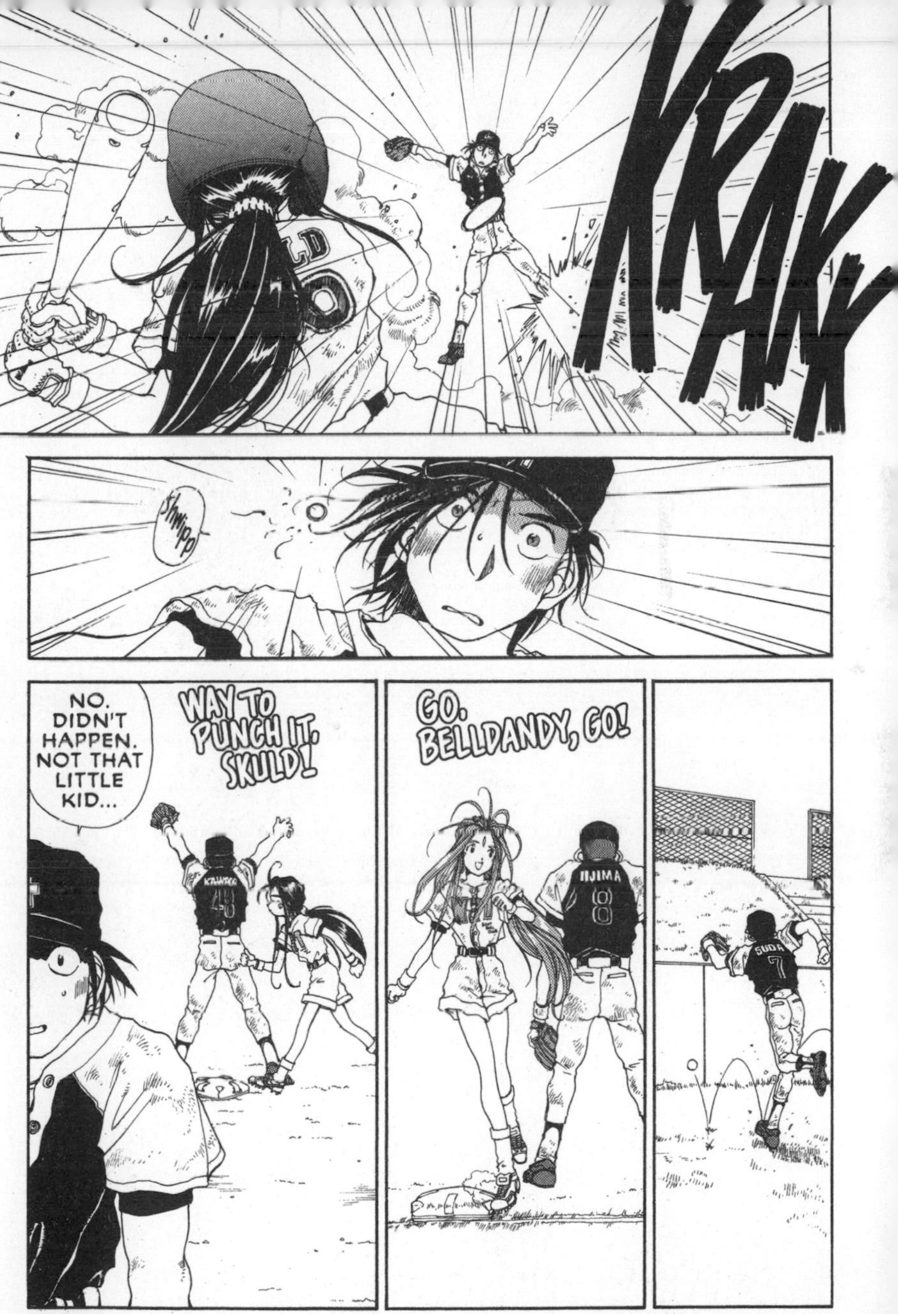
KRAK
shwipp
SUDA
7
GO, BELLDANDY, GO!
IIJIMA
8
WAY TO PUNCH IT, SKULD!
NO. DIDN'T HAPPEN. NOT THAT LITTLE KID...

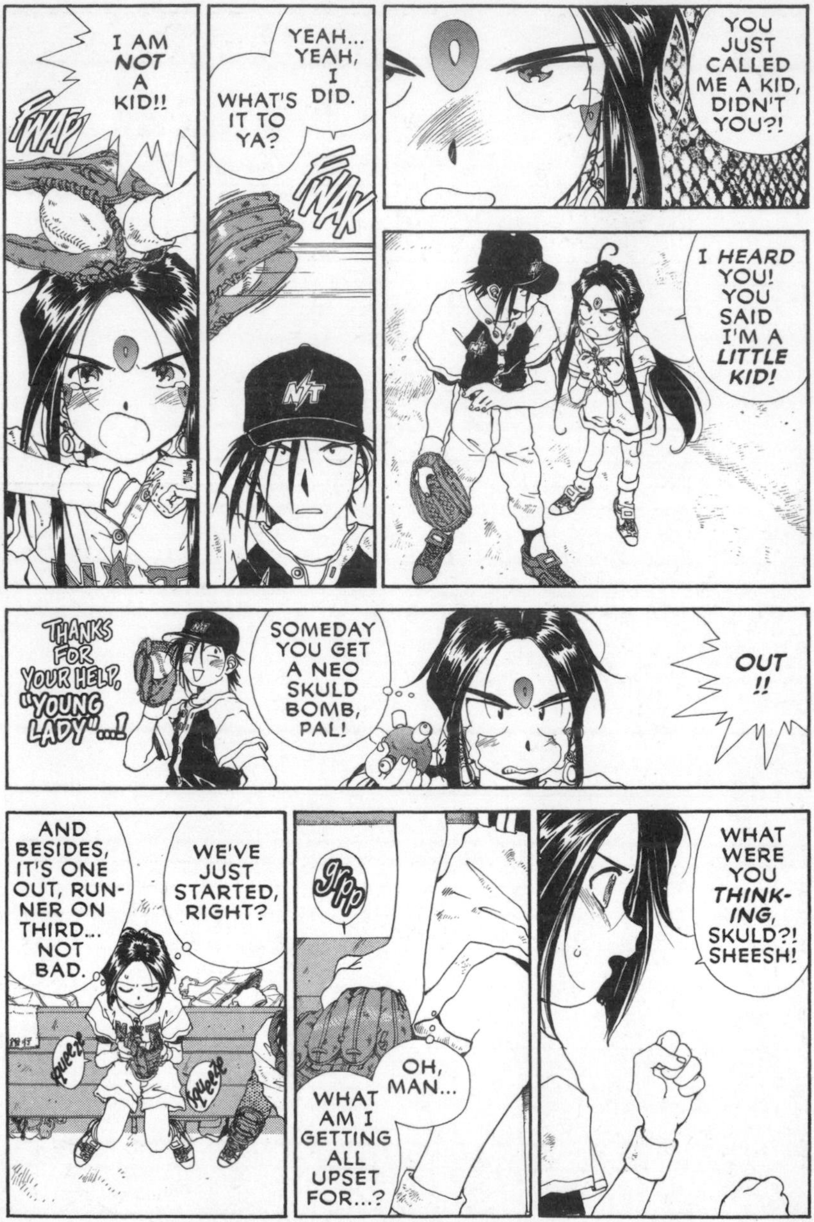
YOU JUST CALLED ME A KID, DIDN'T YOU?!
I HEARD YOU! YOU SAID I'M A LITTLE KID!
YEAH... YEAH, I DID.
WHAT'S IT TO YA?
FWAK
I AM NOT A KID!!
FWAP!
OUT!!
SOMEDAY YOU GET A NEO SKULD BOMB, PAL!
THANKS FOR YOUR HELP, "YOUNG LADY"...!
WHAT WERE YOU THINKING, SKULD?! SHEESH!
grpp
OH, MAN...
WHAT AM I GETTING ALL UPSET FOR...?
WE'VE JUST STARTED, RIGHT?
AND BESIDES, IT'S ONE OUT, RUNNER ON THIRD... NOT BAD.

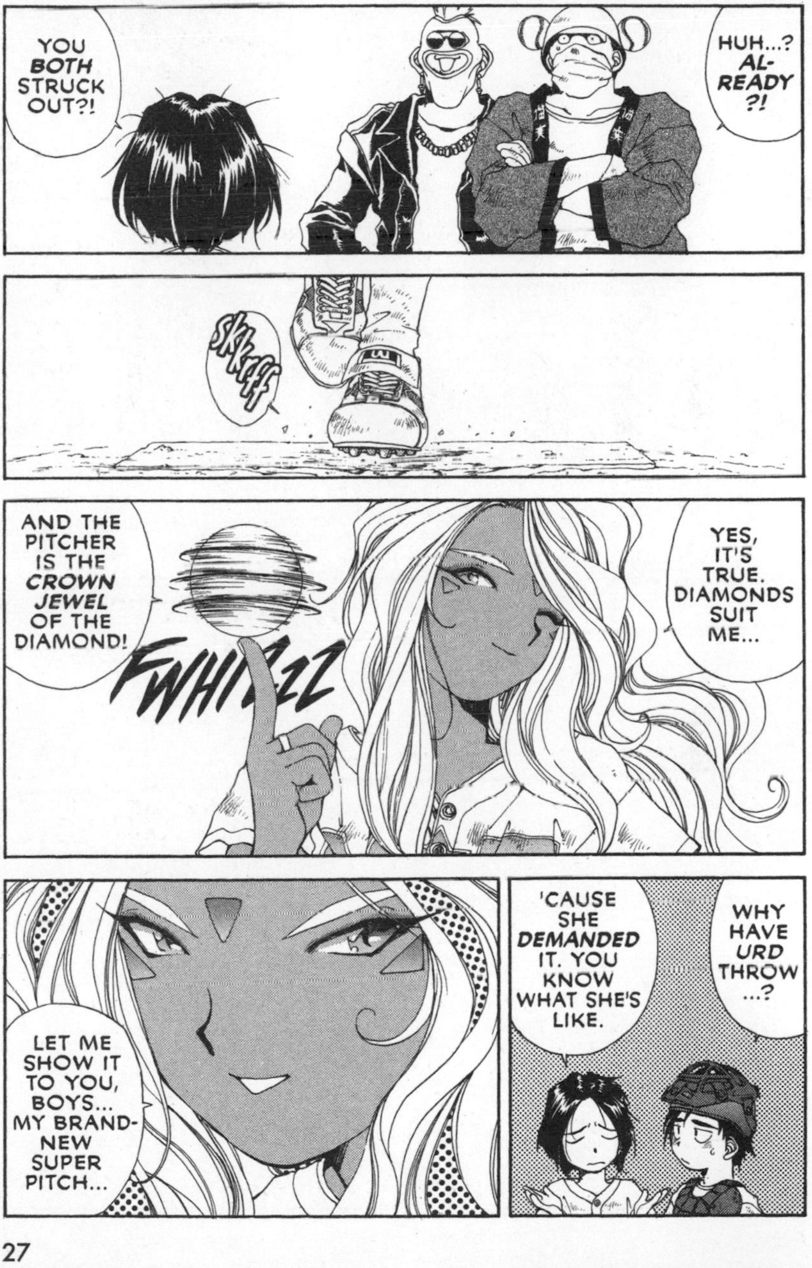
HUH...? AL-READY?!
YOU BOTH STRUCK OUT?!
SKKRFF
YES, IT'S TRUE. DIAMONDS SUIT ME...
AND THE PITCHER IS THE CROWN JEWEL OF THE DIAMOND!
FWHIZZZ
WHY HAVE URD THROW...?
'CAUSE SHE DEMANDED IT. YOU KNOW WHAT SHE'S LIKE.
LET ME SHOW IT TO YOU, BOYS... MY BRAND-NEW SUPER PITCH...

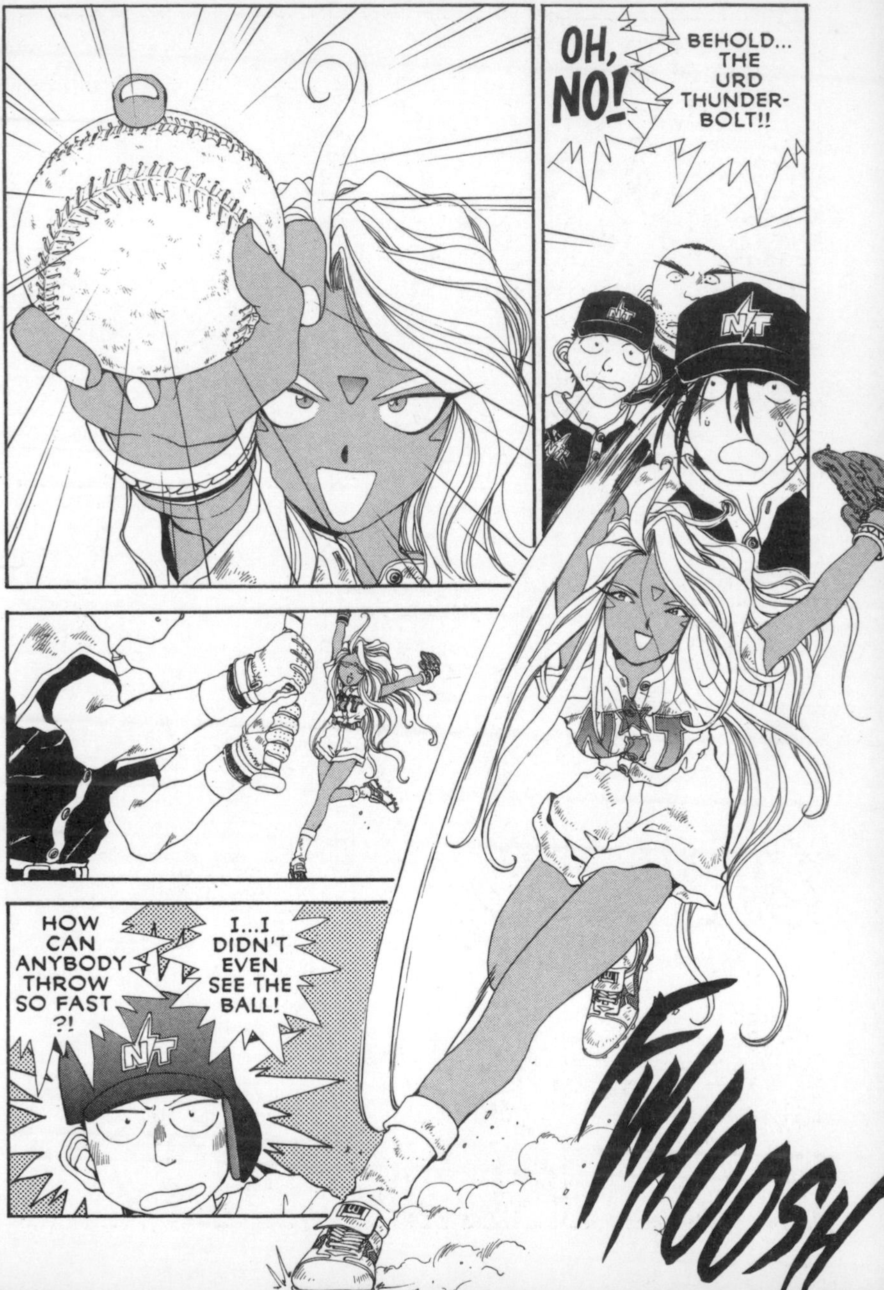
OH, NO!
BEHOLD... THE URD THUNDER-BOLT!!
WHOOSH
I...I DIDN'T EVEN SEE THE BALL!
HOW CAN ANYBODY THROW SO FAST?!

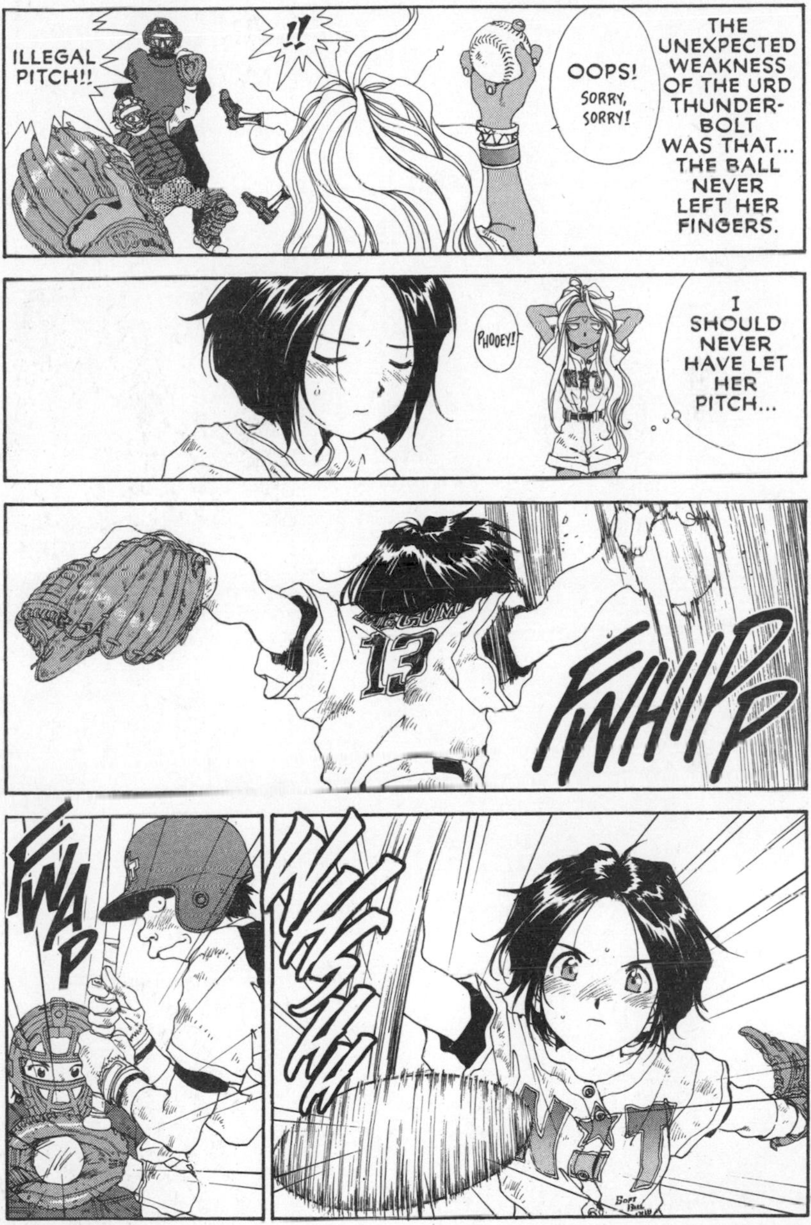
THE UNEXPECTED WEAKNESS OF THE URD THUNDERBOLT WAS THAT... THE BALL NEVER LEFT HER FINGERS.
OOPS!
SORRY, SORRY!
!!
ILLEGAL PITCH!!
I SHOULD NEVER HAVE LET HER PITCH...
PHOOEY!
FWHIPP
FWAP

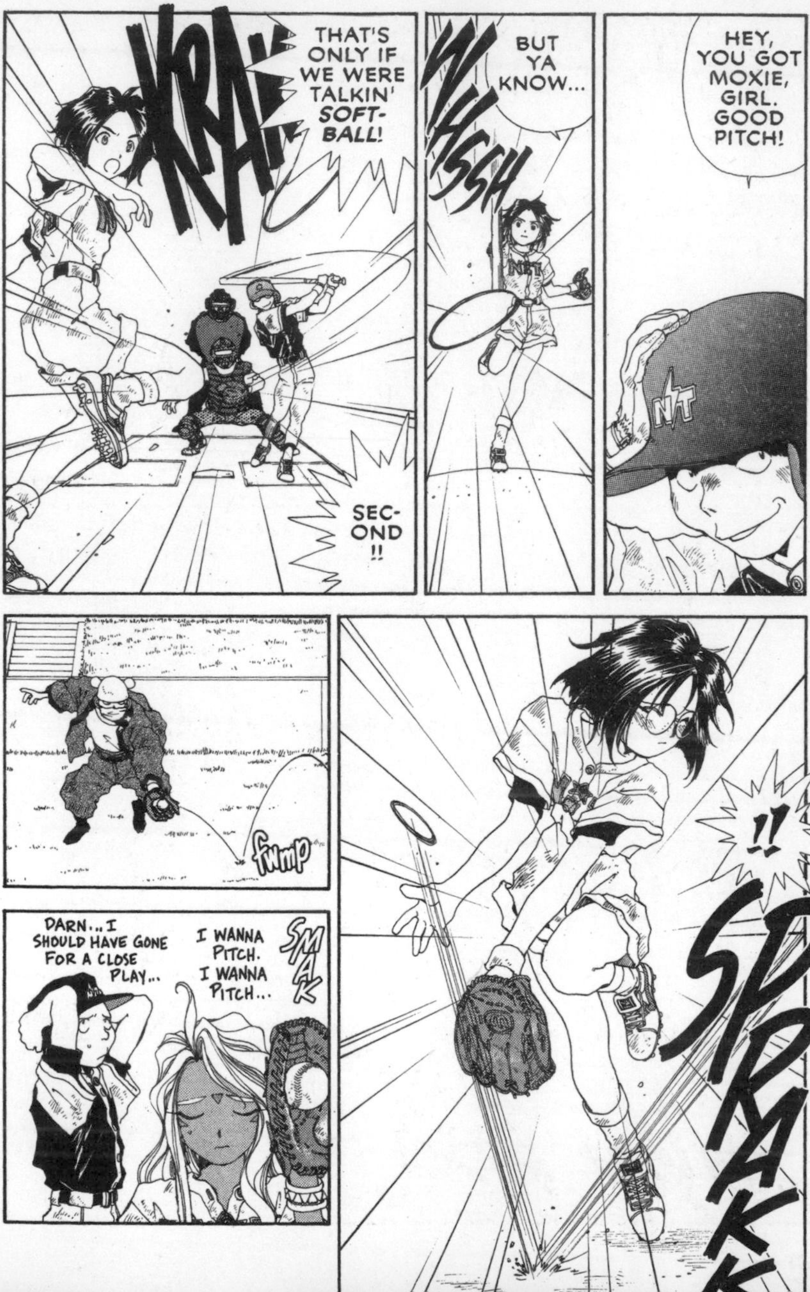
HEY, YOU GOT MOXIE, GIRL. GOOD PITCH!
BUT YA KNOW...
THAT'S ONLY IF WE WERE TALKIN' SOFT-BALL!
SEC-OND !!
!!
fwmp
I WANNA PITCH. I WANNA PITCH...
SMAK
DARN... I SHOULD HAVE GONE FOR A CLOSE PLAY...

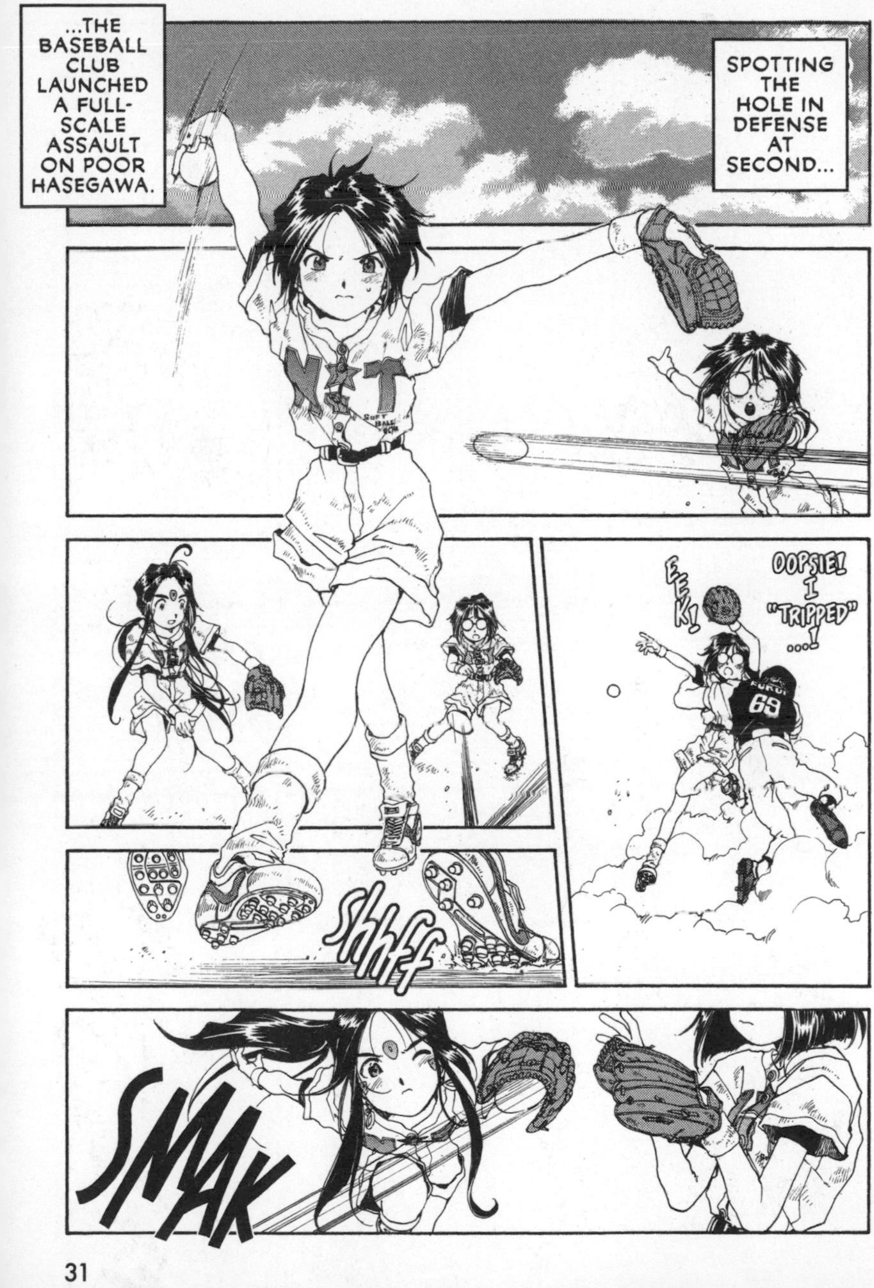
SPOTTING THE HOLE IN DEFENSE AT SECOND...
...THE BASEBALL CLUB LAUNCHED A FULL-SCALE ASSAULT ON POOR HASEGAWA.
OOPSIE! I "TRIPPED"...!
EEK!
shhff
SMAK

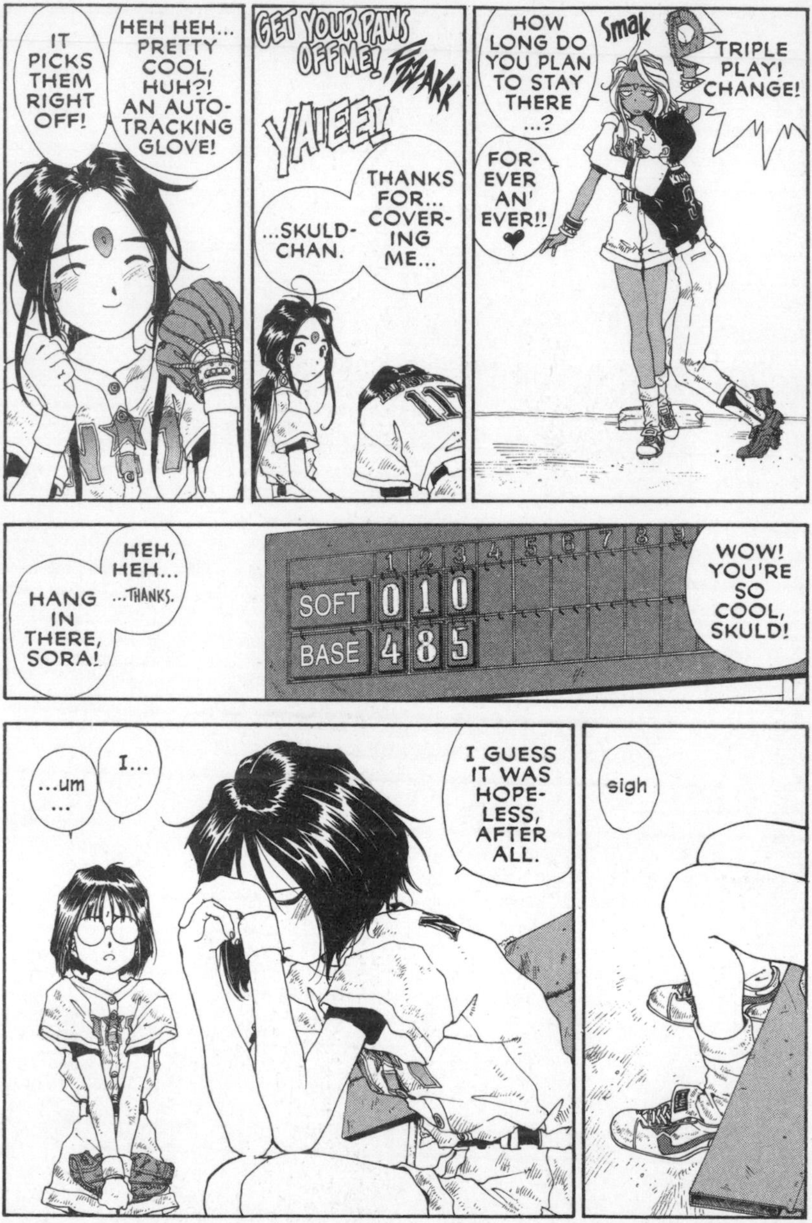
HOW LONG DO YOU PLAN TO STAY THERE ...?
Smak
TRIPLE PLAY! CHANGE!
FOR-EVER AN' EVER!! ❤
GET YOUR PAWS OFFME!
FWAKK
YA!EE!
THANKS FOR... COVER-ING ME...
...SKULD-CHAN.
HEH HEH... PRETTY COOL, HUH?! AN AUTO-TRACKING GLOVE!
IT PICKS THEM RIGHT OFF!
WOW! YOU'RE SO COOL, SKULD!
1 2 3 4 5 6 7 8 9
SOFT 0 1 0
BASE 4 8 5
HEH, HEH... ...THANKS.
HANG IN THERE, SORA!
sigh
I GUESS IT WAS HOPE-LESS, AFTER ALL.
I...
...um ...

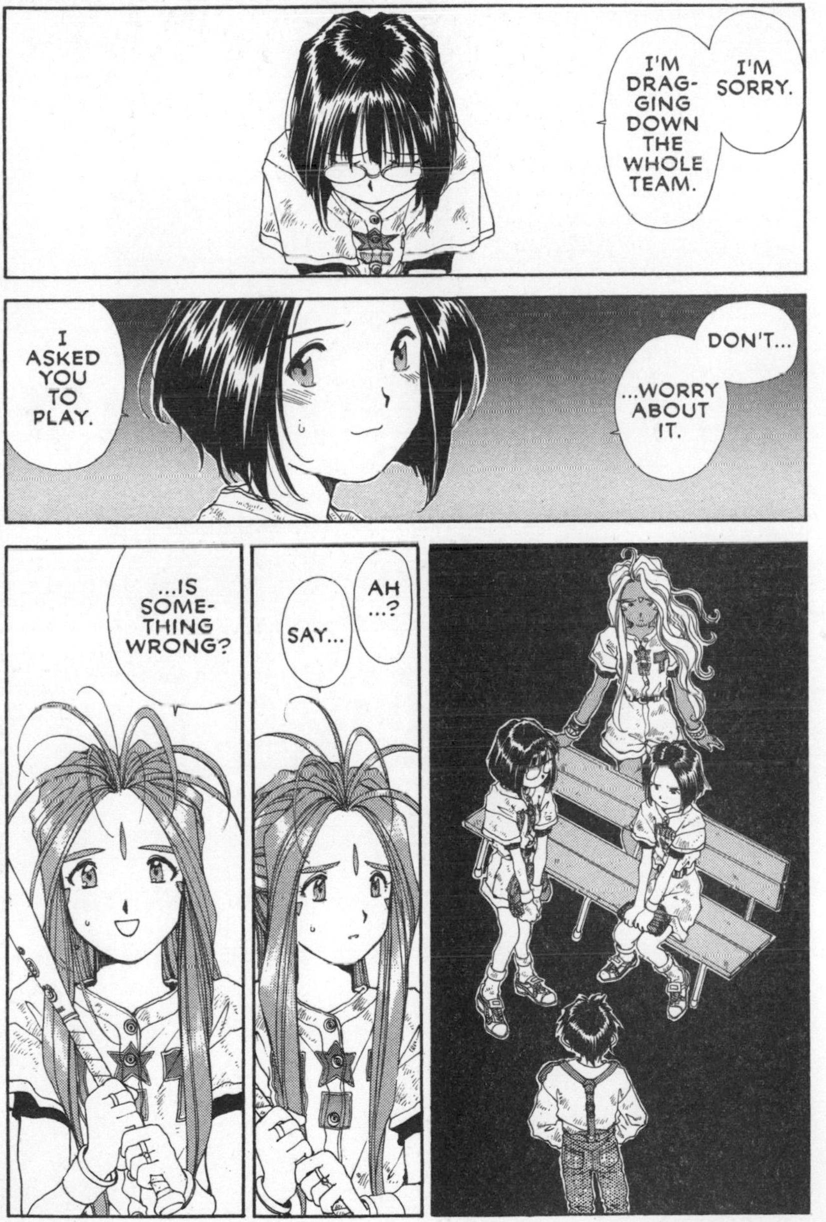
I'M SORRY.
I'M DRAGGING DOWN THE WHOLE TEAM.
DON'T...
...WORRY ABOUT IT.
I ASKED YOU TO PLAY.
AH ...?
SAY...
...IS SOMETHING WRONG?

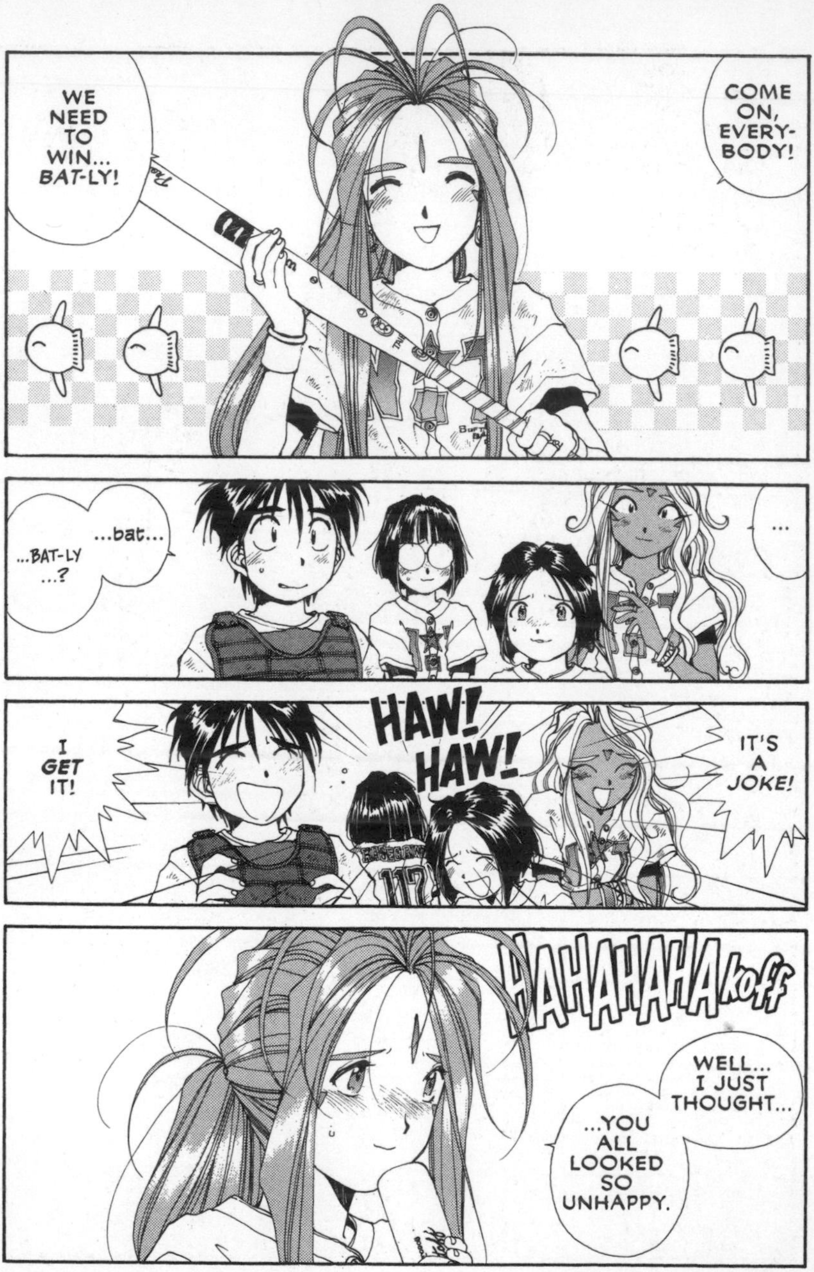
COME ON, EVERY-BODY!
WE NEED TO WIN... BAT-LY!
...
...bat...
...BAT-LY ...?
IT'S A JOKE!
HAW! HAW!
I GET IT!
HAHAHAHAHA koff
WELL... I JUST THOUGHT...
...YOU ALL LOOKED SO UNHAPPY.

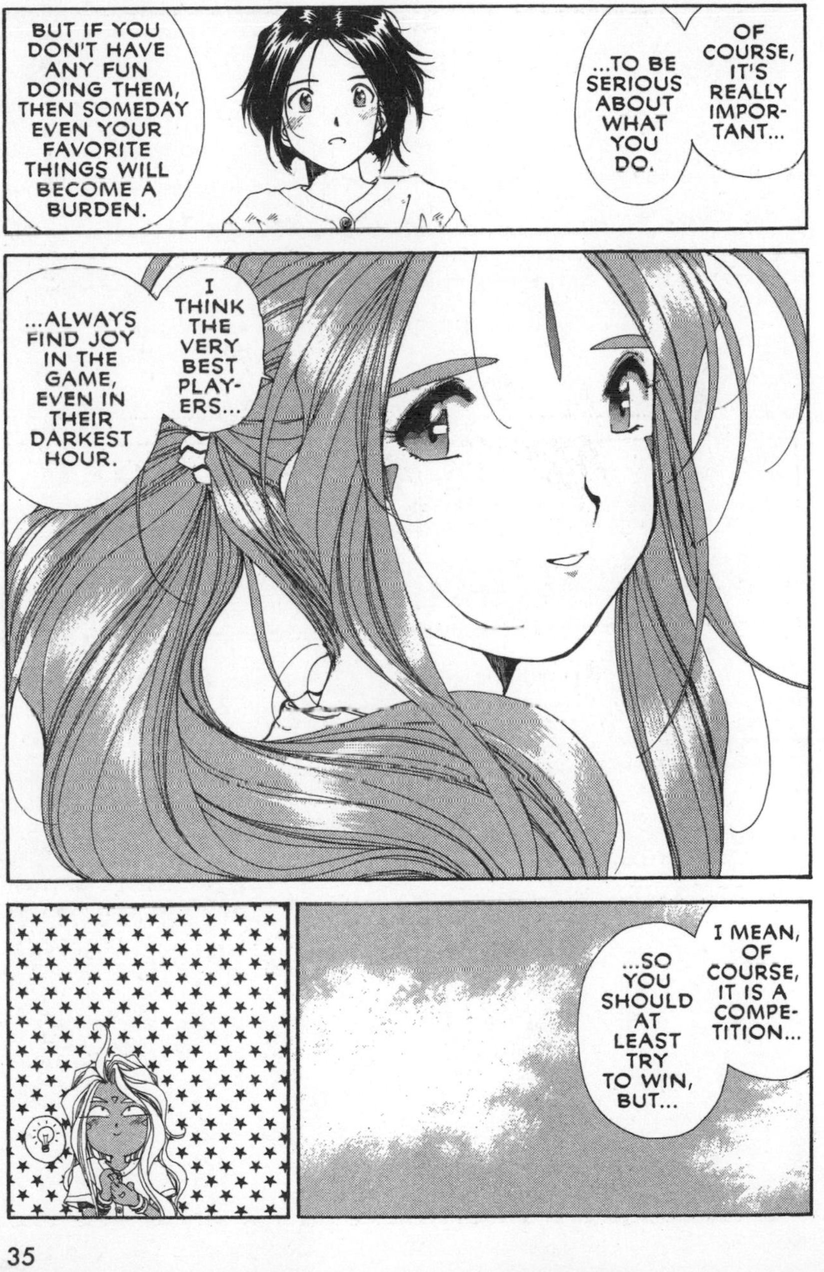
OF COURSE, IT'S REALLY IMPORTANT...
...TO BE SERIOUS ABOUT WHAT YOU DO.
BUT IF YOU DON'T HAVE ANY FUN DOING THEM, THEN SOMEDAY EVEN YOUR FAVORITE THINGS WILL BECOME A BURDEN.
I THINK THE VERY BEST PLAYERS...
...ALWAYS FIND JOY IN THE GAME, EVEN IN THEIR DARKEST HOUR.
I MEAN, OF COURSE, IT IS A COMPETITION...
...SO YOU SHOULD AT LEAST TRY TO WIN, BUT...

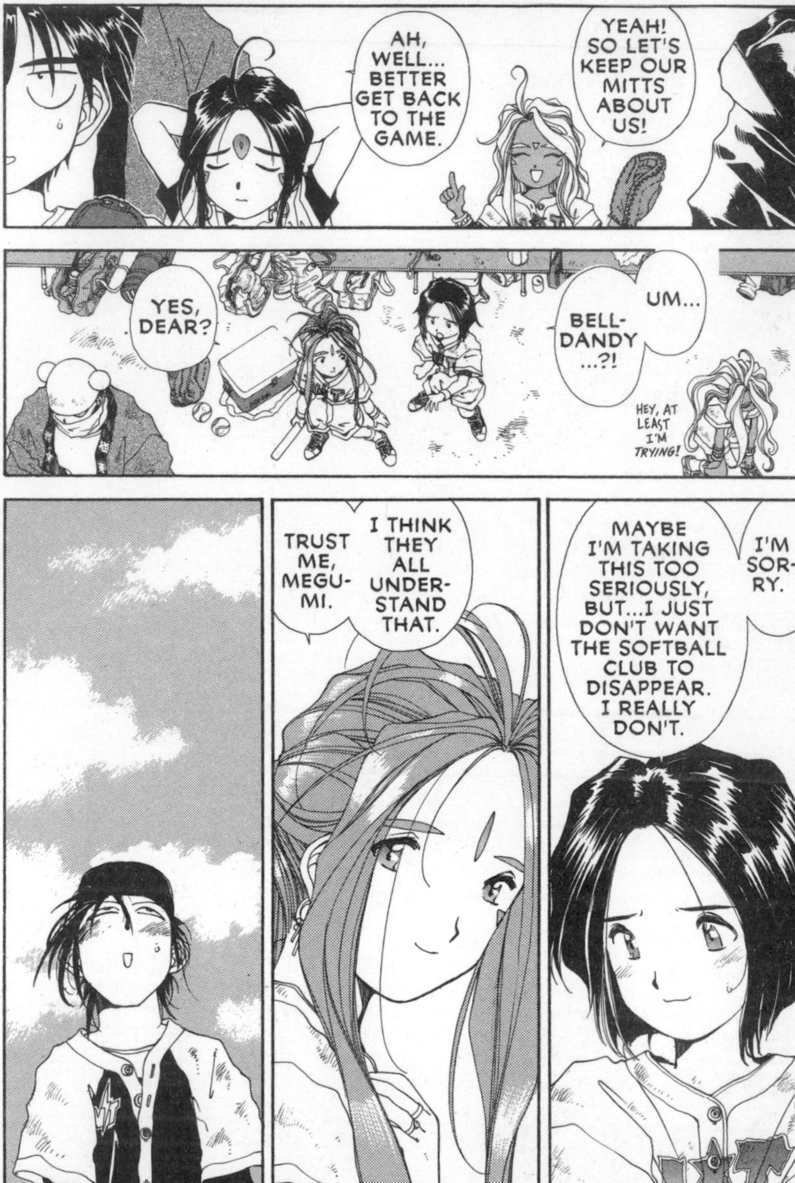
YEAH! SO LET'S KEEP OUR MITTS ABOUT US!
AH, WELL... BETTER GET BACK TO THE GAME.
UM... BELL-DANDY ...?!
YES, DEAR?
HEY, AT LEAST I'M TRYING!
I'M SOR-RY.
MAYBE I'M TAKING THIS TOO SERIOUSLY, BUT...I JUST DON'T WANT THE SOFTBALL CLUB TO DISAPPEAR. I REALLY DON'T.
I THINK THEY ALL UNDER-STAND THAT.
TRUST ME, MEGU-MI.

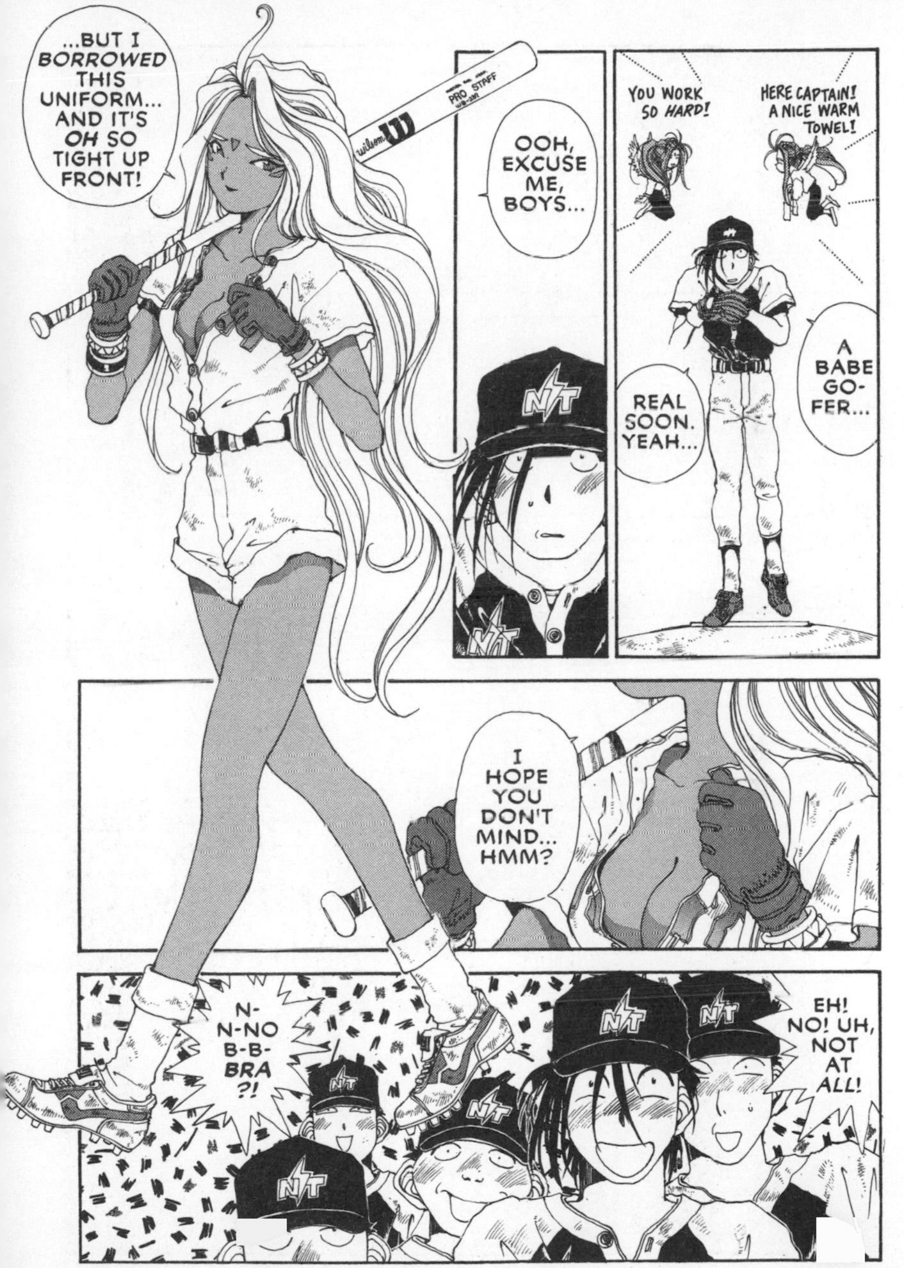
HERE CAPTAIN! A NICE WARM TOWEL!
YOU WORK SO *HARD!*
A BABE GO-FER...
REAL SOON. YEAH...
OOH, EXCUSE ME, BOYS...
...BUT I *BORROWED* THIS UNIFORM... AND IT'S *OH* SO TIGHT UP FRONT!
I HOPE YOU DON'T MIND... HMM?
EH! NO! UH, NOT AT *ALL!*
N-N-NO B-B-*BRA* ?!

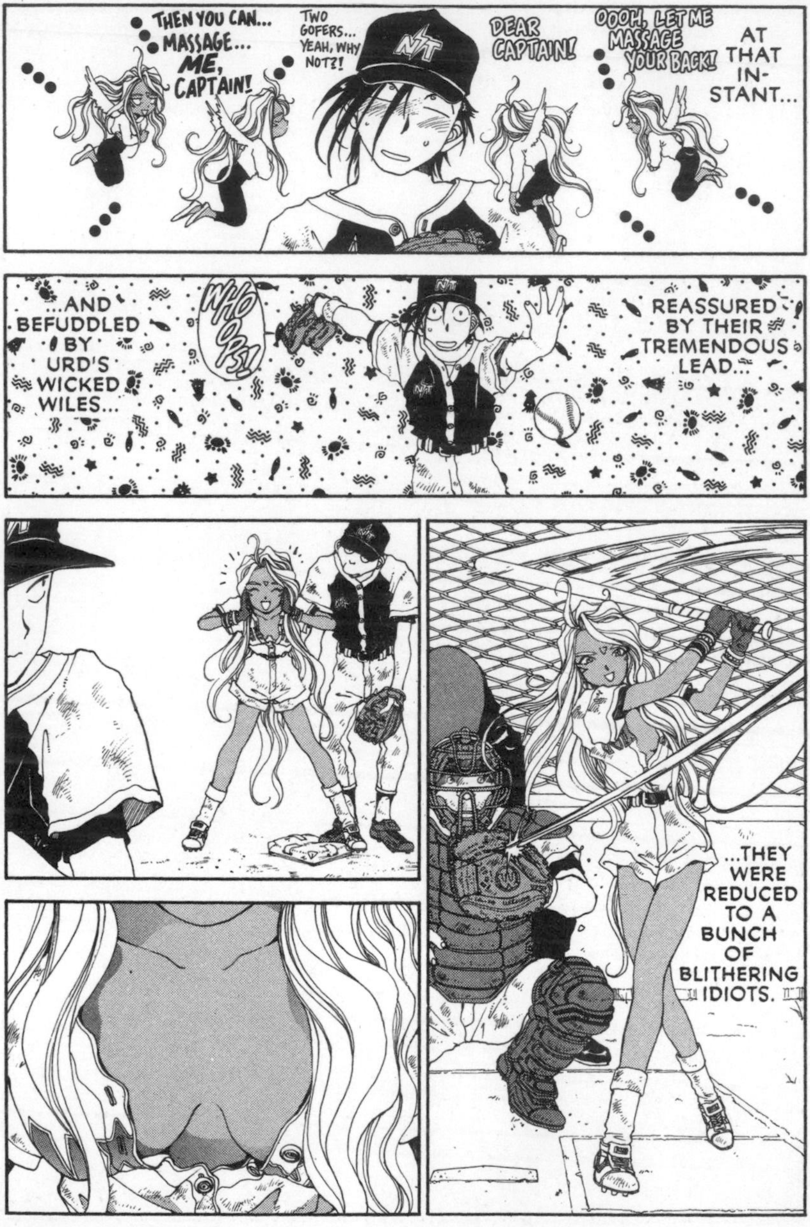
AT THAT IN-STANT...
OOOH, LET ME MASSAGE YOUR BACK!
DEAR CAPTAIN!
TWO GOFERS... YEAH, WHY NOT?!
THEN YOU CAN... MASSAGE... ME, CAPTAIN!
REASSURED BY THEIR TREMENDOUS LEAD...
WHOOPS!
...AND BEFUDDLED BY URD'S WICKED WILES...
...THEY WERE REDUCED TO A BUNCH OF BLITHERING IDIOTS.

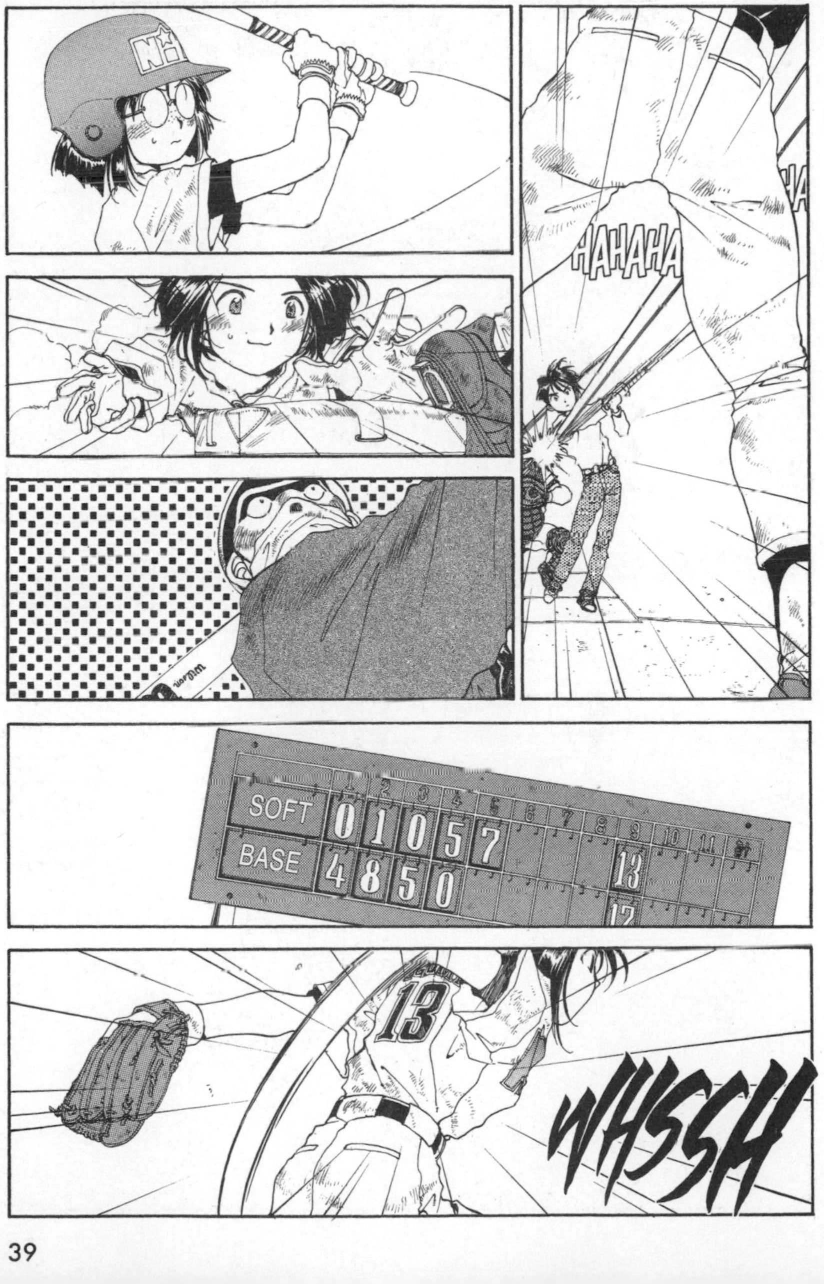
HA
HAHAHA
SOFT 0 1 0 5 7
BASE 4 8 5 0 13
13
WHSSH

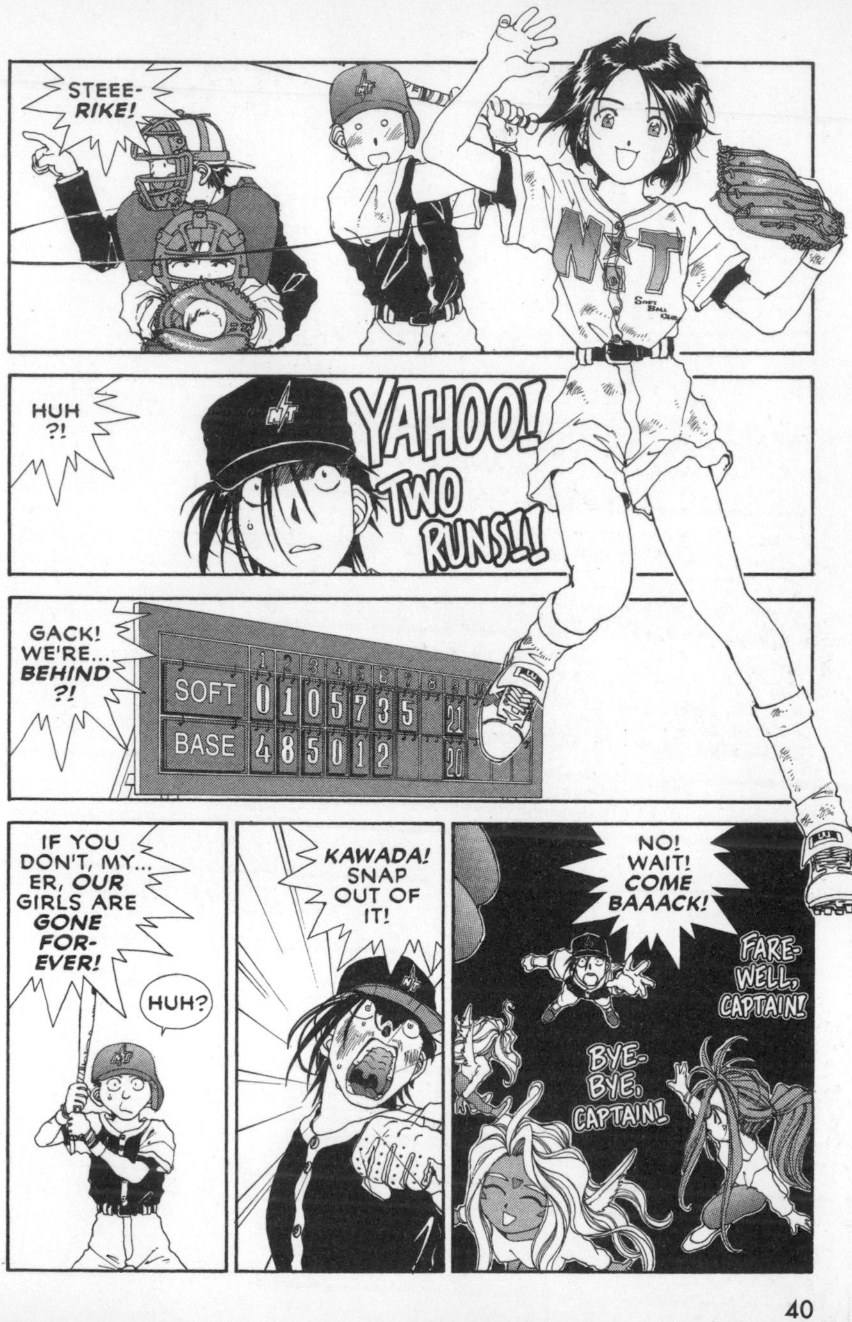
STEEE-RIKE!
YAHOO! TWO RUNS!!
HUH ?!
GACK! WE'RE... BEHIND ?!
SOFT 0 1 0 5 7 3 5 21
BASE 4 8 5 0 1 2 20
NO! WAIT! COME BAAACK!
FARE-WELL, CAPTAIN!
BYE-BYE, CAPTAIN!
KAWADA! SNAP OUT OF IT!
IF YOU DON'T, MY... ER, OUR GIRLS ARE GONE FOR-EVER!
HUH?

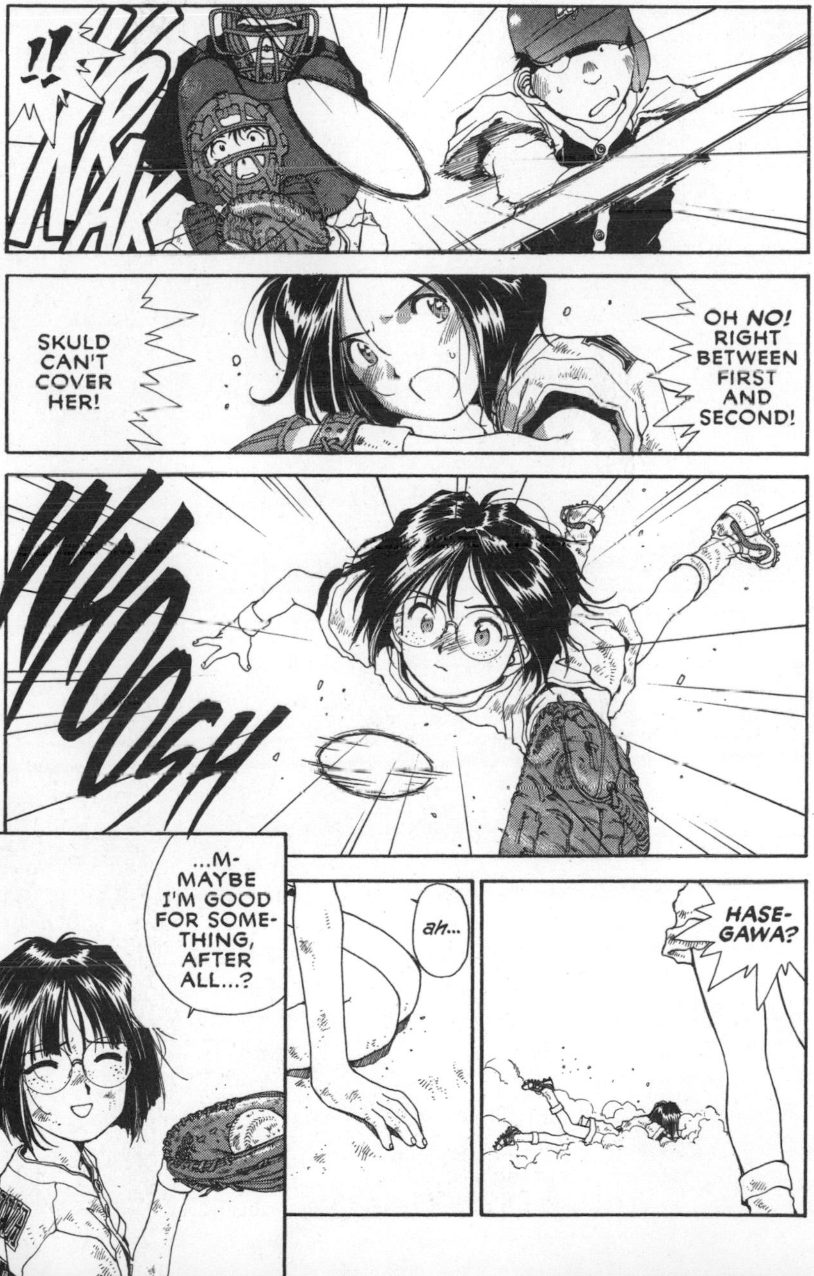
KRAK
!!
OH NO! RIGHT BETWEEN FIRST AND SECOND!
SKULD CAN'T COVER HER!
WHOOSH
HASE-GAWA?
ah...
...M-MAYBE I'M GOOD FOR SOME-THING, AFTER ALL...?

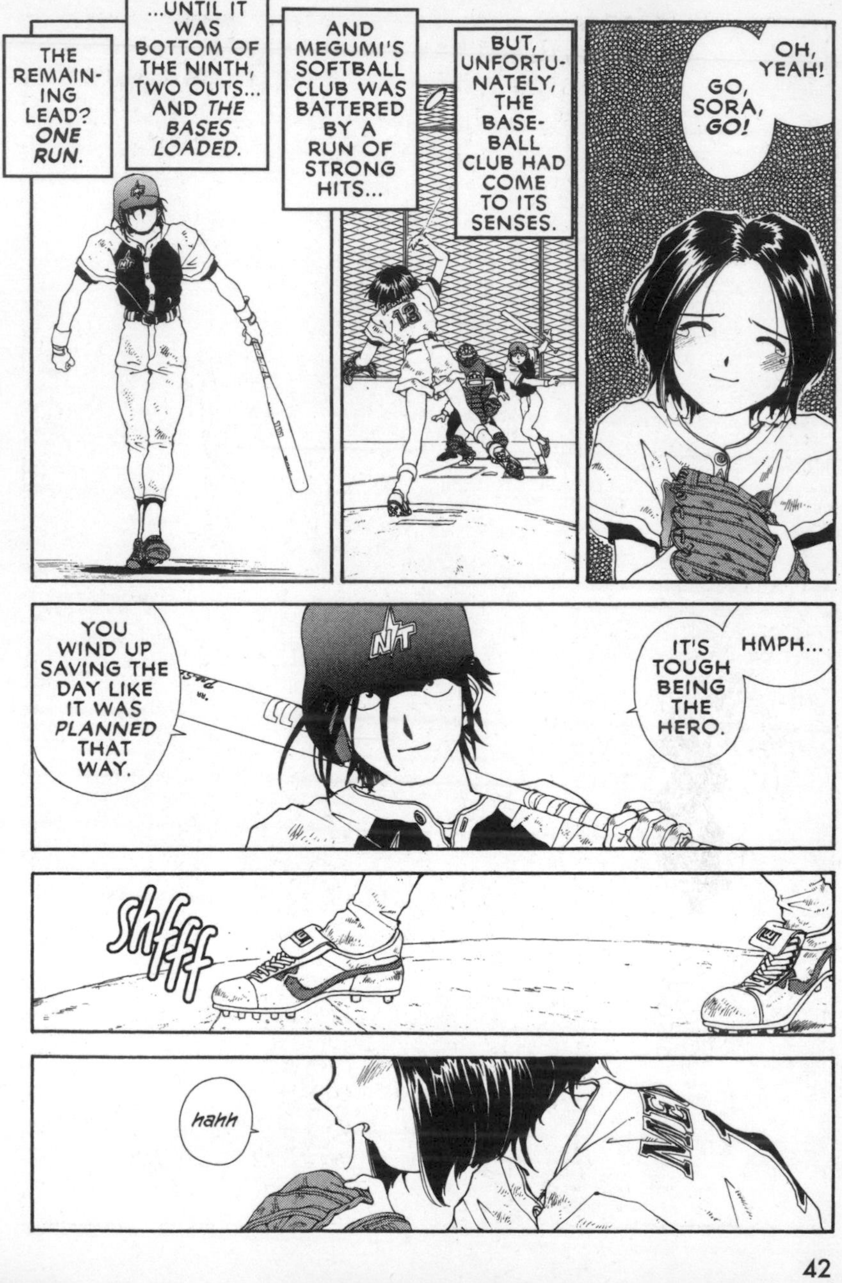
OH, YEAH!
GO, SORA, GO!
BUT, UNFORTUNATELY, THE BASEBALL CLUB HAD COME TO ITS SENSES.
AND MEGUMI'S SOFTBALL CLUB WAS BATTERED BY A RUN OF STRONG HITS...
...UNTIL IT WAS BOTTOM OF THE NINTH, TWO OUTS... AND *THE BASES LOADED.*
THE REMAINING LEAD? *ONE RUN.*
HMPH...
IT'S TOUGH BEING THE HERO.
YOU WIND UP SAVING THE DAY LIKE IT WAS *PLANNED* THAT WAY.
shffff
hahh

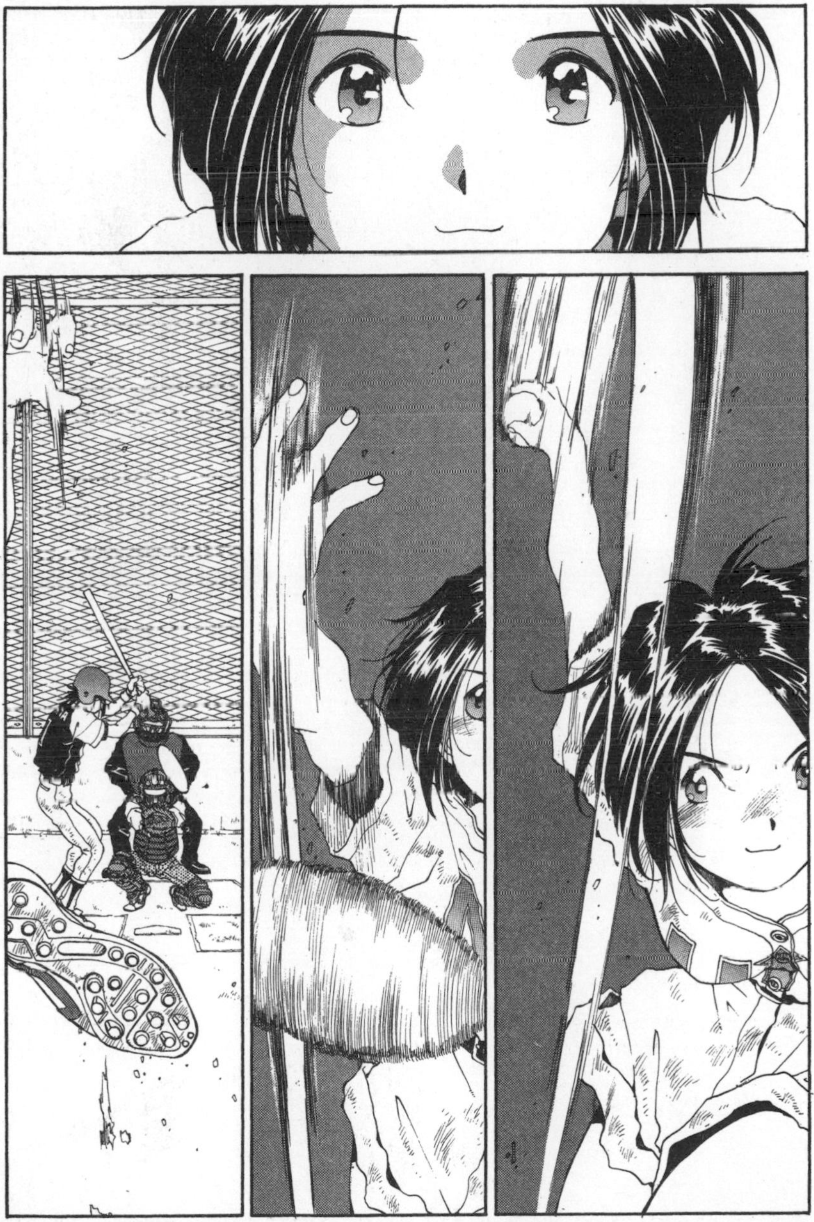

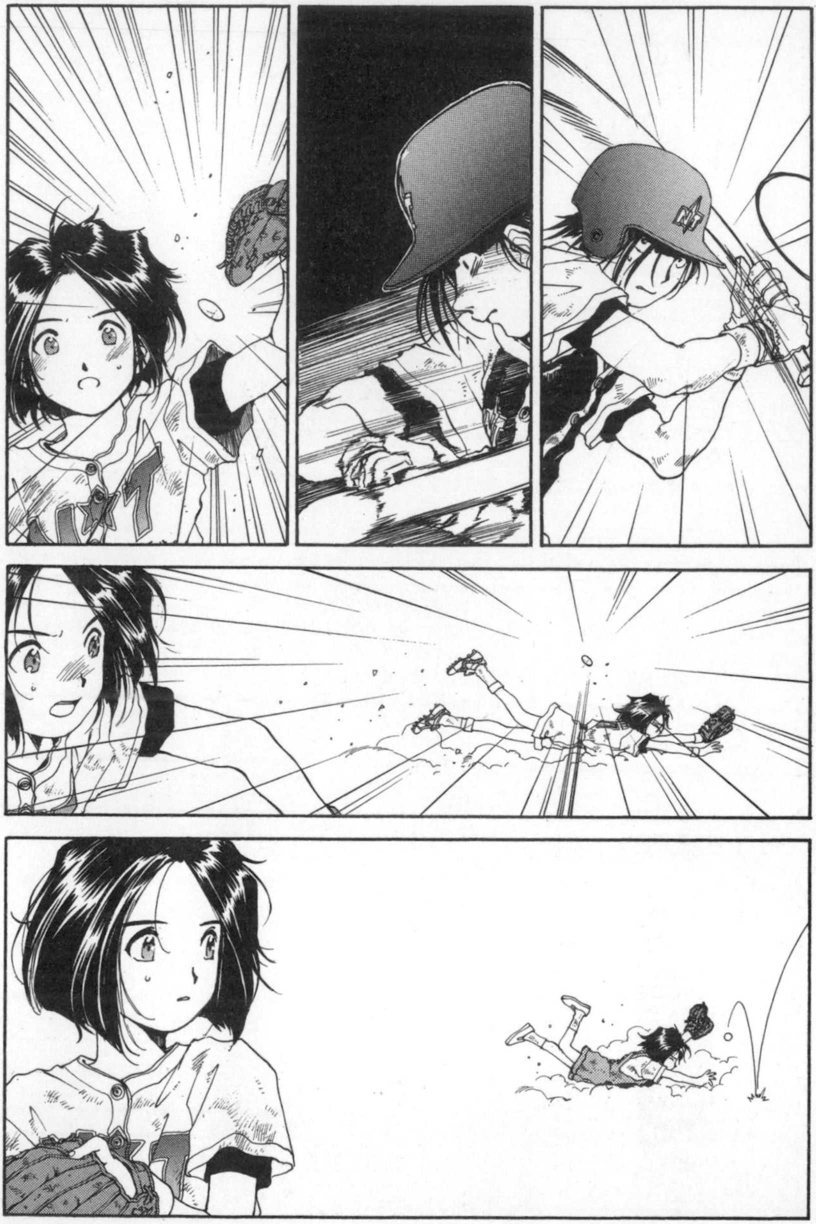

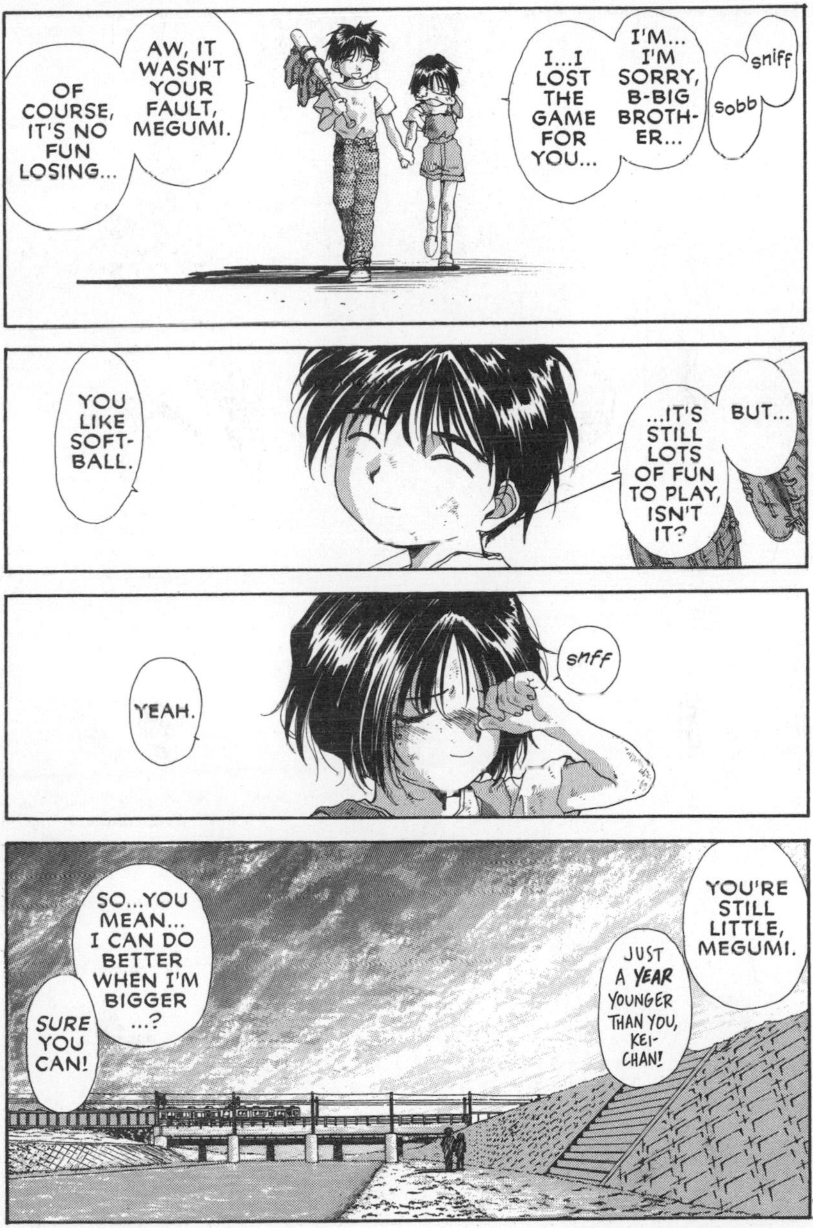
sniff
sobb
I'M... I'M SORRY, B-BIG BROTHER...
I...I LOST THE GAME FOR YOU...
AW, IT WASN'T YOUR FAULT, MEGUMI.
OF COURSE, IT'S NO FUN LOSING...
BUT...
...IT'S STILL LOTS OF FUN TO PLAY, ISN'T IT?
YOU LIKE SOFT-BALL.
snff
YEAH.
YOU'RE STILL LITTLE, MEGUMI.
JUST A *YEAR* YOUNGER THAN YOU, KEI-CHAN!
SO...YOU MEAN... I CAN DO BETTER WHEN I'M BIGGER ...?
SURE YOU CAN!

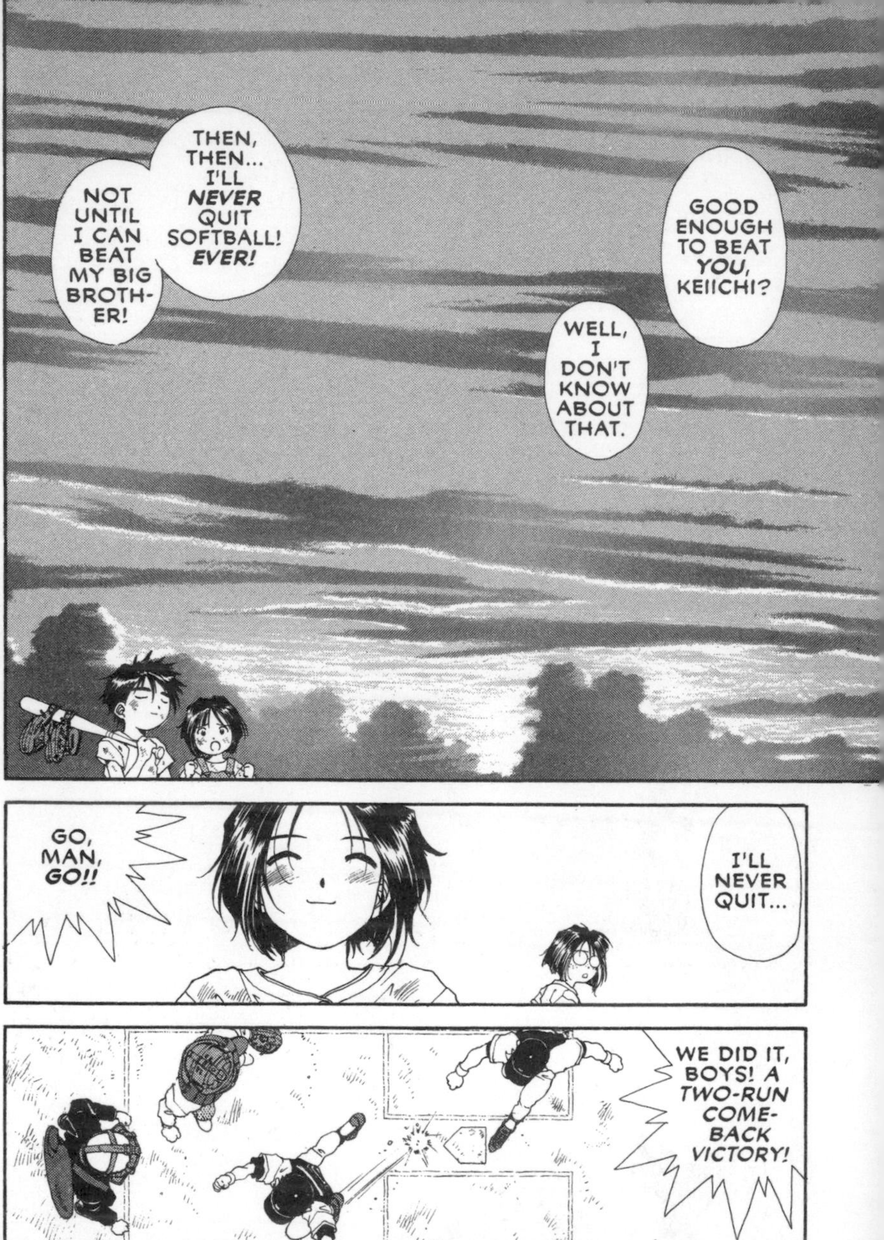
GOOD ENOUGH TO BEAT *YOU*, KEIICHI?
WELL, I DON'T KNOW ABOUT THAT.
THEN, THEN... I'LL *NEVER* QUIT SOFTBALL! *EVER!*
NOT UNTIL I CAN BEAT MY BIG BROTHER!
I'LL NEVER QUIT...
GO, MAN, *GO!!*
WE DID IT, BOYS! A *TWO-RUN* COME-BACK *VICTORY!*

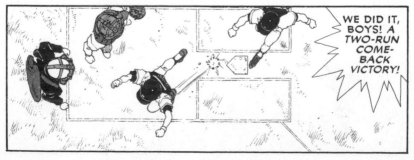

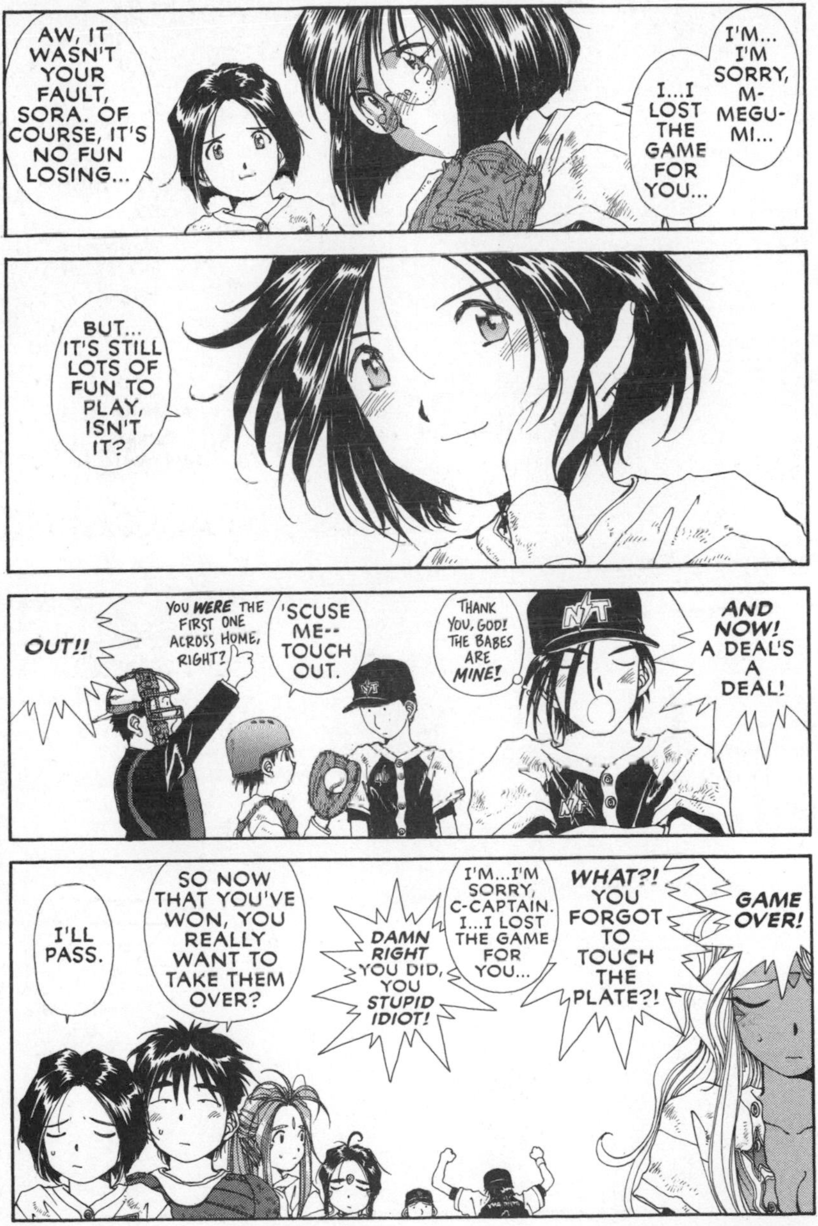
I'M... I'M SORRY, M-MEGUMI...
I...I LOST THE GAME FOR YOU...
AW, IT WASN'T YOUR FAULT, SORA. OF COURSE, IT'S NO FUN LOSING...
BUT... IT'S STILL LOTS OF FUN TO PLAY, ISN'T IT?
AND NOW! A DEAL'S A DEAL!
THANK YOU, GOD! THE BABES ARE MINE!
'SCUSE ME-- TOUCH OUT.
YOU WERE THE FIRST ONE ACROSS HOME, RIGHT?
OUT!!
GAME OVER!
WHAT?! YOU FORGOT TO TOUCH THE PLATE?!
I'M...I'M SORRY, C-CAPTAIN. I...I LOST THE GAME FOR YOU...
DAMN RIGHT YOU DID, YOU STUPID IDIOT!
SO NOW THAT YOU'VE WON, YOU REALLY WANT TO TAKE THEM OVER?
I'LL PASS.

THE ADVENTURES OF THE MINI-GODDESSES

◆ REVIVAL! A BAND REBORN! ◆

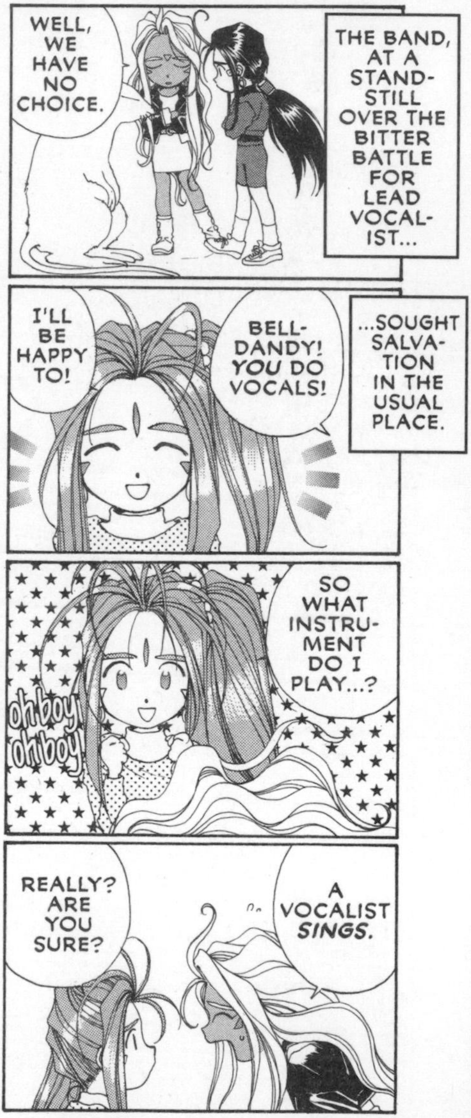
THE BAND, AT A STAND-STILL OVER THE BITTER BATTLE FOR LEAD VOCAL-IST...
WELL, WE HAVE NO CHOICE.
...SOUGHT SALVA-TION IN THE USUAL PLACE.
BELL-DANDY! *YOU* DO VOCALS!
I'LL BE HAPPY TO!
SO WHAT INSTRU-MENT DO I PLAY...?
oh boy oh boy
A VOCALIST *SINGS.*
REALLY? ARE YOU SURE?

◆ THE INVINCIBLE VOCALIST ◆

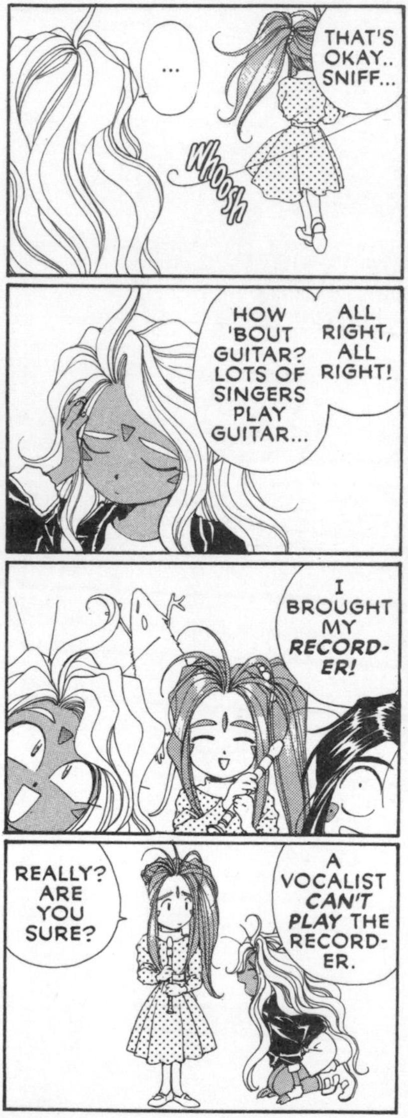
THAT'S OKAY.. SNIFF...
whoosh
...
ALL RIGHT, ALL RIGHT!
HOW 'BOUT GUITAR? LOTS OF SINGERS PLAY GUITAR...
I BROUGHT MY *RECORD-ER!*
A VOCALIST *CAN'T PLAY* THE RECORD-ER.
REALLY? ARE YOU SURE?

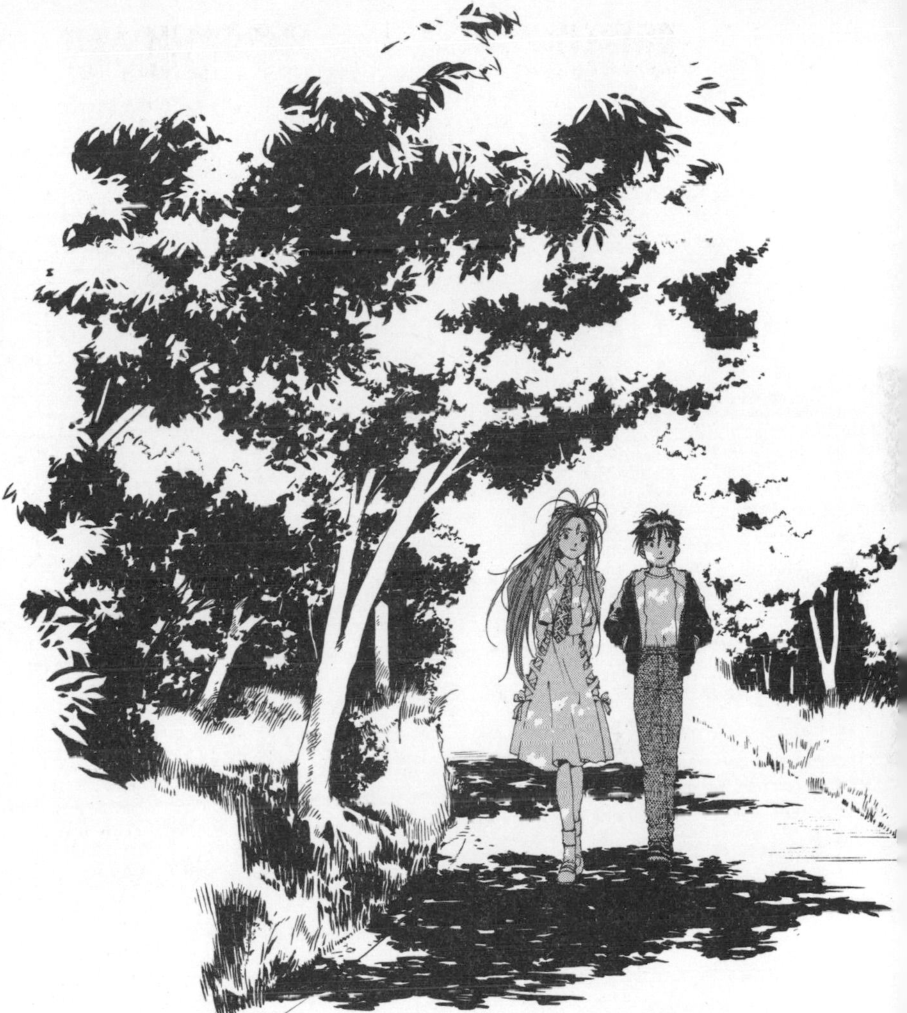

CHAPTER 59

Remember the Sad Times

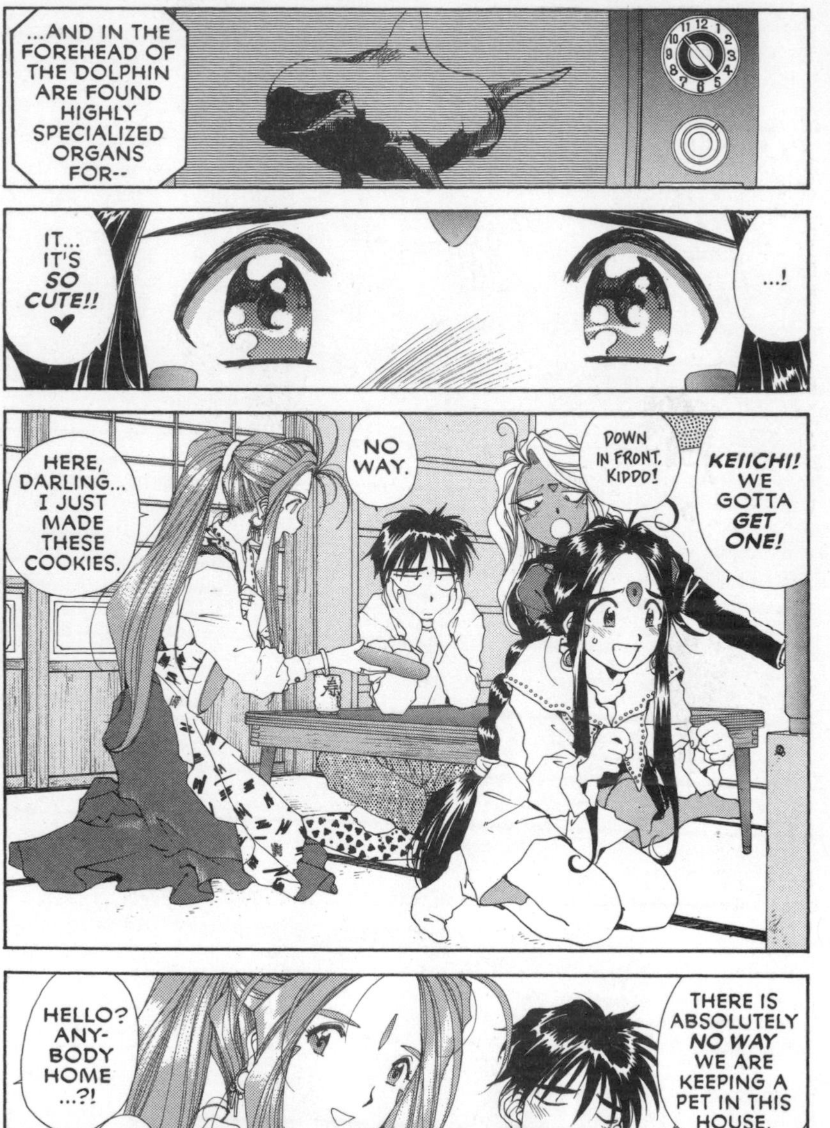
...AND IN THE FOREHEAD OF THE DOLPHIN ARE FOUND HIGHLY SPECIALIZED ORGANS FOR--
...!
IT... IT'S *SO CUTE!!* ❤
KEIICHI! WE GOTTA *GET ONE!*
DOWN IN FRONT, KIDDO!
NO WAY.
HERE, DARLING... I JUST MADE THESE COOKIES.
THERE IS ABSOLUTELY *NO WAY* WE ARE KEEPING A PET IN THIS HOUSE.
HELLO? ANY-BODY HOME ...?!
COME IN!

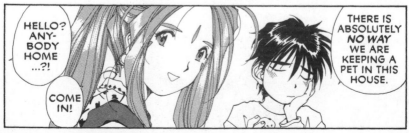

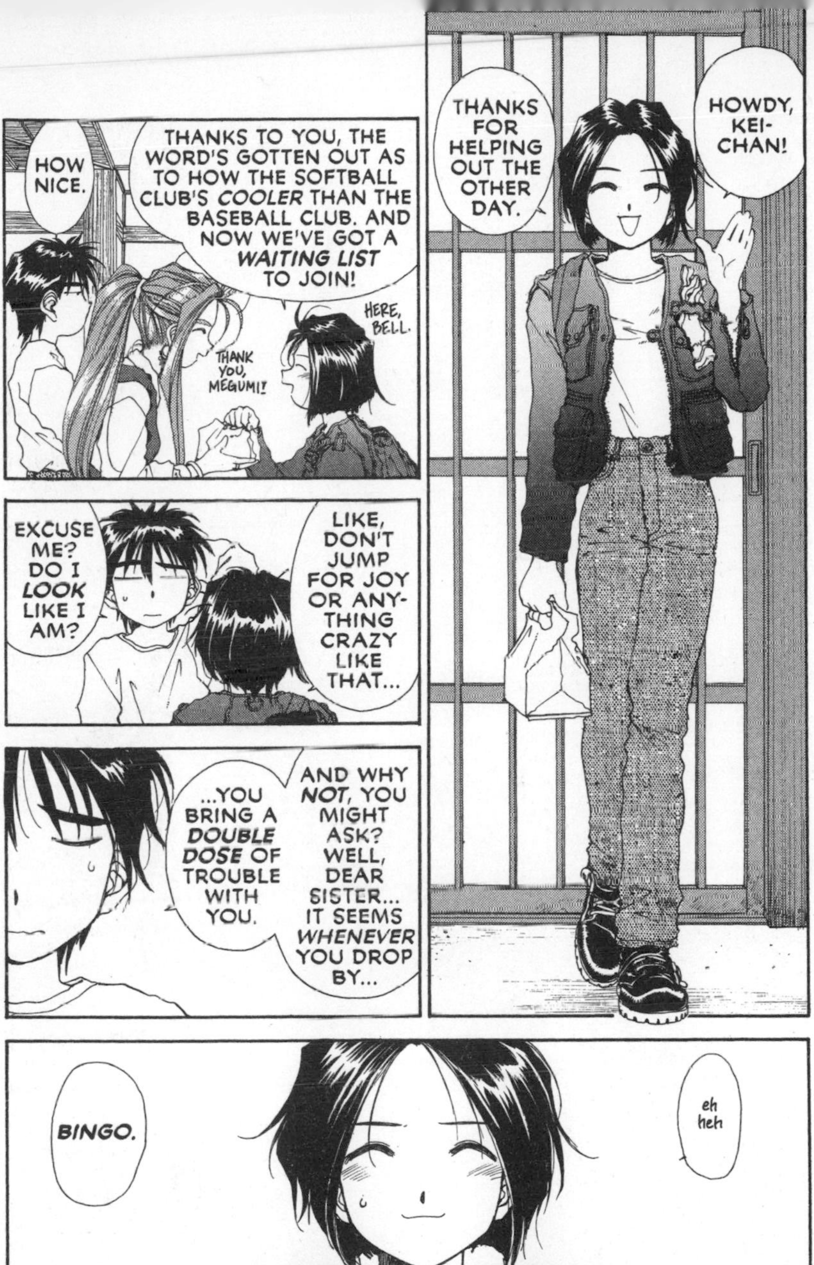
HOWDY, KEI-CHAN!
THANKS FOR HELPING OUT THE OTHER DAY.
THANKS TO YOU, THE WORD'S GOTTEN OUT AS TO HOW THE SOFTBALL CLUB'S *COOLER* THAN THE BASEBALL CLUB. AND NOW WE'VE GOT A ***WAITING LIST*** TO JOIN!
HOW NICE.
HERE, BELL.
THANK YOU, MEGUMI!
LIKE, DON'T JUMP FOR JOY OR ANY-THING CRAZY LIKE THAT...
EXCUSE ME? DO I *LOOK* LIKE I AM?
AND WHY *NOT*, YOU MIGHT ASK? WELL, DEAR SISTER... IT SEEMS *WHENEVER* YOU DROP BY...
...YOU BRING A ***DOUBLE DOSE*** OF TROUBLE WITH YOU.
eh heh
BINGO.

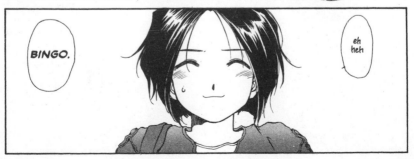

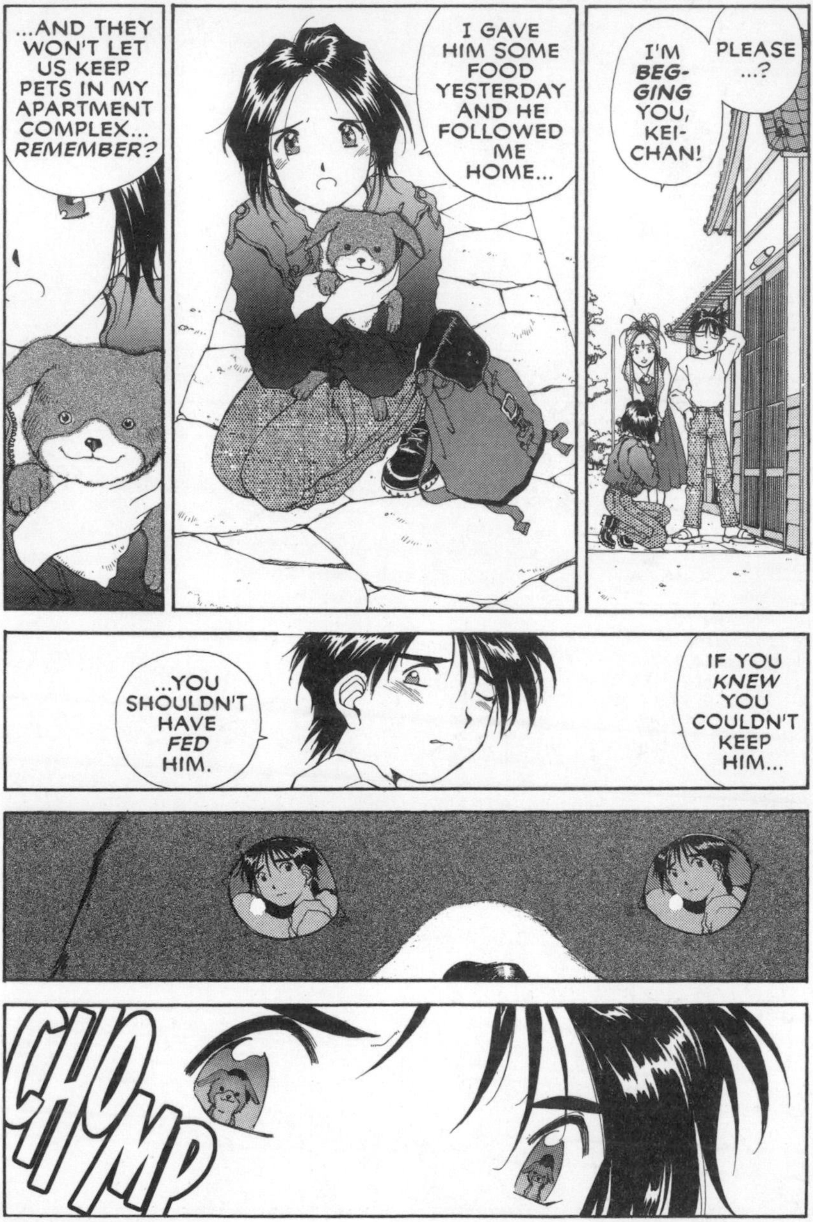
PLEASE ...?
I'M BEGGING YOU, KEI-CHAN!
I GAVE HIM SOME FOOD YESTERDAY AND HE FOLLOWED ME HOME...
...AND THEY WON'T LET US KEEP PETS IN MY APARTMENT COMPLEX... REMEMBER?
IF YOU KNEW YOU COULDN'T KEEP HIM...
...YOU SHOULDN'T HAVE FED HIM.
CHOMP

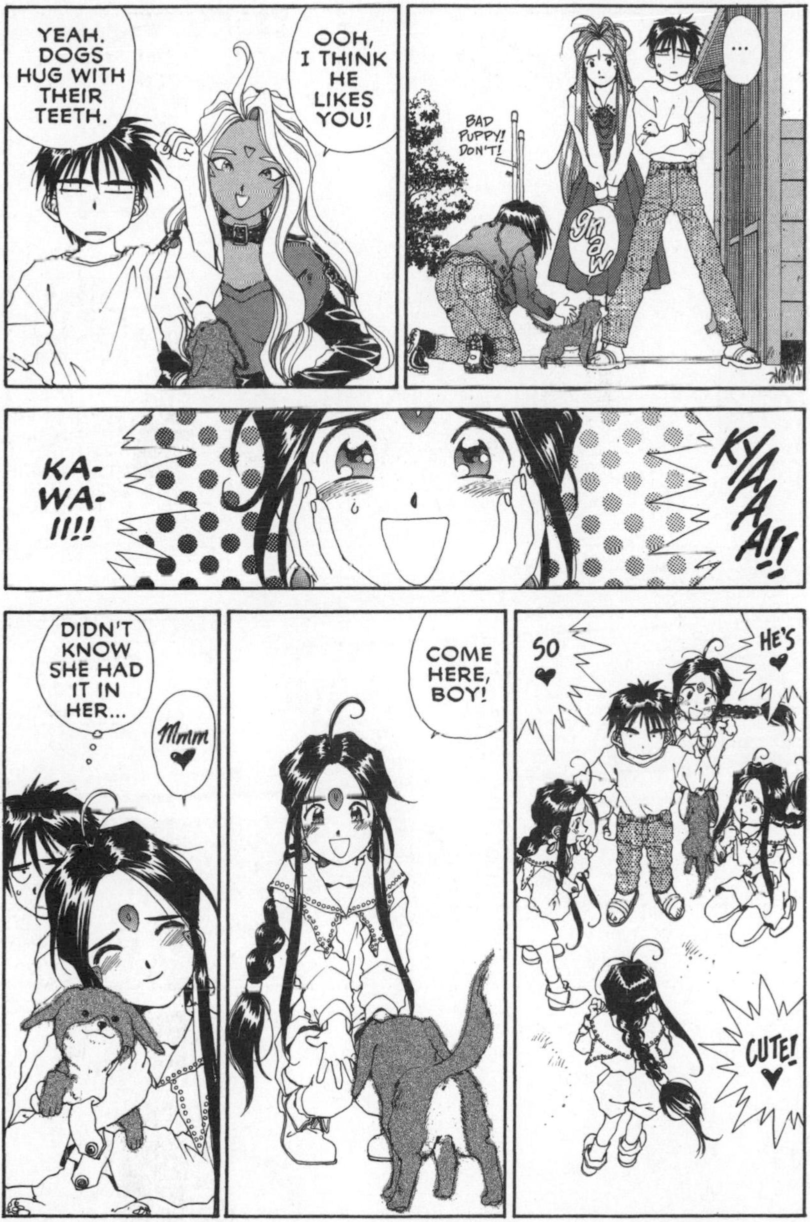
...
BAD PUPPY! DON'T!
gnaw
OOH, I THINK HE LIKES YOU!
YEAH. DOGS HUG WITH THEIR TEETH.
KYAAAA!!!
KA-WA-II!!!
HE'S ♥
SO ♥
CUTE! ♥
COME HERE, BOY!
DIDN'T KNOW SHE HAD IT IN HER...
Mmm ♥

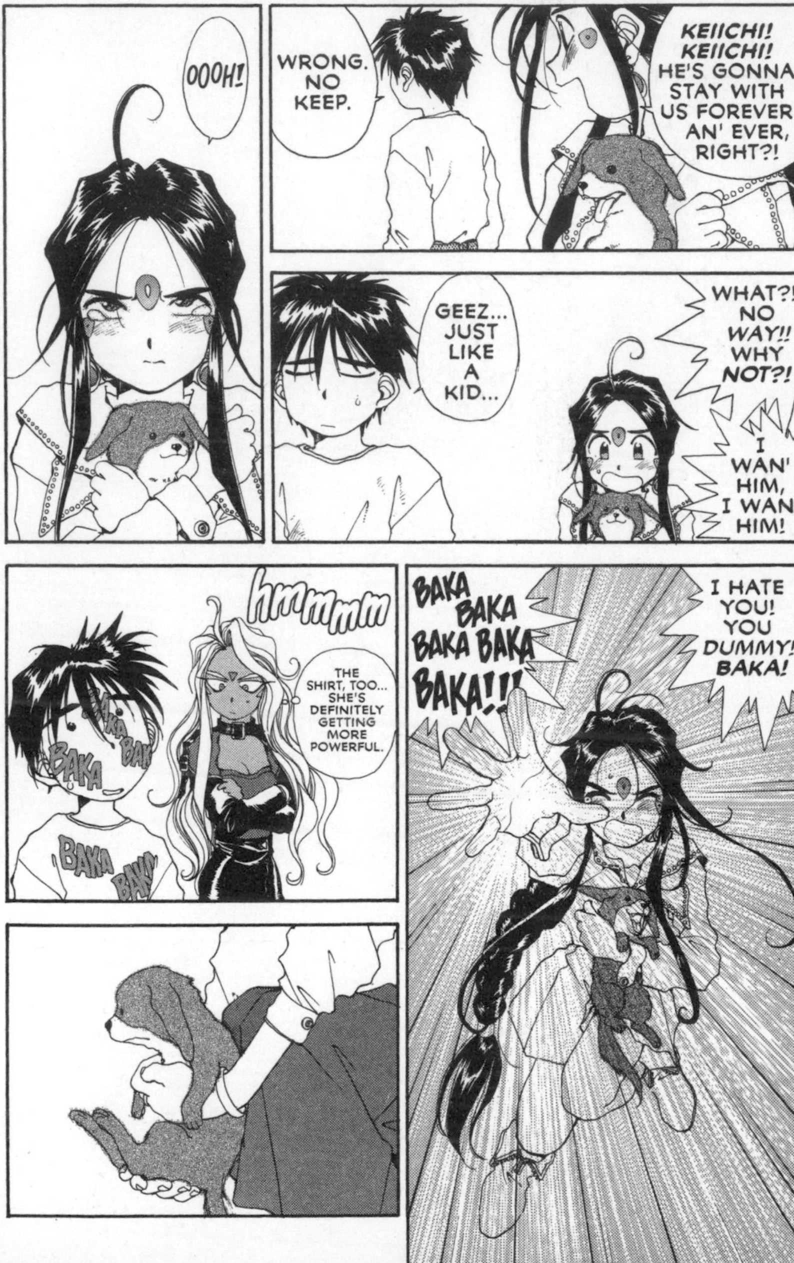
KEIICHI! KEIICHI! HE'S GONNA STAY WITH US FOREVER AN' EVER, RIGHT?!
WRONG. NO KEEP.
WHAT?! NO WAY!! WHY NOT?!
I WAN' HIM, I WAN' HIM!
GEEZ... JUST LIKE A KID...
OOOH!
I HATE YOU! YOU DUMMY! BAKA!
BAKA BAKA BAKA BAKA BAKA!!!
hmmmmm
THE SHIRT, TOO... SHE'S DEFINITELY GETTING MORE POWERFUL.

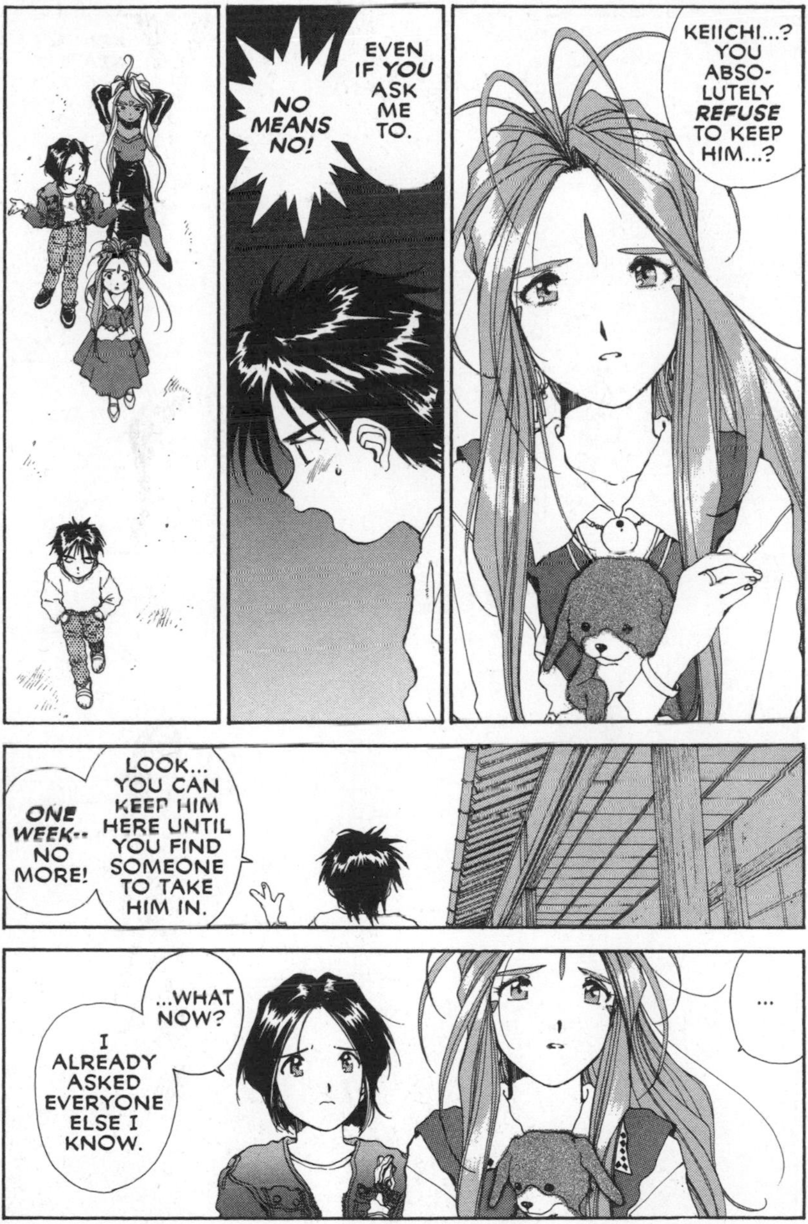
KEIICHI...? YOU ABSOLUTELY *REFUSE* TO KEEP HIM...?
EVEN IF *YOU* ASK ME TO.
NO MEANS NO!
LOOK... YOU CAN KEEP HIM HERE UNTIL YOU FIND SOMEONE TO TAKE HIM IN.
ONE WEEK-- NO MORE!
...
...WHAT NOW?
I ALREADY ASKED EVERYONE ELSE I KNOW.

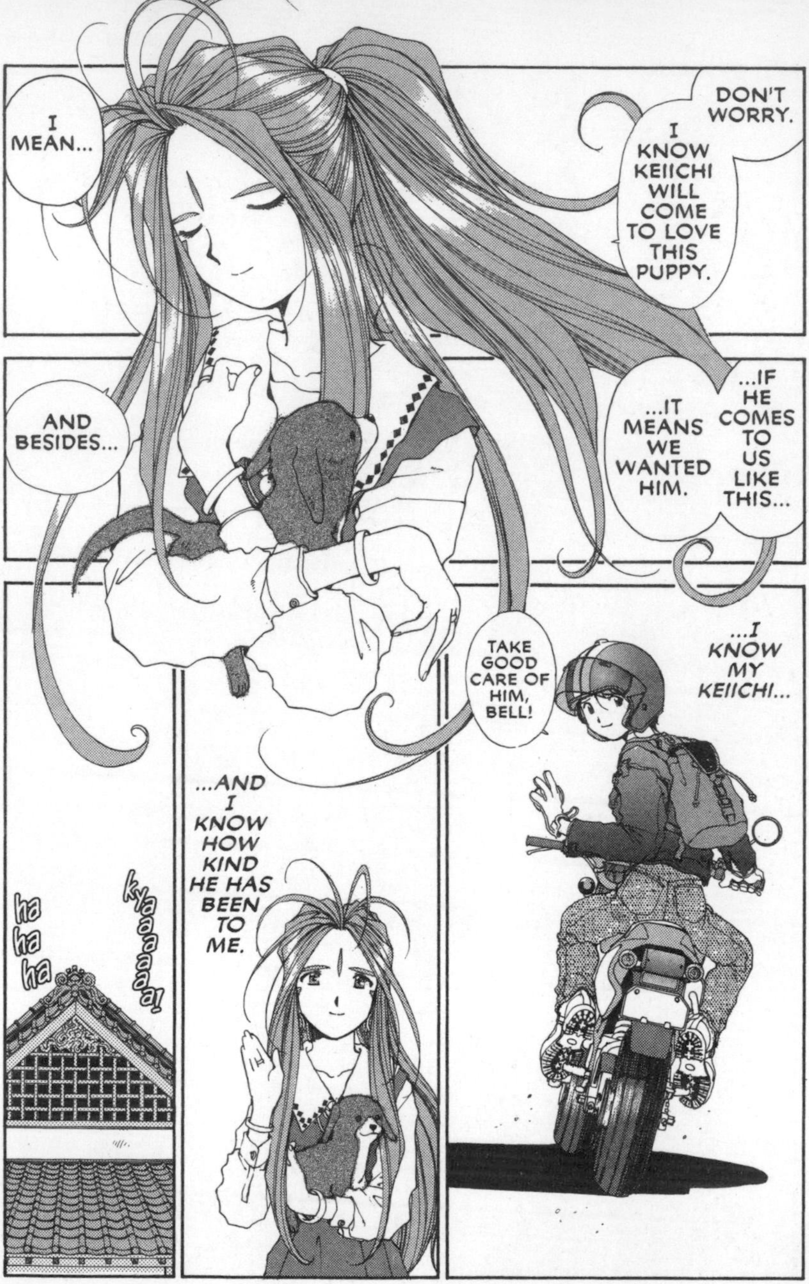
DON'T WORRY. I KNOW KEIICHI WILL COME TO LOVE THIS PUPPY.
I MEAN...
...IF HE COMES TO US LIKE THIS...
...IT MEANS WE WANTED HIM.
AND BESIDES...
...I KNOW MY KEIICHI...
TAKE GOOD CARE OF HIM, BELL!
...AND I KNOW HOW KIND HE HAS BEEN TO ME.
kyaaaaaaa!
ha ha ha

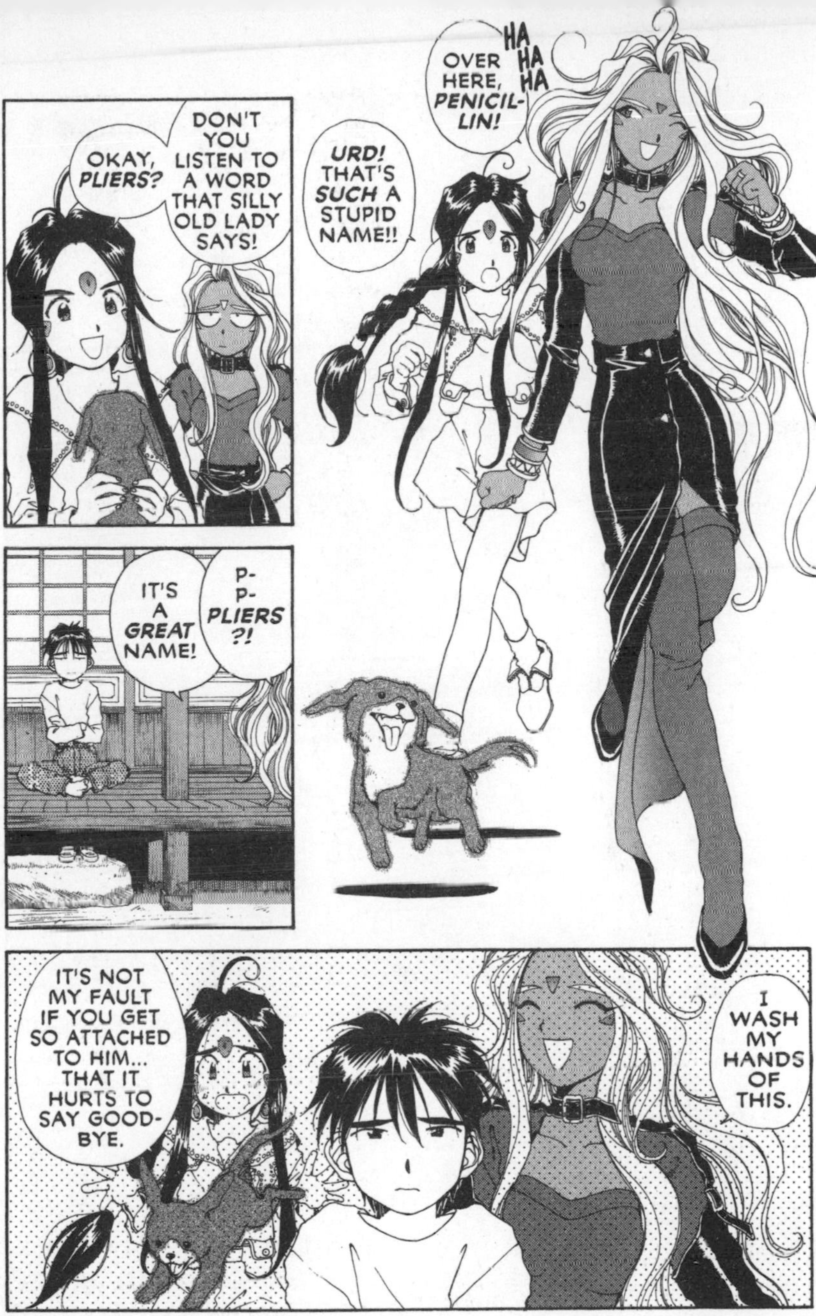
HA HA HA
OVER HERE, PENICILLIN!
URD! THAT'S SUCH A STUPID NAME!!
DON'T YOU LISTEN TO A WORD THAT SILLY OLD LADY SAYS!
OKAY, PLIERS?
P-P-PLIERS?!
IT'S A GREAT NAME!
I WASH MY HANDS OF THIS.
IT'S NOT MY FAULT IF YOU GET SO ATTACHED TO HIM... THAT IT HURTS TO SAY GOOD-BYE.

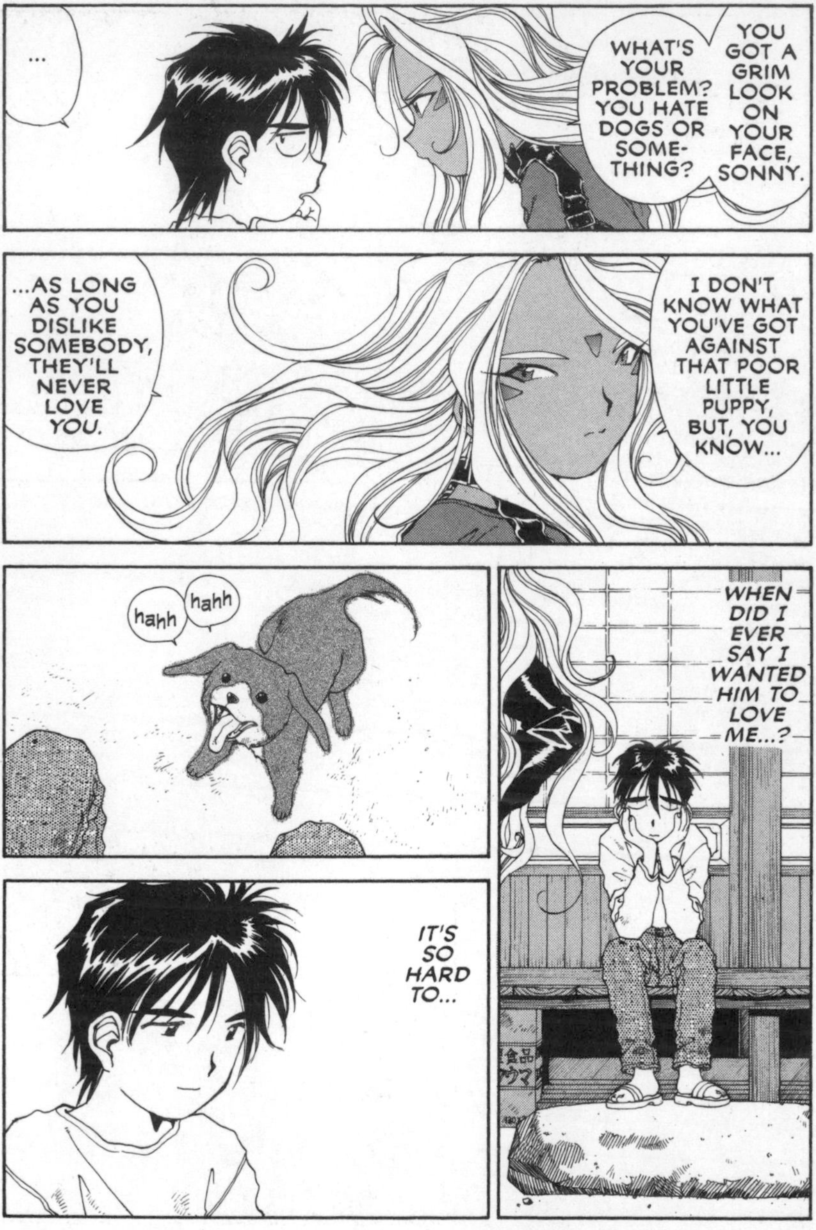
YOU GOT A GRIM LOOK ON YOUR FACE, SONNY.
WHAT'S YOUR PROBLEM? YOU HATE DOGS OR SOME-THING?
...
I DON'T KNOW WHAT YOU'VE GOT AGAINST THAT POOR LITTLE PUPPY, BUT, YOU KNOW...
...AS LONG AS YOU DISLIKE SOMEBODY, THEY'LL NEVER LOVE YOU.
WHEN DID I EVER SAY I WANTED HIM TO LOVE ME...?
hahh
hahh
IT'S SO HARD TO...

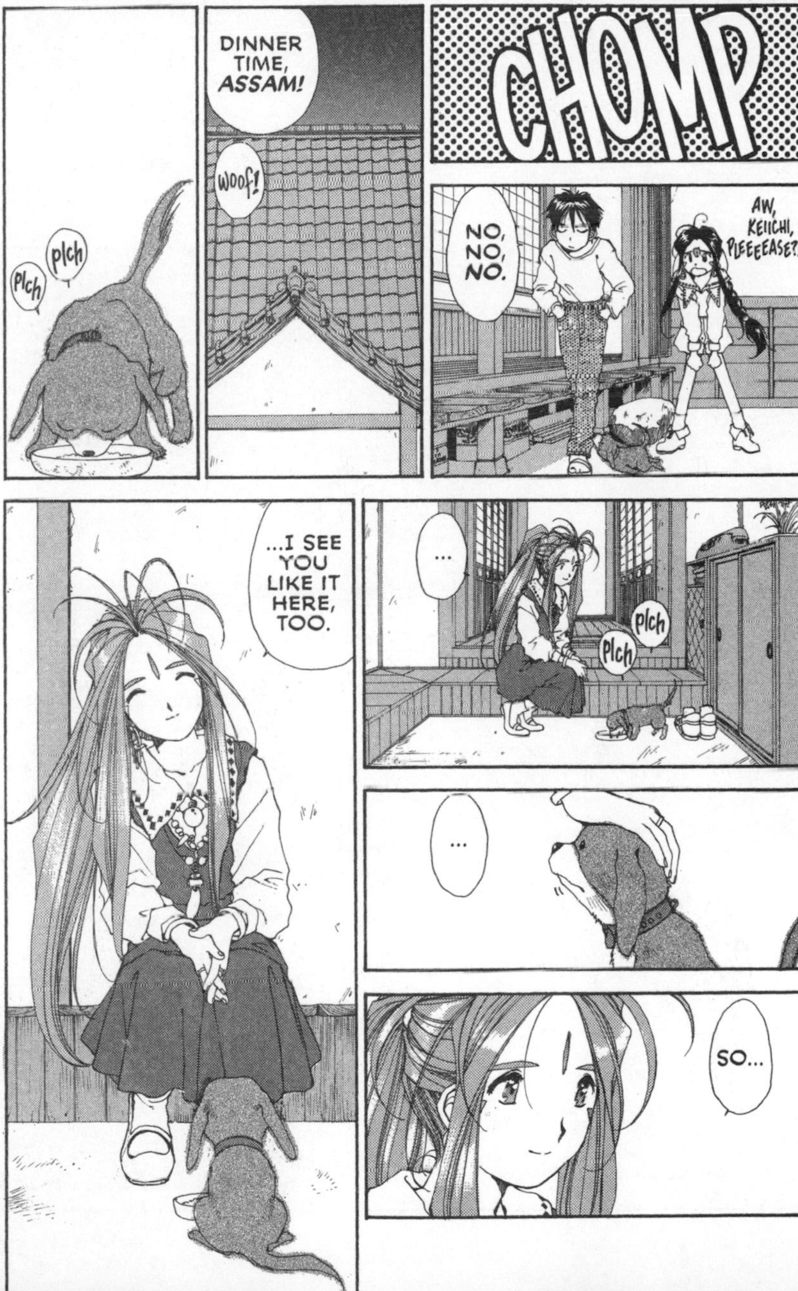
CHOMP
AW, KEIICHI, PLEEEEASE?!
NO, NO, NO.
DINNER TIME, ASSAM!
woof!
plch
plch
...
plch
plch
...
SO...
...I SEE YOU LIKE IT HERE, TOO.

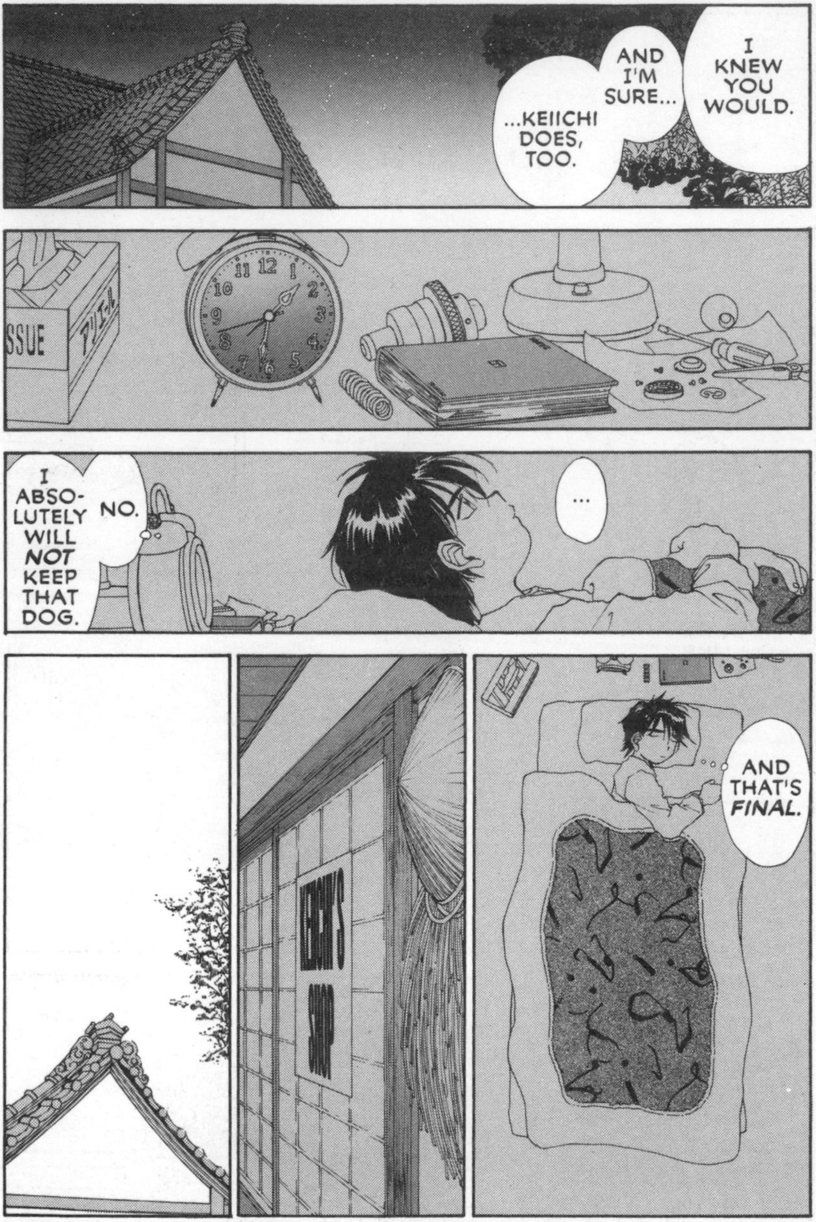
I KNEW YOU WOULD.
AND I'M SURE...
...KEIICHI DOES, TOO.
...
NO.
I ABSO-LUTELY WILL *NOT* KEEP THAT DOG.
KEIICHI'S SHOP
AND THAT'S *FINAL.*

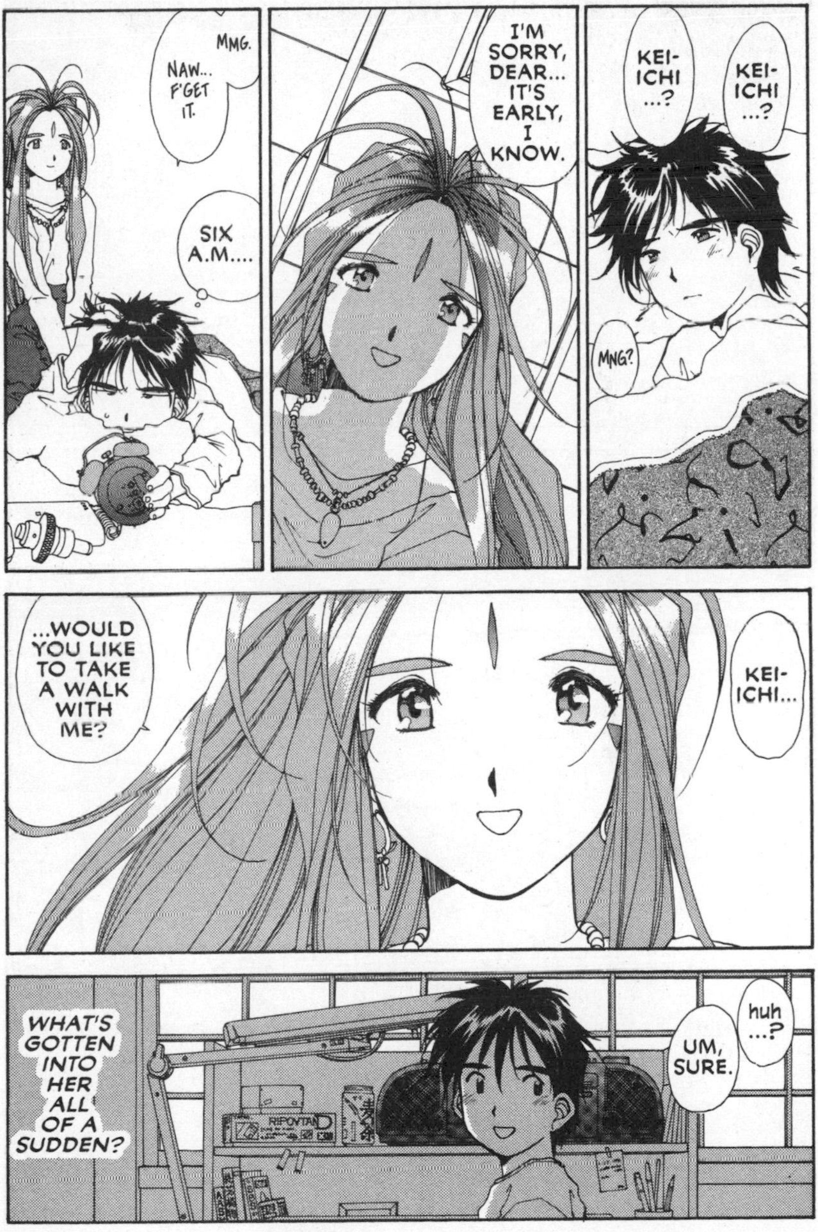
KEI-ICHI ...?
KEI-ICHI ...?
MNG?
I'M SORRY, DEAR... IT'S EARLY, I KNOW.
MMG.
NAW... F'GET IT.
SIX A.M....
KEI-ICHI...
...WOULD YOU LIKE TO TAKE A WALK WITH ME?
huh ...?
UM, SURE.
WHAT'S GOTTEN INTO HER ALL OF A SUDDEN?

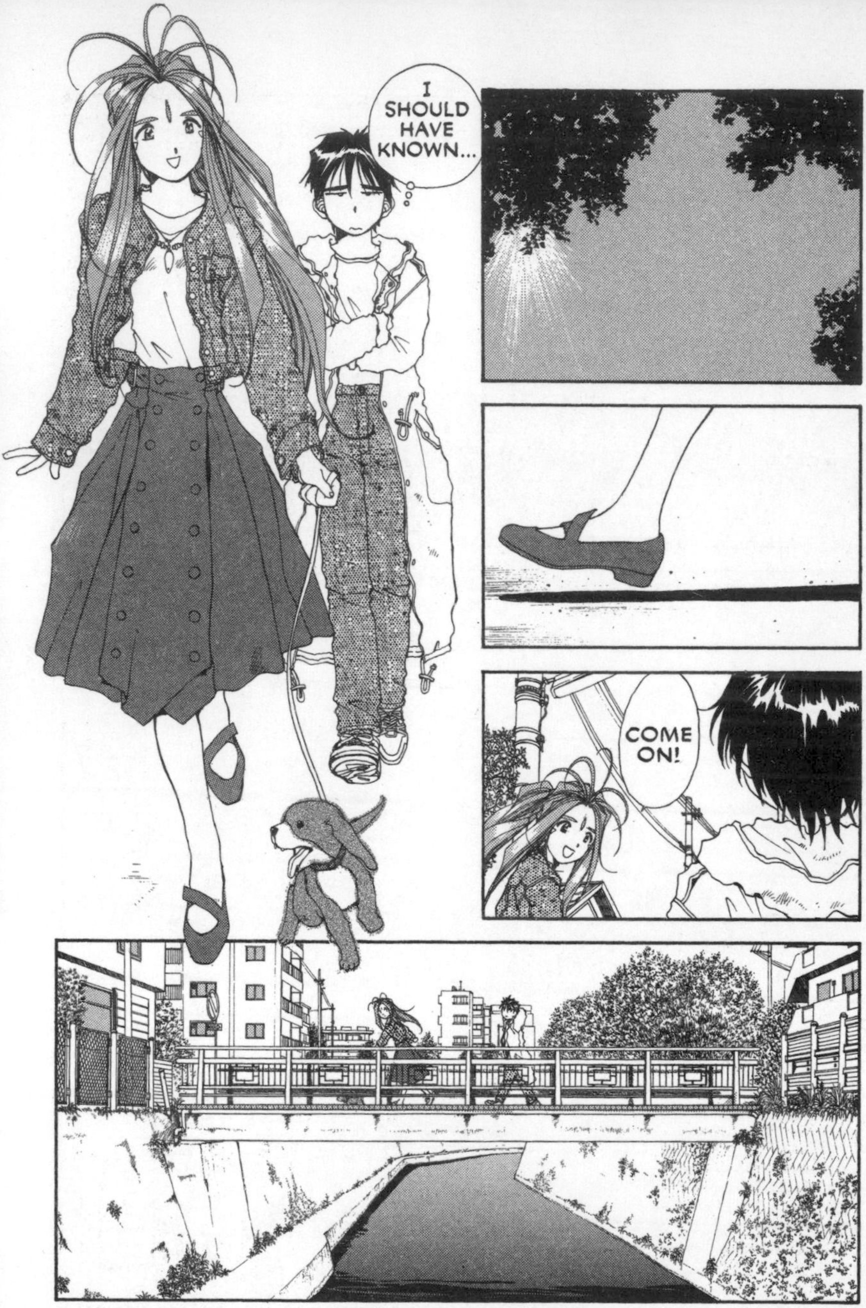
COME ON!
I SHOULD HAVE KNOWN...

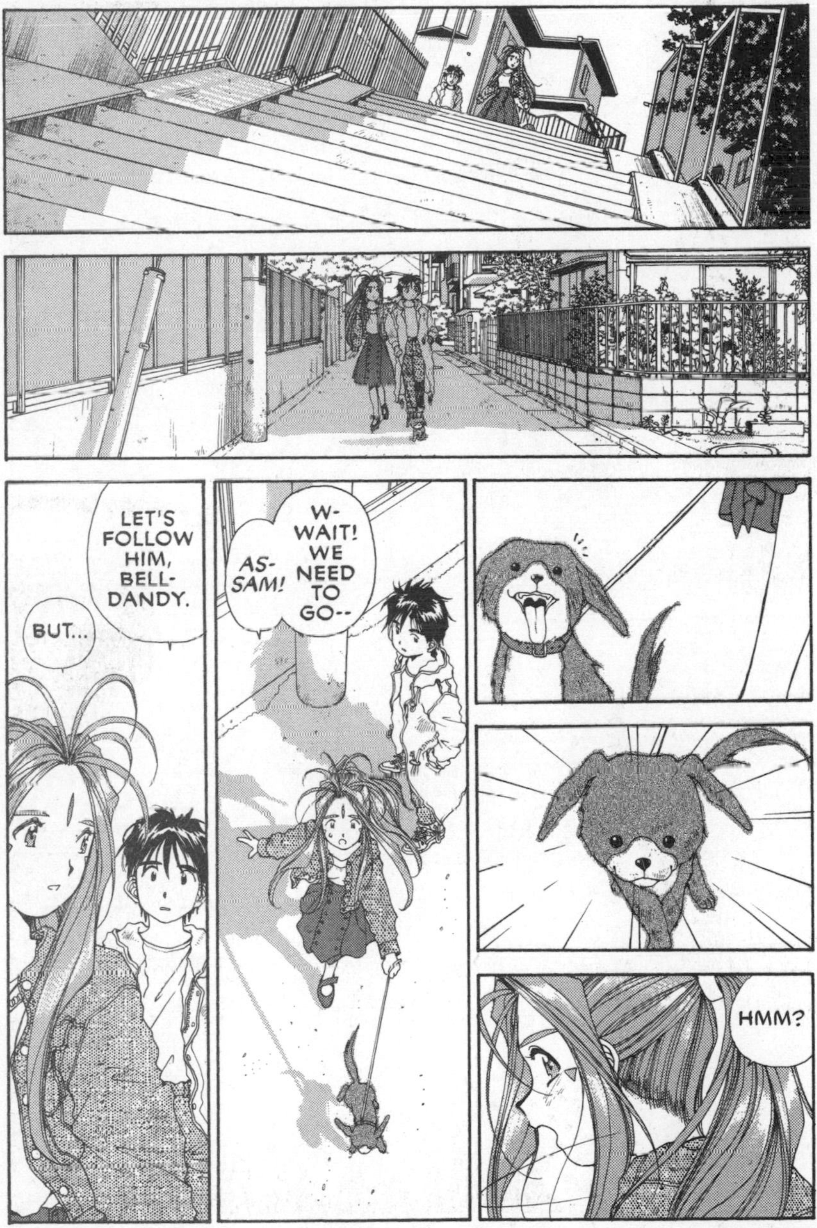
HMM?
W-WAIT! WE NEED TO GO--
AS-SAM!
LET'S FOLLOW HIM, BELL-DANDY.
BUT...

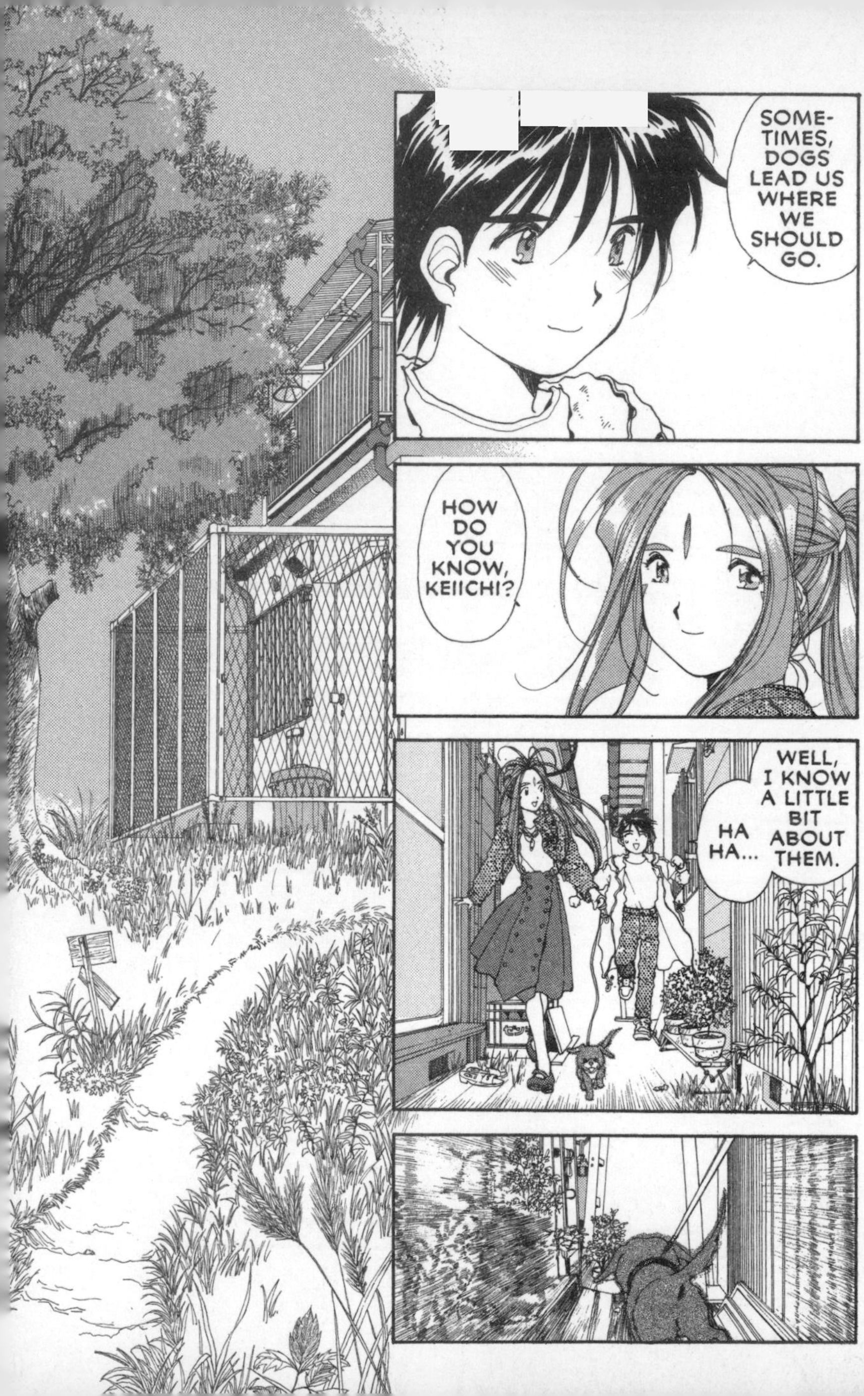
SOME-TIMES, DOGS LEAD US WHERE WE SHOULD GO.
HOW DO YOU KNOW, KEIICHI?
WELL, I KNOW A LITTLE BIT ABOUT THEM.
HA HA...

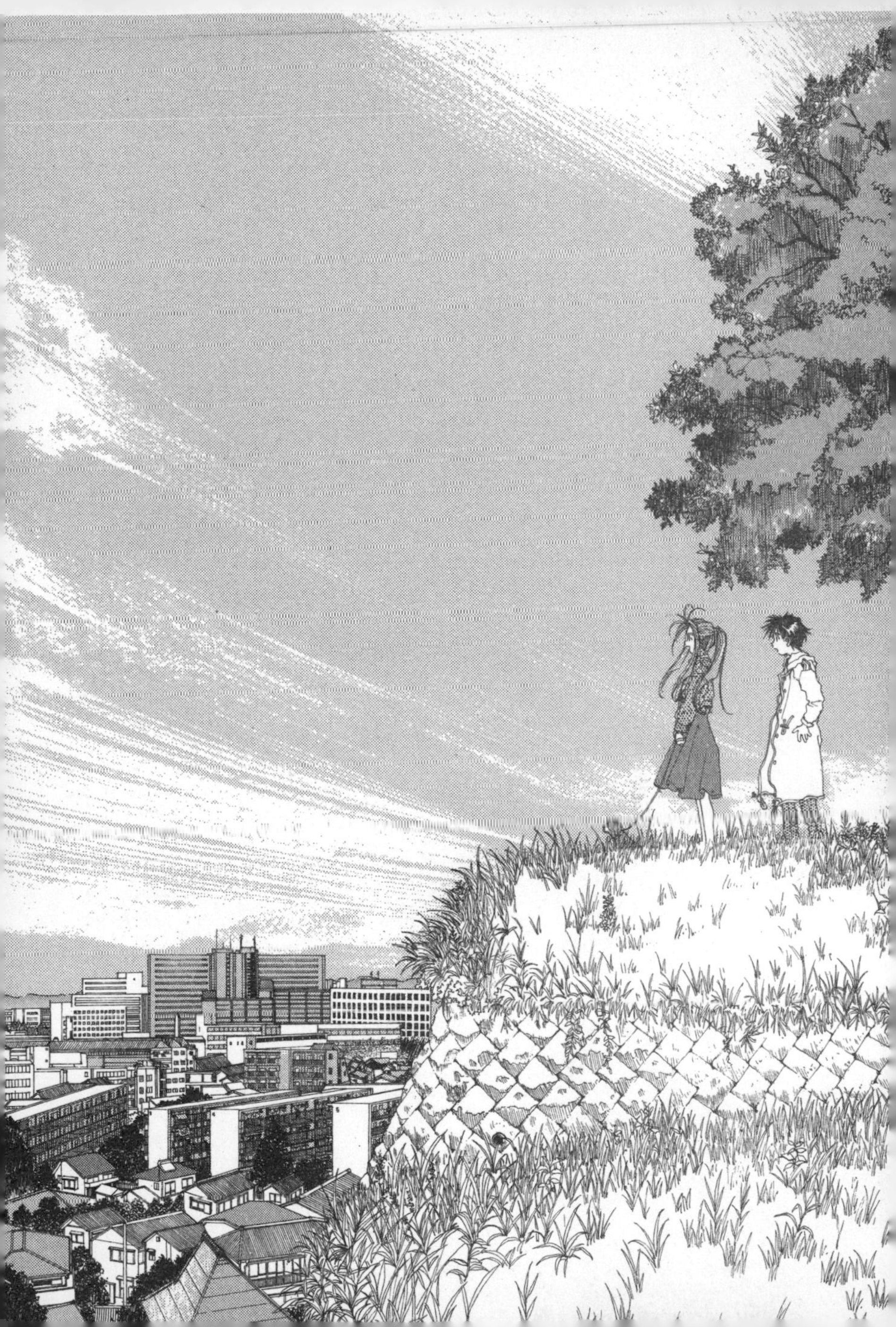

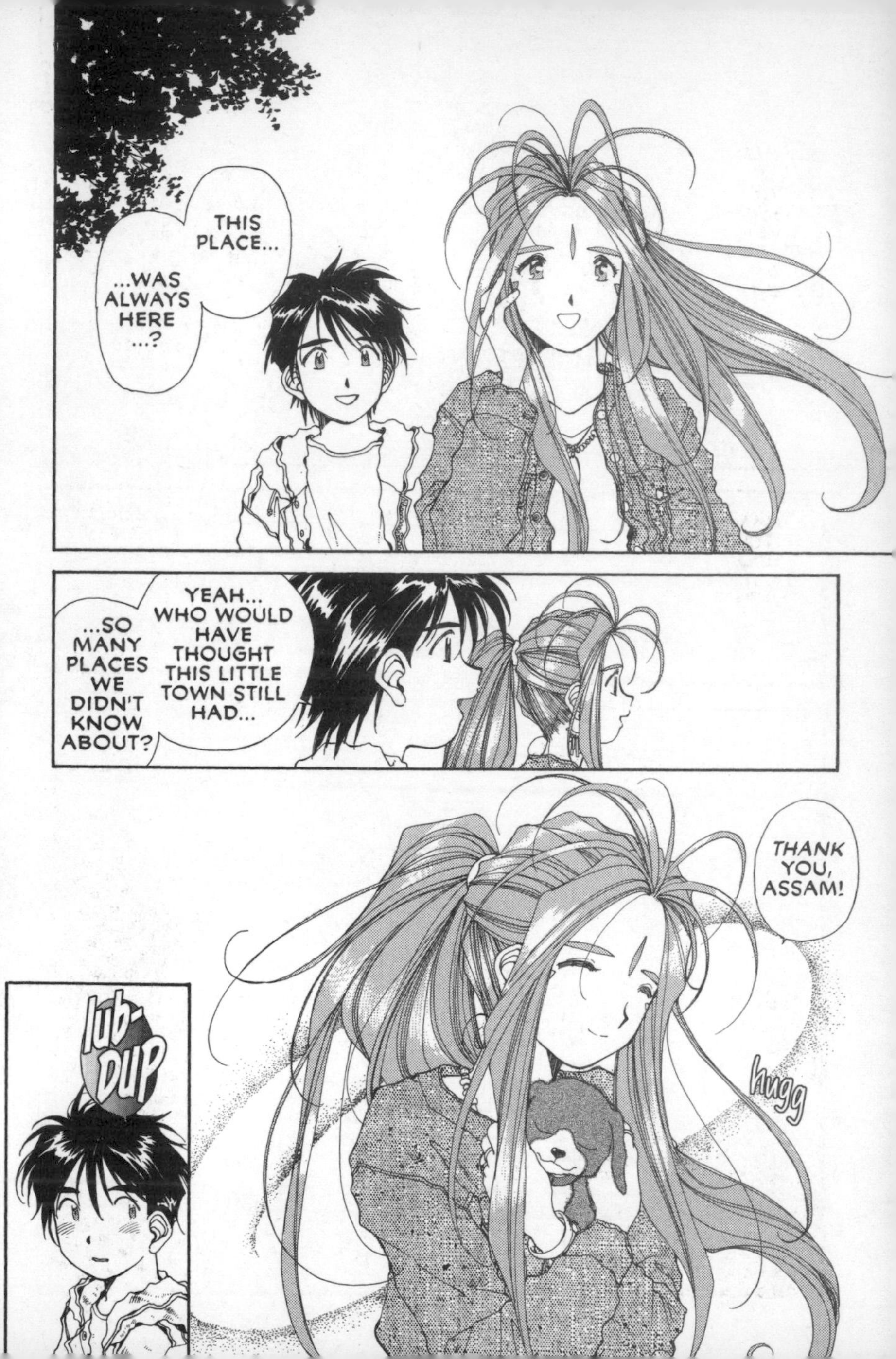
THIS PLACE...
...WAS ALWAYS HERE ...?
YEAH... WHO WOULD HAVE THOUGHT THIS LITTLE TOWN STILL HAD...
...SO MANY PLACES WE DIDN'T KNOW ABOUT?
THANK YOU, ASSAM!
hugg
lub-DUP

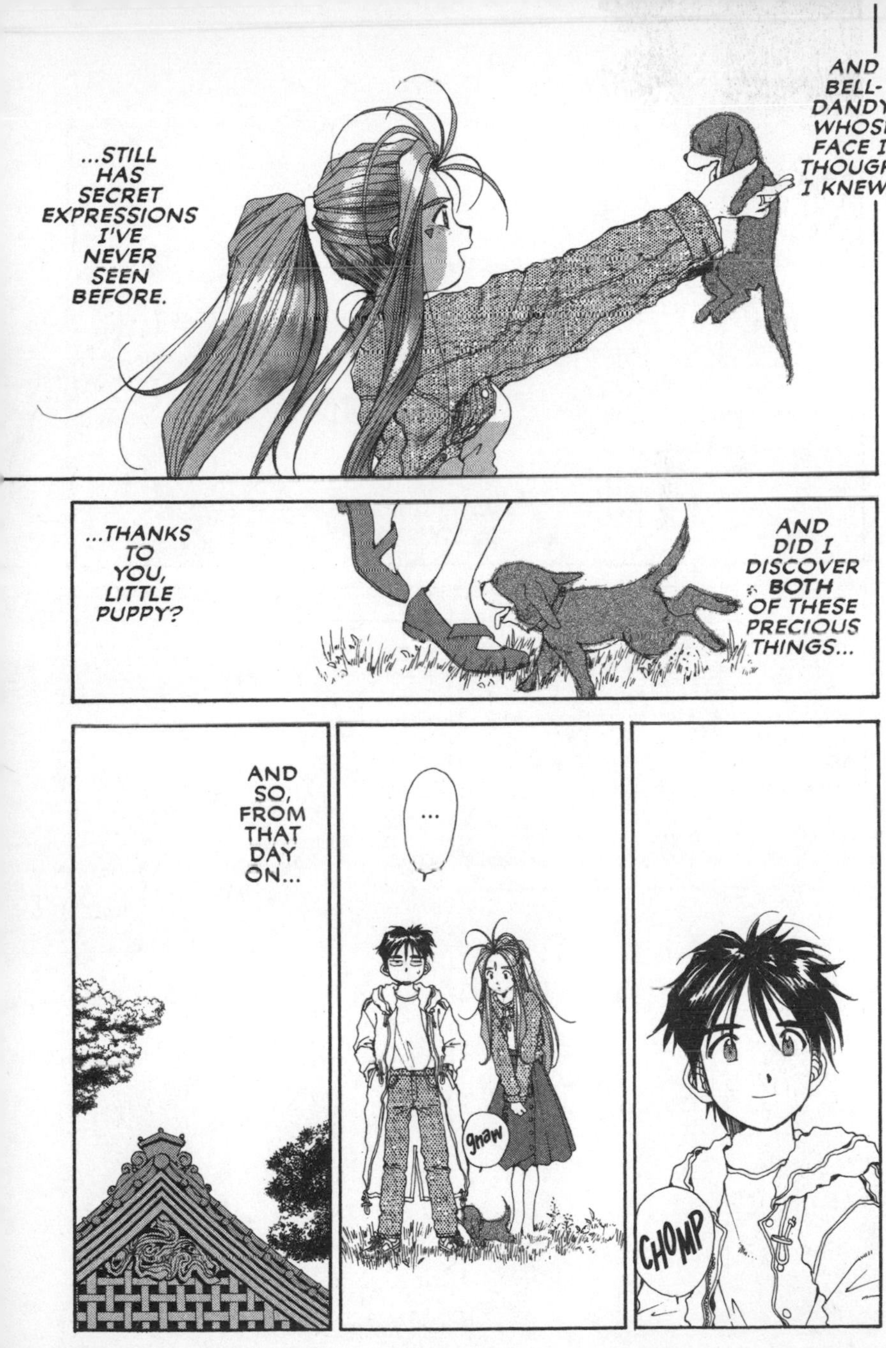
AND BELL-DANDY, WHOSE FACE I THOUGHT I KNEW...
...STILL HAS SECRET EXPRESSIONS I'VE NEVER SEEN BEFORE.
AND DID I DISCOVER BOTH OF THESE PRECIOUS THINGS...
...THANKS TO YOU, LITTLE PUPPY?
CHOMP
...
gnaw
AND SO, FROM THAT DAY ON...

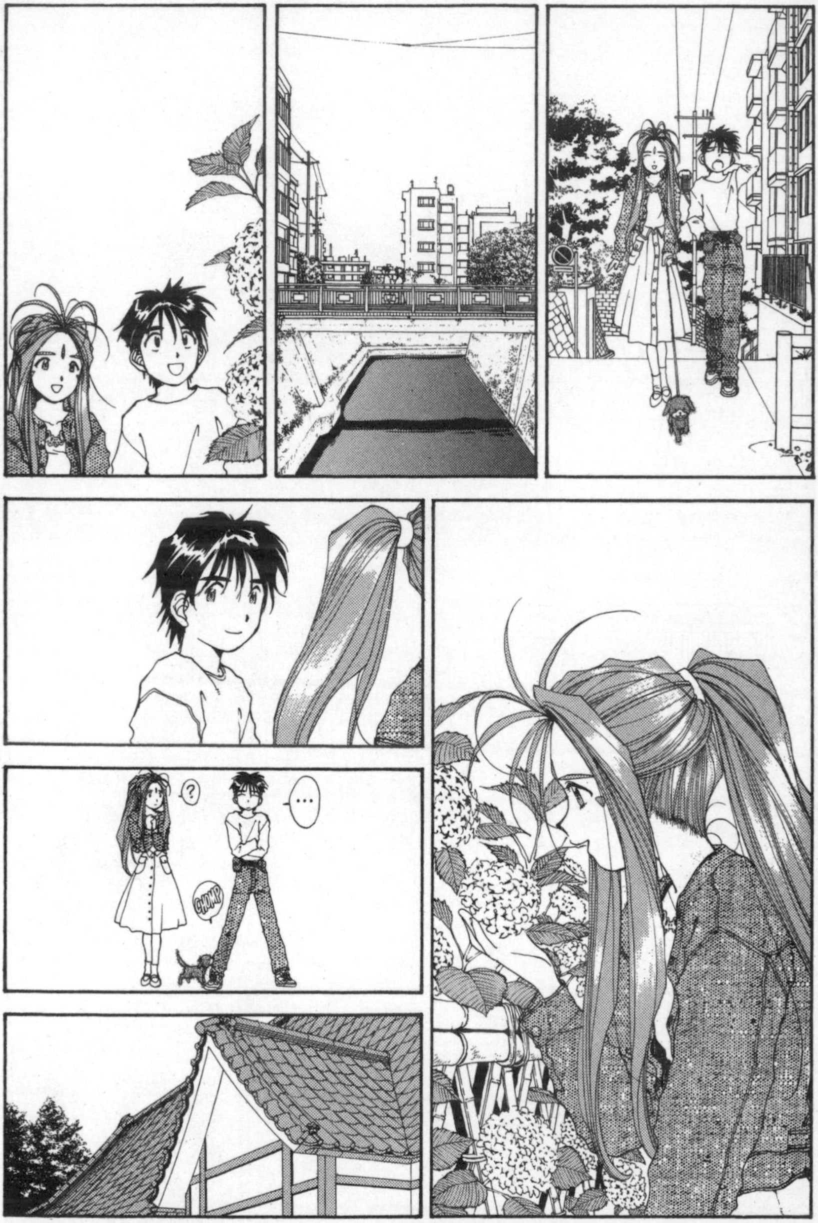
...
?
CHOMP!

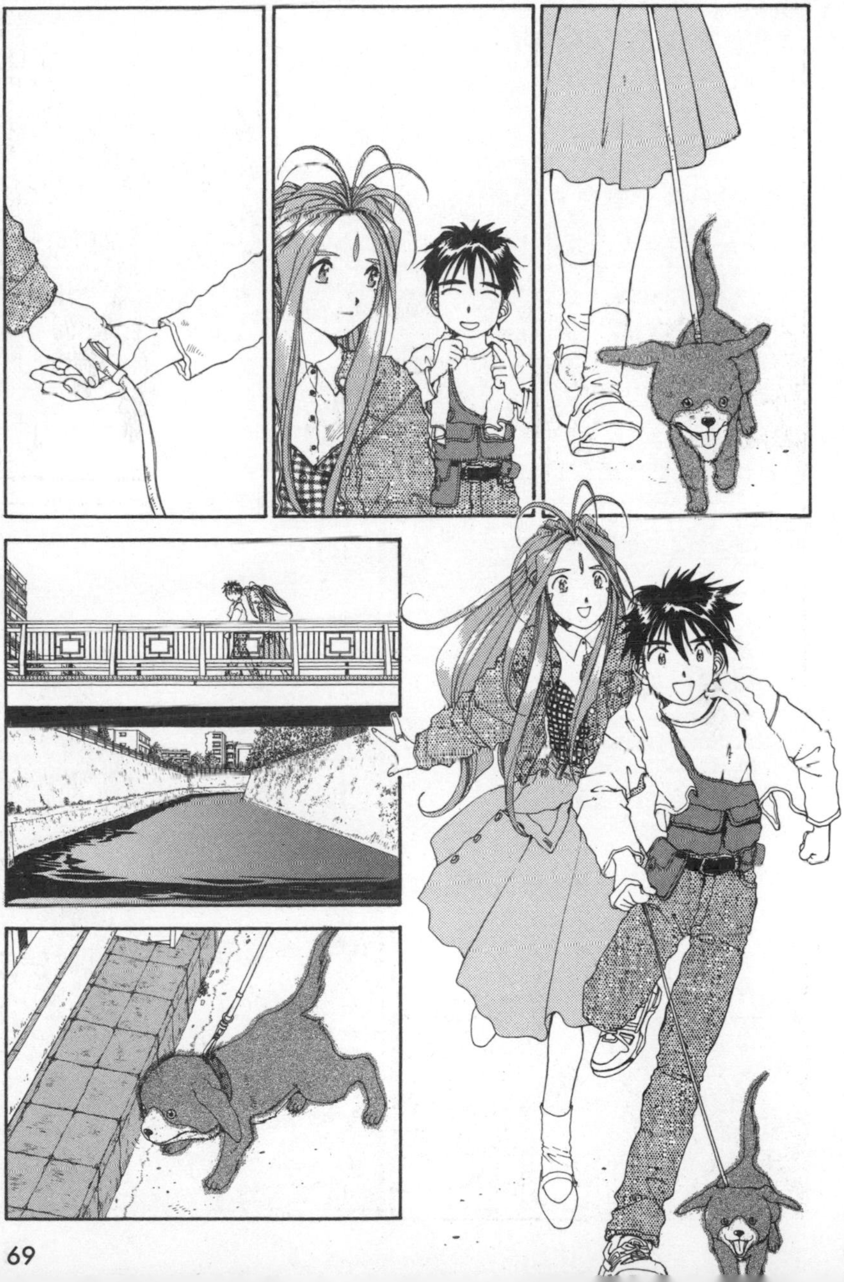

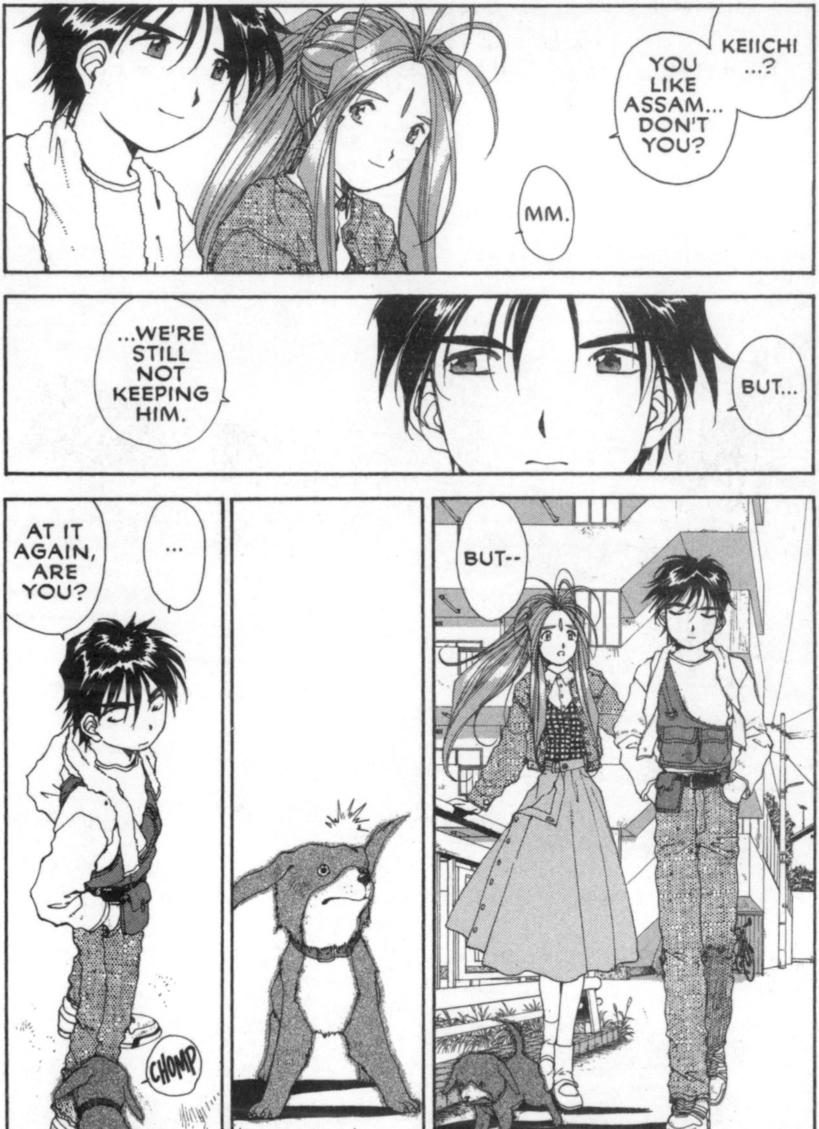
KEIICHI ...?
YOU LIKE ASSAM... DON'T YOU?
MM.
BUT...
...WE'RE STILL NOT KEEPING HIM.
BUT--
...
AT IT AGAIN, ARE YOU?
CHOMP

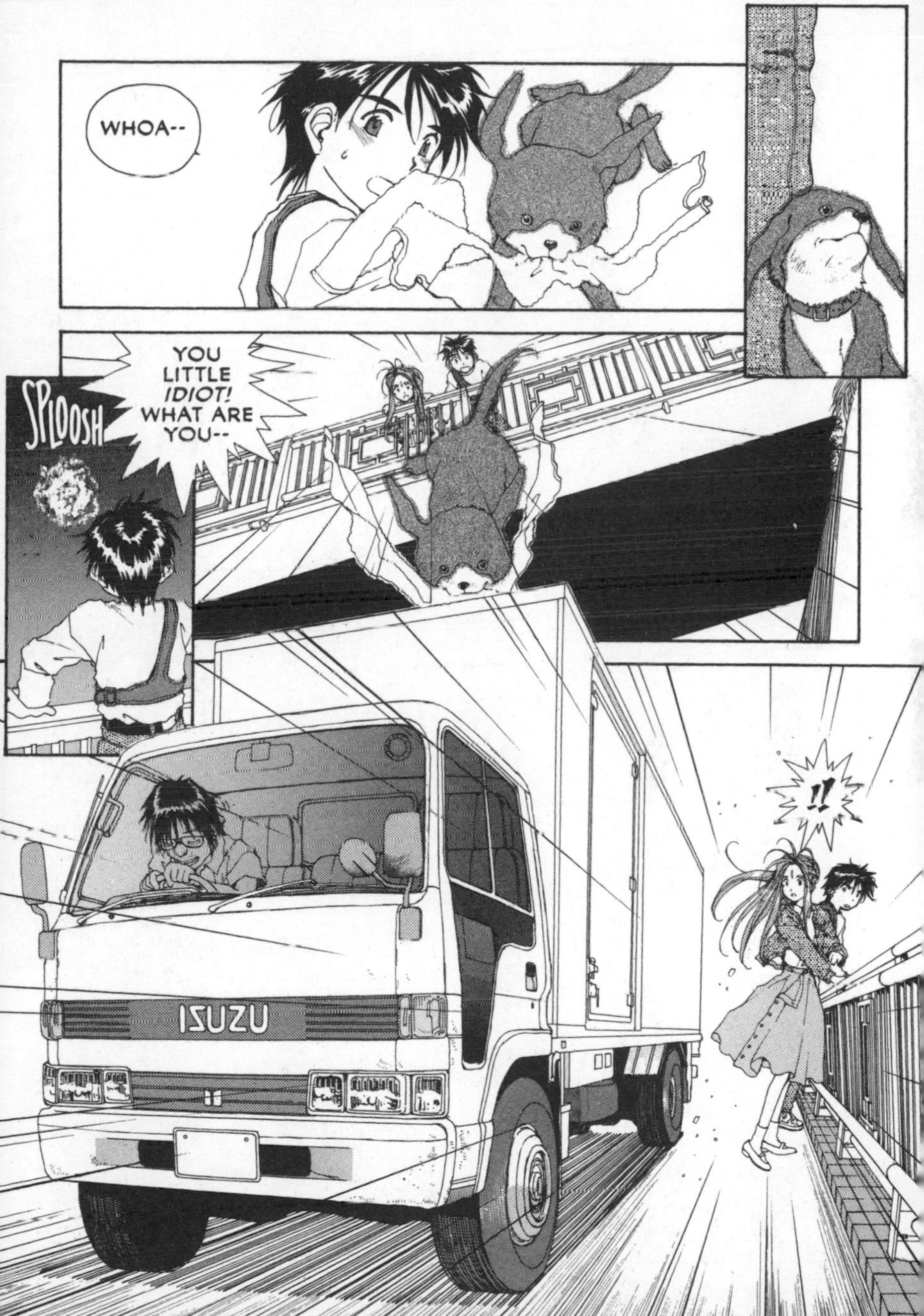
WHOA--
YOU LITTLE *IDIOT!* WHAT ARE YOU--
SPLOOSH
ISUZU
!!

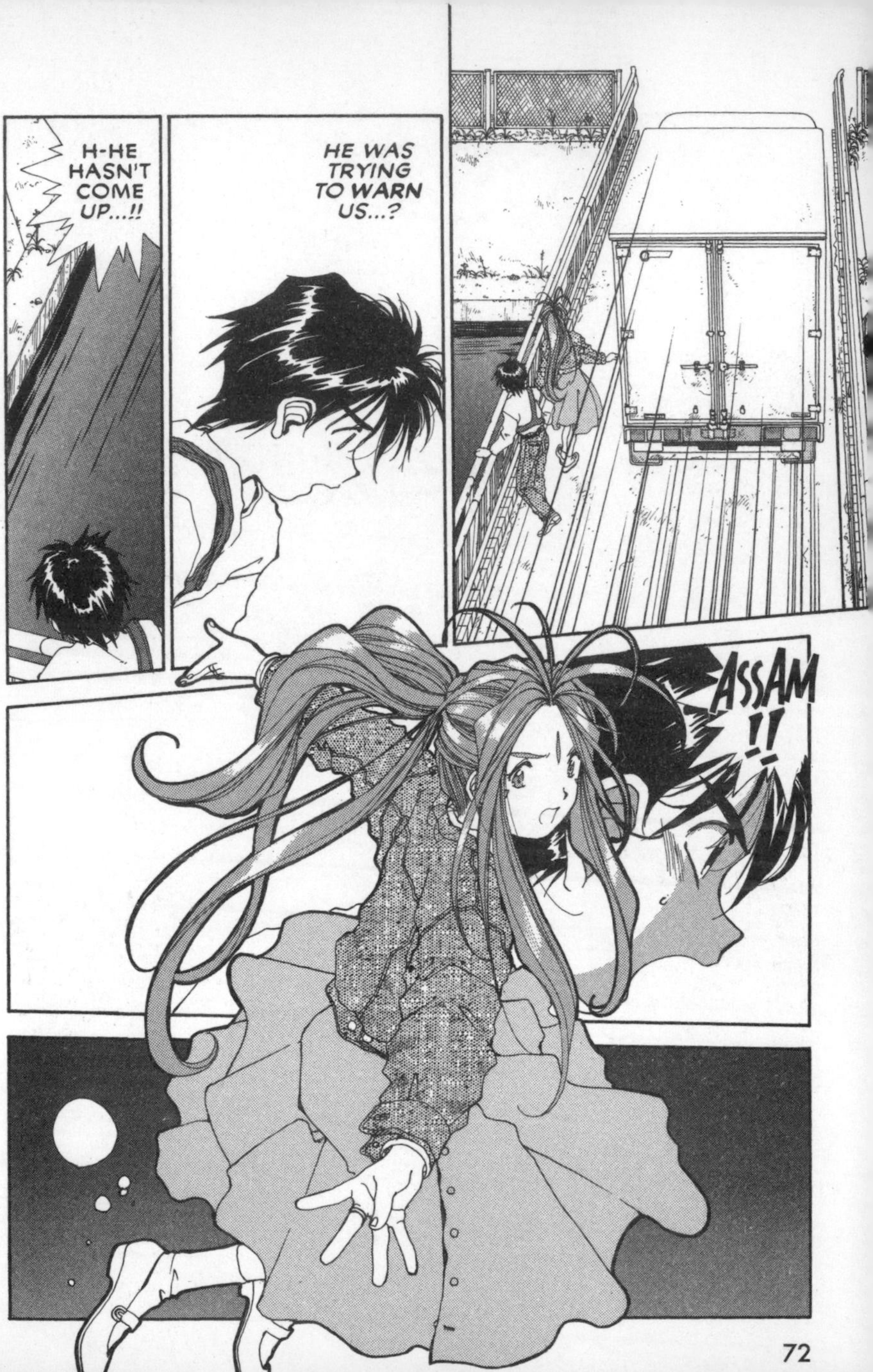
HE WAS TRYING TO WARN US...?
H-HE HASN'T COME UP...!!
ASSAM !!

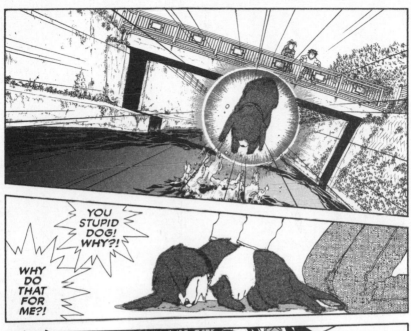

YOU STUPID DOG! WHY?!

WHY DO THAT FOR ME?!

NIHON-MARU!

OH, NO!!

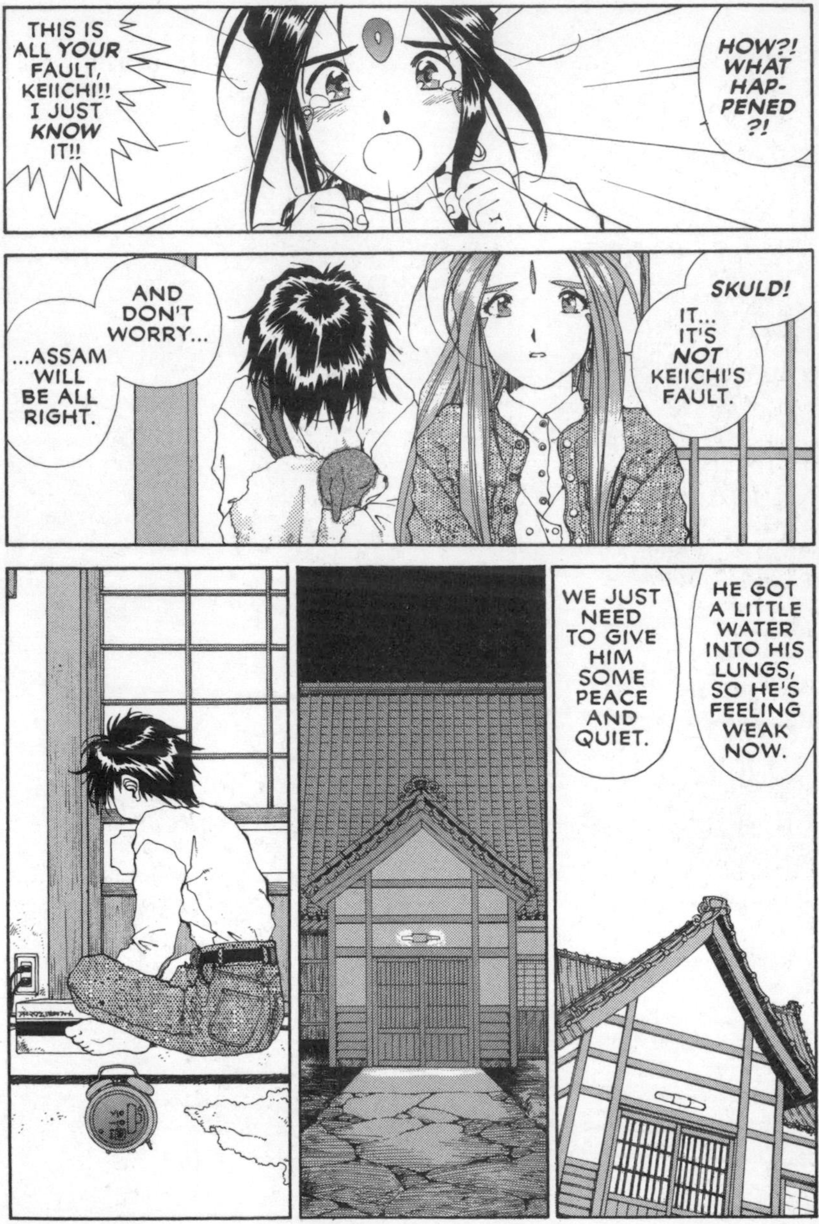
HOW?! WHAT HAPPENED?!
THIS IS ALL YOUR FAULT, KEIICHI!! I JUST KNOW IT!!
SKULD! IT... IT'S NOT KEIICHI'S FAULT.
AND DON'T WORRY... ...ASSAM WILL BE ALL RIGHT.
HE GOT A LITTLE WATER INTO HIS LUNGS, SO HE'S FEELING WEAK NOW.
WE JUST NEED TO GIVE HIM SOME PEACE AND QUIET.

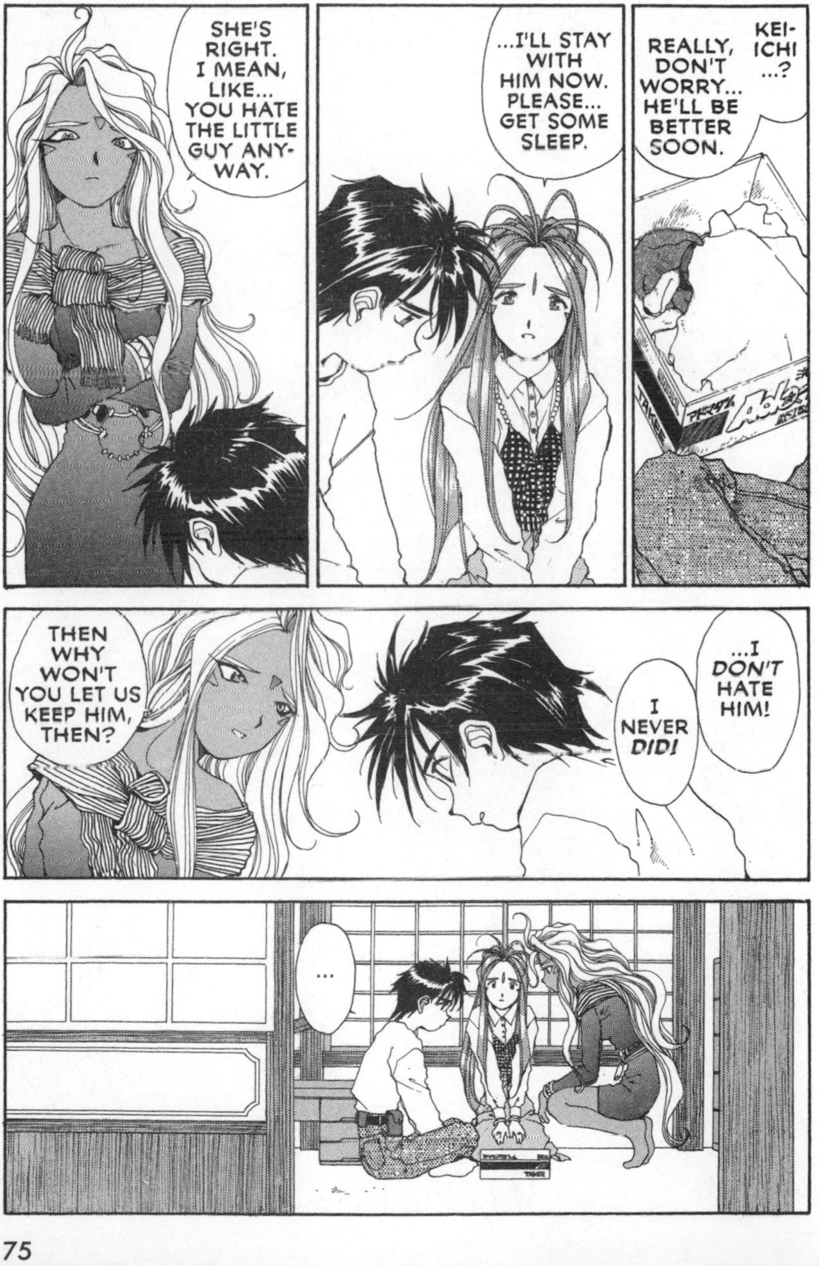
KEI-ICHI ...?
REALLY, DON'T WORRY... HE'LL BE BETTER SOON.
...I'LL STAY WITH HIM NOW. PLEASE... GET SOME SLEEP.
SHE'S RIGHT. I MEAN, LIKE... YOU HATE THE LITTLE GUY ANY-WAY.
...I *DON'T* HATE HIM!
I NEVER *DID!*
THEN WHY WON'T YOU LET US KEEP HIM, THEN?
...

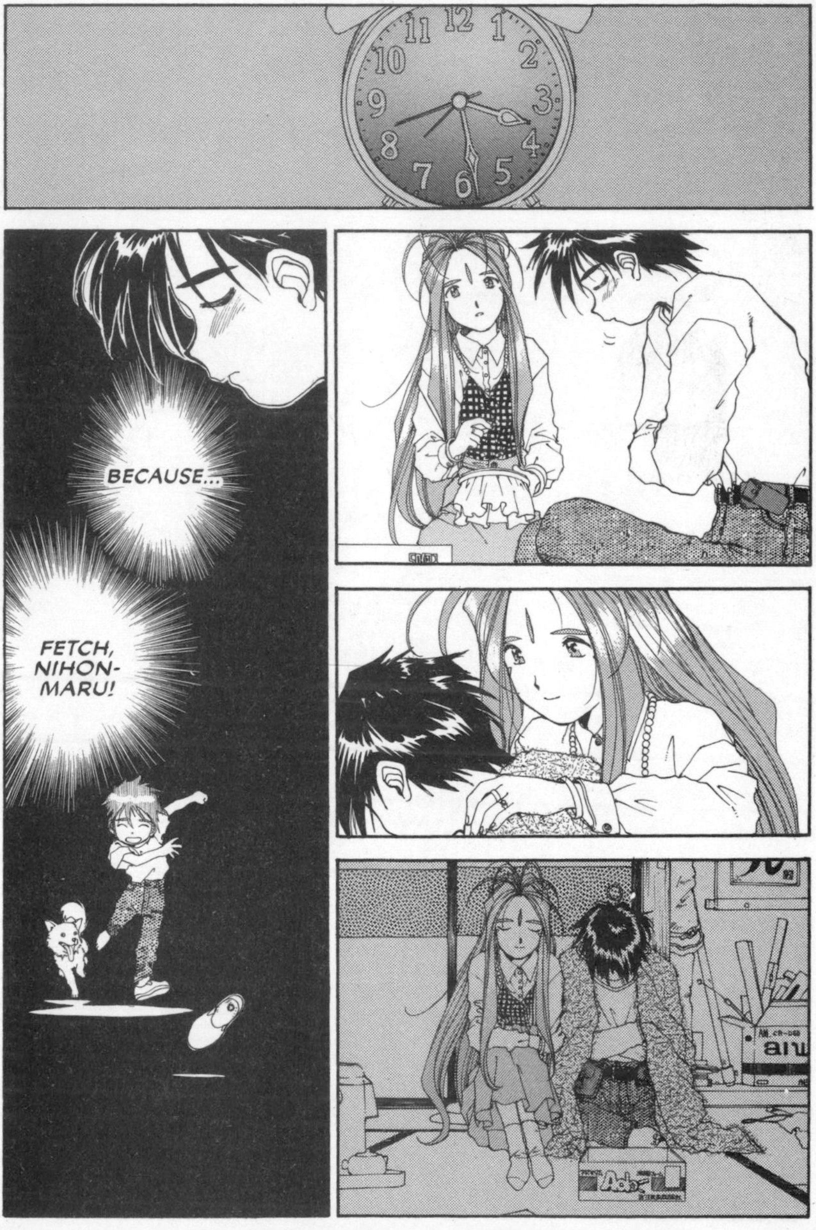

BECAUSE...
FETCH, NIHON-MARU!

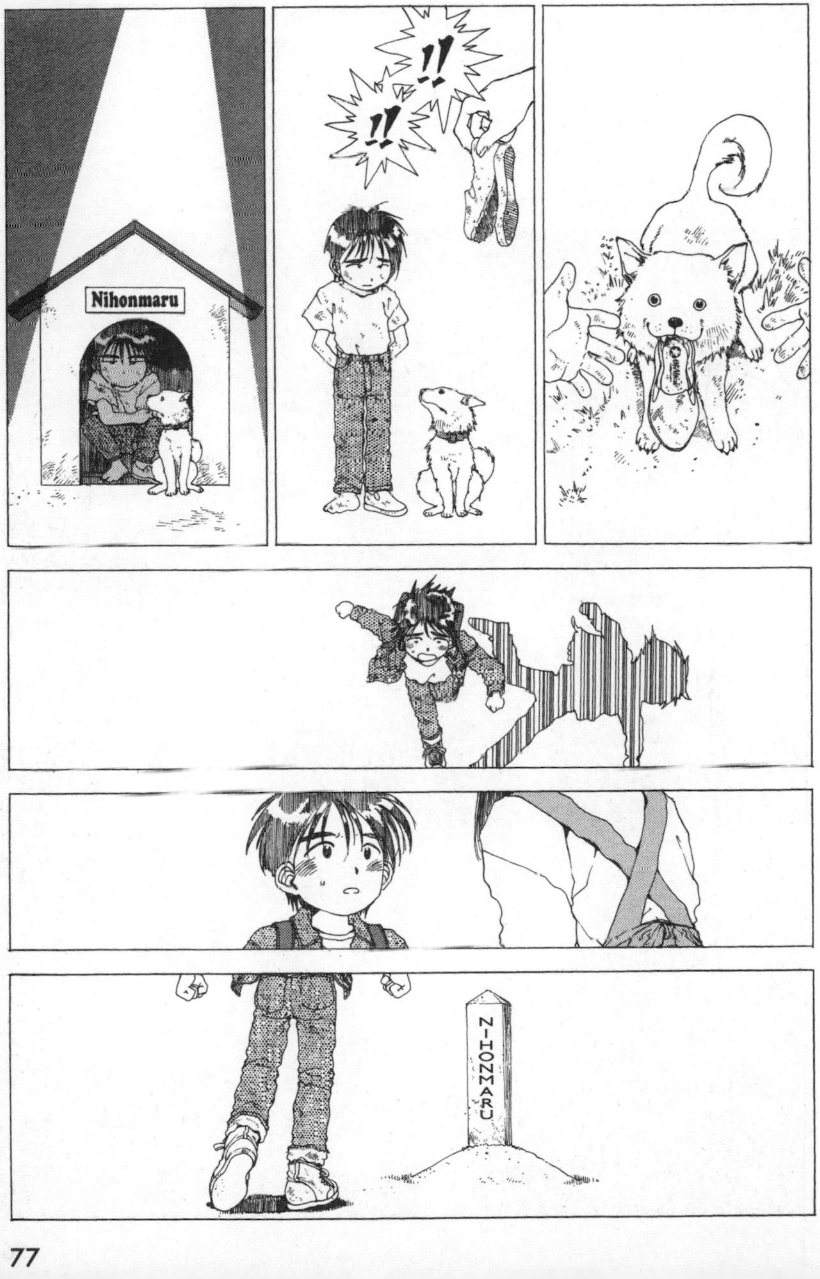
!!
!!
Nihonmaru
NIHONMARU

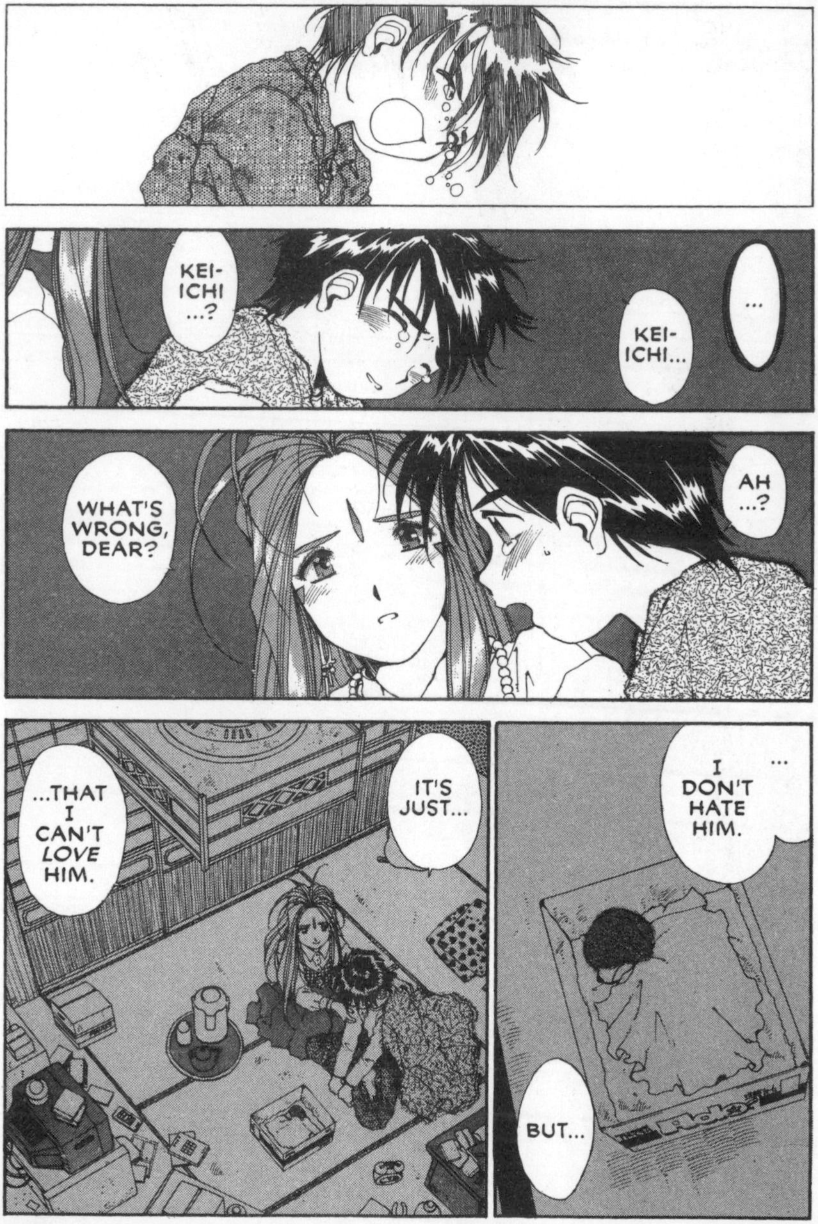
...
KEI-ICHI...
KEI-ICHI...?
AH ...?
WHAT'S WRONG, DEAR?
... I DON'T HATE HIM.
BUT...
IT'S JUST...
...THAT I CAN'T *LOVE* HIM.

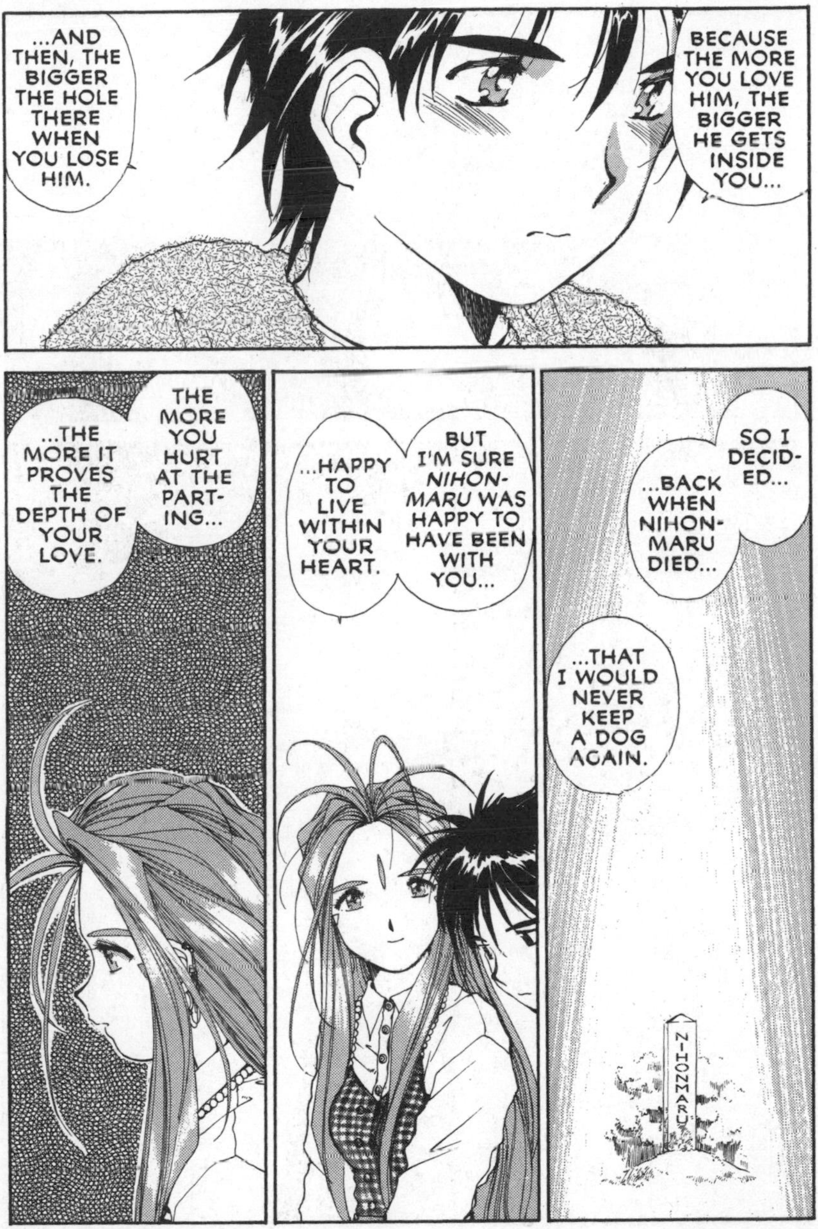
BECAUSE THE MORE YOU LOVE HIM, THE BIGGER HE GETS INSIDE YOU...
...AND THEN, THE BIGGER THE HOLE THERE WHEN YOU LOSE HIM.
SO I DECIDED...
...BACK WHEN NIHONMARU DIED...
...THAT I WOULD NEVER KEEP A DOG AGAIN.
NIHONMARU
BUT I'M SURE *NIHONMARU* WAS HAPPY TO HAVE BEEN WITH YOU...
...HAPPY TO LIVE WITHIN YOUR HEART.
THE MORE YOU HURT AT THE PARTING...
...THE MORE IT PROVES THE DEPTH OF YOUR LOVE.

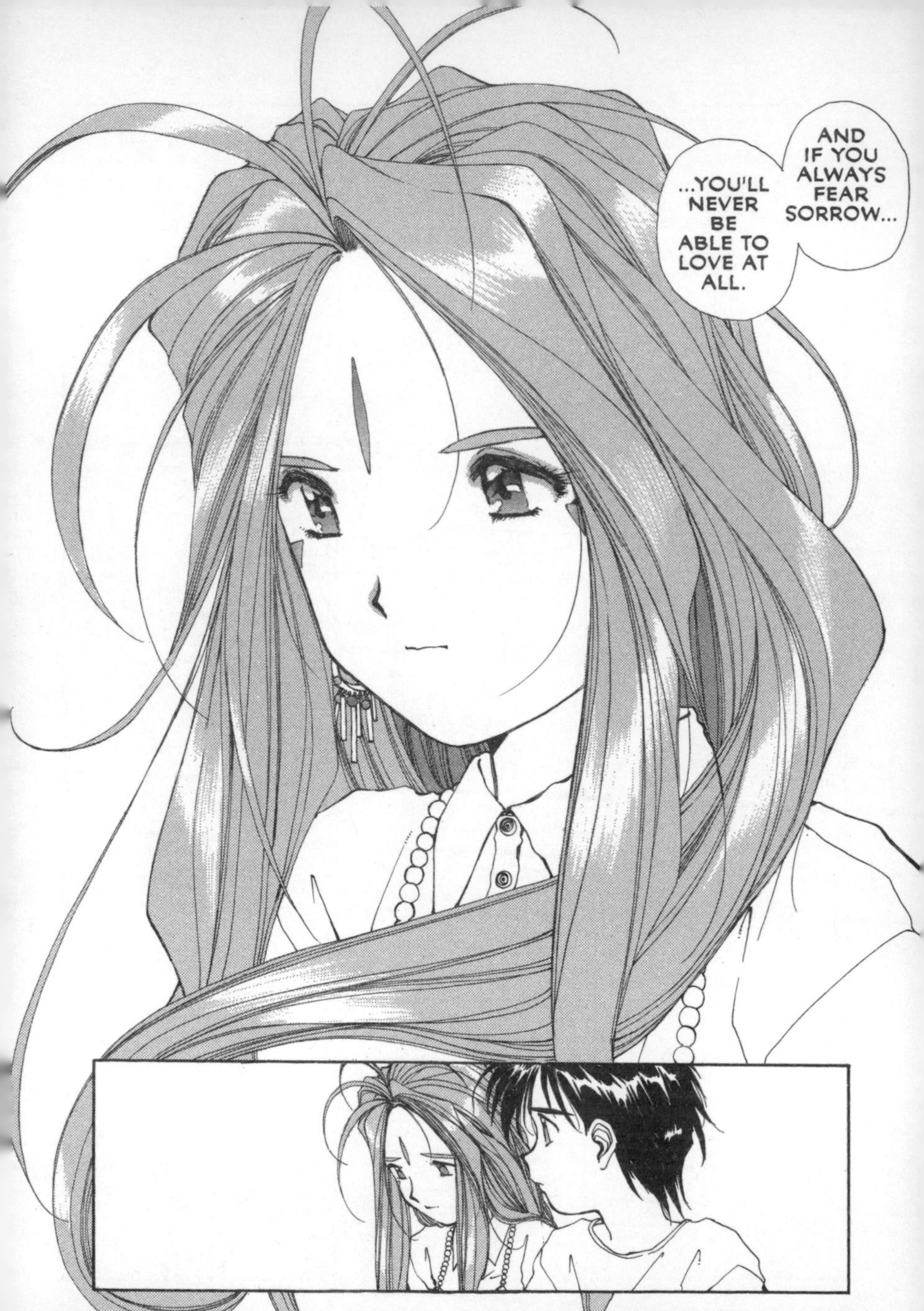
AND IF YOU ALWAYS FEAR SORROW...
...YOU'LL NEVER BE ABLE TO LOVE AT ALL.

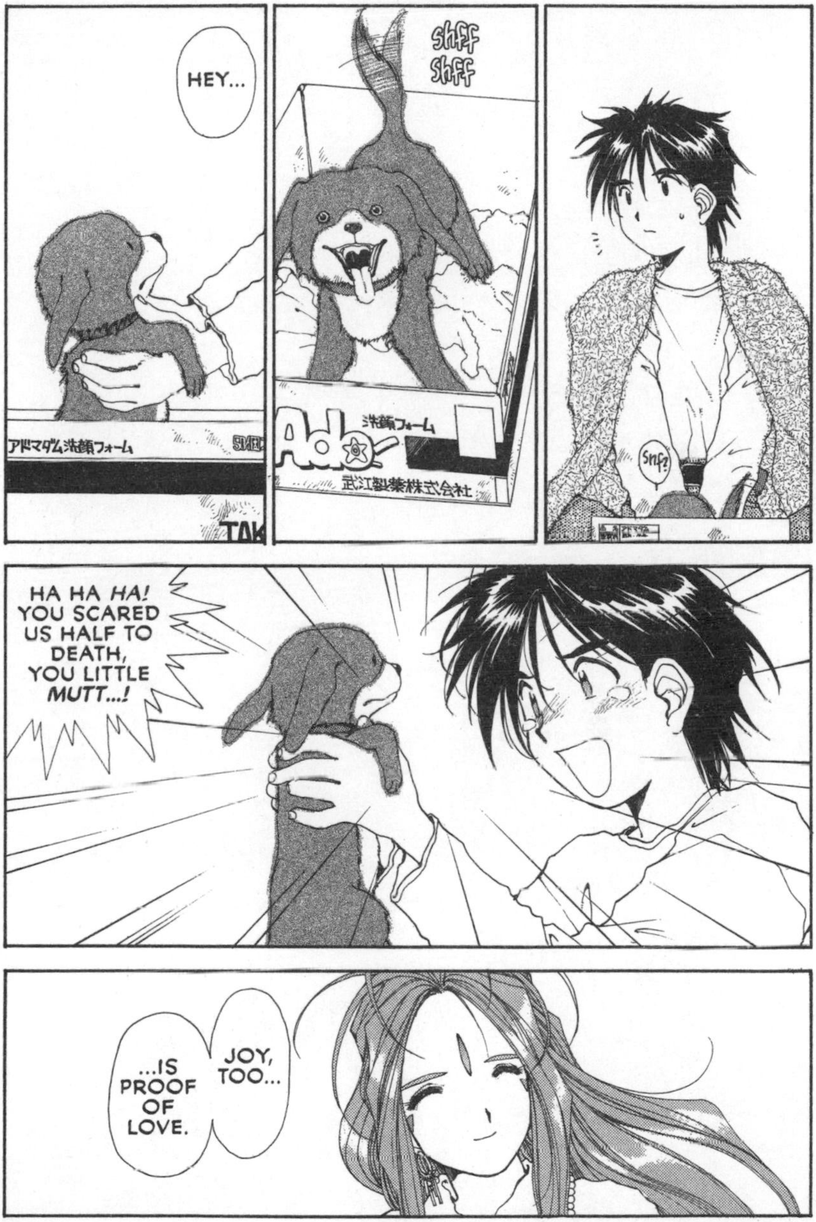
snf?
shff
shff
Ado
洗顔フォーム
武江製薬株式会社
HEY...
アドマダム洗顔フォーム
HA HA HA! YOU SCARED US HALF TO DEATH, YOU LITTLE MUTT...!
JOY, TOO...
...IS PROOF OF LOVE.

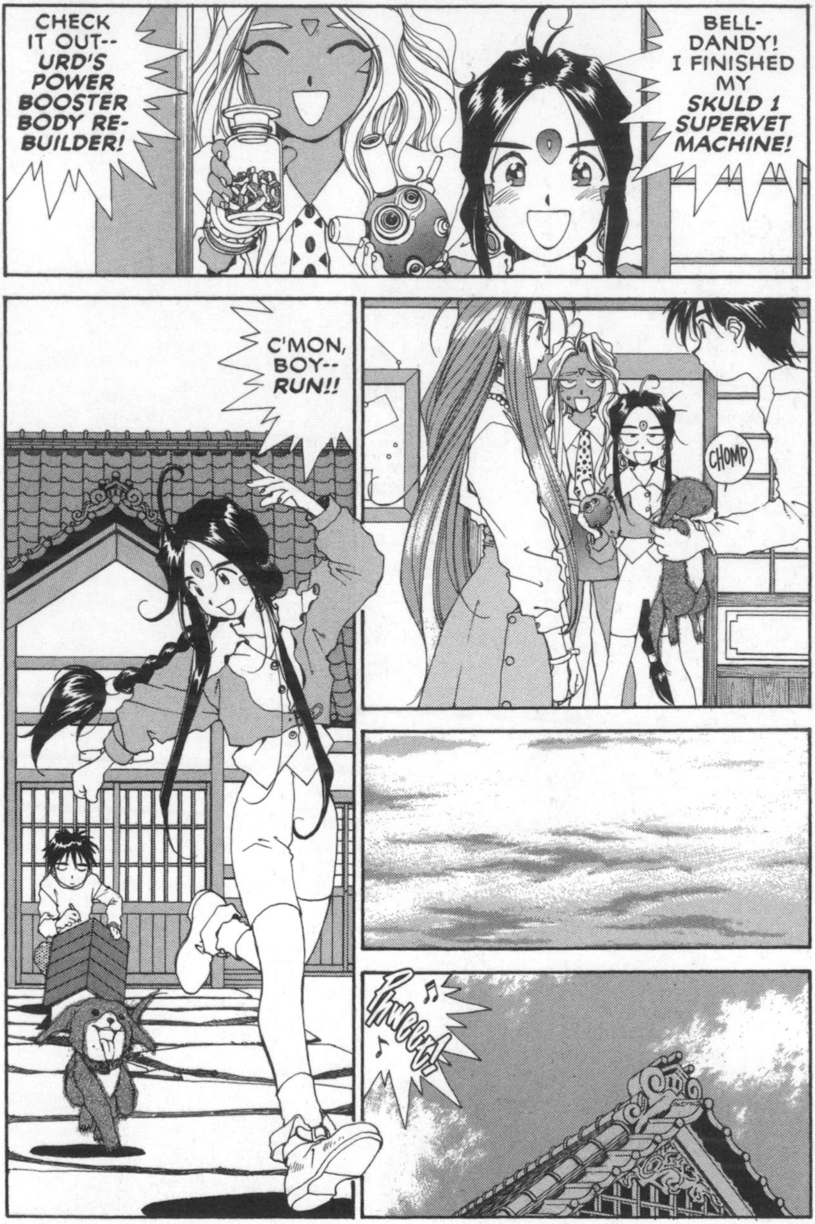
BELL-DANDY! I FINISHED MY SKULD 1 SUPERVET MACHINE!
CHECK IT OUT-- URD'S POWER BOOSTER BODY RE-BUILDER!
CHOMP
Phweeet!
C'MON, BOY-- RUN!!

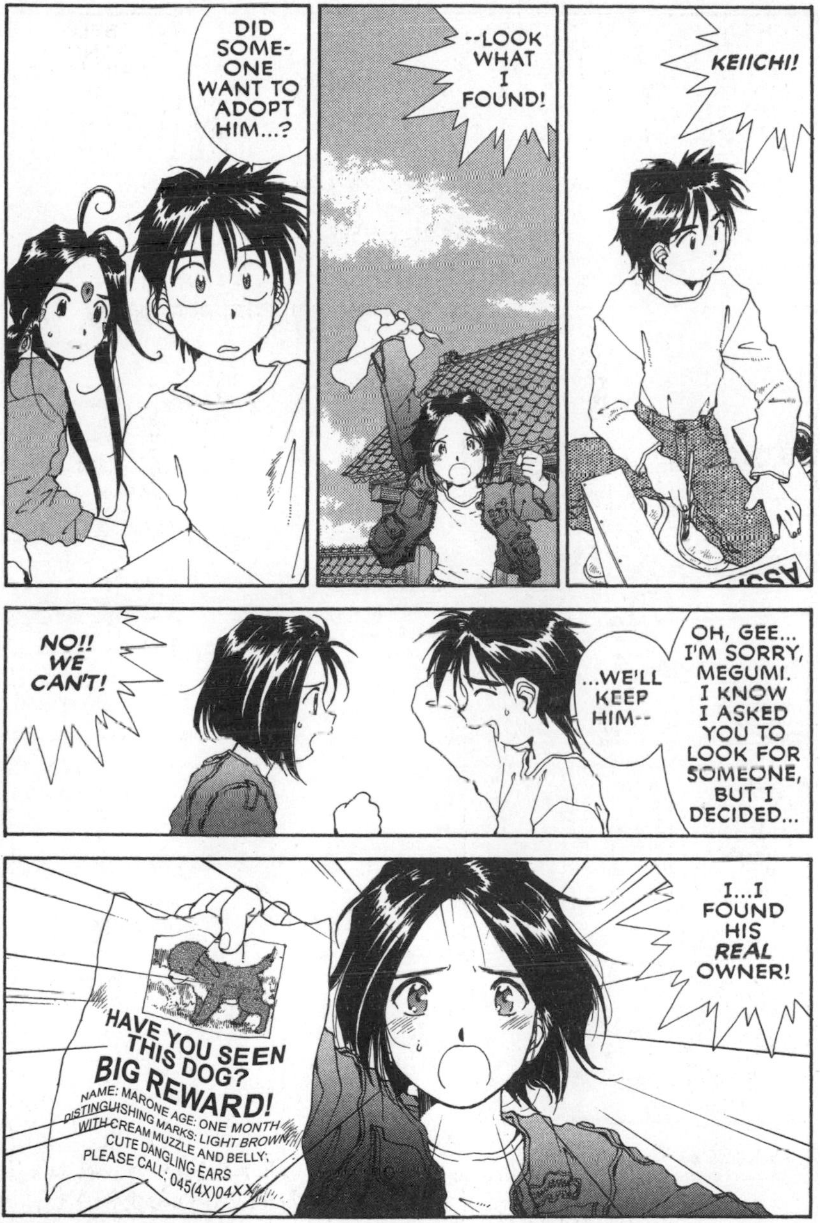
KEIICHI!
--LOOK WHAT I FOUND!
DID SOME-ONE WANT TO ADOPT HIM...?
OH, GEE... I'M SORRY, MEGUMI. I KNOW I ASKED YOU TO LOOK FOR SOMEONE, BUT I DECIDED...
...WE'LL KEEP HIM--
NO!! WE CAN'T!
I...I FOUND HIS REAL OWNER!
HAVE YOU SEEN THIS DOG?
BIG REWARD!
NAME: MARONE AGE: ONE MONTH
DISTINGUISHING MARKS: LIGHT BROWN WITH CREAM MUZZLE AND BELLY; CUTE DANGLING EARS
PLEASE CALL: 045(4X)04XX

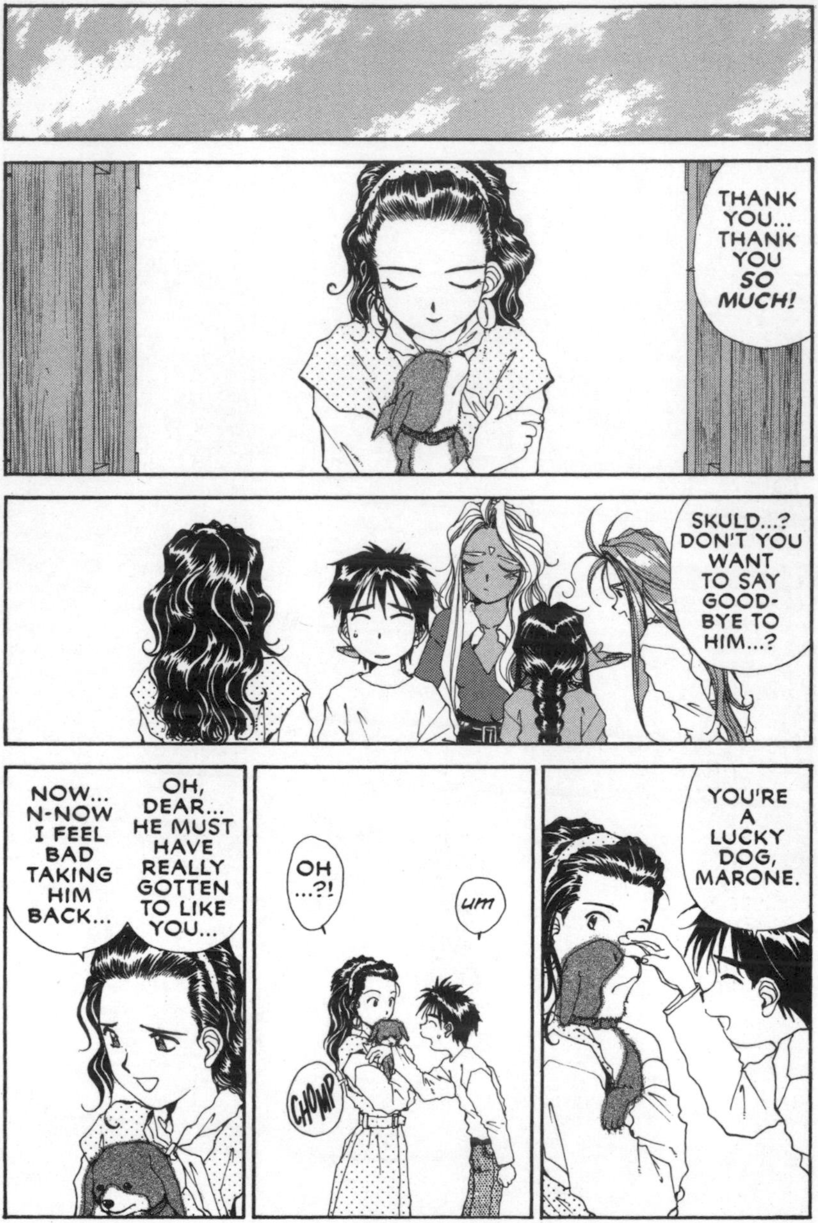
THANK YOU... THANK YOU *SO MUCH!*
SKULD...? DON'T YOU WANT TO SAY GOOD-BYE TO HIM...?
YOU'RE A LUCKY DOG, MARONE.
OH ...?!
um
CHOMP
OH, DEAR... HE MUST HAVE REALLY GOTTEN TO LIKE YOU...
NOW... N-NOW I FEEL BAD TAKING HIM BACK...

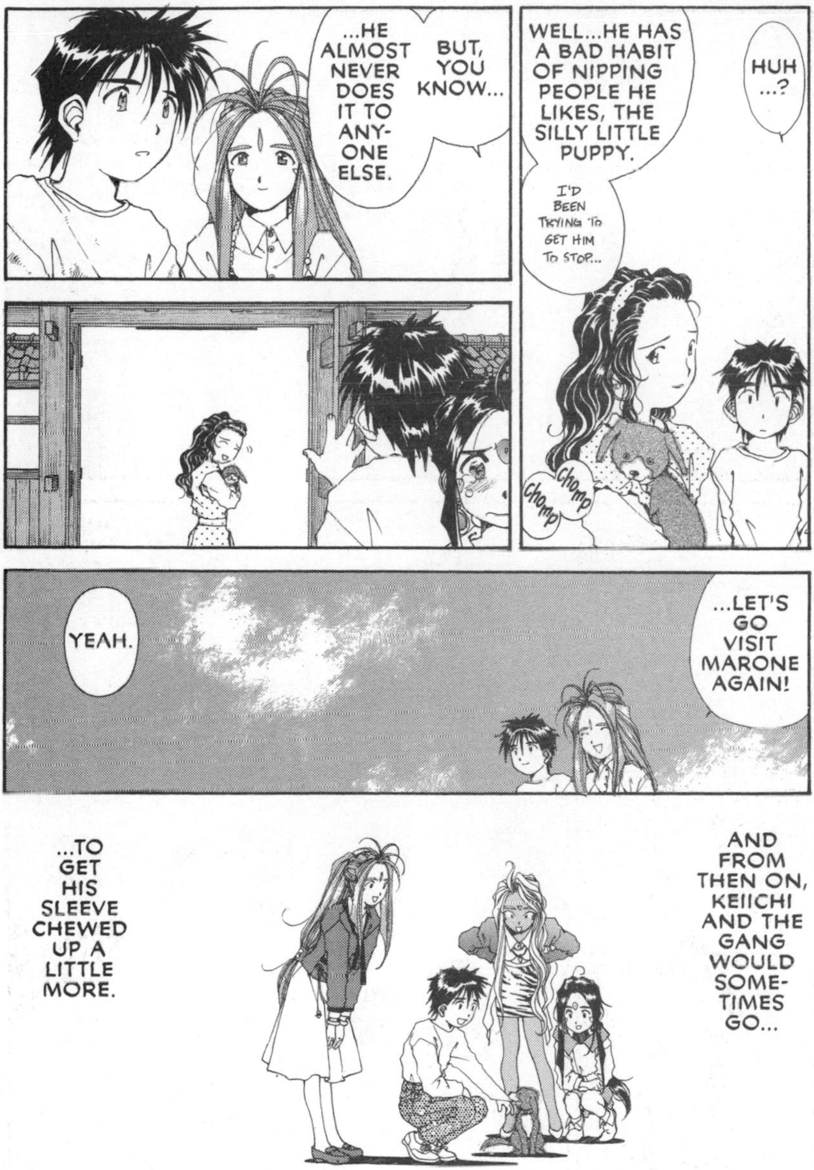
HUH ...?
WELL...HE HAS A BAD HABIT OF NIPPING PEOPLE HE LIKES, THE SILLY LITTLE PUPPY.
I'D BEEN TRYING TO GET HIM TO STOP...
Chomp
Chomp
BUT, YOU KNOW...
...HE ALMOST NEVER DOES IT TO ANYONE ELSE.
...LET'S GO VISIT MARONE AGAIN!
YEAH.
AND FROM THEN ON, KEIICHI AND THE GANG WOULD SOMETIMES GO...
...TO GET HIS SLEEVE CHEWED UP A LITTLE MORE.

THE ADVENTURES OF THE MINI-GODDESSES

◆BACK AGAIN! THE "OH MY ROCK GODDESS" GRAND PRIX!◆

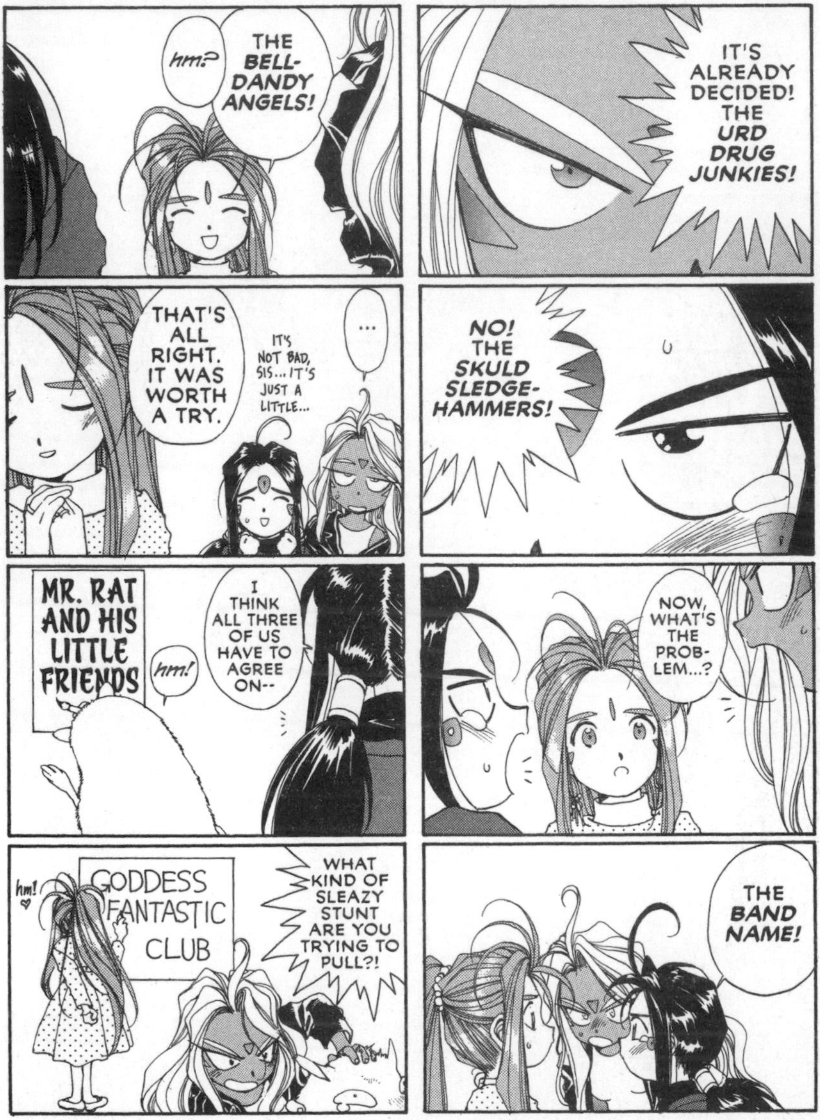

IT'S ALREADY DECIDED! THE URD DRUG JUNKIES!
THE BELL-DANDY ANGELS!
hm?
NO! THE SKULD SLEDGE-HAMMERS!
...
IT'S NOT BAD, SIS... IT'S JUST A LITTLE...
THAT'S ALL RIGHT. IT WAS WORTH A TRY.
NOW, WHAT'S THE PROB-LEM...?
I THINK ALL THREE OF US HAVE TO AGREE ON--
hm!
MR. RAT AND HIS LITTLE FRIENDS
THE BAND NAME!
WHAT KIND OF SLEAZY STUNT ARE YOU TRYING TO PULL?!
GODDESS FANTASTIC CLUB
hm! ♡

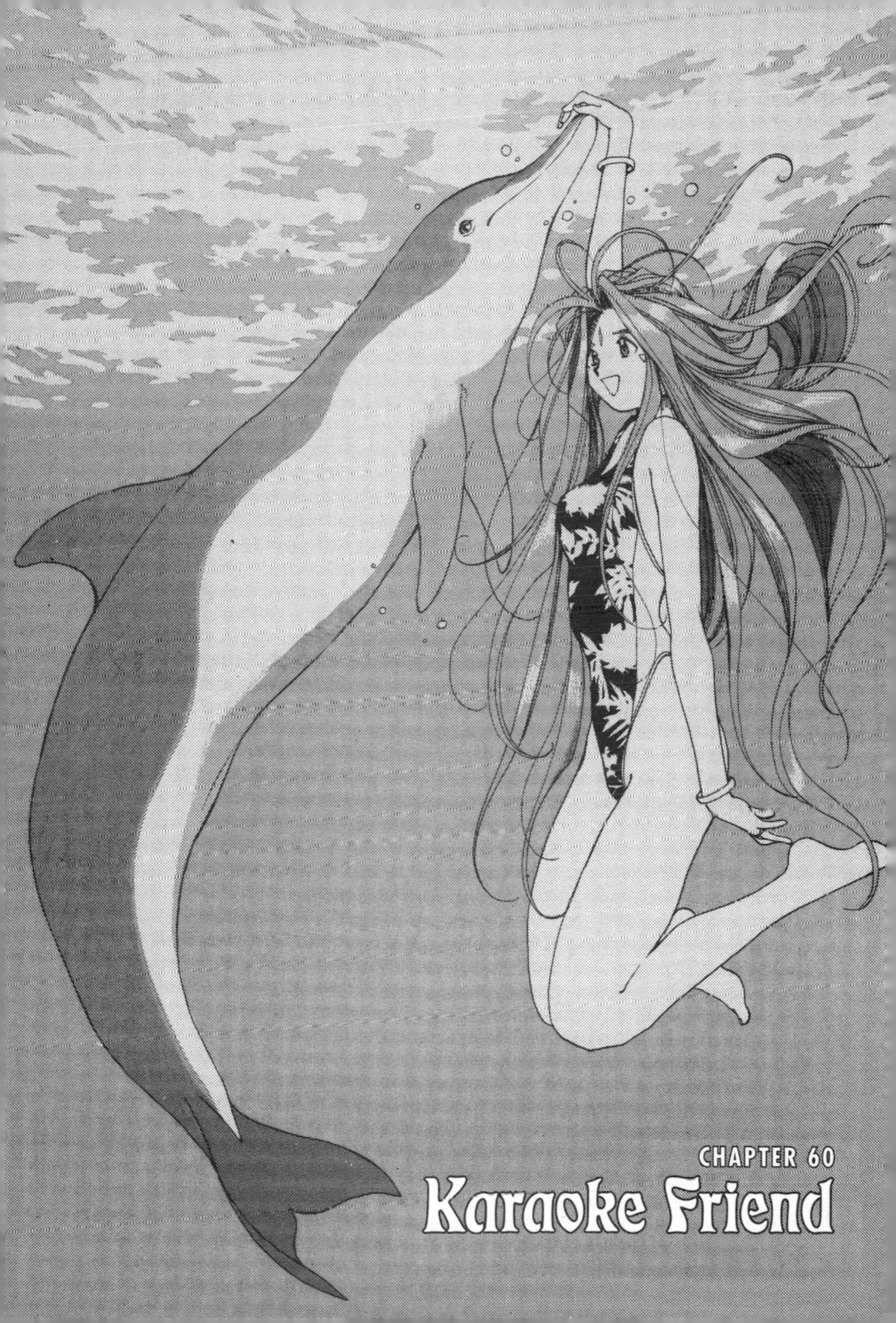

CHAPTER 60
Karaoke Friend

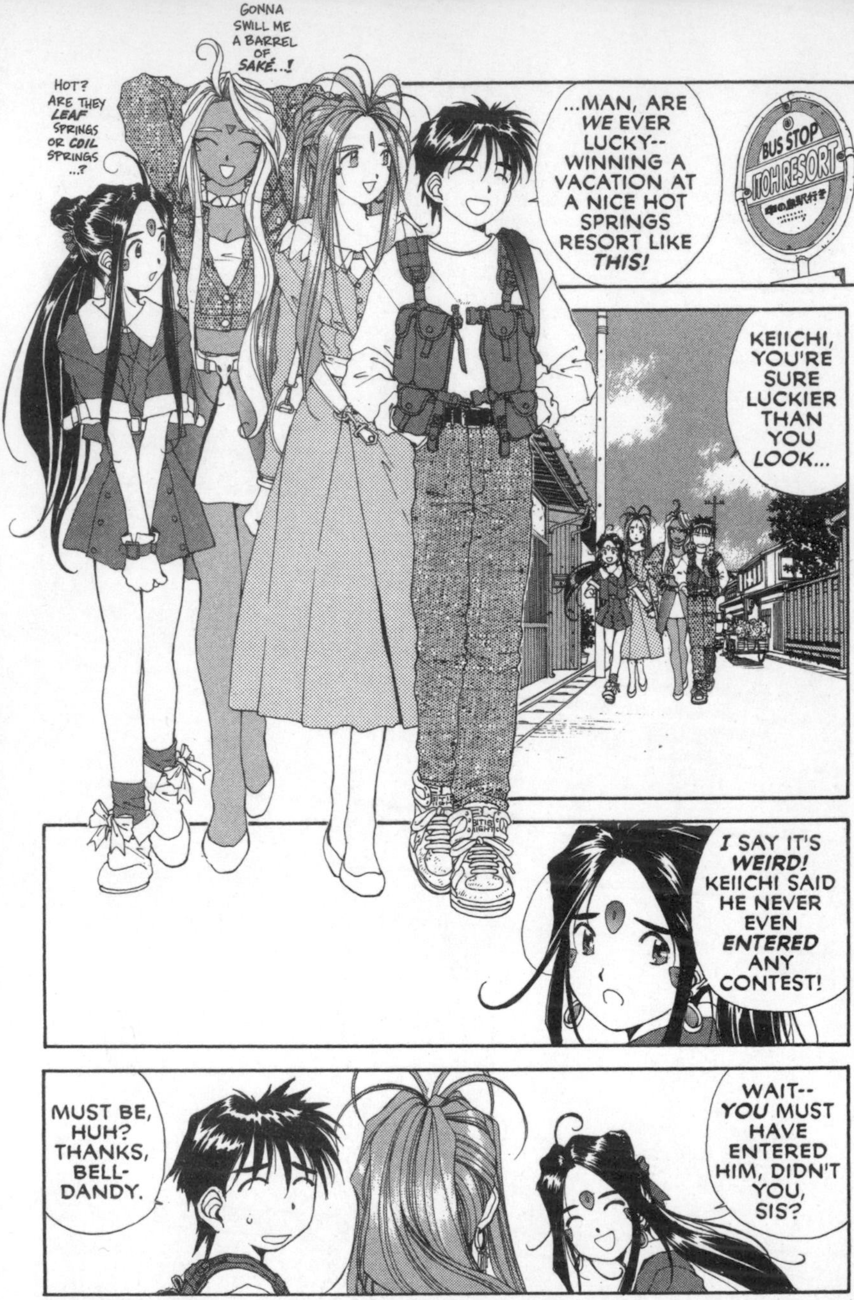
BUS STOP
ITOH RESORT
...MAN, ARE *WE* EVER LUCKY-- WINNING A VACATION AT A NICE HOT SPRINGS RESORT LIKE *THIS!*
KEIICHI, YOU'RE SURE LUCKIER THAN YOU *LOOK...*
GONNA SWILL ME A BARREL OF *SAKÉ..!*
HOT? ARE THEY *LEAF* SPRINGS OR *COIL* SPRINGS ...?
I SAY IT'S *WEIRD!* KEIICHI SAID HE NEVER EVEN *ENTERED* ANY CONTEST!
WAIT-- *YOU* MUST HAVE ENTERED HIM, DIDN'T YOU, SIS?
MUST BE, HUH? THANKS, BELL-DANDY.

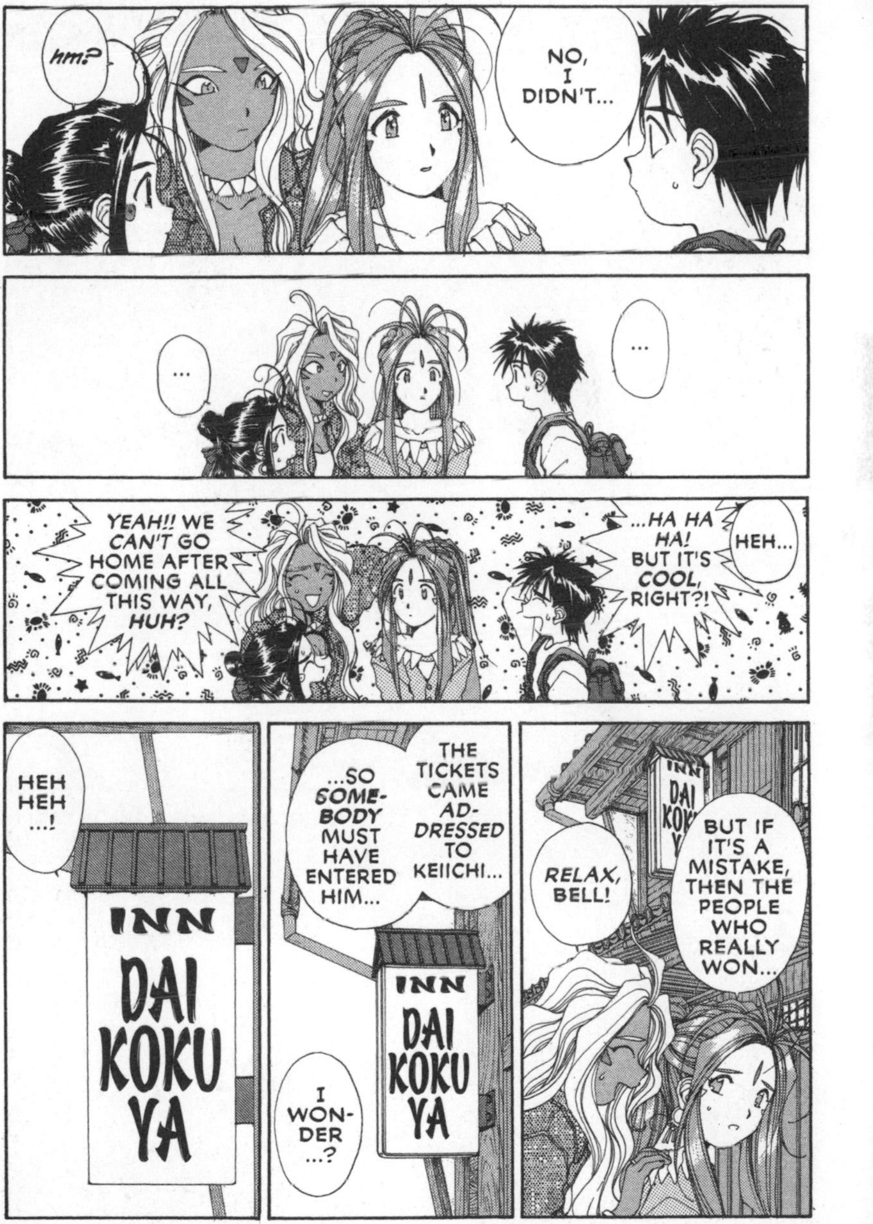
NO, I DIDN'T...
hm?
...
...
HEH...
...*HA HA HA!* BUT IT'S *COOL,* RIGHT?!
YEAH!! WE *CAN'T* GO HOME AFTER COMING ALL THIS WAY, *HUH?*
INN DAI KOKU YA
BUT IF IT'S A MISTAKE, THEN THE PEOPLE WHO REALLY WON...
RELAX, BELL!
THE TICKETS CAME *AD-DRESSED* TO KEIICHI...
...SO *SOME-BODY* MUST HAVE ENTERED HIM...
INN DAI KOKU YA
I WON-DER ...?
HEH HEH ...!
INN DAI KOKU YA

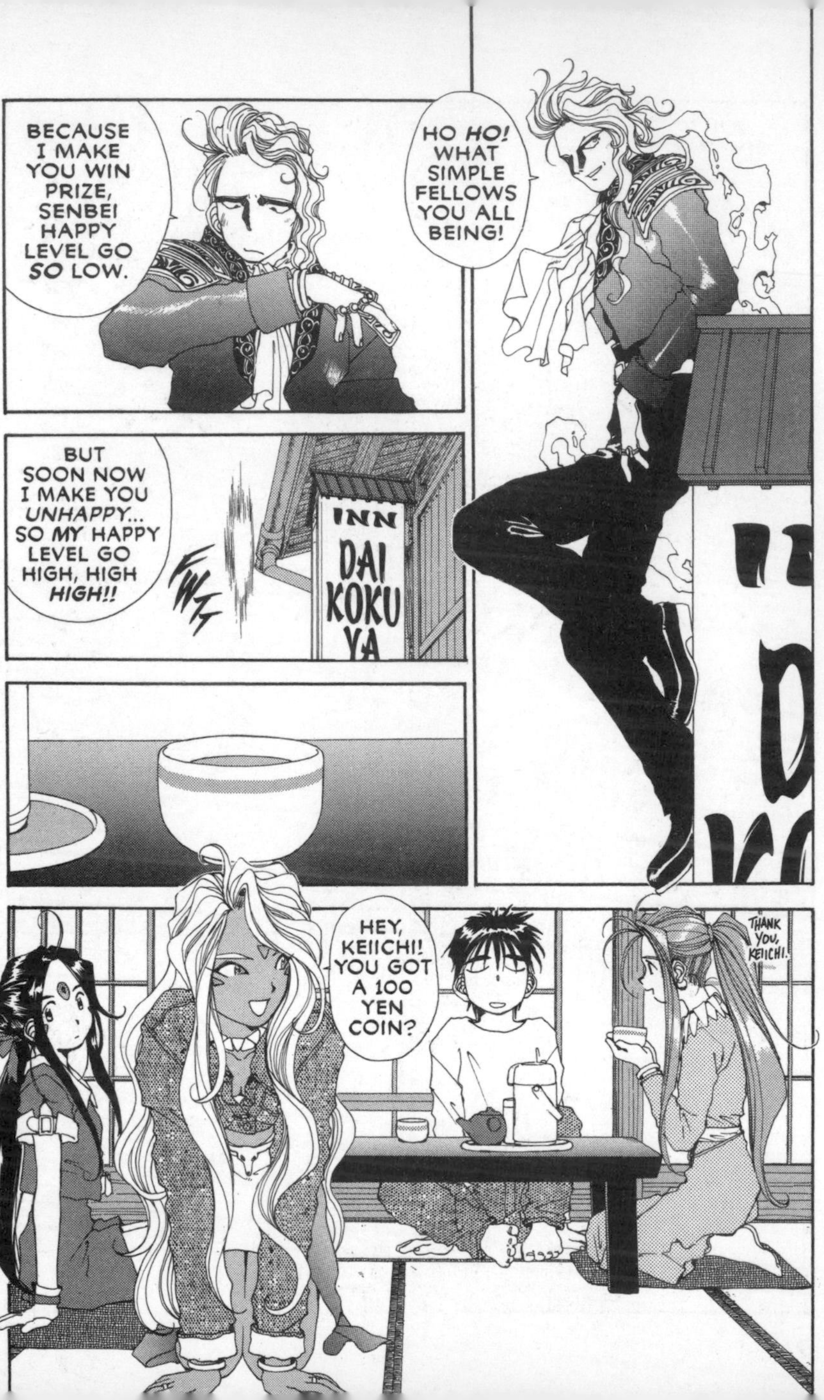
HO *HO!* WHAT SIMPLE FELLOWS YOU ALL BEING!
BECAUSE I MAKE YOU WIN PRIZE, SENBEI HAPPY LEVEL GO *SO* LOW.
BUT SOON NOW I MAKE YOU *UNHAPPY*... SO *MY* HAPPY LEVEL GO HIGH, HIGH *HIGH!!*
INN
DAI KOKU YA
THANK YOU, KEIICHI!
HEY, KEIICHI! YOU GOT A 100 YEN COIN?

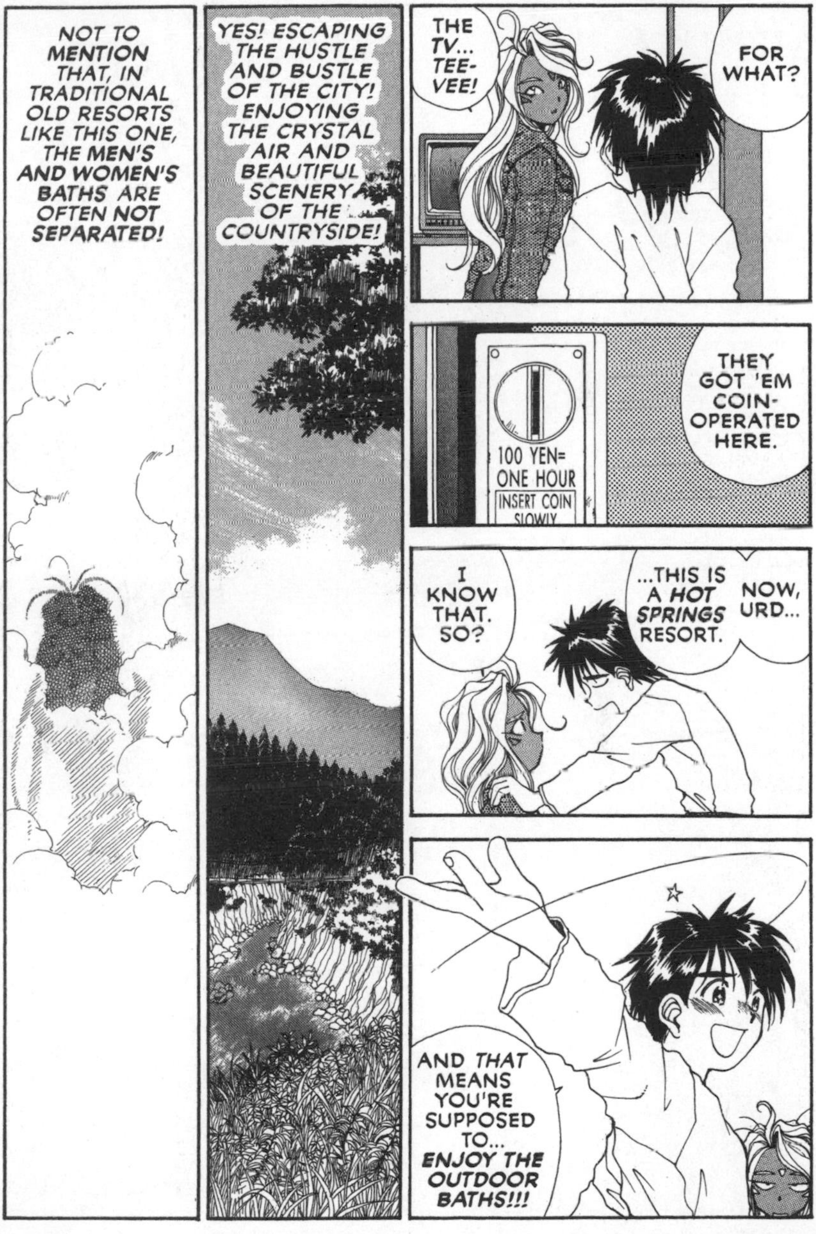
FOR WHAT?
THE *TV*... TEE-VEE!
THEY GOT 'EM COIN-OPERATED HERE.
100 YEN= ONE HOUR
INSERT COIN SLOWLY
NOW, URD...
...THIS IS A *HOT SPRINGS* RESORT.
I KNOW THAT. SO?
AND *THAT* MEANS YOU'RE SUPPOSED TO... ***ENJOY THE OUTDOOR BATHS!!!***
YES! ESCAPING THE HUSTLE AND BUSTLE OF THE CITY! ENJOYING THE CRYSTAL AIR AND BEAUTIFUL SCENERY OF THE COUNTRYSIDE!
NOT TO **MENTION** THAT, IN TRADITIONAL OLD RESORTS LIKE THIS ONE, THE **MEN'S AND WOMEN'S BATHS** ARE OFTEN **NOT SEPARATED!**

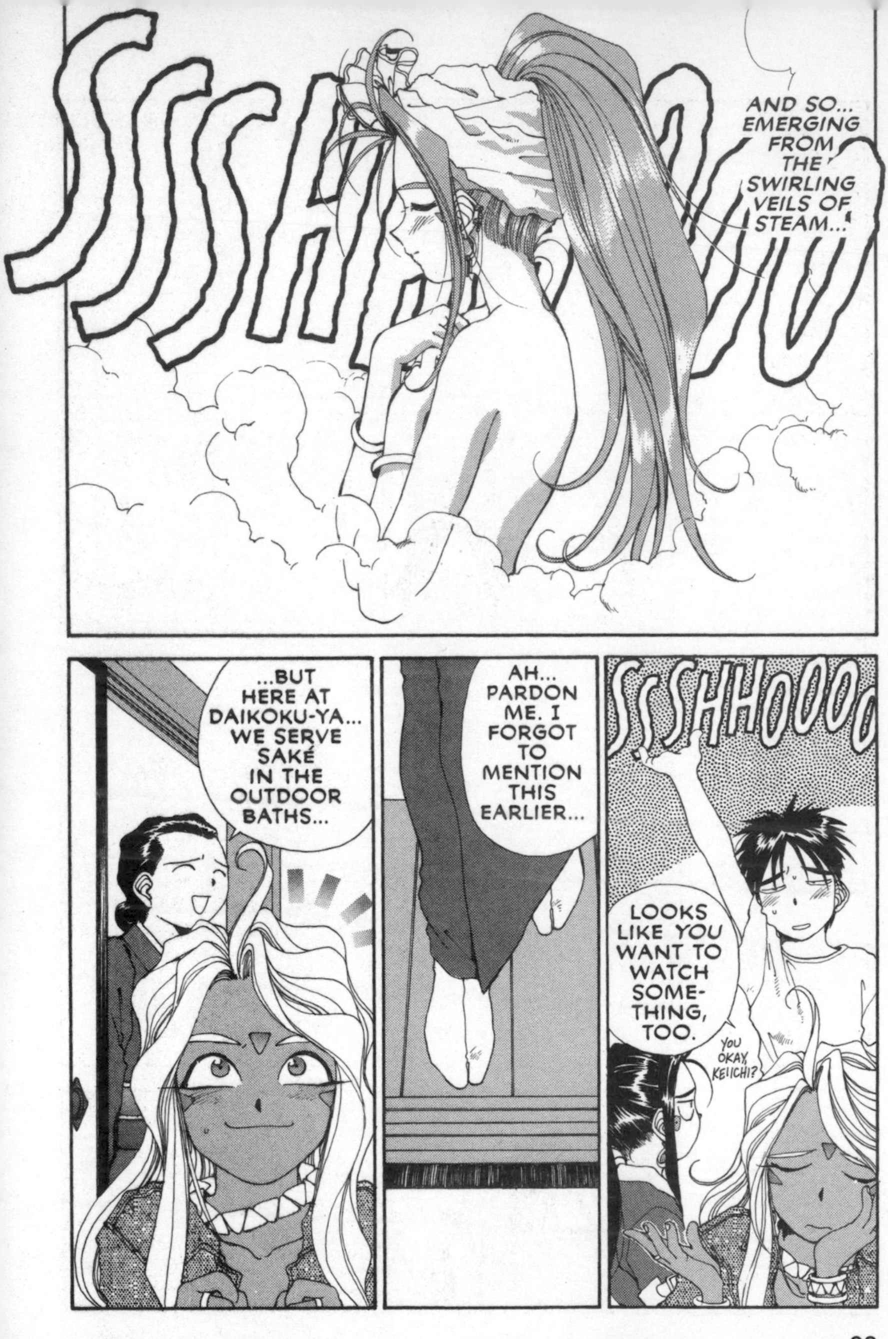
SSSHHOOOO
AND SO... EMERGING FROM THE SWIRLING VEILS OF STEAM...
SSSHHOOOO
LOOKS LIKE YOU WANT TO WATCH SOME-THING, TOO.
YOU OKAY, KEIICHI?
AH... PARDON ME. I FORGOT TO MENTION THIS EARLIER...
...BUT HERE AT DAIKOKU-YA... WE SERVE SAKÉ IN THE OUTDOOR BATHS...

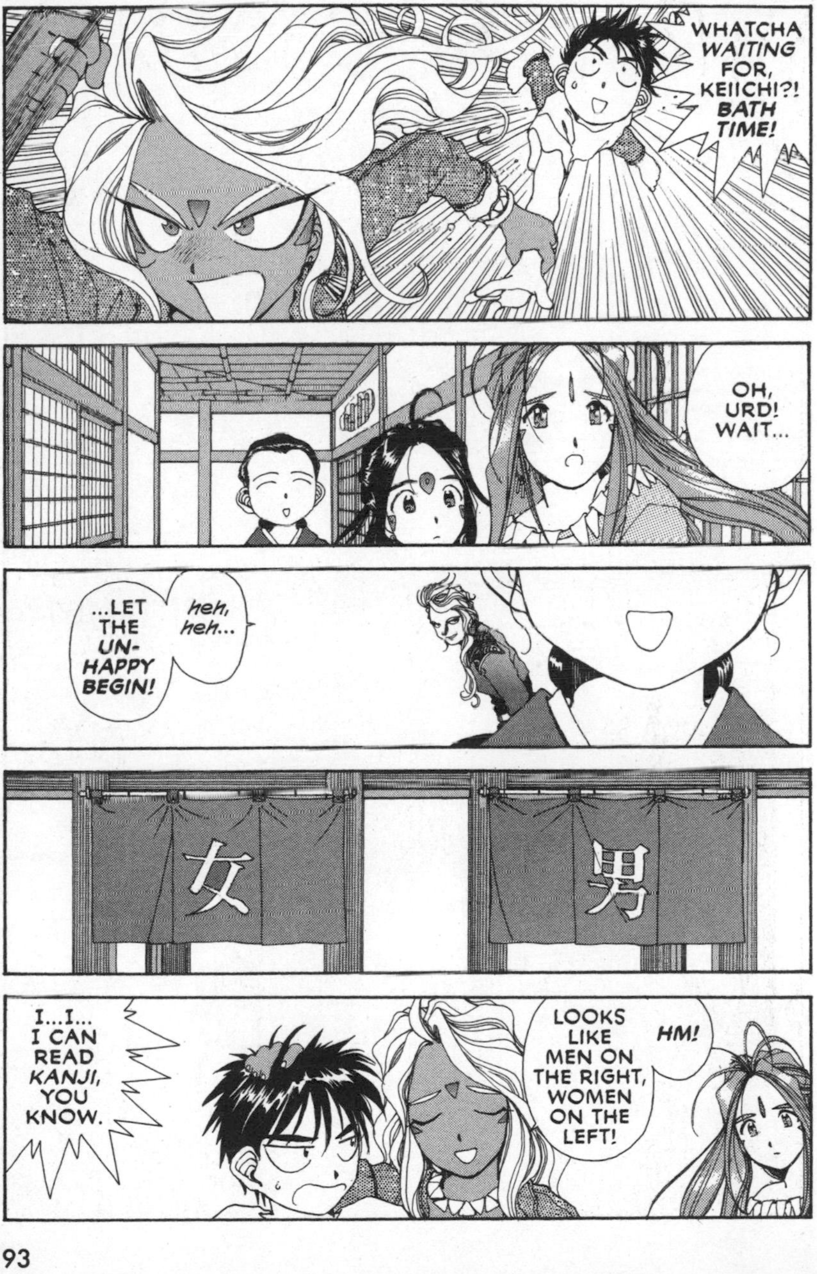
WHATCHA WAITING FOR, KEIICHI?! BATH TIME!
OH, URD! WAIT...
heh, heh...
...LET THE UN-HAPPY BEGIN!
男
女
HM!
LOOKS LIKE MEN ON THE RIGHT, WOMEN ON THE LEFT!
I...I... I CAN READ KANJI, YOU KNOW.

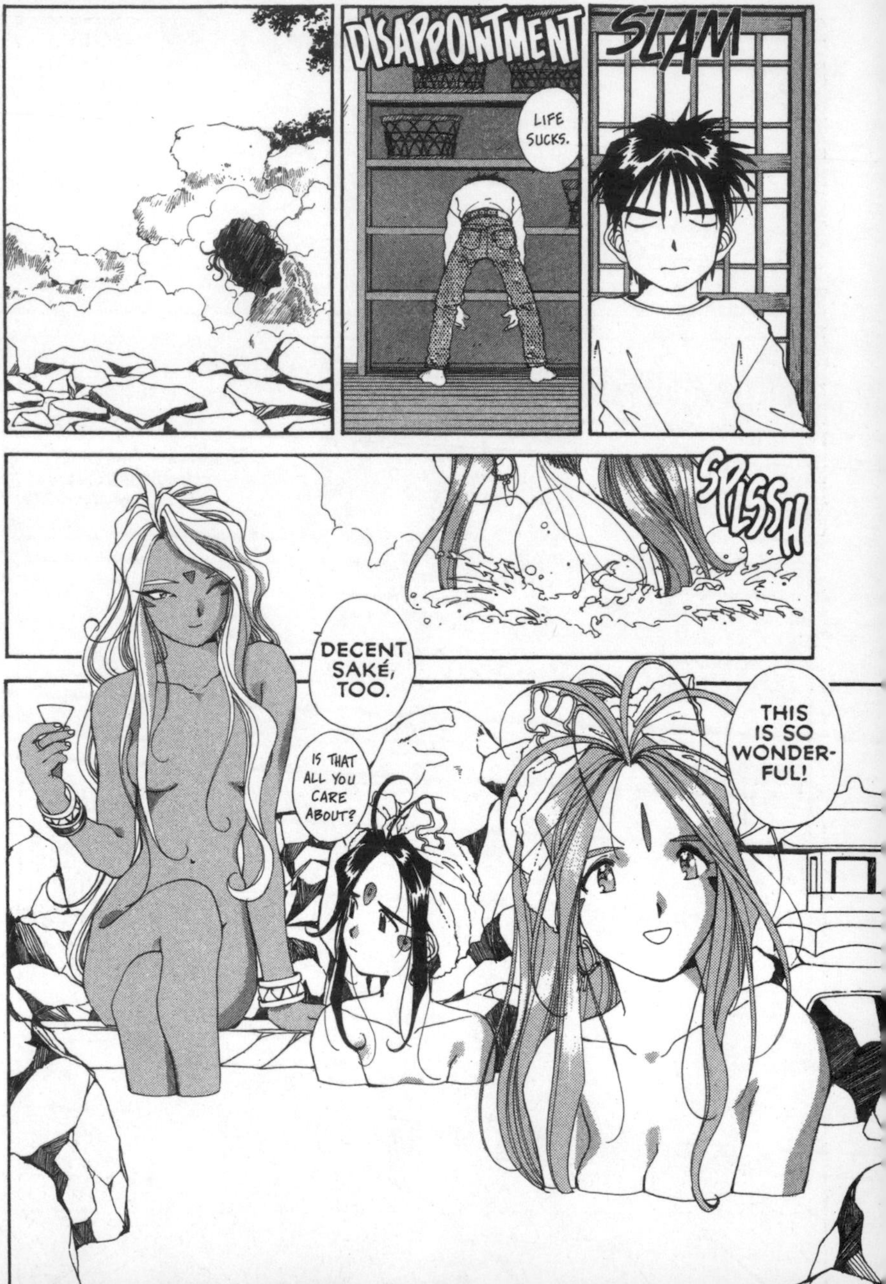
SLAM
DISAPPOINTMENT
LIFE SUCKS.
SPLSSH
THIS IS SO WONDERFUL!
DECENT SAKÉ, TOO.
IS THAT ALL YOU CARE ABOUT?

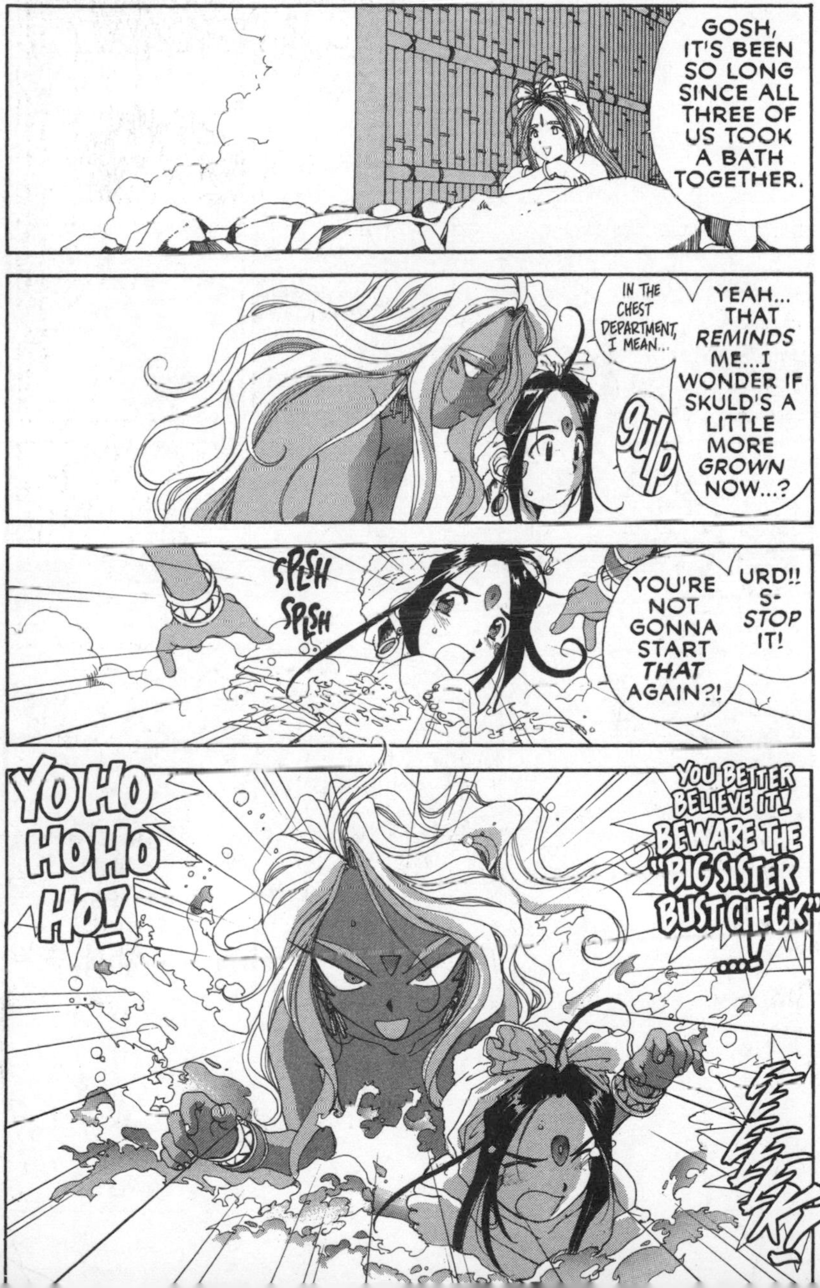
GOSH, IT'S BEEN SO LONG SINCE ALL THREE OF US TOOK A BATH TOGETHER.
YEAH... THAT *REMINDS* ME...I WONDER IF SKULD'S A LITTLE MORE *GROWN* NOW...?
IN THE CHEST DEPARTMENT, I MEAN...
gulp
URD!! S-*STOP* IT!
YOU'RE NOT GONNA START *THAT* AGAIN?!
SPLSH
SPLSH
YOU BETTER BELIEVE IT! BEWARE THE "BIG SISTER BUST CHECK"...!
YO HO HOHO HO!
EEEEEK!

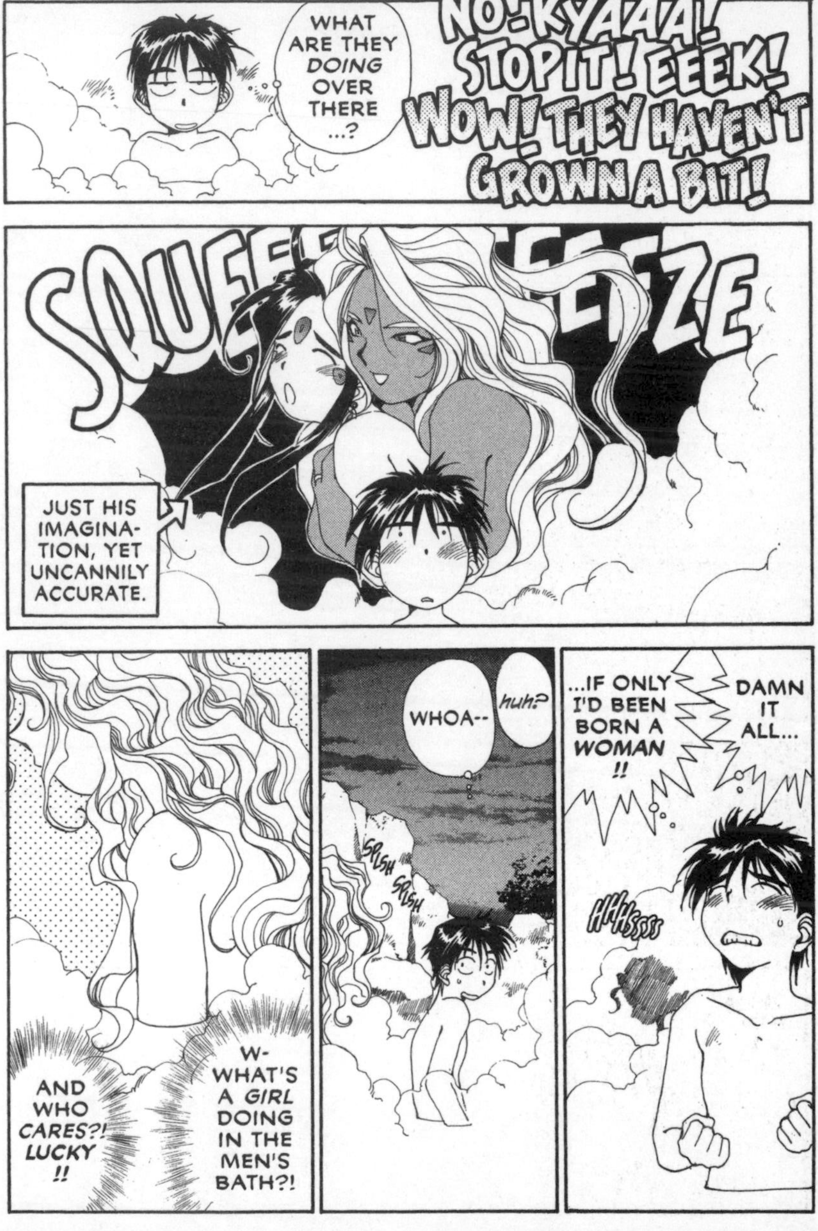
NO! KYAAA! STOPIT! EEEK! WOW! THEY HAVEN'T GROWN A BIT!
WHAT ARE THEY DOING OVER THERE ...?
SQUEEEEEEZE
JUST HIS IMAGINATION, YET UNCANNILY ACCURATE.
DAMN IT ALL...
...IF ONLY I'D BEEN BORN A WOMAN !!
HHHSSSS
huh?
WHOA--
SPLSH
SPLSH
W- WHAT'S A GIRL DOING IN THE MEN'S BATH?!
AND WHO CARES?! LUCKY !!

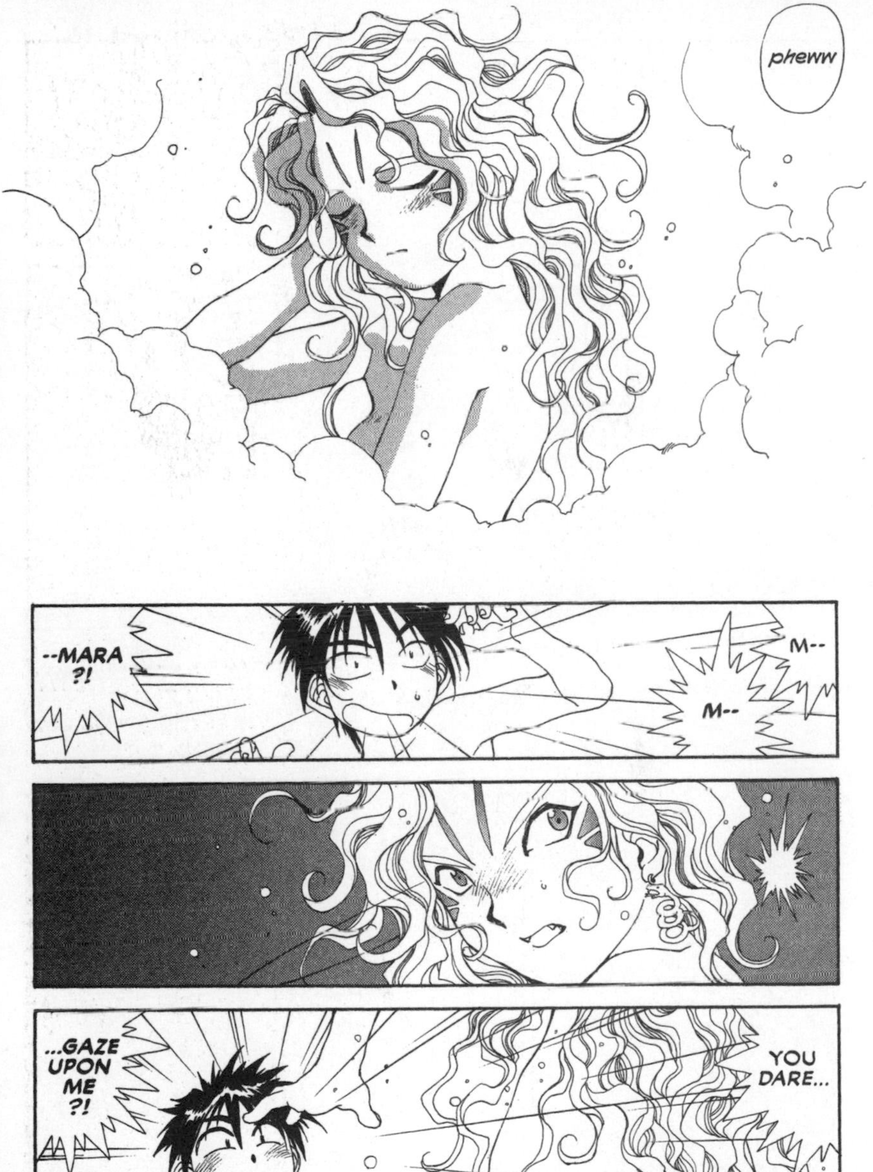
pheww
M--
M--
--MARA ?!
YOU DARE...
...GAZE UPON ME ?!

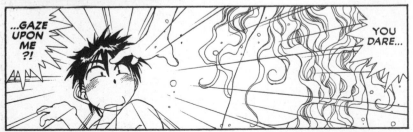

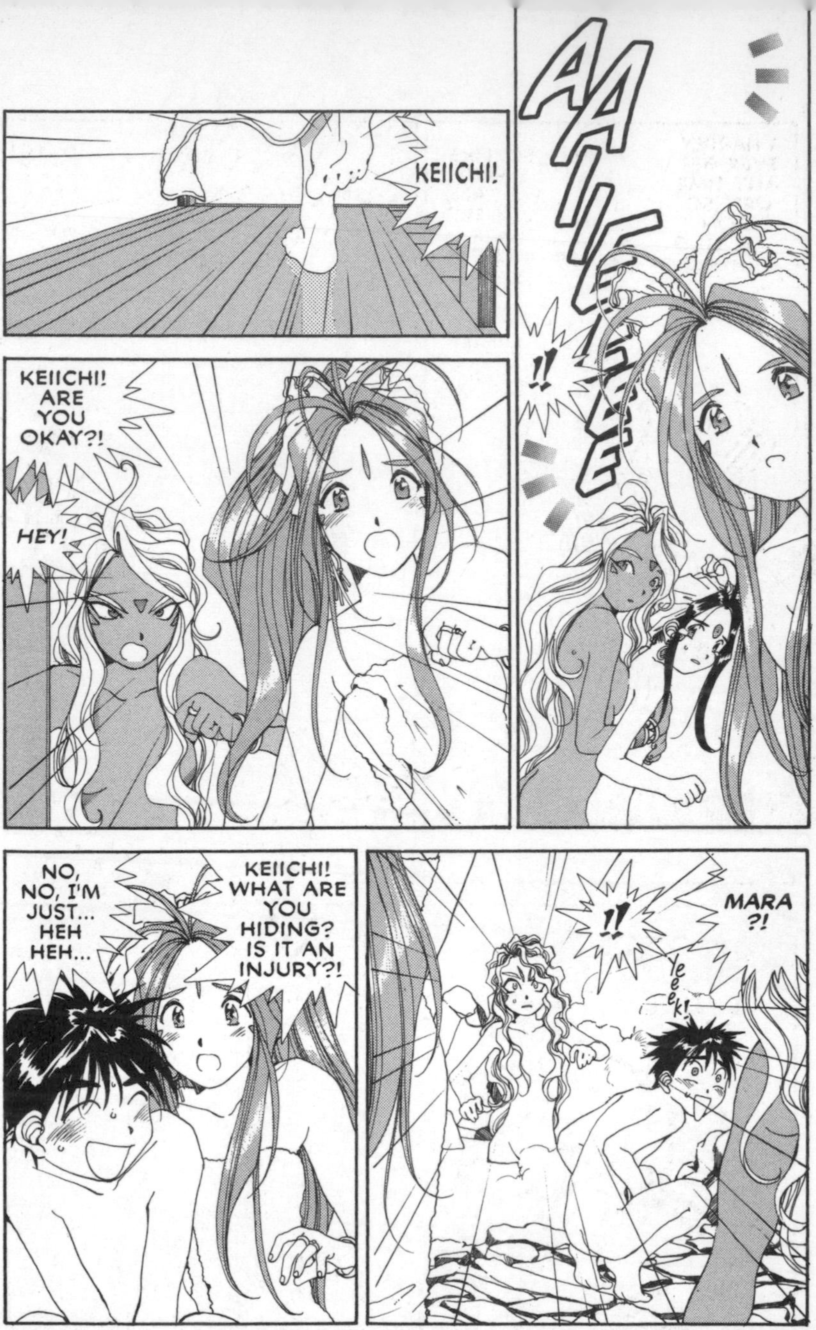
AAIIEEEEE
!!
KEIICHI!
KEIICHI! ARE YOU OKAY?!
HEY!
!!
MARA ?!
Yeeek!
KEIICHI! WHAT ARE YOU HIDING? IS IT AN INJURY?!
NO, NO, I'M JUST... HEH HEH...

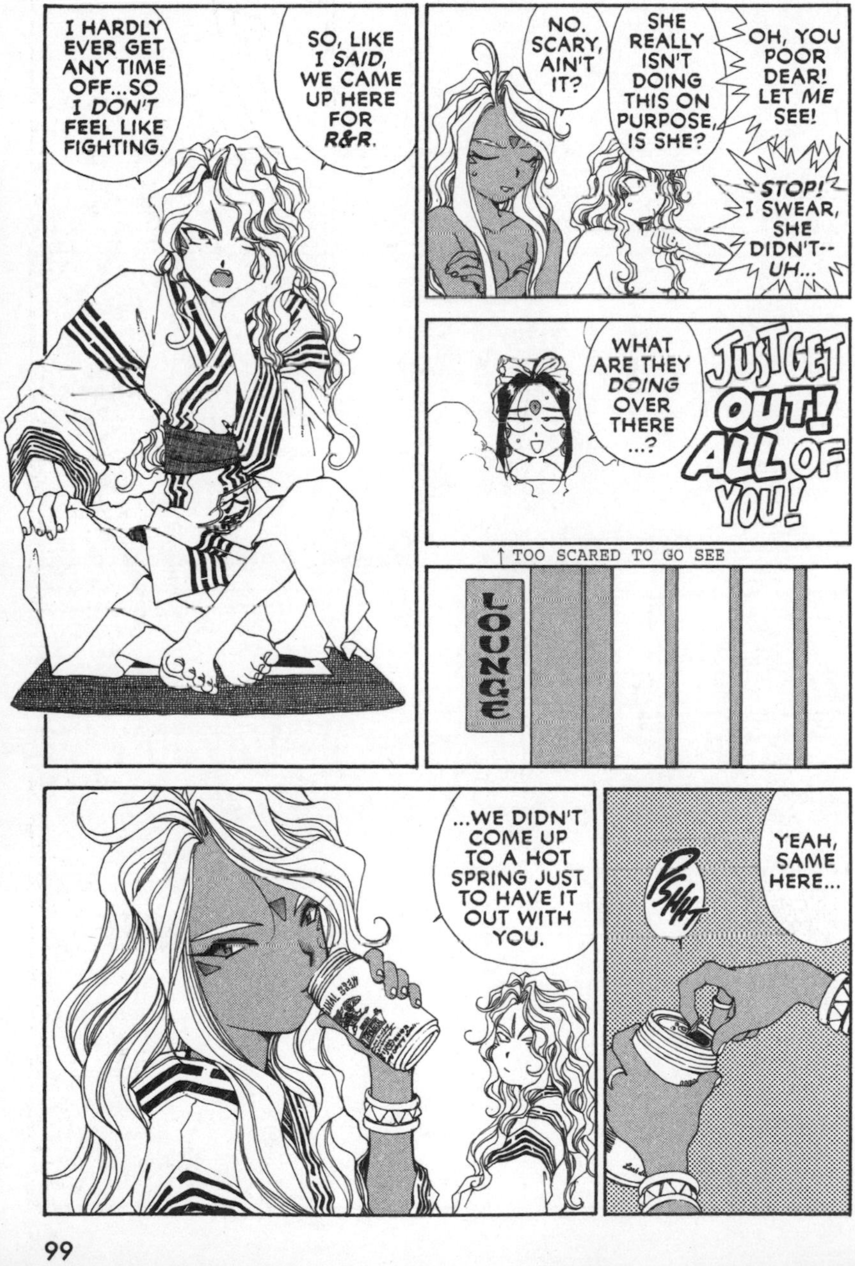
OH, YOU POOR DEAR! LET ME SEE!
STOP! I SWEAR, SHE DIDN'T--UH...
SHE REALLY ISN'T DOING THIS ON PURPOSE, IS SHE?
NO. SCARY, AIN'T IT?
JUST GET OUT! ALL OF YOU!
WHAT ARE THEY DOING OVER THERE ...?
↑ TOO SCARED TO GO SEE
LOUNGE
SO, LIKE I SAID, WE CAME UP HERE FOR R&R.
I HARDLY EVER GET ANY TIME OFF...SO I DON'T FEEL LIKE FIGHTING.
YEAH, SAME HERE...
PSHH
...WE DIDN'T COME UP TO A HOT SPRING JUST TO HAVE IT OUT WITH YOU.

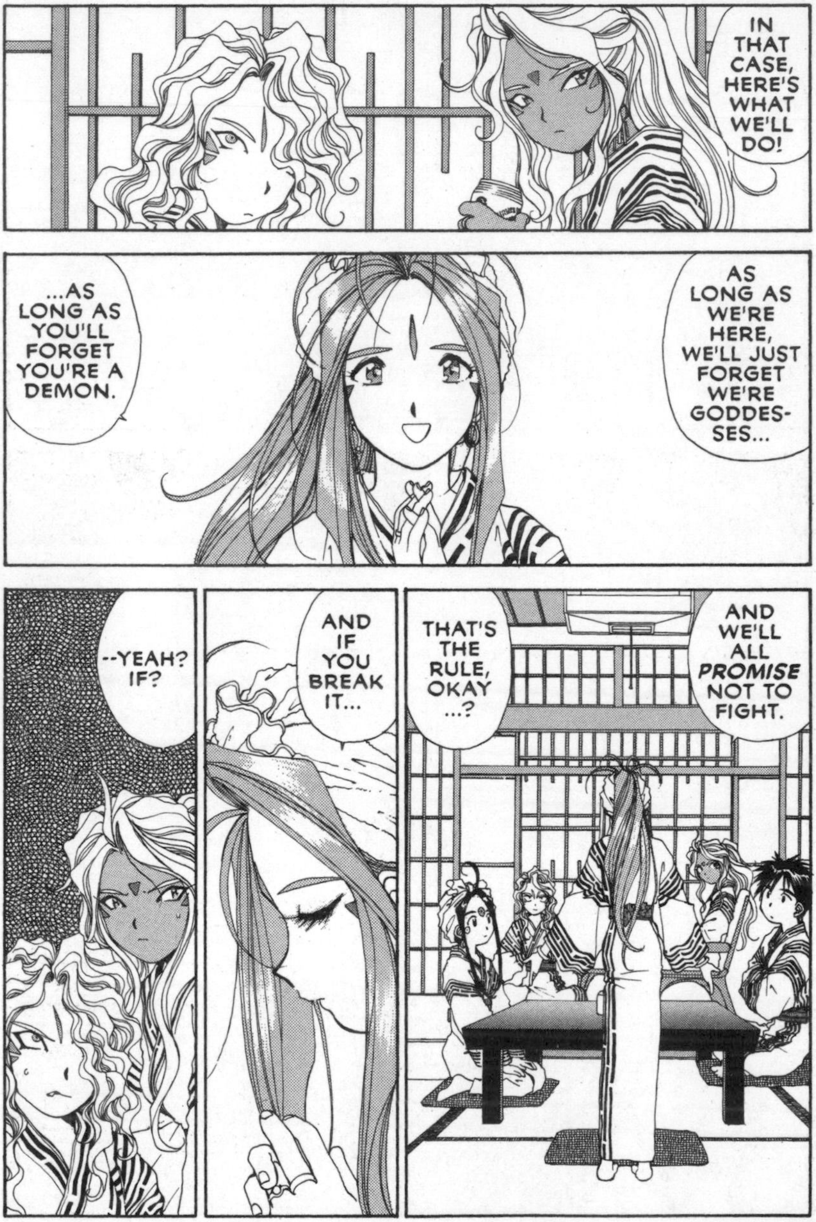
IN THAT CASE, HERE'S WHAT WE'LL DO!
AS LONG AS WE'RE HERE, WE'LL JUST FORGET WE'RE GODDESSES...
...AS LONG AS YOU'LL FORGET YOU'RE A DEMON.
AND WE'LL ALL *PROMISE* NOT TO FIGHT.
THAT'S THE RULE, OKAY ...?
AND IF YOU BREAK IT...
--YEAH? IF?

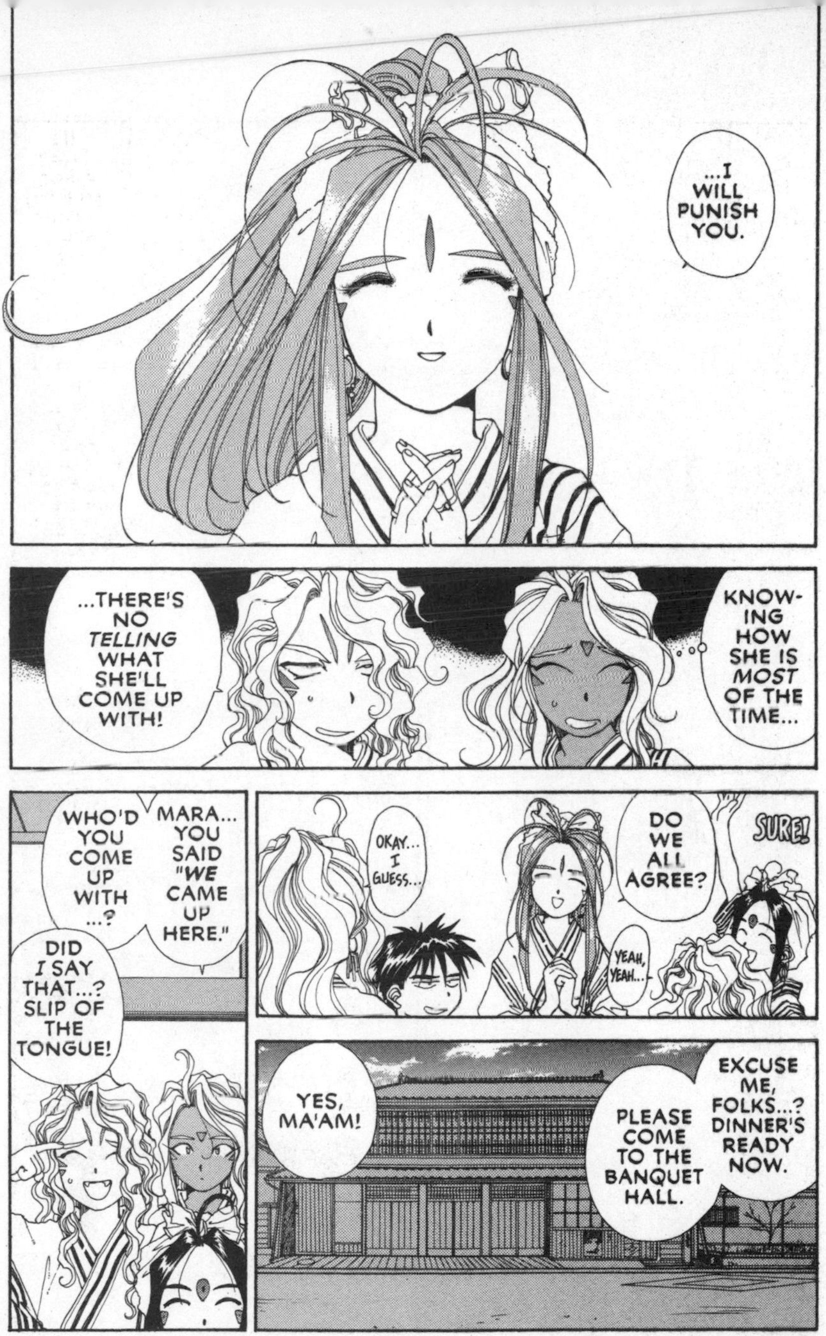
...I WILL PUNISH YOU.
KNOWING HOW SHE IS *MOST* OF THE TIME...
...THERE'S NO *TELLING* WHAT SHE'LL COME UP WITH!
SURE!
DO WE ALL AGREE?
OKAY... I GUESS...
YEAH, YEAH...
EXCUSE ME, FOLKS...? DINNER'S READY NOW.
PLEASE COME TO THE BANQUET HALL.
YES, MA'AM!
MARA... YOU SAID "*WE* CAME UP HERE."
WHO'D YOU COME UP WITH...?
DID *I* SAY THAT...? SLIP OF THE TONGUE!

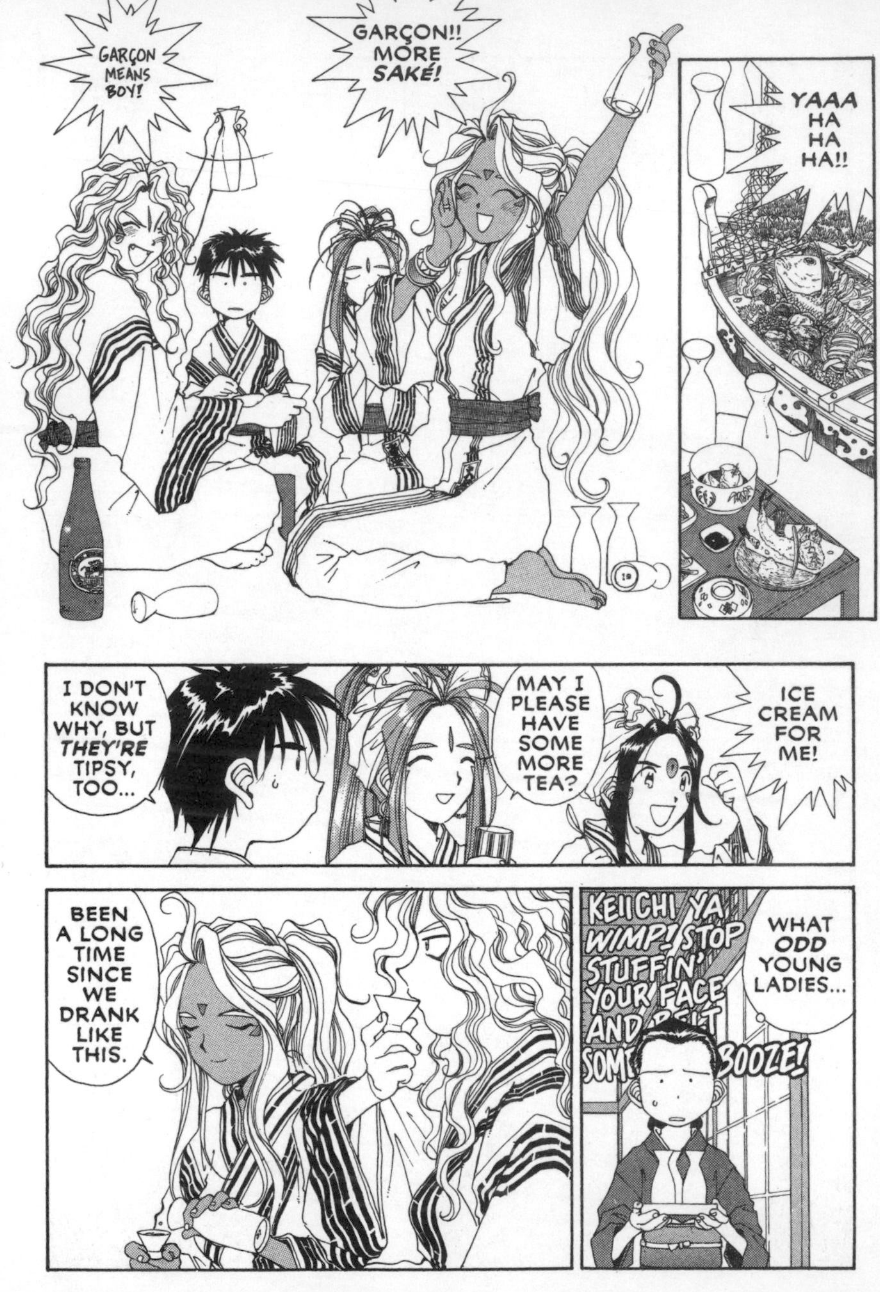
YAAA HA HA HA!!
GARÇON!! MORE SAKÉ!
GARÇON MEANS BOY!
ICE CREAM FOR ME!
MAY I PLEASE HAVE SOME MORE TEA?
I DON'T KNOW WHY, BUT THEY'RE TIPSY, TOO...
WHAT ODD YOUNG LADIES...
KEIICHI YA WIMP! STOP STUFFIN' YOUR FACE AND
BOOZE!
BEEN A LONG TIME SINCE WE DRANK LIKE THIS.

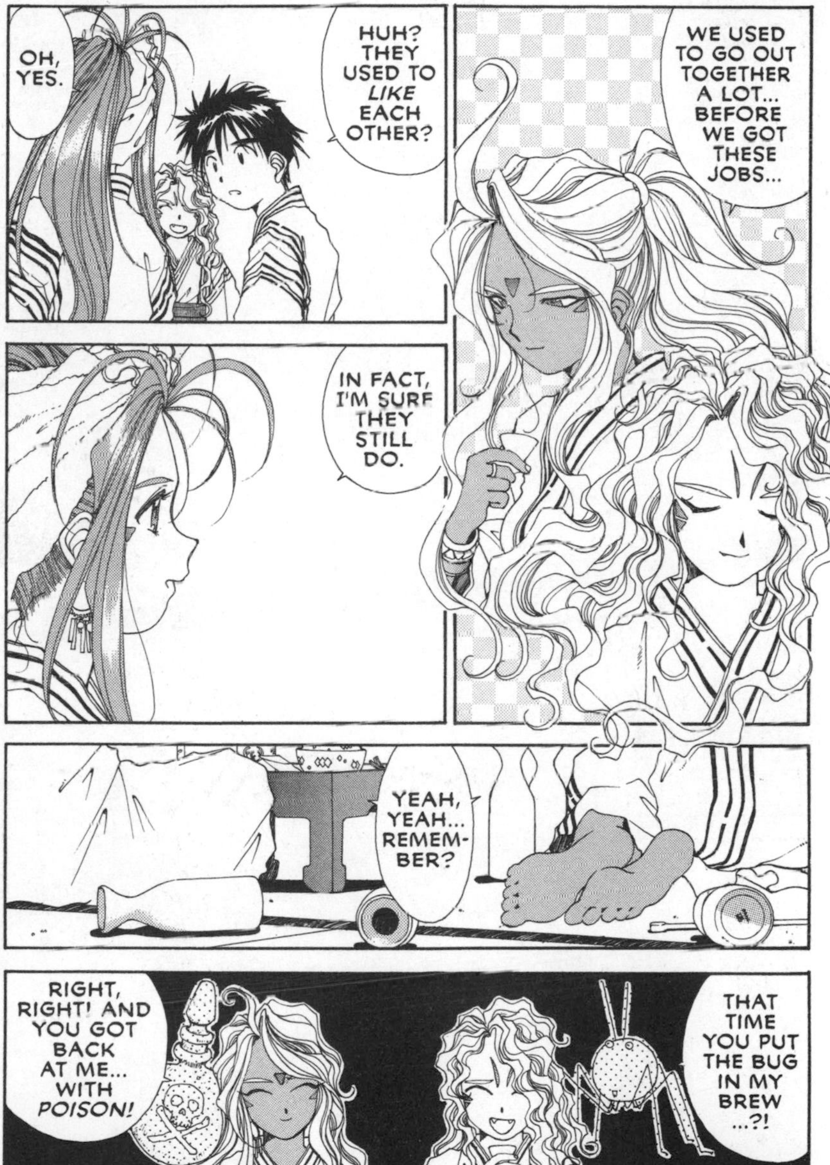

WE USED TO GO OUT TOGETHER A LOT... BEFORE WE GOT THESE JOBS...
HUH? THEY USED TO *LIKE* EACH OTHER?
OH, YES.
IN FACT, I'M SURF THEY STILL DO.
YEAH, YEAH... REMEMBER?
THAT TIME YOU PUT THE BUG IN MY BREW ...?!
RIGHT, RIGHT! AND YOU GOT BACK AT ME... WITH *POISON!*

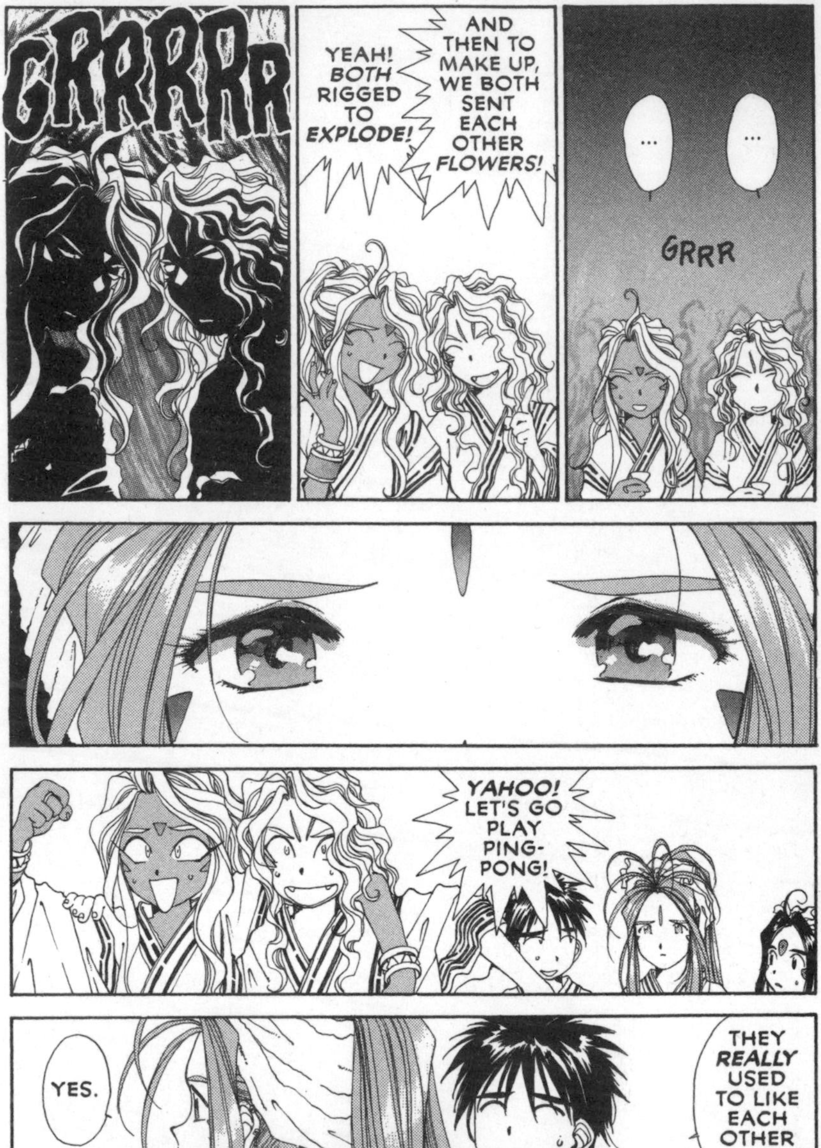
...
...
GRRR
AND THEN TO MAKE UP, WE BOTH SENT EACH OTHER *FLOWERS!*
YEAH! *BOTH* RIGGED TO *EXPLODE!*
GRRRRR
YAHOO! LET'S GO PLAY PING-PONG!
THEY *REALLY* USED TO LIKE EACH OTHER ...?
YES.

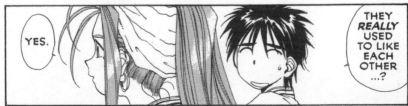

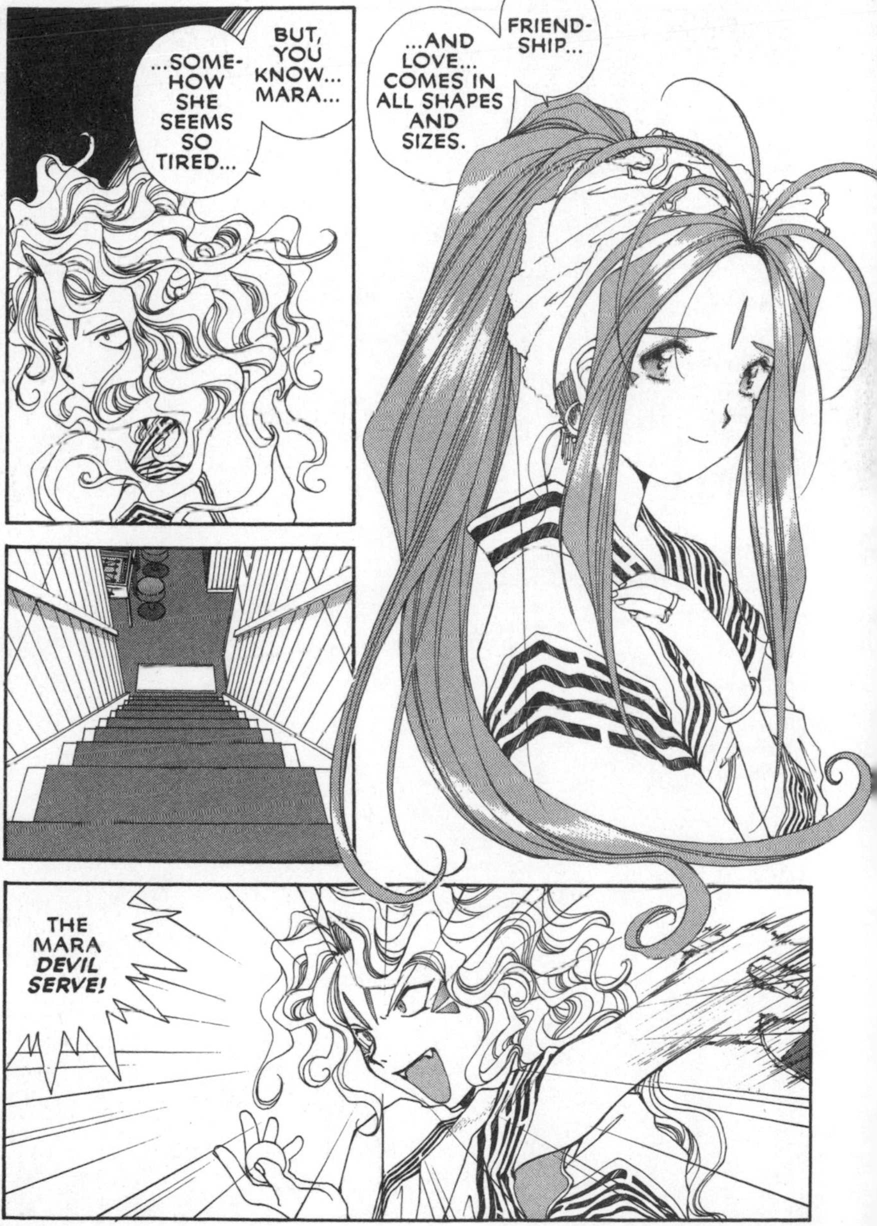
FRIEND-SHIP...
...AND LOVE... COMES IN ALL SHAPES AND SIZES.
BUT, YOU KNOW... MARA...
...SOME-HOW SHE SEEMS SO TIRED...
THE MARA *DEVIL SERVE!*

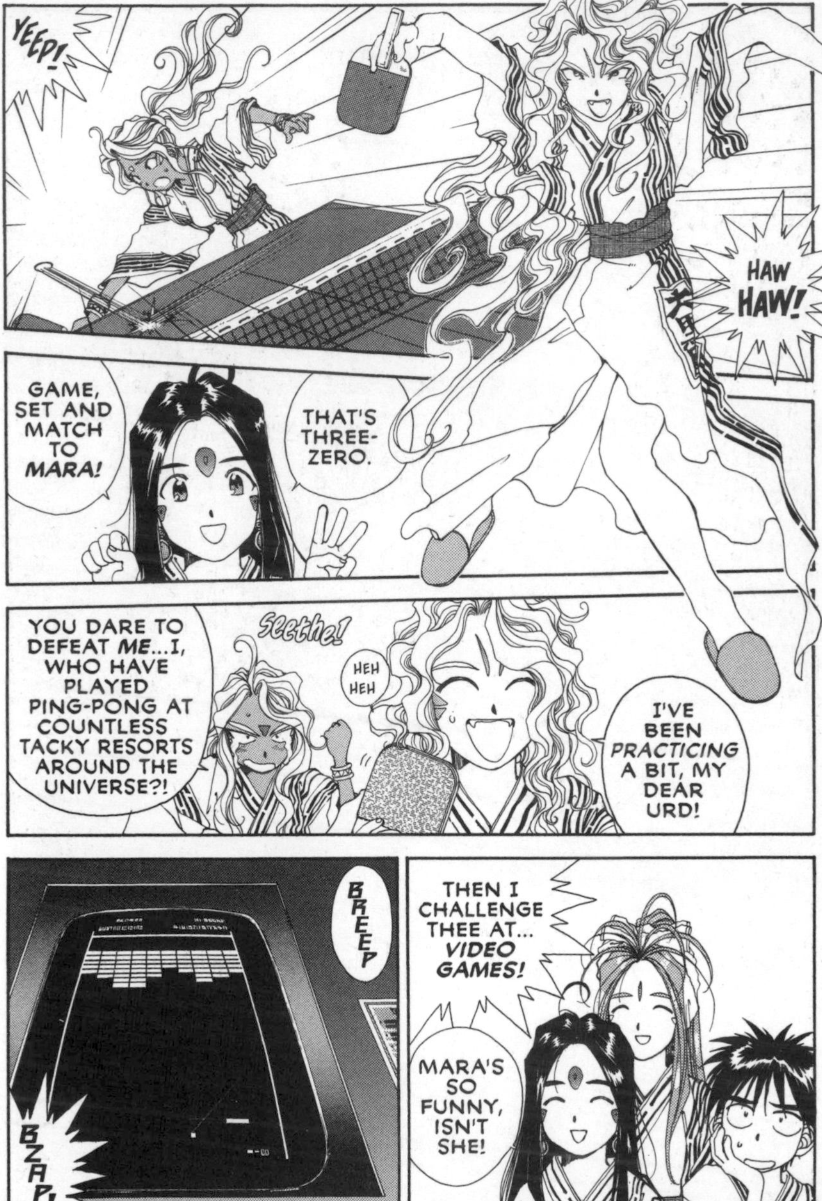
HAW HAW!
YEEP!
THAT'S THREE-ZERO.
GAME, SET AND MATCH TO MARA!
I'VE BEEN PRACTICING A BIT, MY DEAR URD!
HEH HEH
Seethe!
YOU DARE TO DEFEAT ME...I, WHO HAVE PLAYED PING-PONG AT COUNTLESS TACKY RESORTS AROUND THE UNIVERSE?!
THEN I CHALLENGE THEE AT... VIDEO GAMES!
MARA'S SO FUNNY, ISN'T SHE!
BREEP
BZAP!

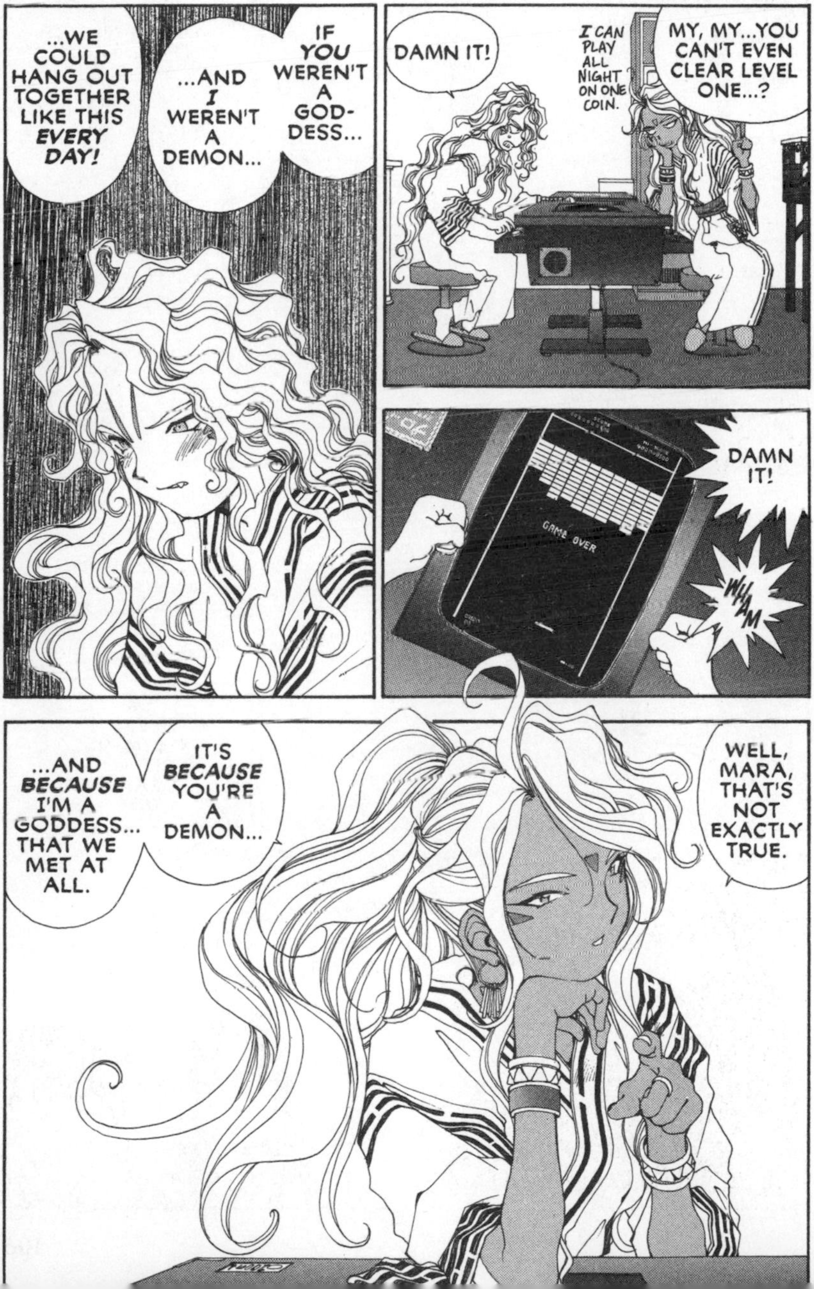
MY, MY...YOU CAN'T EVEN CLEAR LEVEL ONE...?
I CAN PLAY ALL NIGHT ON ONE COIN.
DAMN IT!
GAME OVER
DAMN IT!
WHAM
IF YOU WEREN'T A GOD-DESS...
...AND I WEREN'T A DEMON...
...WE COULD HANG OUT TOGETHER LIKE THIS EVERY DAY!
WELL, MARA, THAT'S NOT EXACTLY TRUE.
IT'S BECAUSE YOU'RE A DEMON...
...AND BECAUSE I'M A GODDESS... THAT WE MET AT ALL.

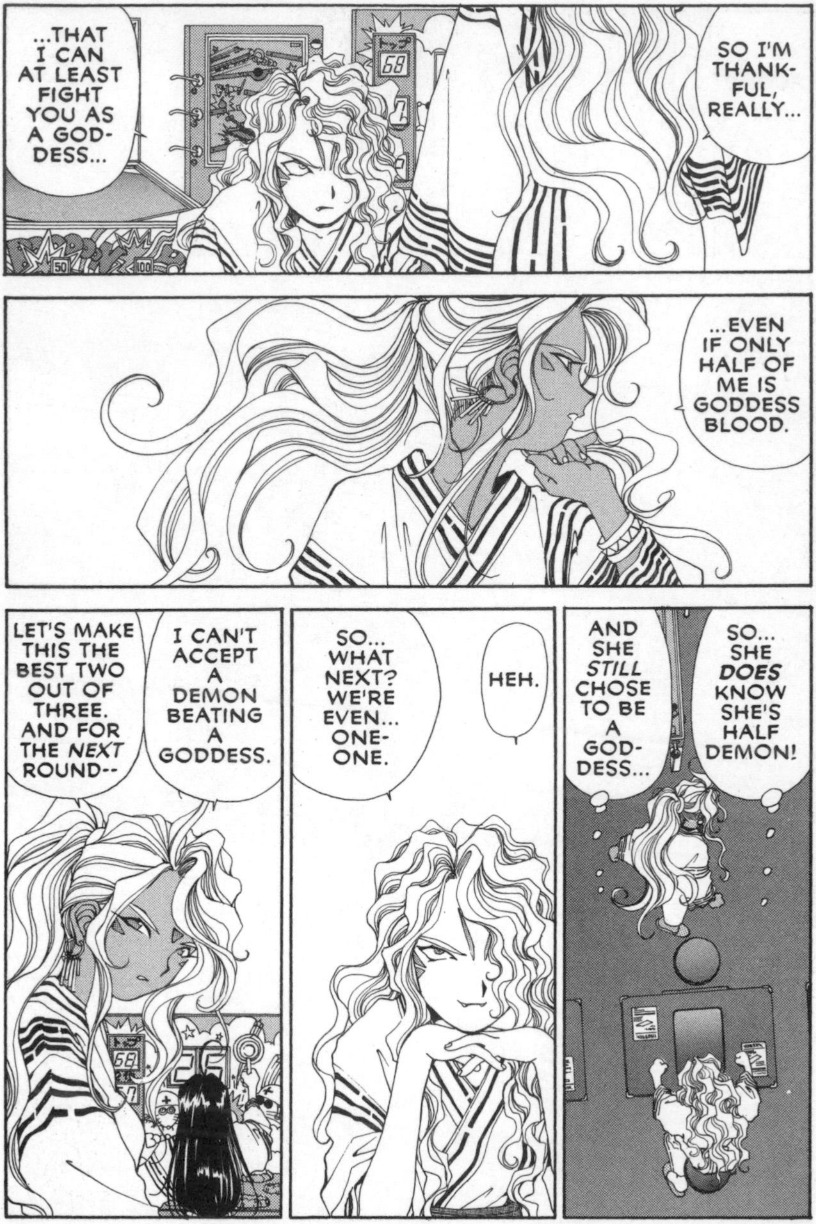
SO I'M THANKFUL, REALLY...
...THAT I CAN AT LEAST FIGHT YOU AS A GODDESS...
...EVEN IF ONLY HALF OF ME IS GODDESS BLOOD.
SO... SHE *DOES* KNOW SHE'S HALF DEMON!
AND SHE *STILL* CHOSE TO BE A GODDESS...
HEH.
SO... WHAT NEXT? WE'RE EVEN... ONE-ONE.
I CAN'T ACCEPT A DEMON BEATING A GODDESS.
LET'S MAKE THIS THE BEST TWO OUT OF THREE. AND FOR THE *NEXT* ROUND--

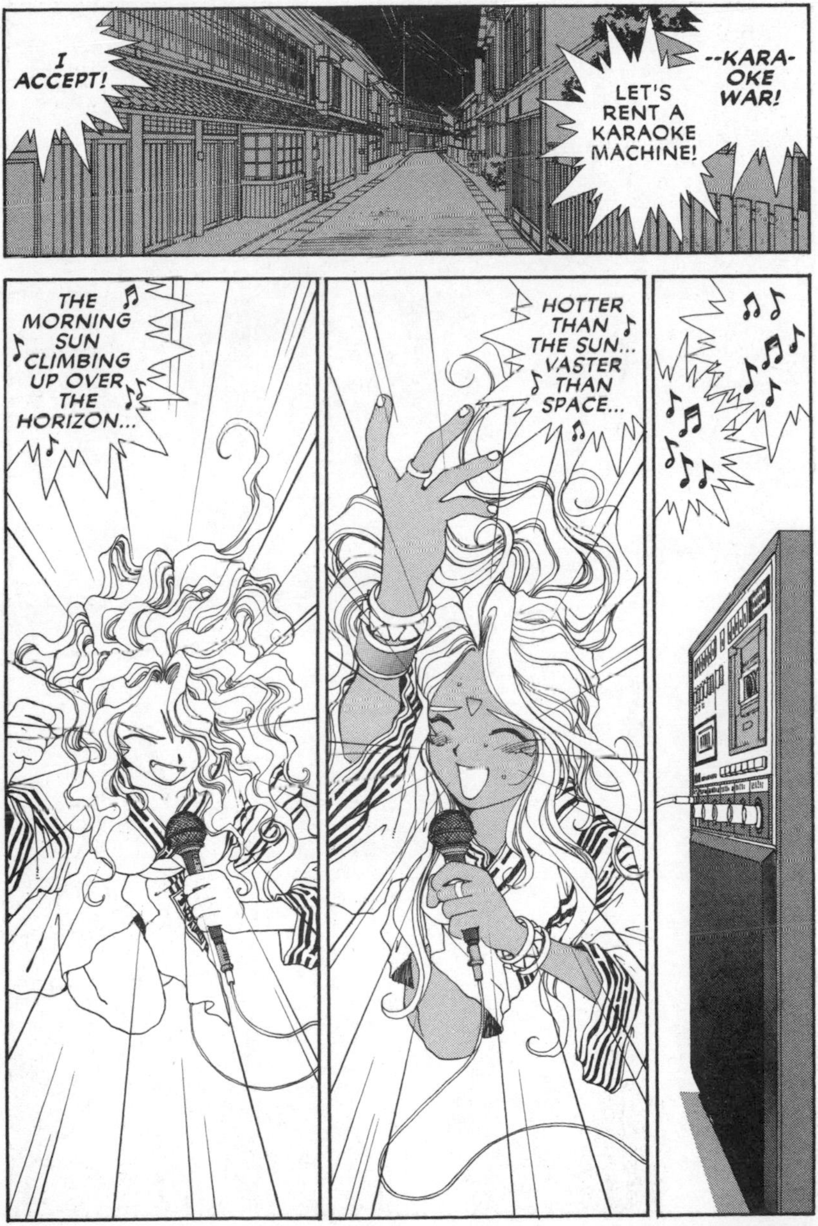
LET'S RENT A KARAOKE MACHINE!
--KARA-OKE WAR!
I ACCEPT!
HOTTER THAN THE SUN... VASTER THAN SPACE...
THE MORNING SUN CLIMBING UP OVER THE HORIZON...

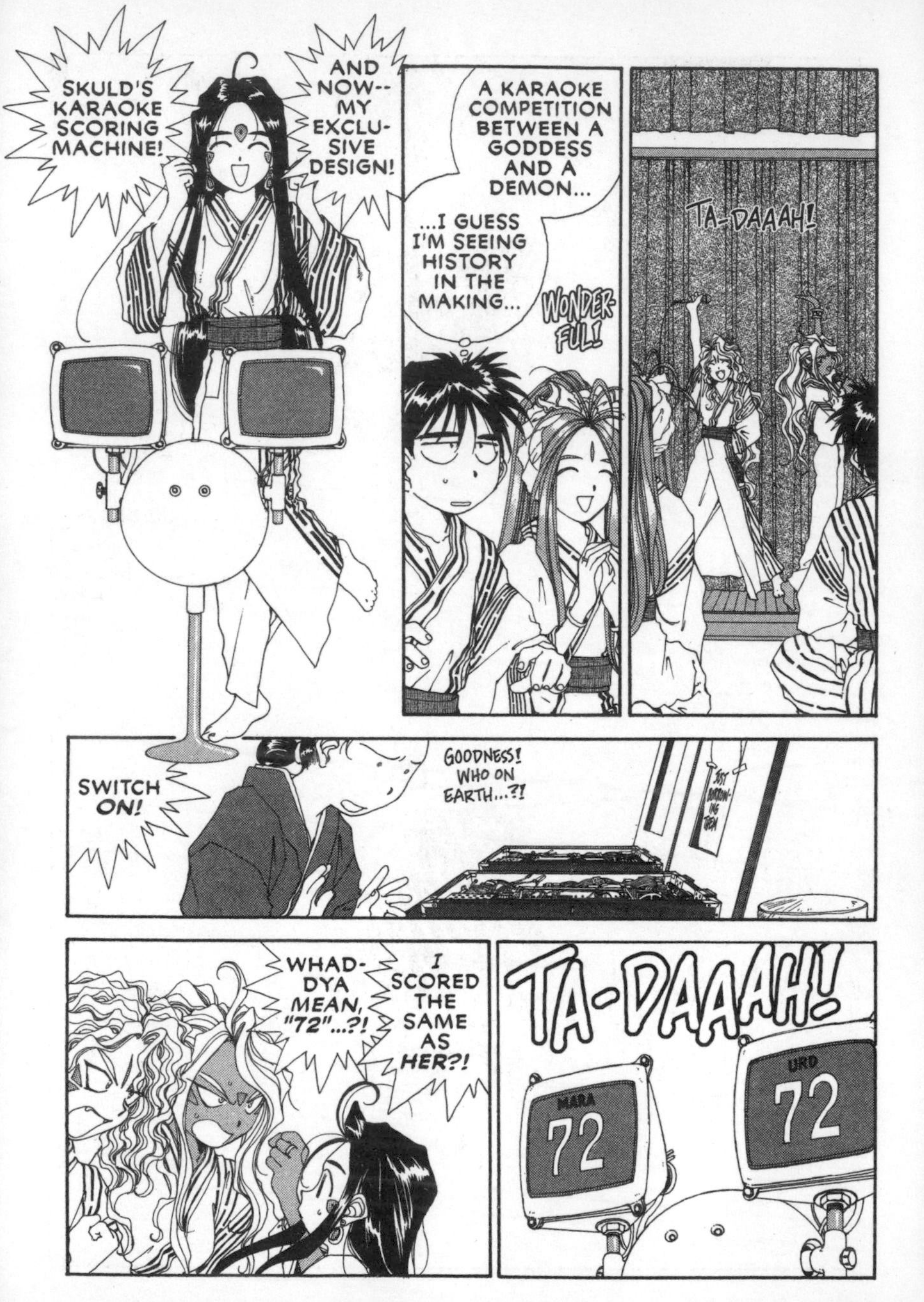
AND NOW-- MY EXCLUSIVE DESIGN!
SKULD'S KARAOKE SCORING MACHINE!
A KARAOKE COMPETITION BETWEEN A GODDESS AND A DEMON...
...I GUESS I'M SEEING HISTORY IN THE MAKING...
WONDERFUL!
TA-DAAAH!
SWITCH ON!
GOODNESS! WHO ON EARTH...?!
JUST BORROWING THEM
WHADDYA MEAN, "72"...?!
I SCORED THE SAME AS HER?!
TA-DAAAH!
MARA
72
URD
72

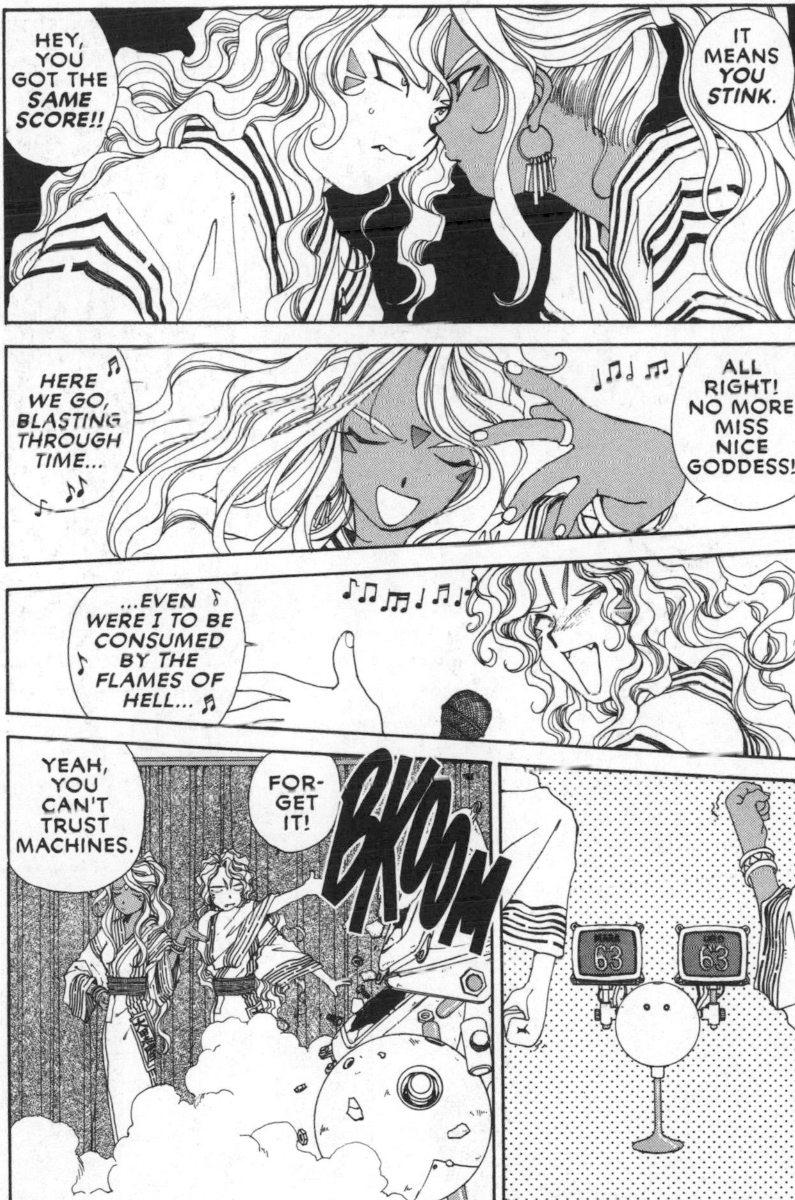
IT MEANS YOU STINK.
HEY, YOU GOT THE SAME SCORE!!
ALL RIGHT! NO MORE MISS NICE GODDESS!
HERE WE GO, BLASTING THROUGH TIME...
...EVEN WERE I TO BE CONSUMED BY THE FLAMES OF HELL...
63
63
FOR-GET IT!
BKOOM
YEAH, YOU CAN'T TRUST MACHINES.

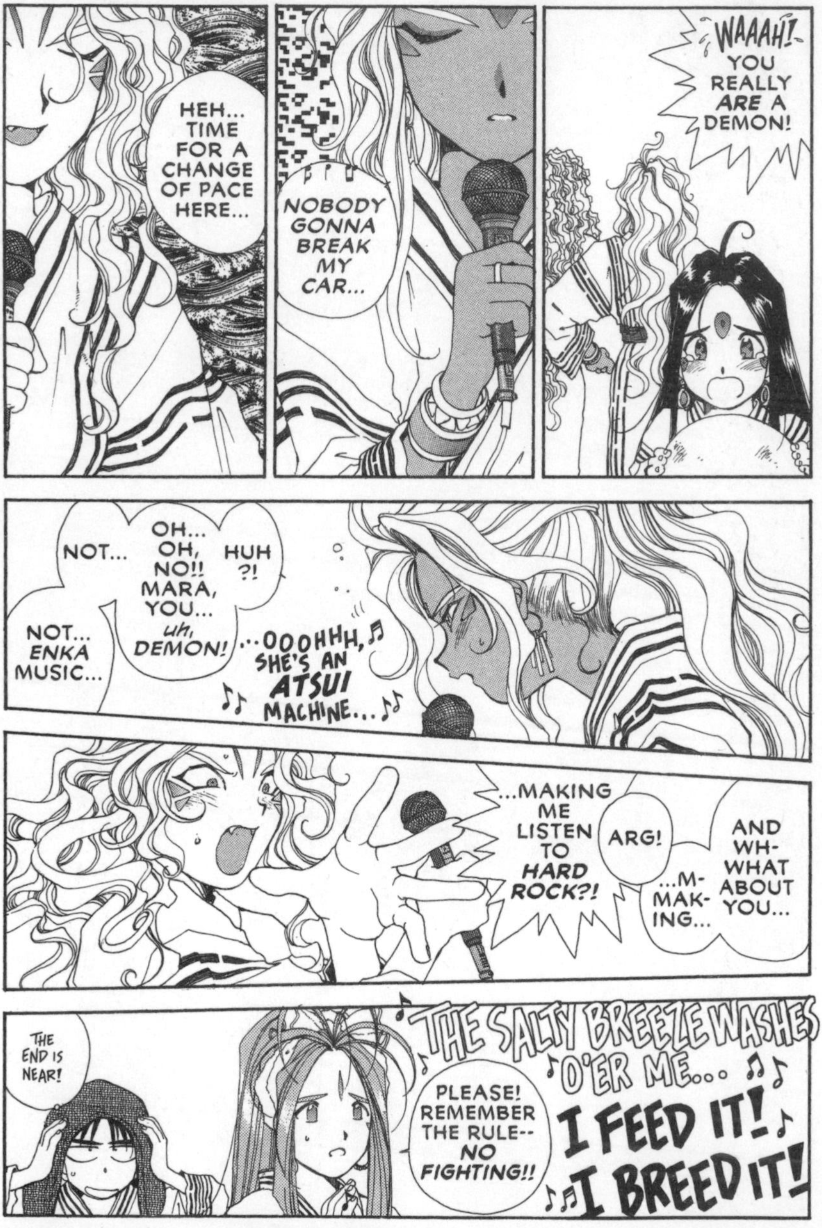
WAAAH! YOU REALLY ARE A DEMON!
NOBODY GONNA BREAK MY CAR...
HEH... TIME FOR A CHANGE OF PACE HERE...
...OOOHHH, SHE'S AN ATSUI MACHINE...
HUH ?!
OH... OH, NO!! MARA, YOU... uh, DEMON!
NOT... NOT... ENKA MUSIC...
AND WH- WHAT ABOUT YOU...
...M- MAK- ING...
ARG!
...MAKING ME LISTEN TO HARD ROCK?!
THE SALTY BREEZE WASHES O'ER ME...
I FEED IT! I BREED IT!
PLEASE! REMEMBER THE RULE-- NO FIGHTING!!
THE END IS NEAR!

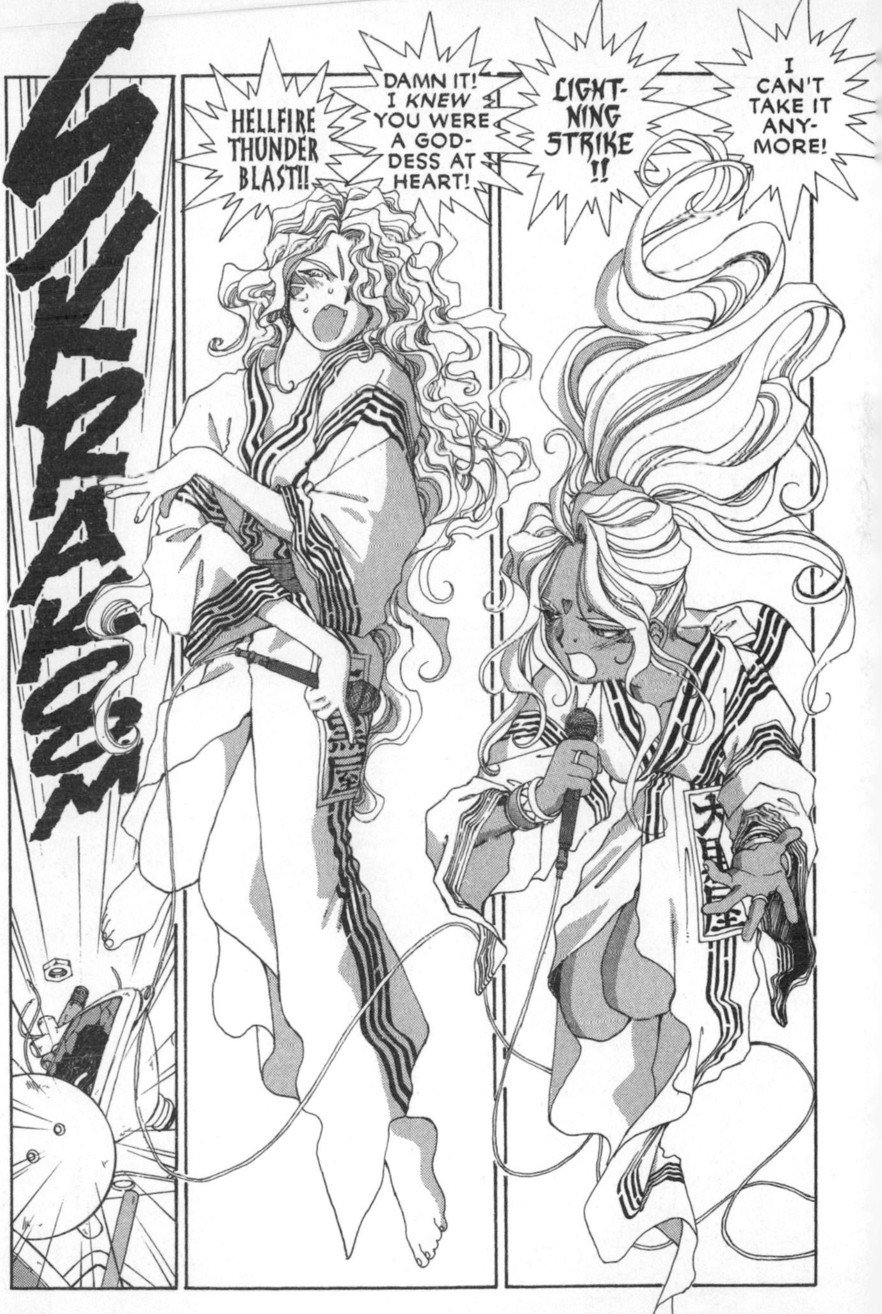
I CAN'T TAKE IT ANY-MORE!
LIGHT-NING STRIKE !!
DAMN IT! I KNEW YOU WERE A GOD-DESS AT HEART!
HELLFIRE THUNDER BLAST!!

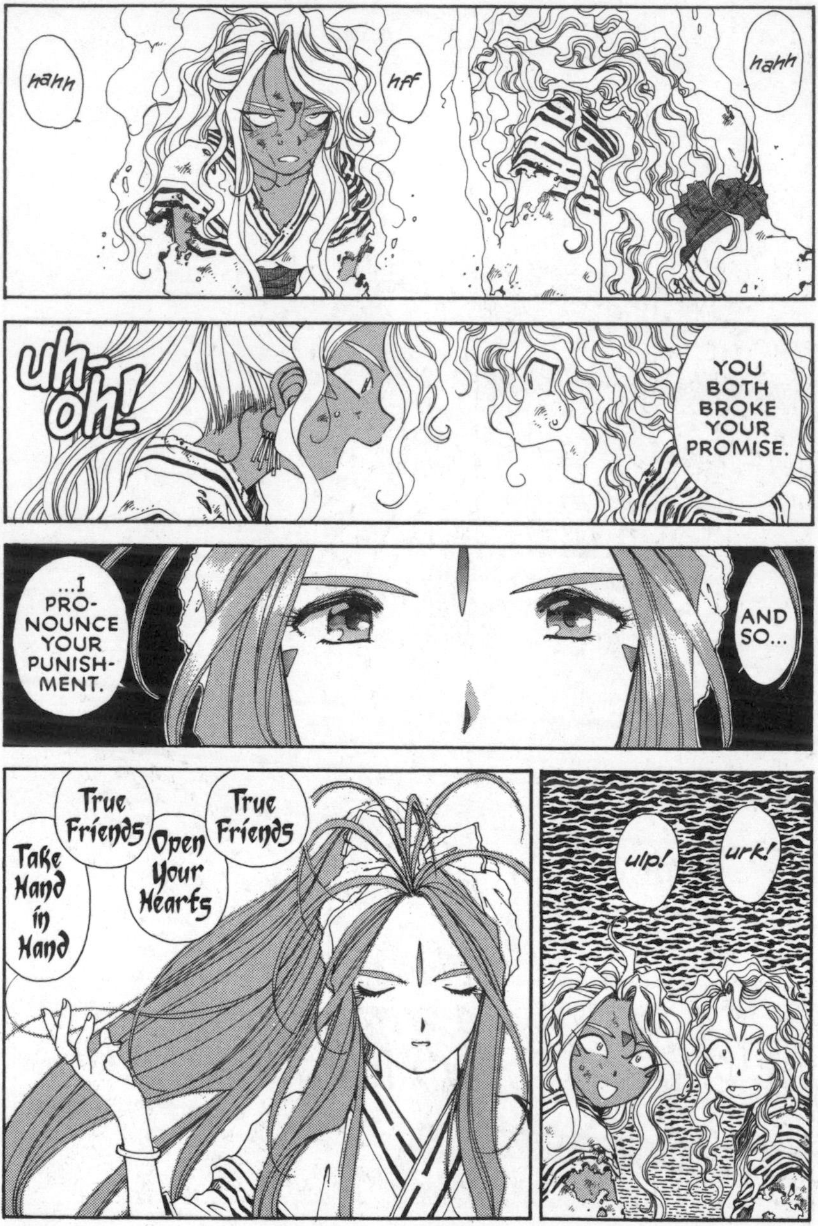
hahh
hff
hahh
YOU BOTH BROKE YOUR PROMISE.
uh-oh!
AND SO...
...I PRONOUNCE YOUR PUNISHMENT.
urk!
ulp!
True Friends
True Friends
Open Your Hearts
Take Hand in Hand

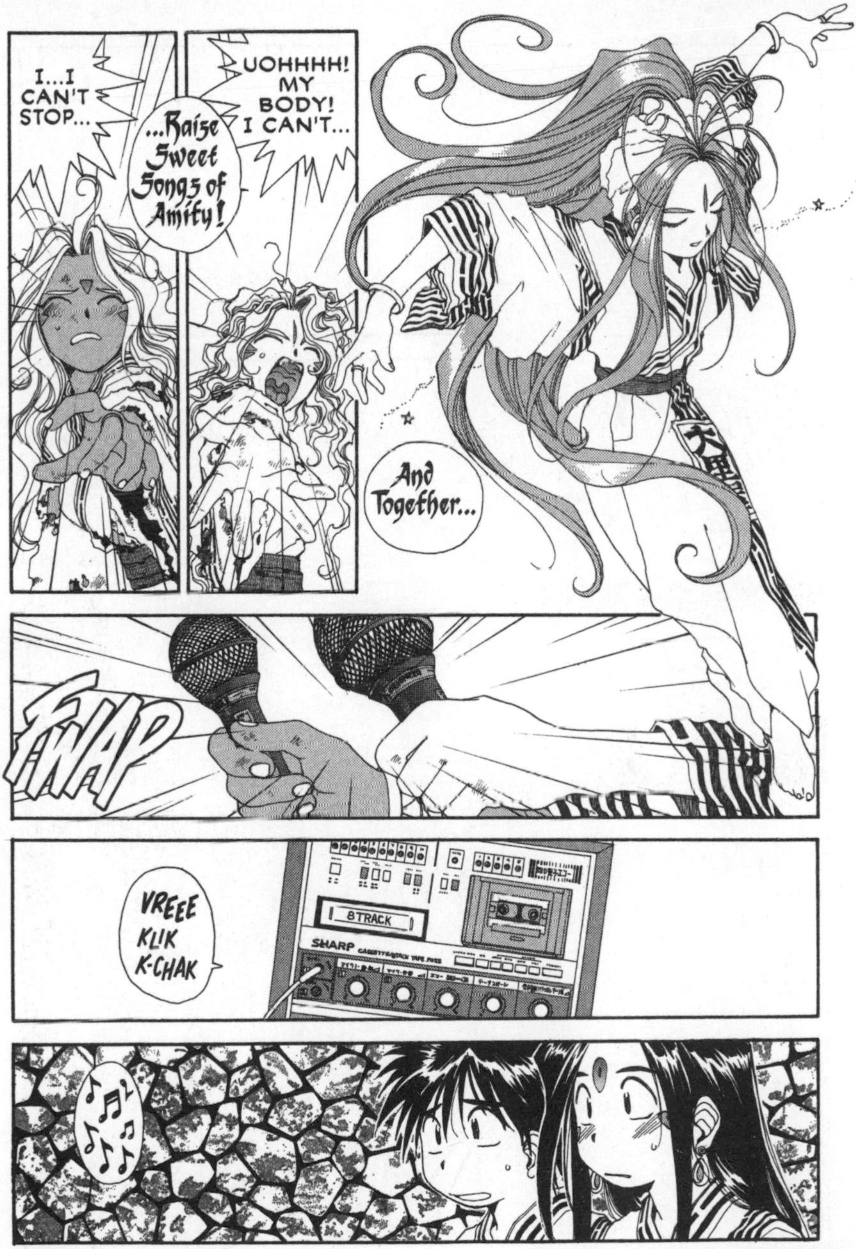
And Together...
UOHHHH! MY BODY! I CAN'T...
...Raise Sweet Songs of Amity!
I...I CAN'T STOP...
FWAP
VREEE KLIK K-CHAK
8TRACK
SHARP

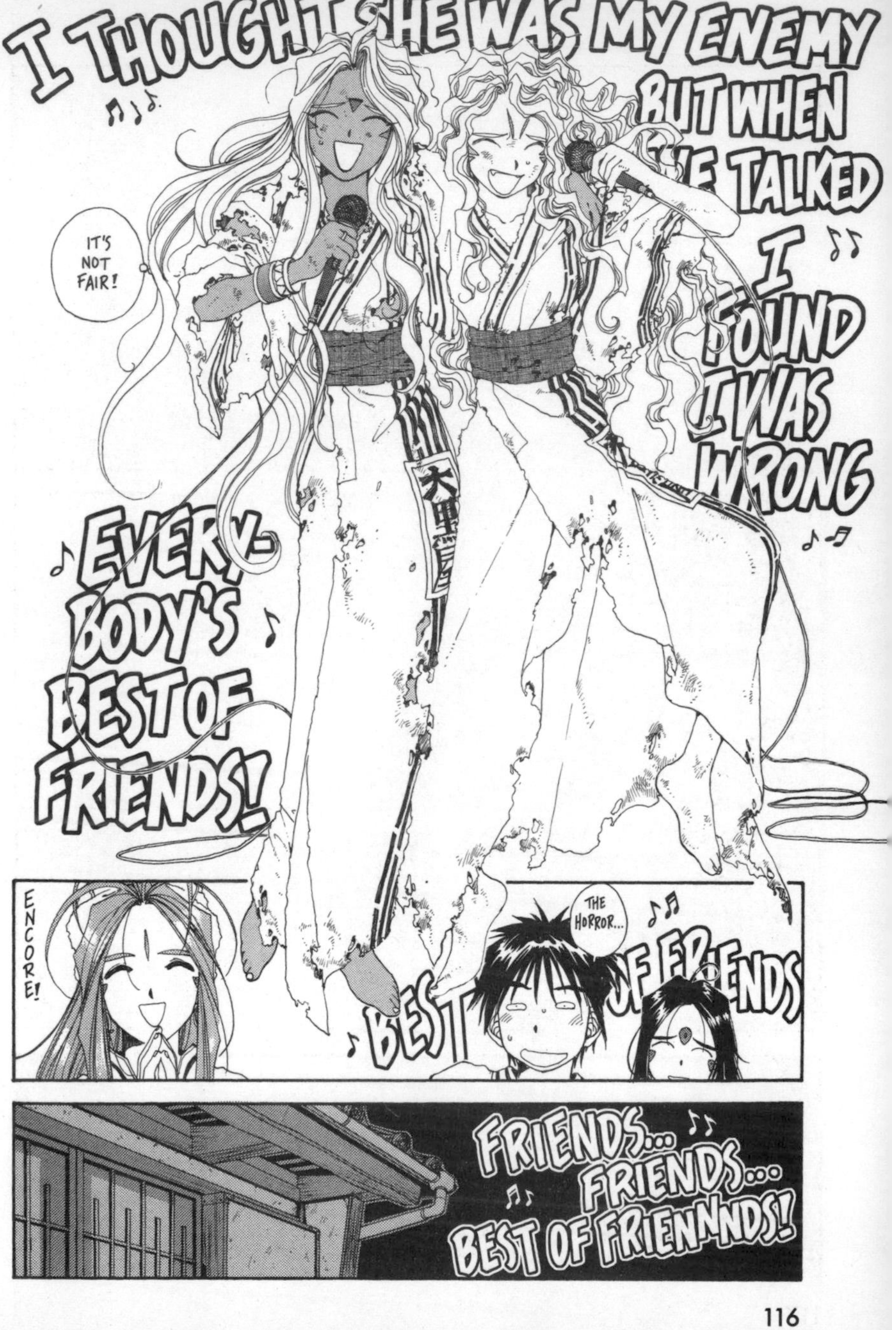
I THOUGHT SHE WAS MY ENEMY
BUT WHEN
E TALKED
I FOUND I WAS WRONG
IT'S NOT FAIR!
EVERY-BODY'S BEST OF FRIENDS!
THE HORROR...
BEST
OF FRIENDS
ENCORE!
FRIENDS... FRIENDS... BEST OF FRIENNNDS!

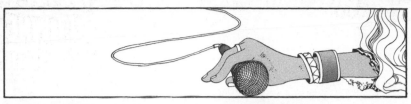

SHEESH...IF SHE HADN'T RESISTED SO MUCH, SHE WOULDN'T HAVE COLLAPSED LIKE THIS...

MARA... I...

...WELL, MY JOB DOESN'T LET ME WISH YOU *LUCK.*

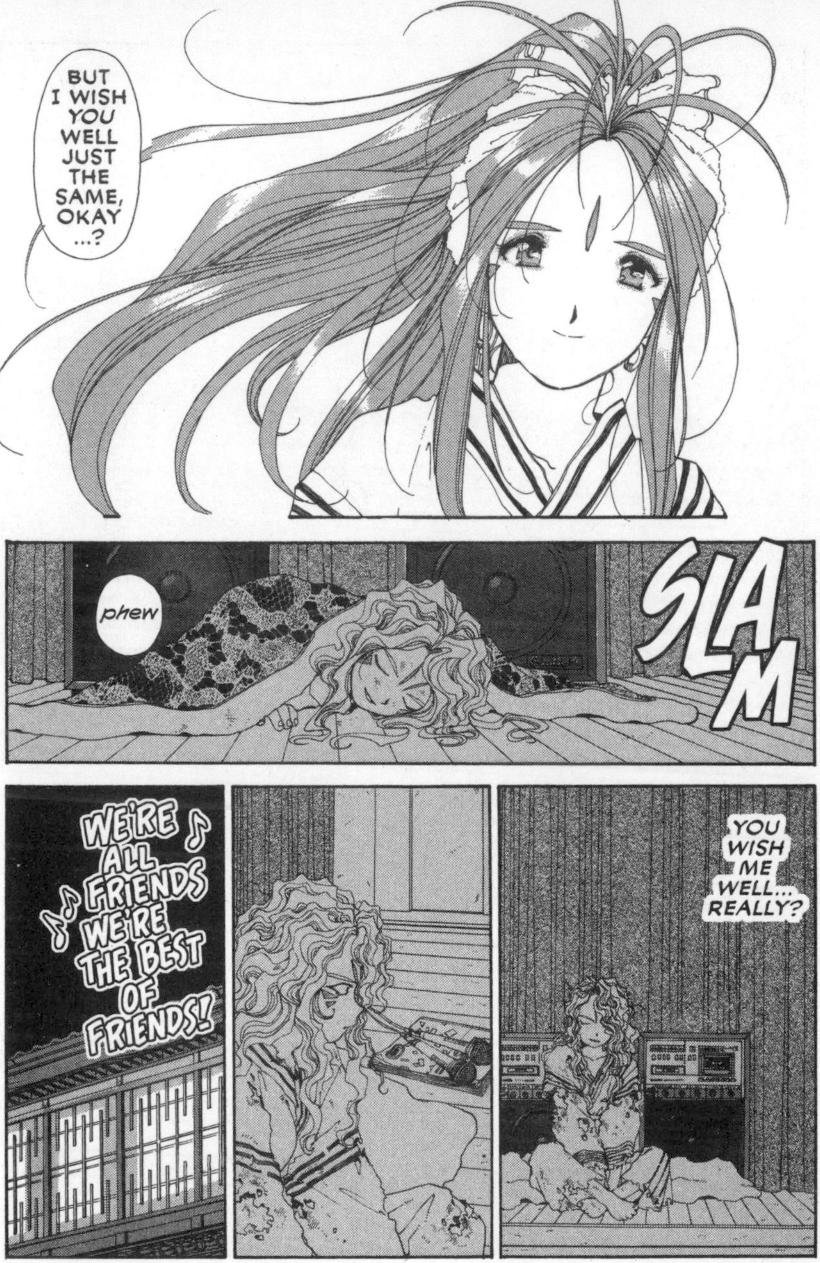

BUT I WISH *YOU* WELL JUST THE SAME, OKAY ...?
SLAM
phew
YOU WISH ME WELL... REALLY?
WE'RE ♪ ALL FRIENDS ♪♪ WE'RE THE BEST OF FRIENDS!

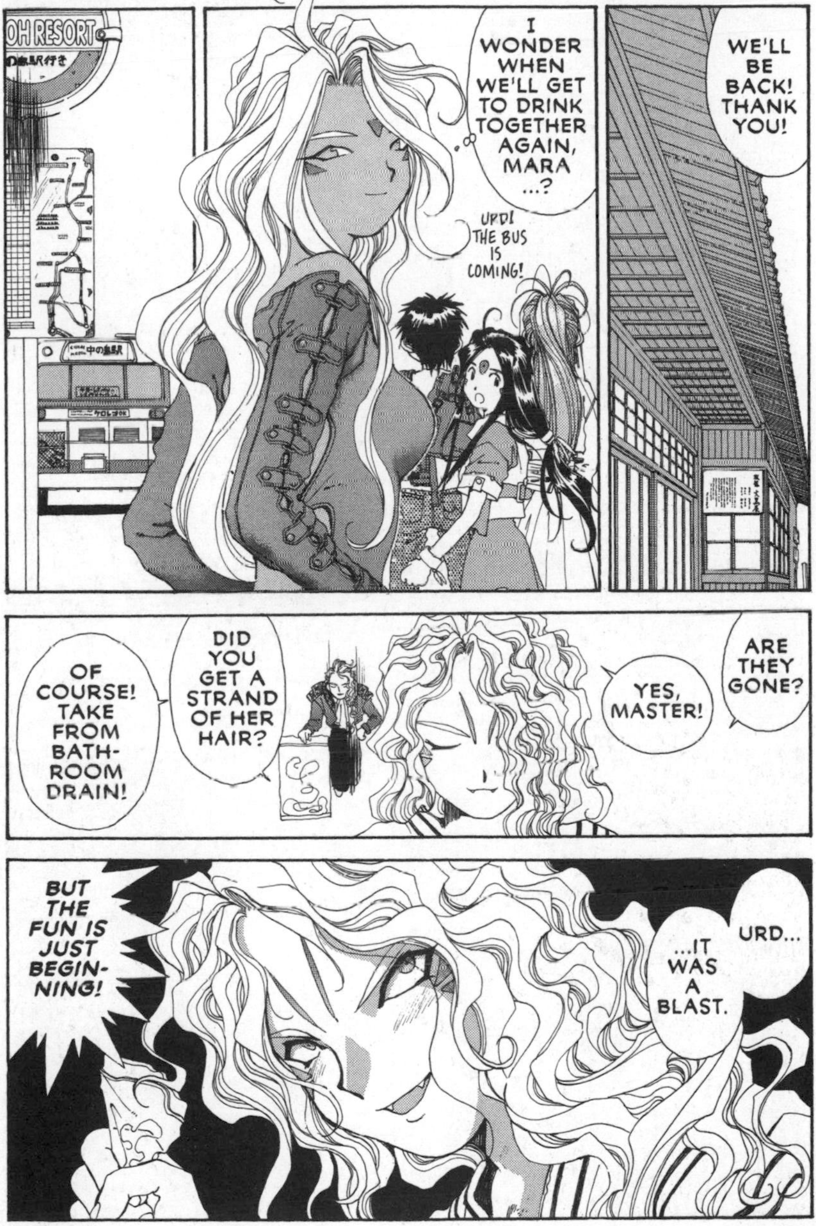
WE'LL BE BACK! THANK YOU!
I WONDER WHEN WE'LL GET TO DRINK TOGETHER AGAIN, MARA ...?
URD! THE BUS IS COMING!
OH RESORT
ARE THEY GONE?
YES, MASTER!
DID YOU GET A STRAND OF HER HAIR?
OF COURSE! TAKE FROM BATH-ROOM DRAIN!
URD...
...IT WAS A BLAST.
BUT THE FUN IS JUST BEGIN-NING!

THE ADVENTURES OF THE MINI-GODDESSES

◆ THE TRAGIC FLYING "V"! AND BELLDANDY! AND MR. RAT! ◆

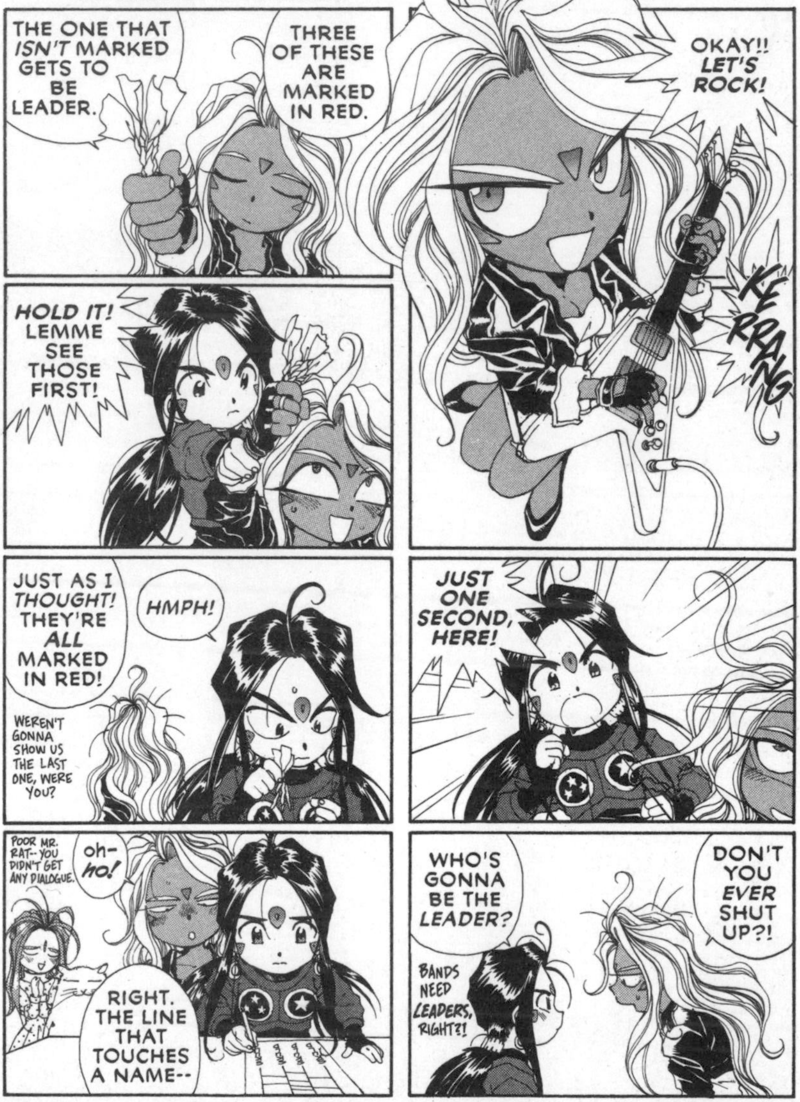
OKAY!! LET'S ROCK!
KE-RRANG
THREE OF THESE ARE MARKED IN RED.
THE ONE THAT ISN'T MARKED GETS TO BE LEADER.
HOLD IT! LEMME SEE THOSE FIRST!
JUST ONE SECOND, HERE!
JUST AS I THOUGHT! THEY'RE ALL MARKED IN RED!
HMPH!
WEREN'T GONNA SHOW US THE LAST ONE, WERE YOU?
DON'T YOU EVER SHUT UP?!
WHO'S GONNA BE THE LEADER?
BANDS NEED LEADERS, RIGHT?!
oh-ho!
POOR MR. RAT-- YOU DIDN'T GET ANY DIALOGUE.
RIGHT. THE LINE THAT TOUCHES A NAME--

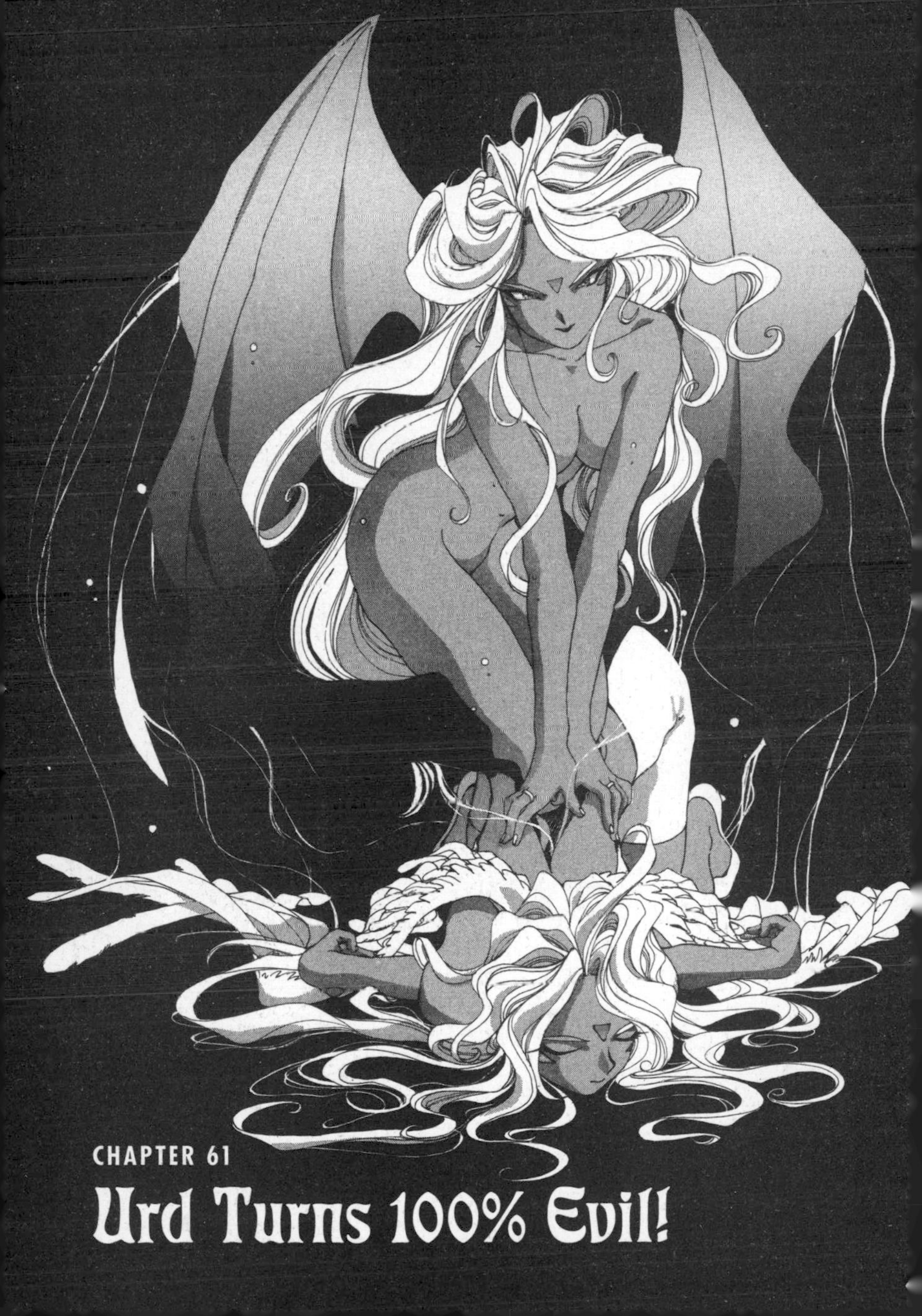

CHAPTER 61

Urd Turns 100% Evil!

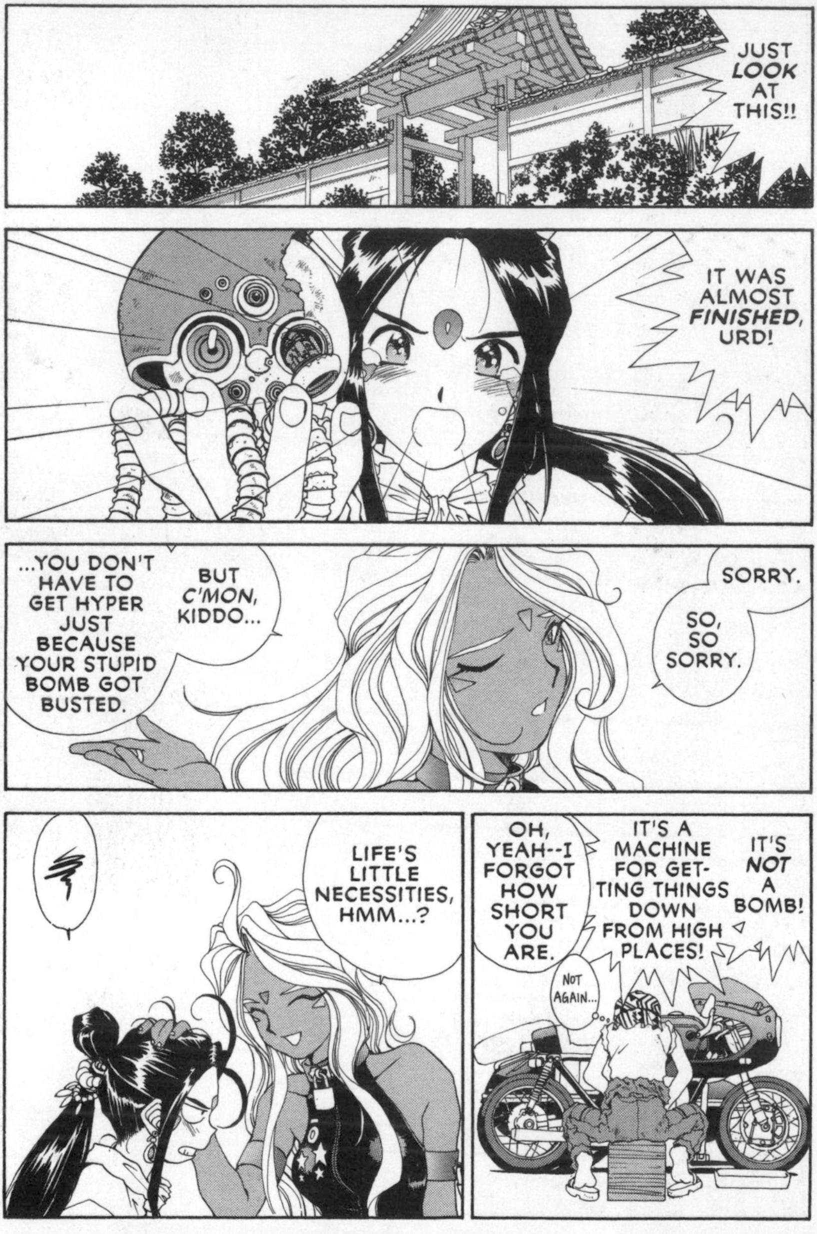
JUST *LOOK* AT THIS!!
IT WAS ALMOST *FINISHED*, URD!
SORRY.
SO, SO SORRY.
BUT *C'MON*, KIDDO...
...YOU DON'T HAVE TO GET HYPER JUST BECAUSE YOUR STUPID BOMB GOT BUSTED.
IT'S *NOT* A BOMB!
IT'S A MACHINE FOR GET-TING THINGS DOWN FROM HIGH PLACES!
OH, YEAH--I FORGOT HOW SHORT YOU ARE.
NOT AGAIN...
LIFE'S LITTLE NECESSITIES, HMM...?

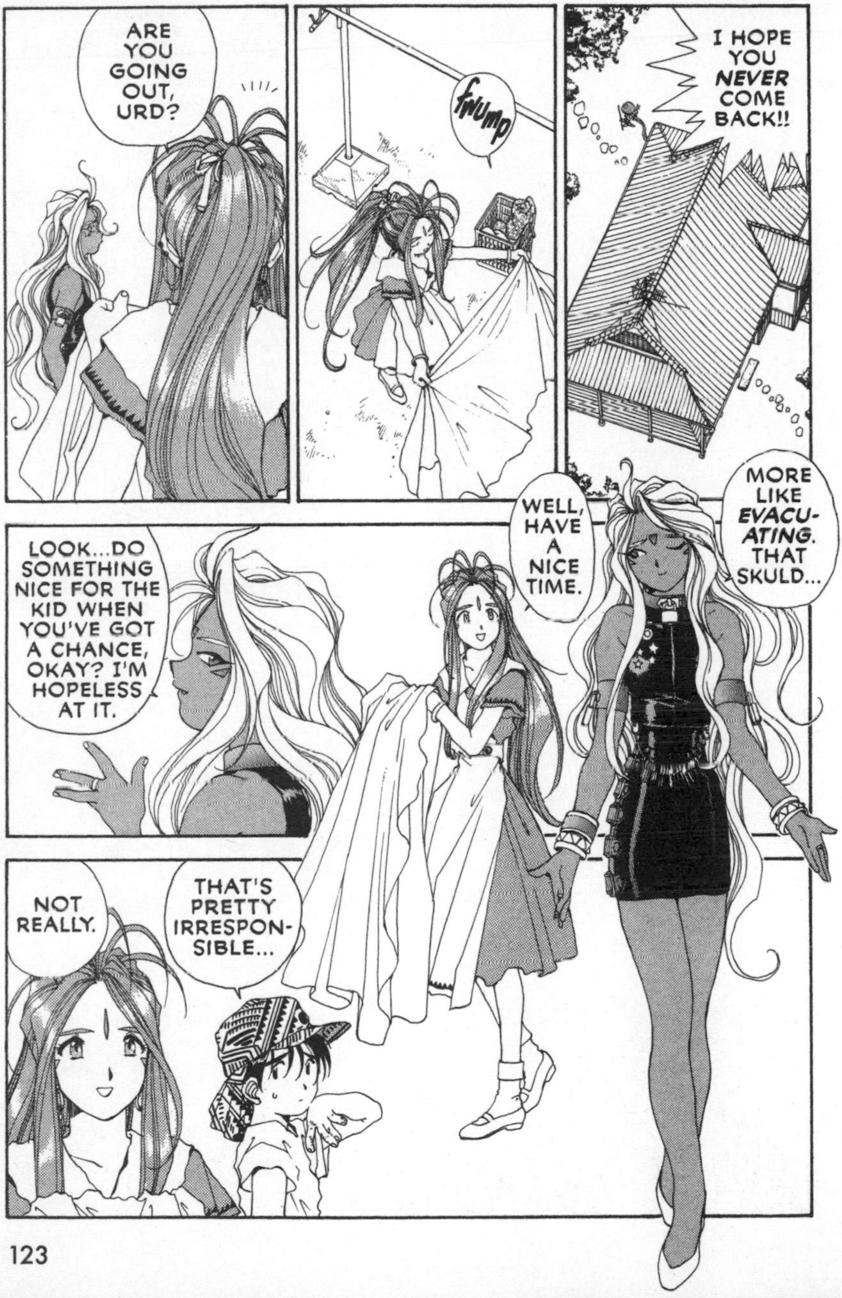
ARE YOU GOING OUT, URD?
frump
I HOPE YOU NEVER COME BACK!!
WELL, HAVE A NICE TIME.
MORE LIKE EVACUATING. THAT SKULD...
LOOK...DO SOMETHING NICE FOR THE KID WHEN YOU'VE GOT A CHANCE, OKAY? I'M HOPELESS AT IT.
THAT'S PRETTY IRRESPONSIBLE...
NOT REALLY.

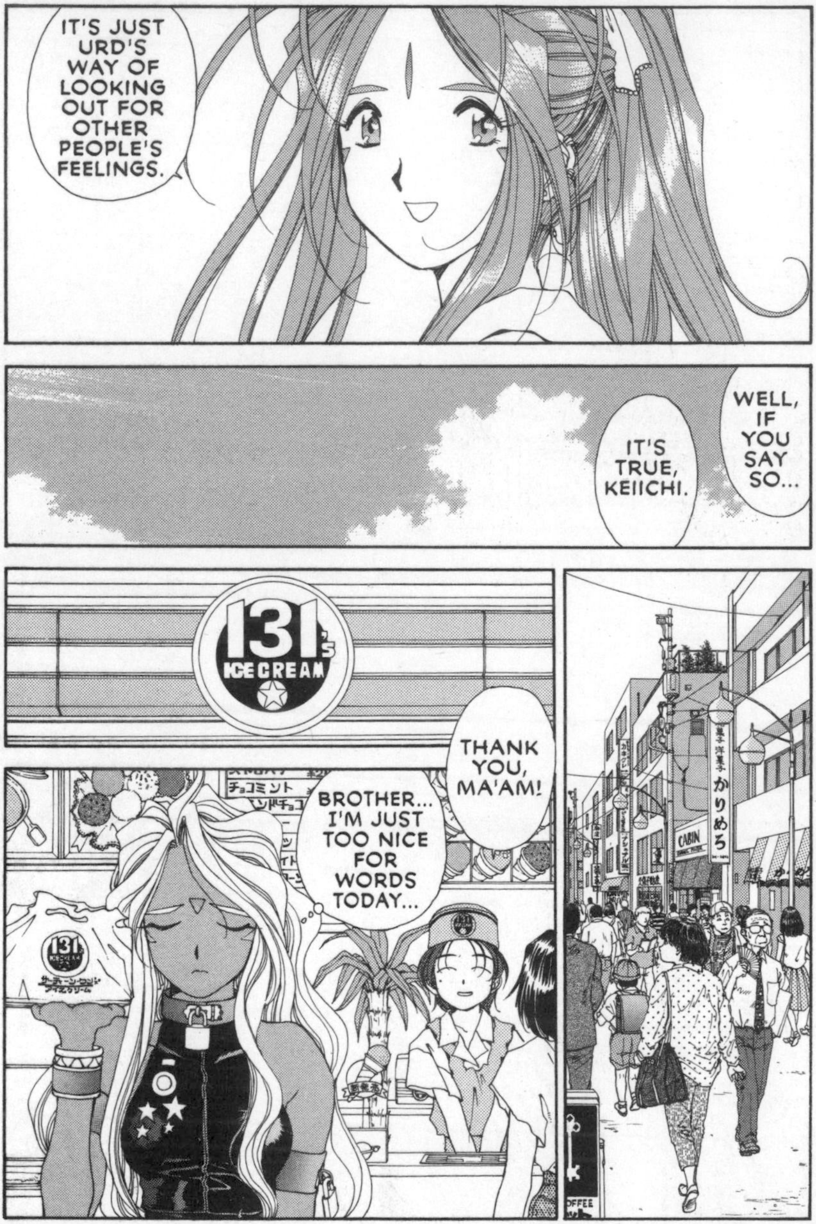
IT'S JUST URD'S WAY OF LOOKING OUT FOR OTHER PEOPLE'S FEELINGS.
WELL, IF YOU SAY SO...
IT'S TRUE, KEIICHI.
かりめろ
CABIN
131's ICE CREAM
THANK YOU, MA'AM!
BROTHER... I'M JUST TOO NICE FOR WORDS TODAY...
チョコミント

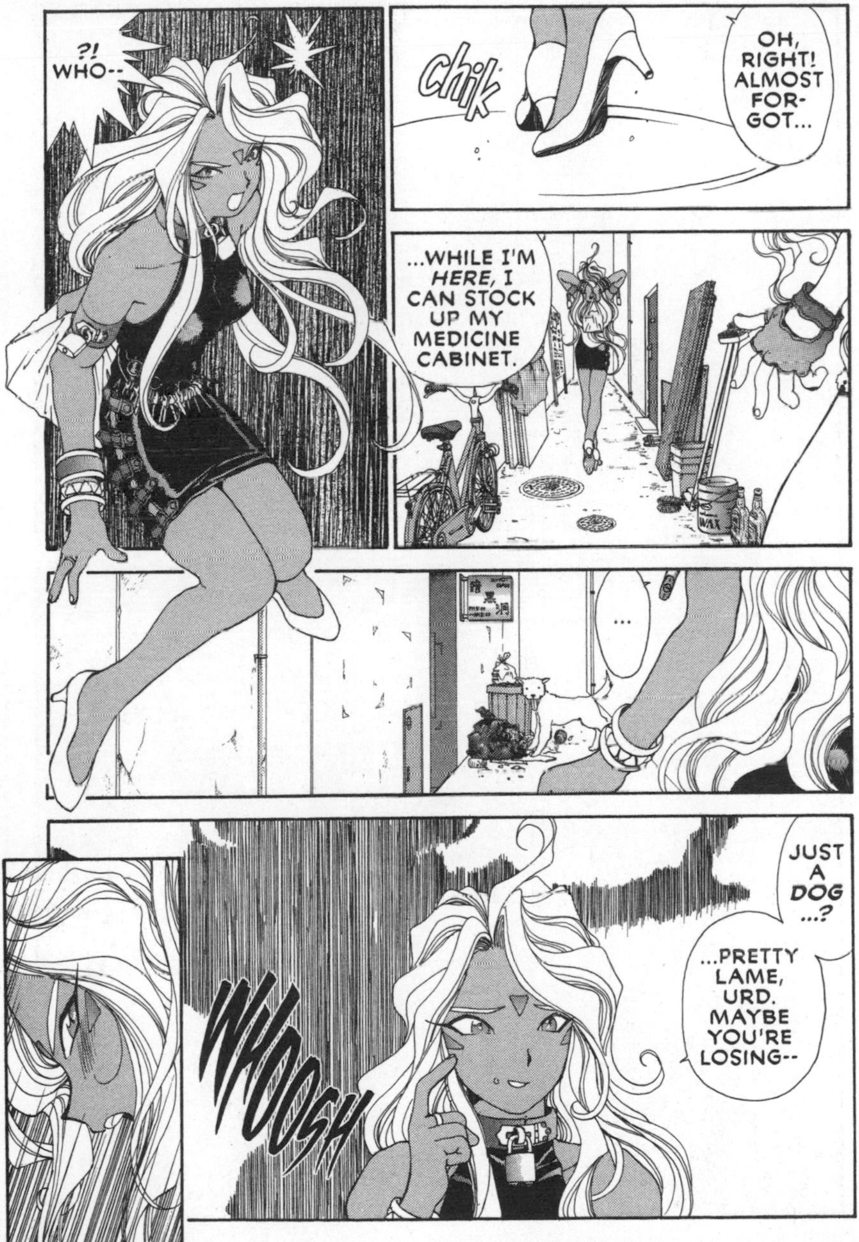
chik
OH, RIGHT! ALMOST FOR-GOT...
...WHILE I'M *HERE,* I CAN STOCK UP MY MEDICINE CABINET.
...
JUST A *DOG* ...?
...PRETTY LAME, URD. MAYBE YOU'RE LOSING--
WHOOSH
?! WHO--

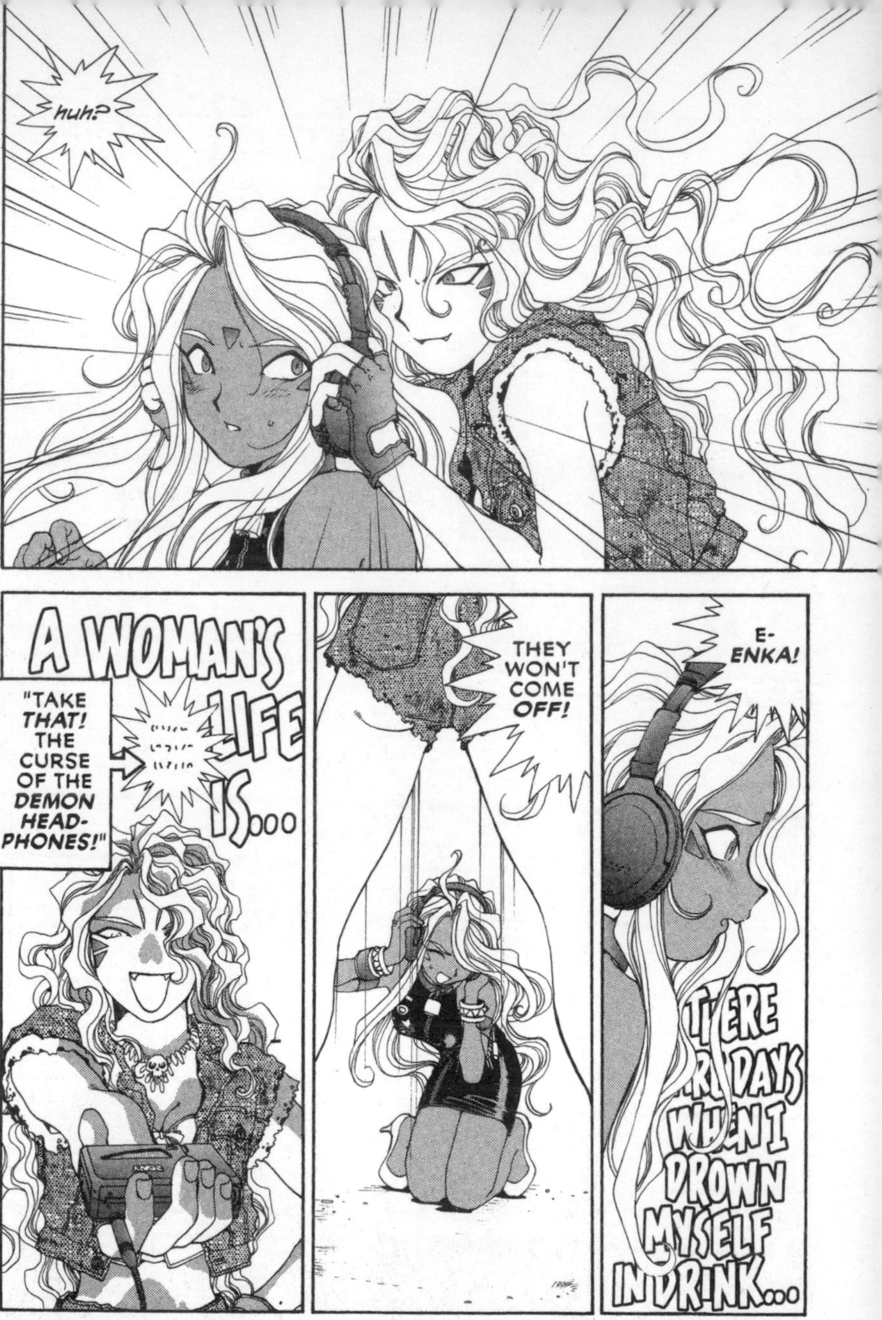
huh?
E-ENKA!
THERE ARE DAYS WHEN I DROWN MYSELF IN DRINK...
THEY WON'T COME OFF!
A WOMAN'S LIFE IS...
"TAKE THAT! THE CURSE OF THE DEMON HEAD-PHONES!"

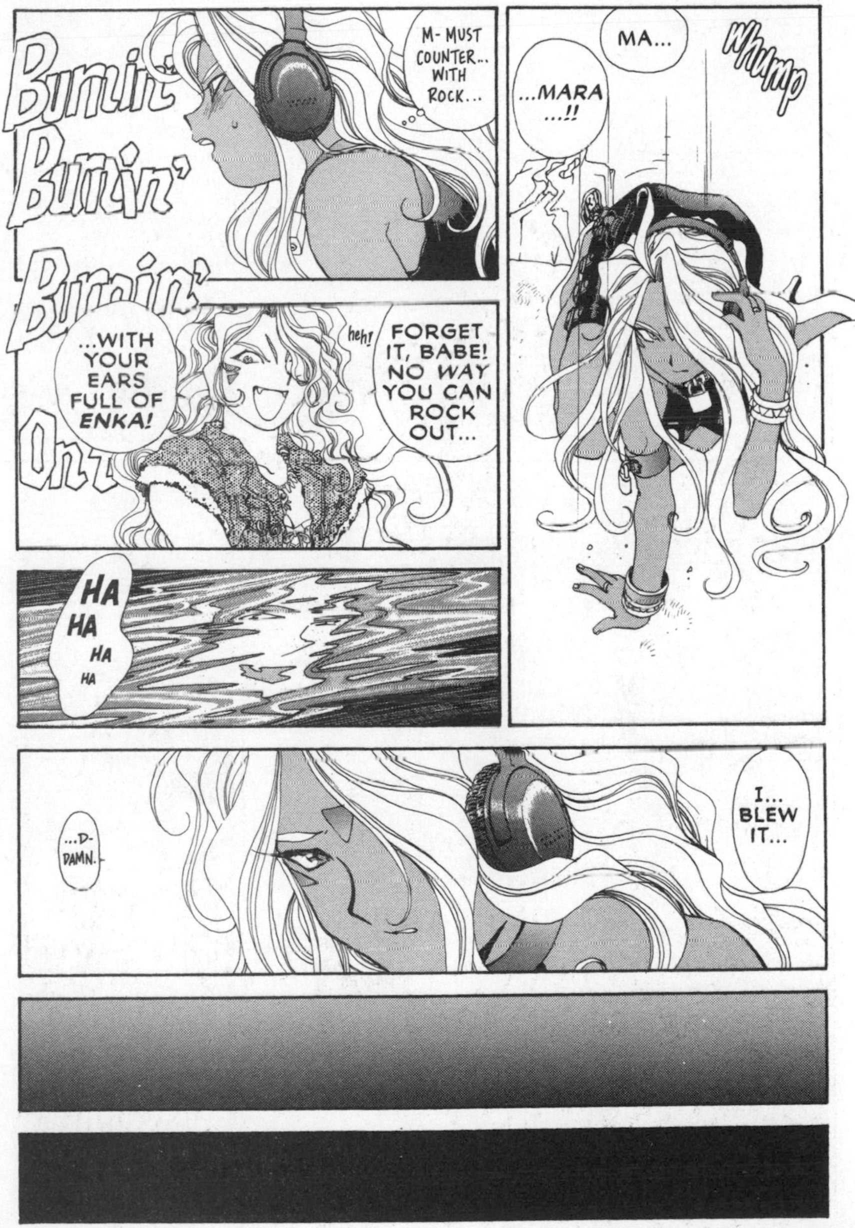
WHUMP
MA...
...MARA ...!!
M-MUST COUNTER... WITH ROCK...
Burnin'
Burnin'
Burnin'
FORGET IT, BABE! NO WAY YOU CAN ROCK OUT...
heh!
...WITH YOUR EARS FULL OF ENKA!
On!
HA HA HA HA
I... BLEW IT...
...D-DAMN.

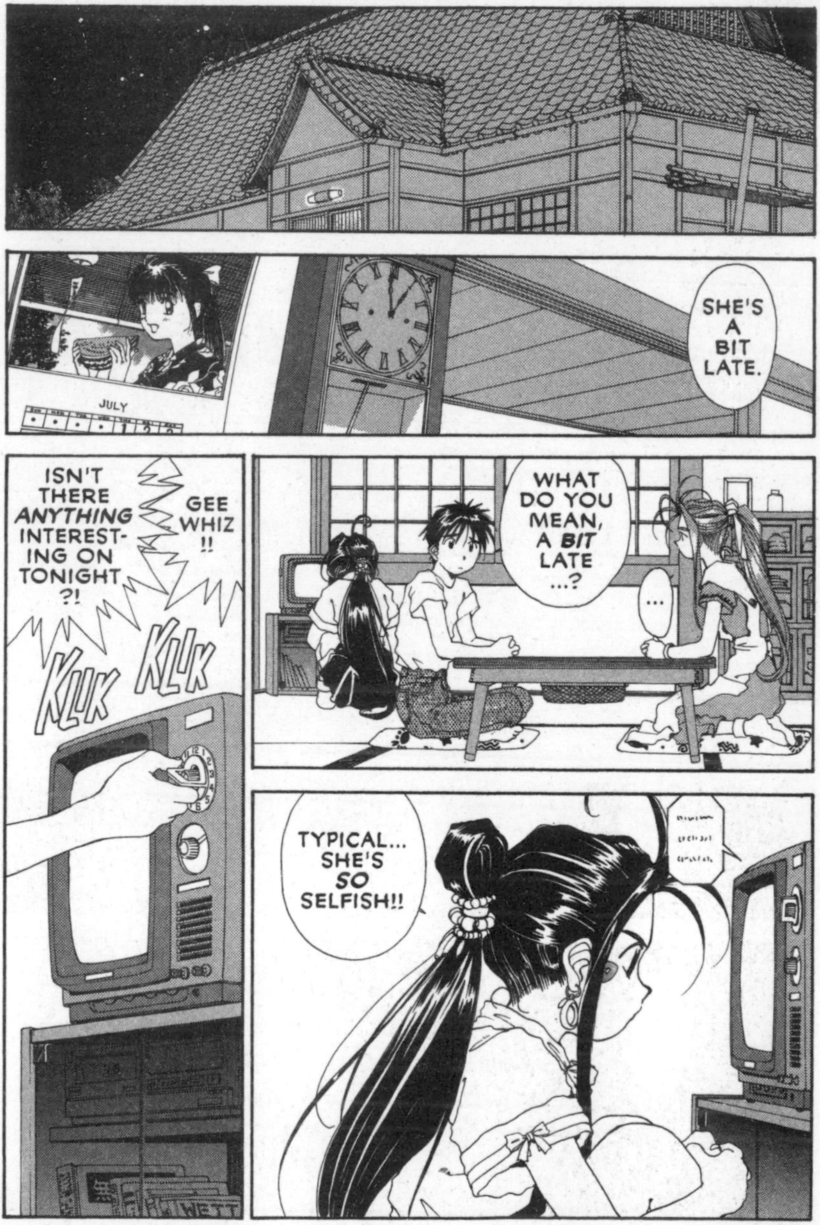
SHE'S A BIT LATE.
JULY
WHAT DO YOU MEAN, A *BIT* LATE ...?
...
TYPICAL... SHE'S *SO* SELFISH!!
ISN'T THERE *ANYTHING* INTERESTING ON TONIGHT ?!
GEE WHIZ !!
KLIK KLIK

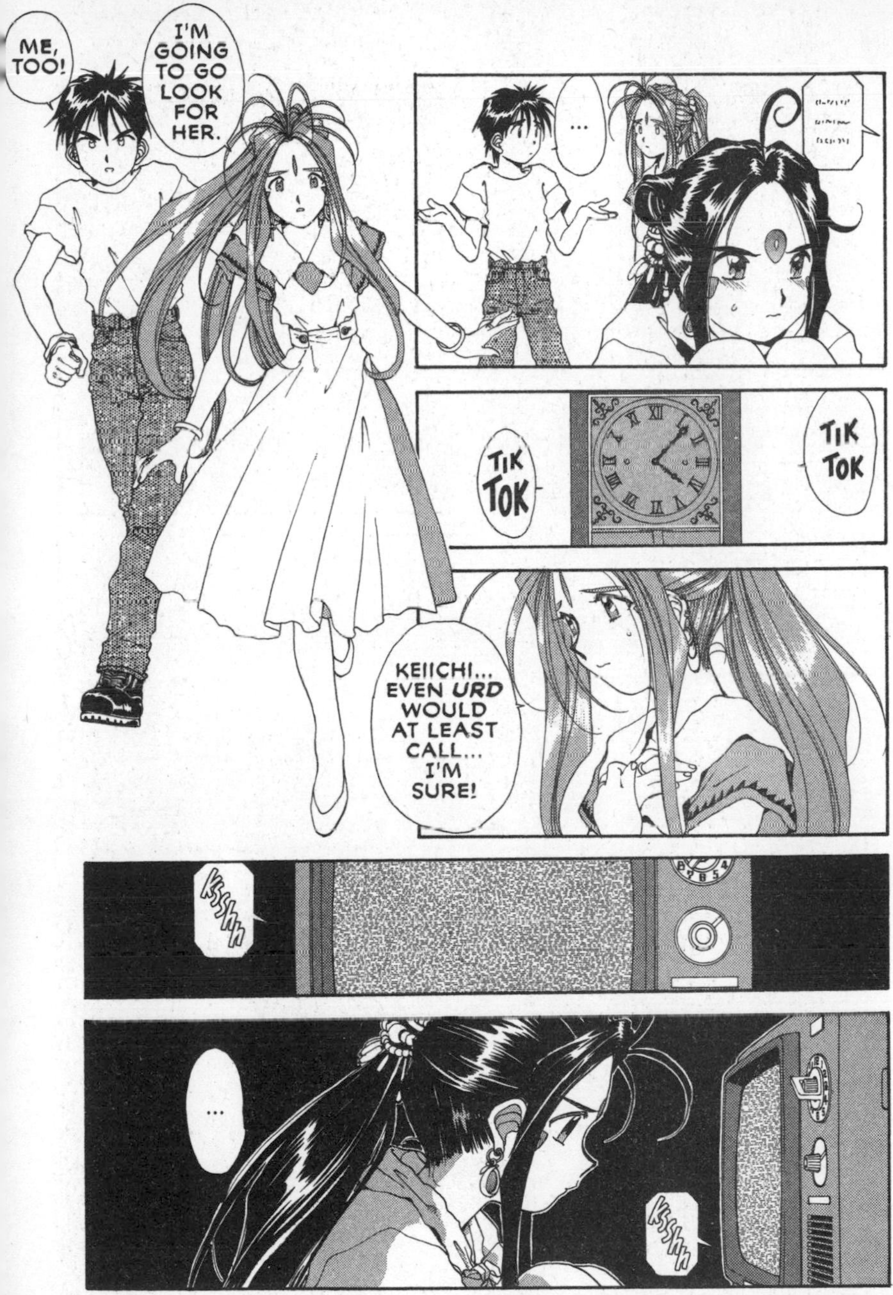
...
TIK TOK
TIK TOK
KEIICHI... EVEN *URD* WOULD AT LEAST CALL... I'M SURE!
I'M GOING TO GO LOOK FOR HER.
ME, TOO!
KSSHH
KSSHH
...

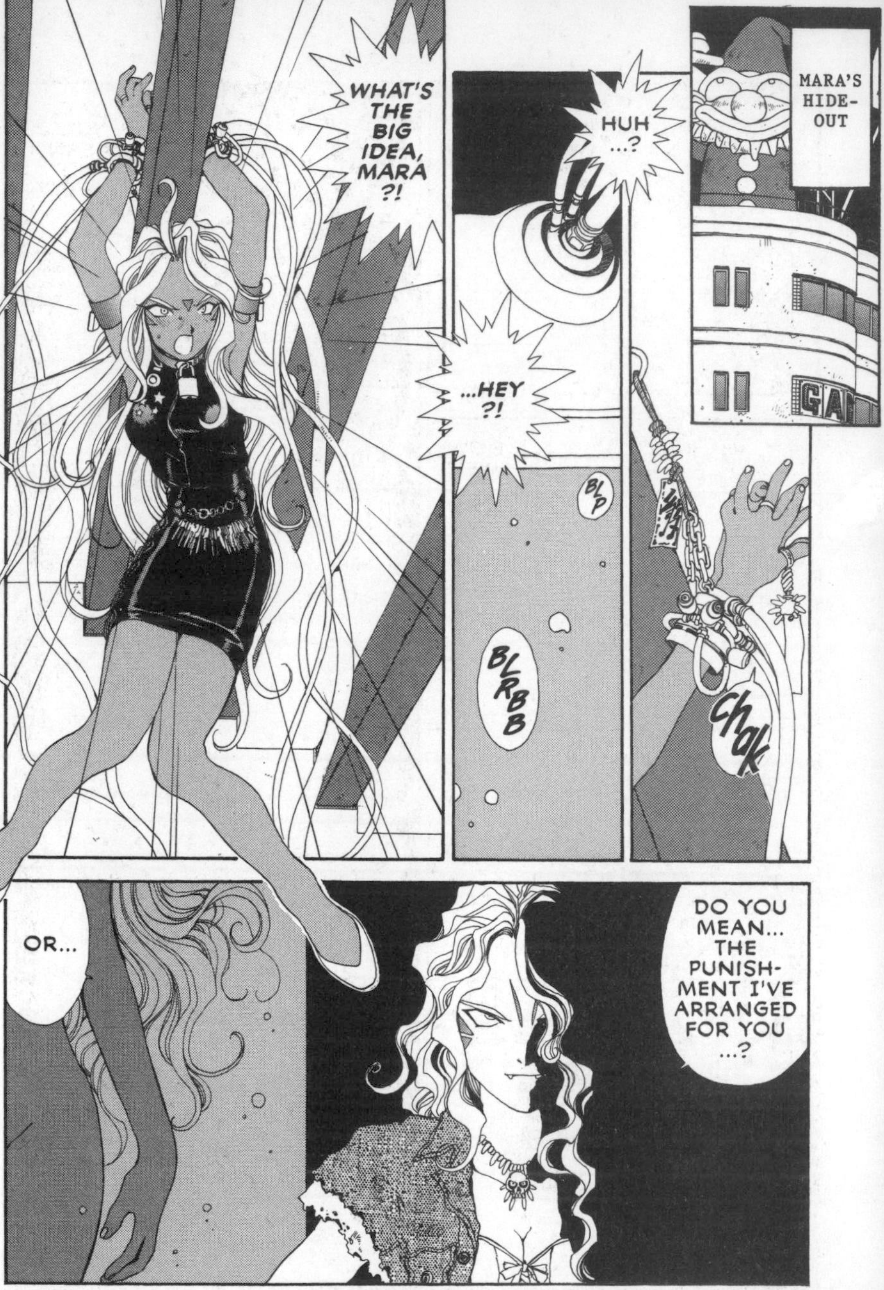
MARA'S HIDE-OUT
CHOK
HUH ...?
...HEY ?!
BLP
BLRBB
WHAT'S THE BIG IDEA, MARA ?!
DO YOU MEAN... THE PUNISHMENT I'VE ARRANGED FOR YOU ...?
OR...

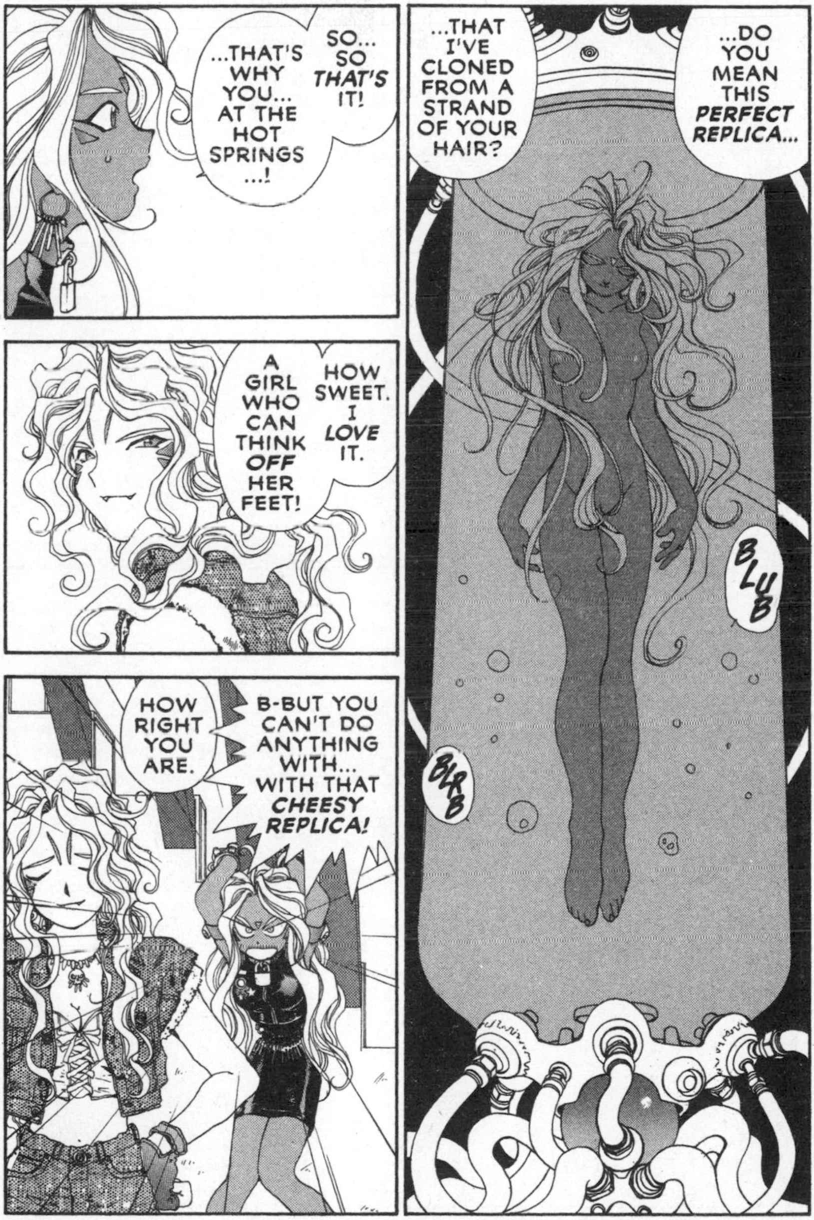
...DO YOU MEAN THIS PERFECT REPLICA...
...THAT I'VE CLONED FROM A STRAND OF YOUR HAIR?
BLUB
BLRB
SO... SO THAT'S IT!
...THAT'S WHY YOU... AT THE HOT SPRINGS ...!
HOW SWEET. I LOVE IT.
A GIRL WHO CAN THINK OFF HER FEET!
B-BUT YOU CAN'T DO ANYTHING WITH... WITH THAT CHEESY REPLICA!
HOW RIGHT YOU ARE.

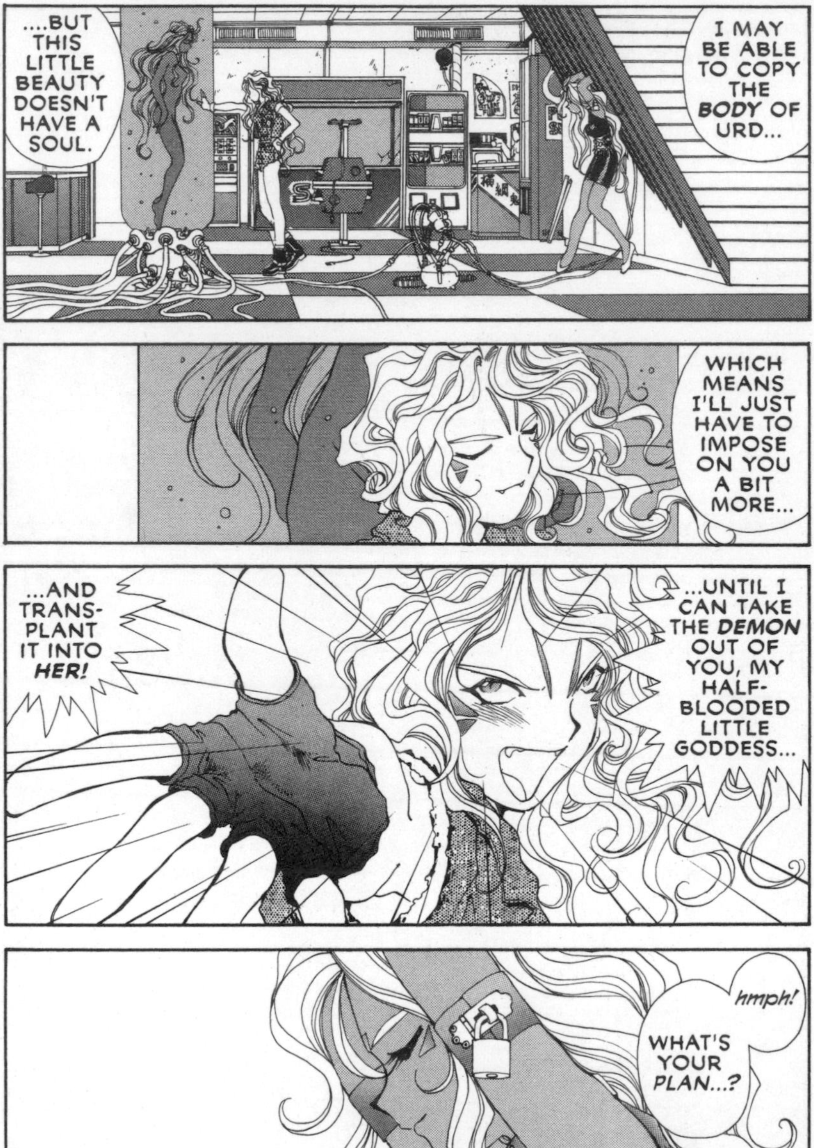
I MAY BE ABLE TO COPY THE BODY OF URD...
....BUT THIS LITTLE BEAUTY DOESN'T HAVE A SOUL.
WHICH MEANS I'LL JUST HAVE TO IMPOSE ON YOU A BIT MORE...
...UNTIL I CAN TAKE THE DEMON OUT OF YOU, MY HALF-BLOODED LITTLE GODDESS...
...AND TRANS-PLANT IT INTO HER!
hmph!
WHAT'S YOUR PLAN...?

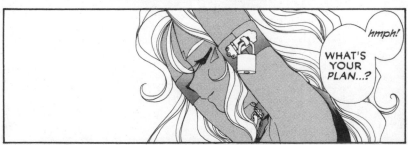

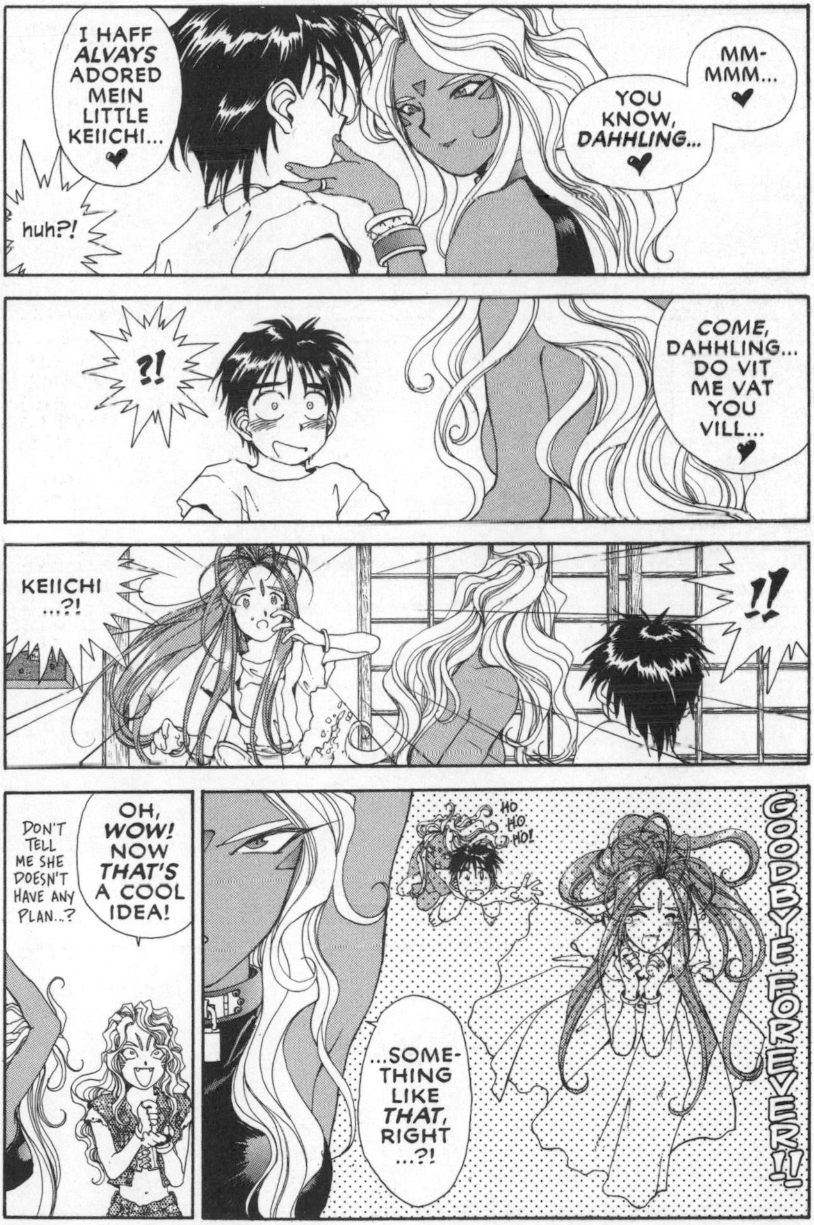
MM-MMM... ♥
YOU KNOW, DAHHLING... ♥
I HAFF ALVAYS ADORED MEIN LITTLE KEIICHI... ♥
huh?!
COME, DAHHLING... DO VIT ME VAT YOU VILL... ♥
?!
!!
KEIICHI ...?!
GOODBYE FOREVER!!
HO HO HO!
...SOME-THING LIKE THAT, RIGHT ...?!
OH, WOW! NOW THAT'S A COOL IDEA!
DON'T TELL ME SHE DOESN'T HAVE ANY PLAN..?

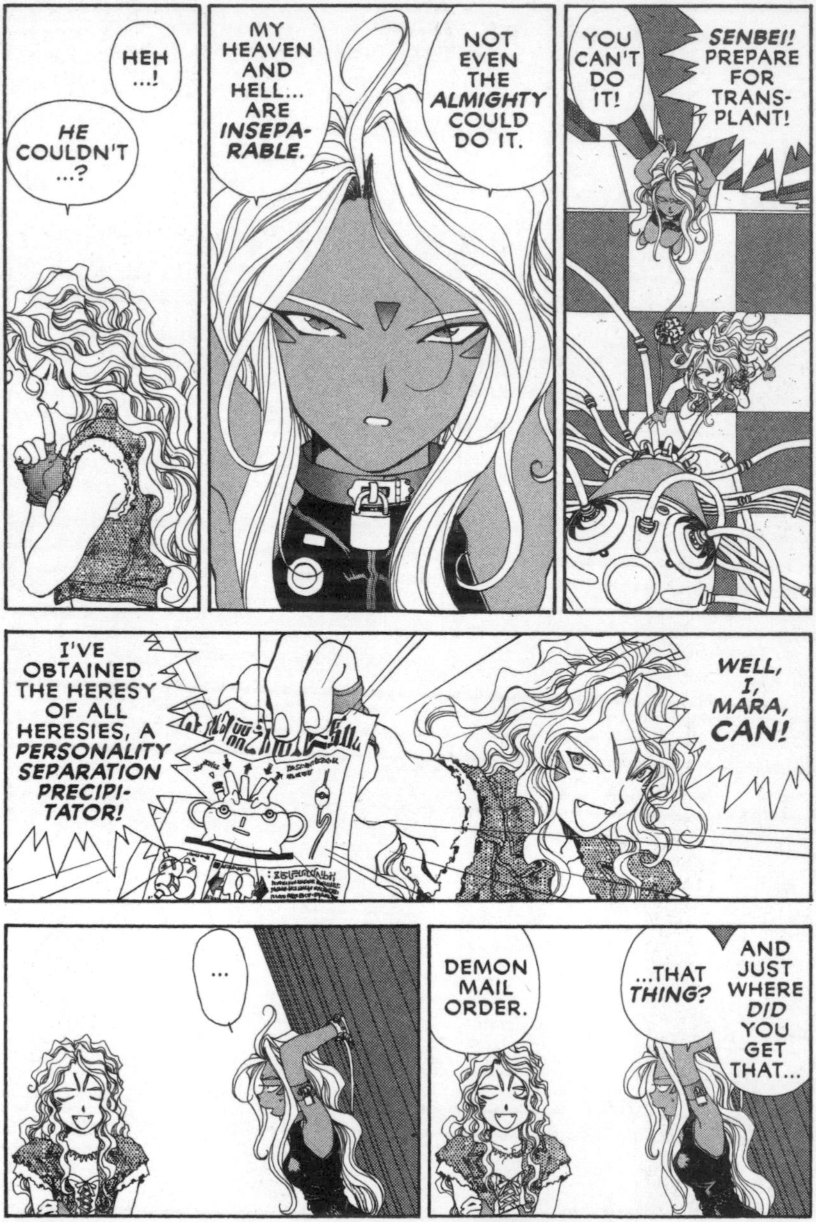
SENBEI! PREPARE FOR TRANS-PLANT!
YOU CAN'T DO IT!
NOT EVEN THE ALMIGHTY COULD DO IT.
MY HEAVEN AND HELL... ARE INSEPARABLE.
HEH ...!
HE COULDN'T ...?
WELL, I, MARA, CAN!
I'VE OBTAINED THE HERESY OF ALL HERESIES, A PERSONALITY SEPARATION PRECIPITATOR!
AND JUST WHERE DID YOU GET THAT...
...THAT THING?
DEMON MAIL ORDER.
...

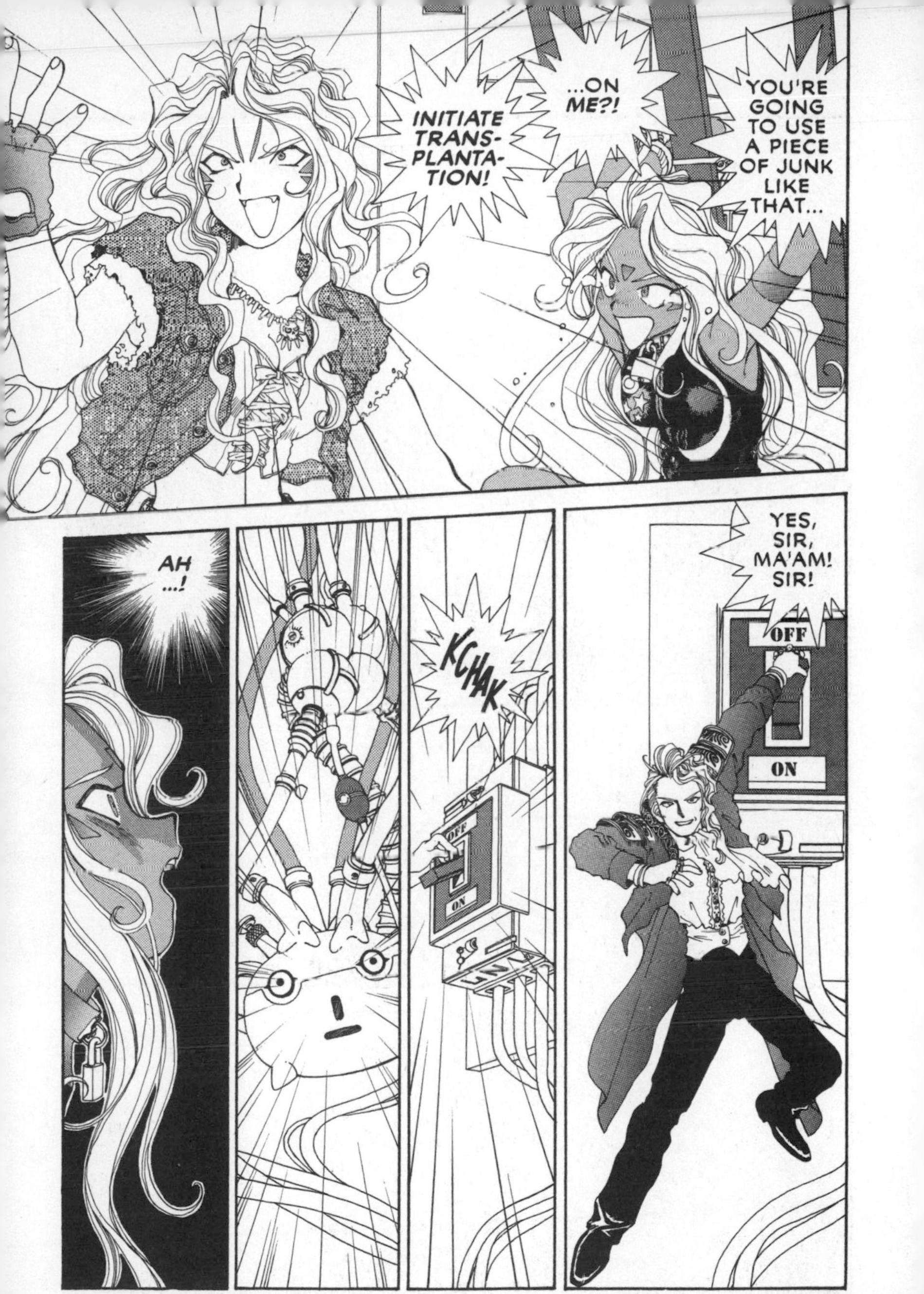
YOU'RE GOING TO USE A PIECE OF JUNK LIKE THAT...
...ON ME?!
INITIATE TRANS-PLANTA-TION!
YES, SIR, MA'AM! SIR!
OFF
ON
KCHAK
OFF
ON
AH ...!

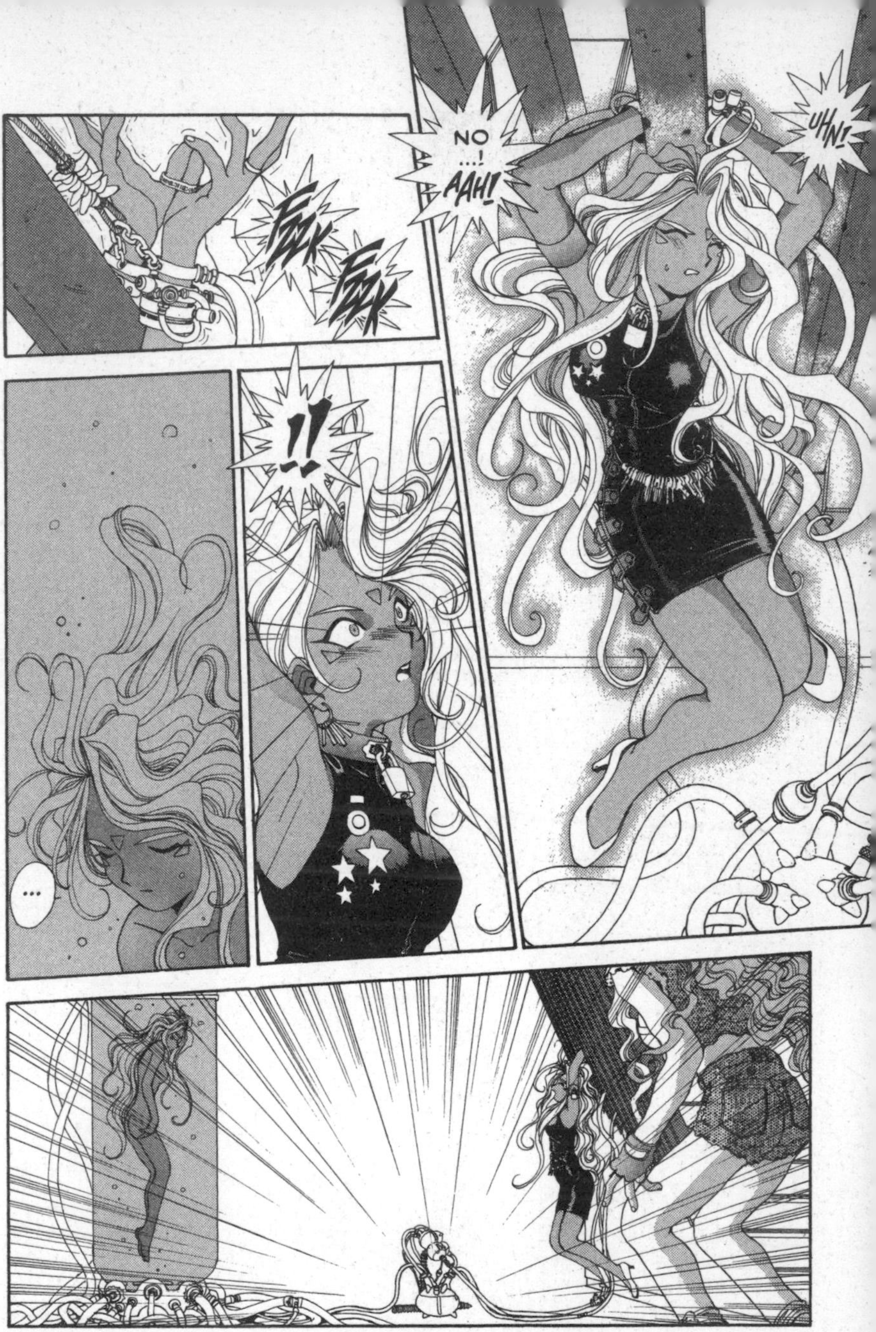

UHN!
NO ...! AAH!
FZZK
FZZK
!!
...

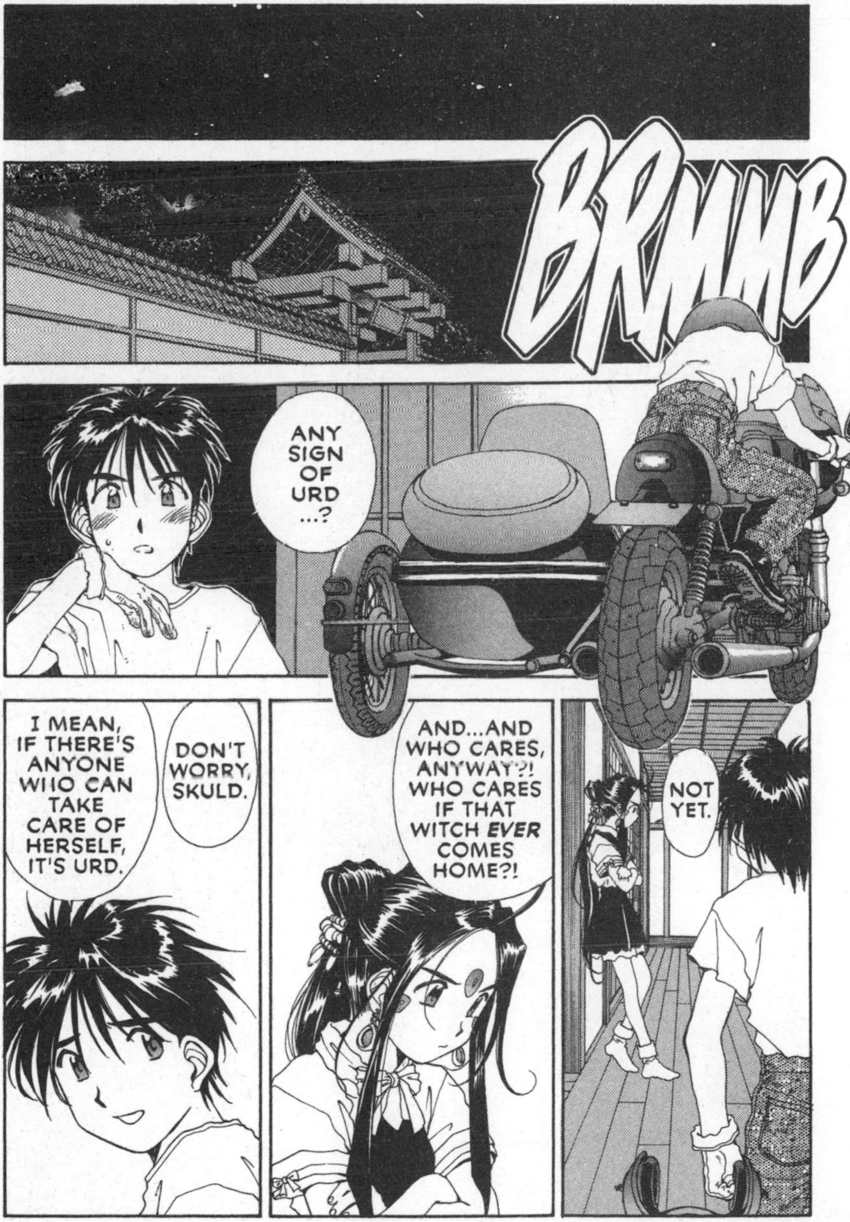
BRMMB
ANY SIGN OF URD ...?
NOT YET.
AND...AND WHO CARES, ANYWAY?! WHO CARES IF THAT WITCH *EVER* COMES HOME?!
DON'T WORRY, SKULD.
I MEAN, IF THERE'S ANYONE WHO CAN TAKE CARE OF HERSELF, IT'S URD.

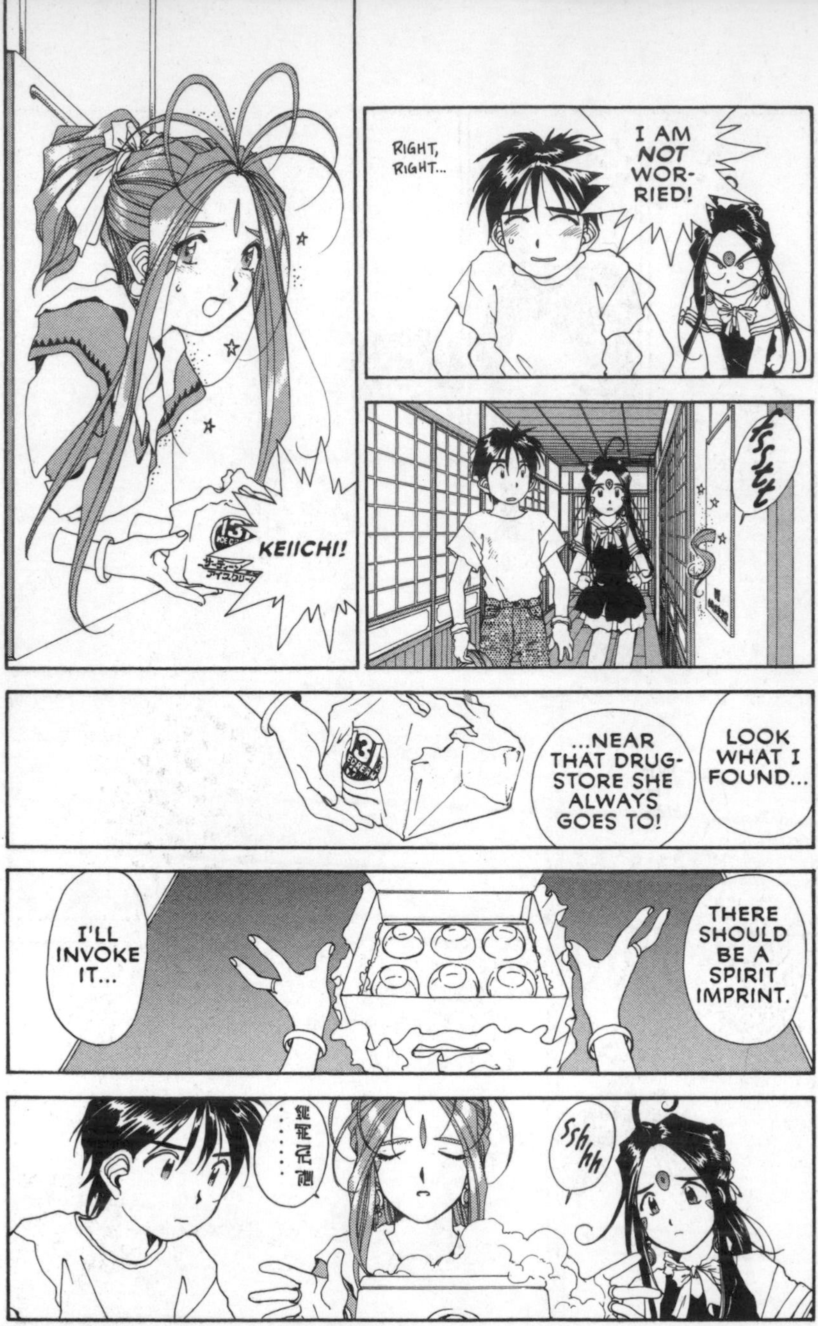
I AM NOT WORRIED!
RIGHT, RIGHT...
KEIICHI!
LOOK WHAT I FOUND...
...NEAR THAT DRUG-STORE SHE ALWAYS GOES TO!
THERE SHOULD BE A SPIRIT IMPRINT.
I'LL INVOKE IT...
sshhh

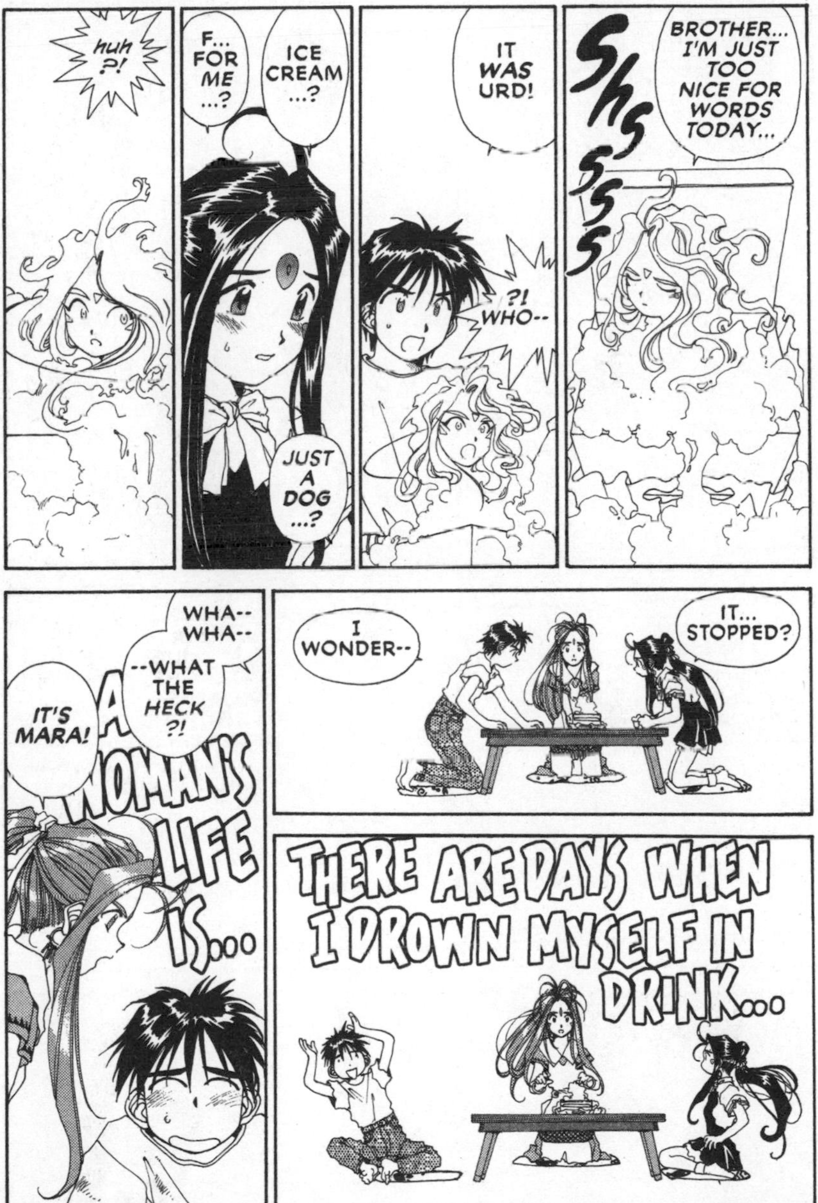
SHSSSS
BROTHER... I'M JUST TOO NICE FOR WORDS TODAY...
IT WAS URD!
?! WHO--
ICE CREAM ...?
F... FOR ME ...?
JUST A DOG ...?
huh ?!
IT... STOPPED?
I WONDER--
THERE ARE DAYS WHEN I DROWN MYSELF IN DRINK...
WHA-- WHA--
--WHAT THE HECK ?!
IT'S MARA!
A WOMAN'S LIFE IS...

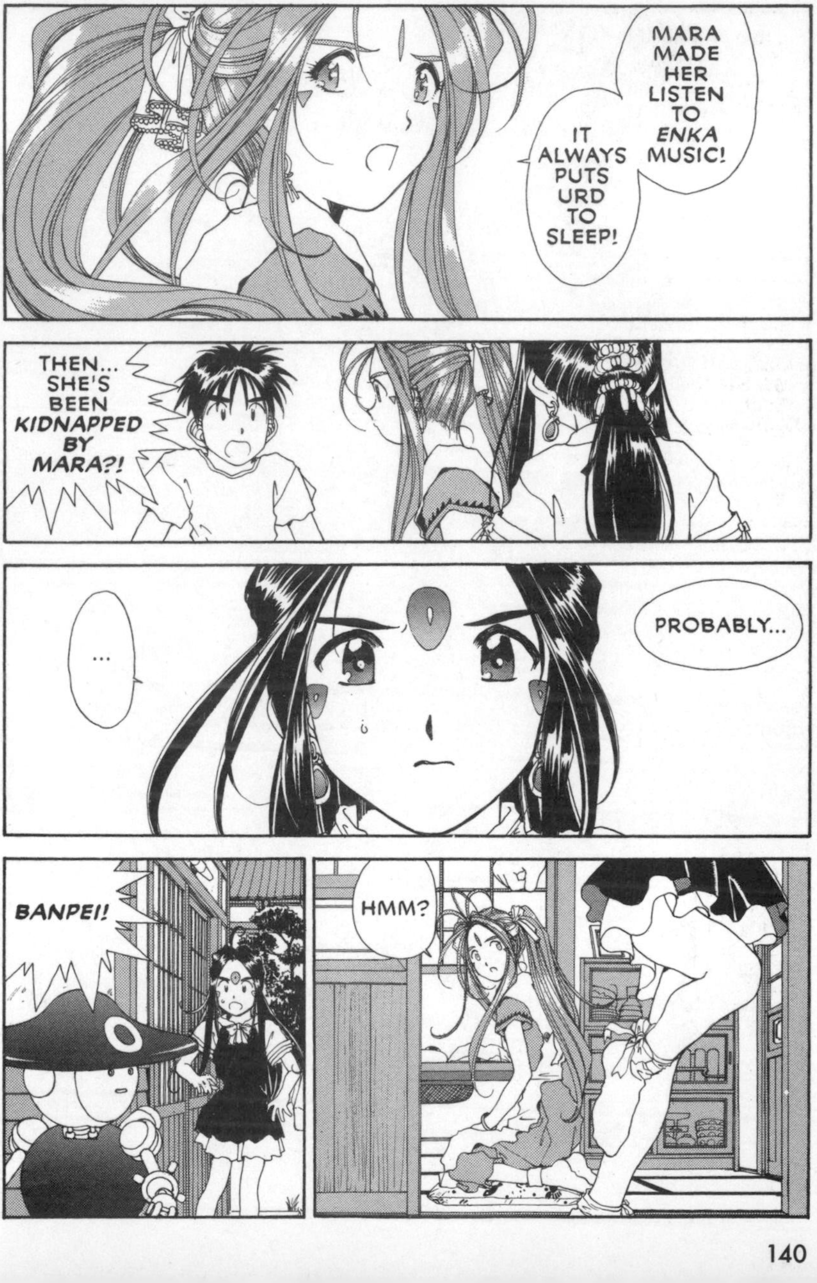
MARA MADE HER LISTEN TO ENKA MUSIC!
IT ALWAYS PUTS URD TO SLEEP!
THEN... SHE'S BEEN KIDNAPPED BY MARA?!
PROBABLY...
...
HMM?
BANPEI!

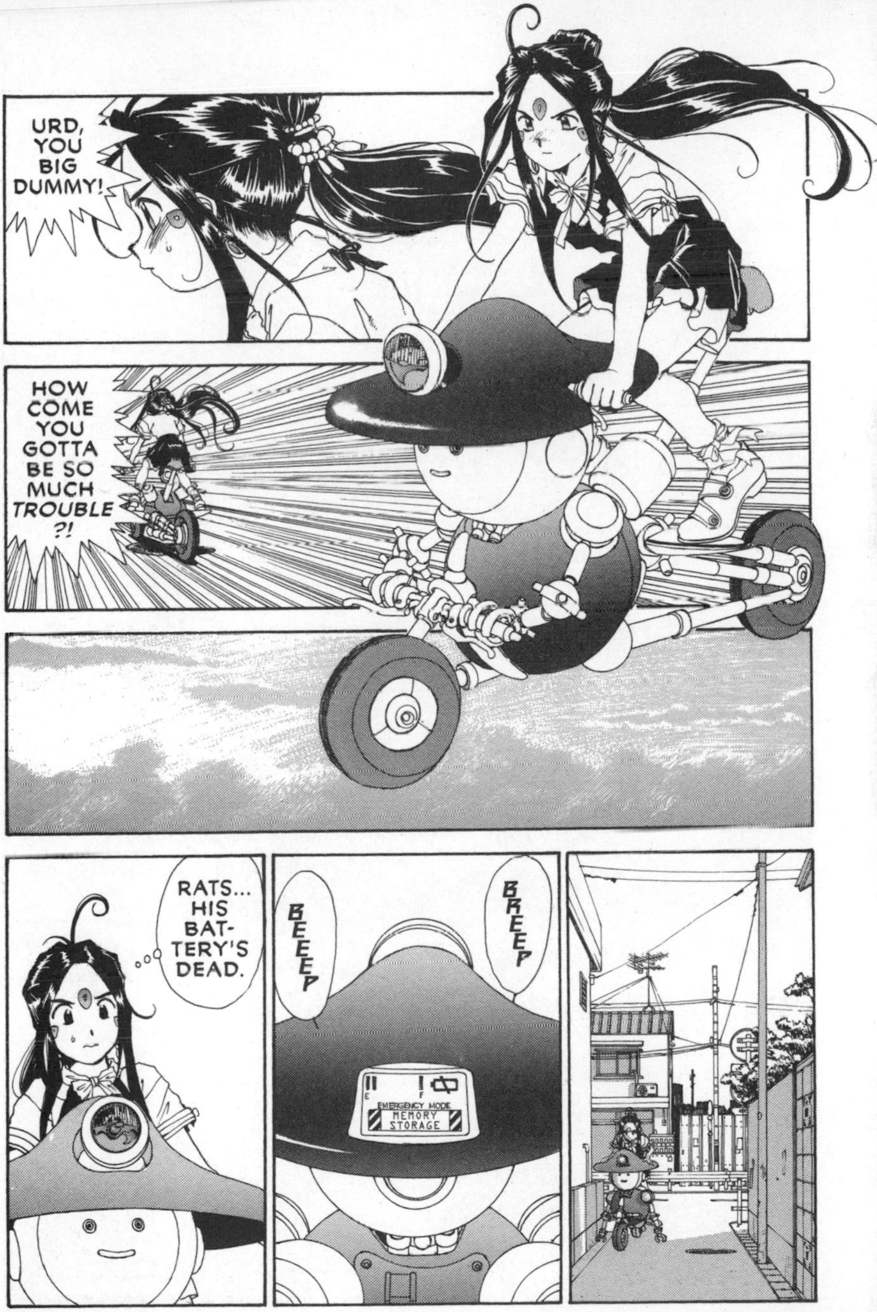
URD, YOU BIG DUMMY!
HOW COME YOU GOTTA BE SO MUCH TROUBLE?!
BREEP
BEEEP
EMERGENCY MODE
MEMORY STORAGE
RATS... HIS BATTERY'S DEAD.

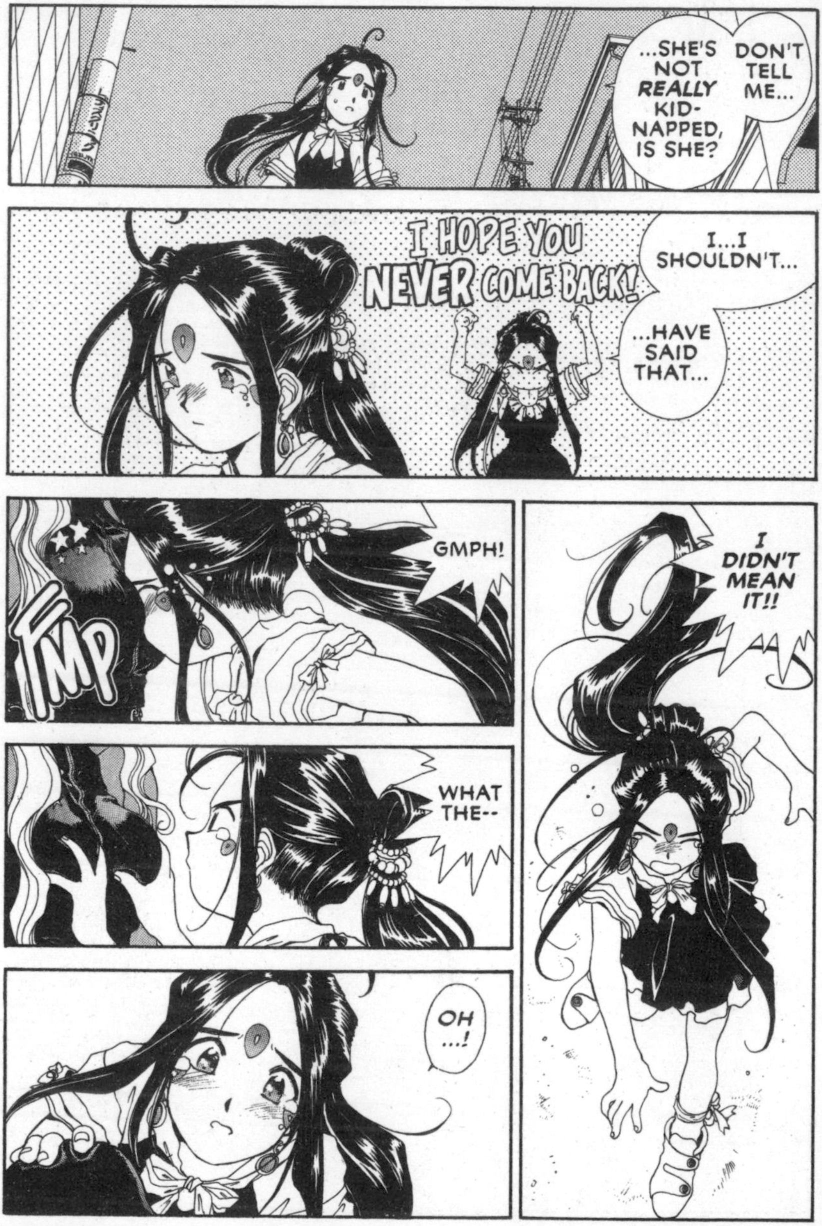
DON'T TELL ME...
...SHE'S NOT *REALLY* KID-NAPPED, IS SHE?
I...I SHOULDN'T...
...HAVE SAID THAT...
I HOPE YOU NEVER COME BACK!
I DIDN'T MEAN IT!!
GMPH!
FMP
WHAT THE--
OH ...!

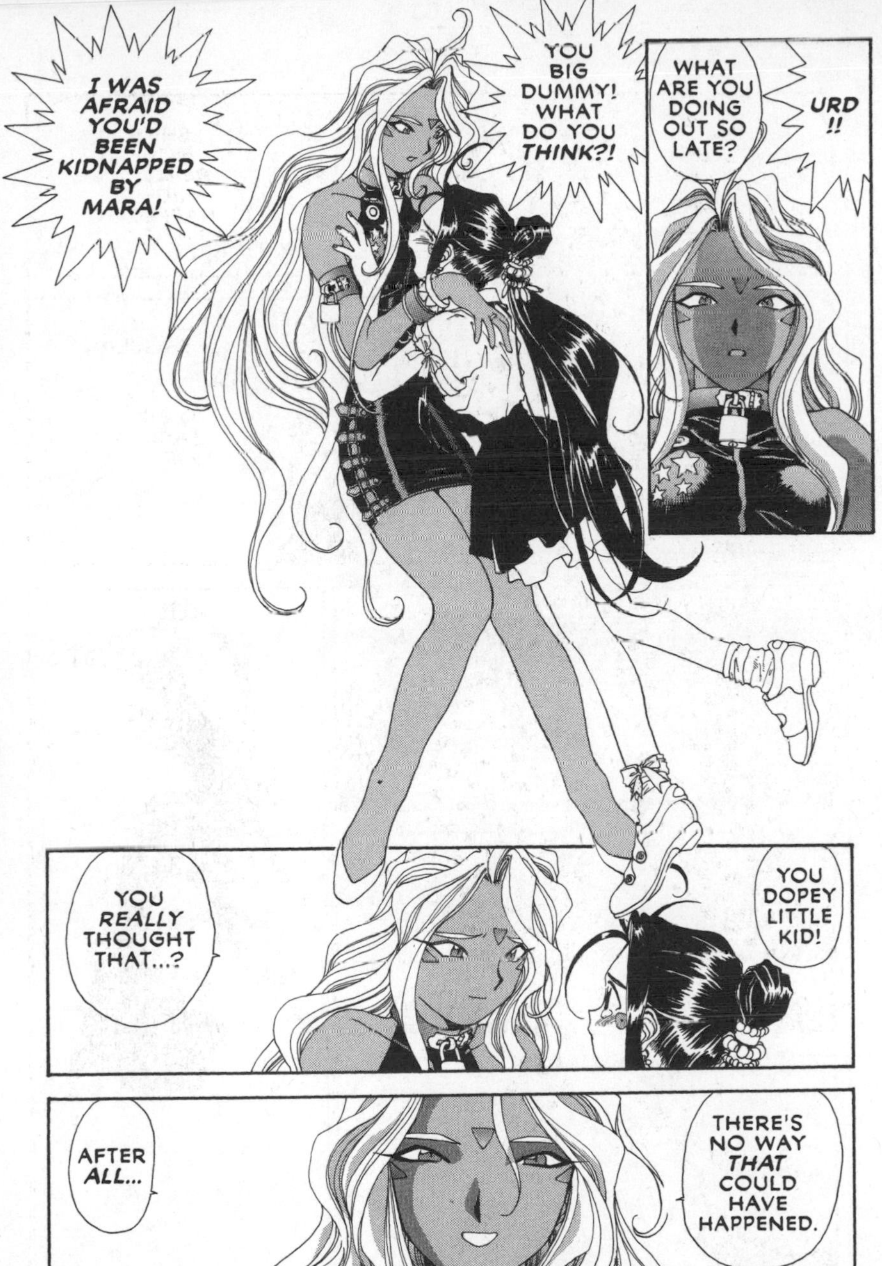
URD !!
WHAT ARE YOU DOING OUT SO LATE?
YOU BIG DUMMY! WHAT DO YOU *THINK?!*
I WAS AFRAID YOU'D BEEN KIDNAPPED BY MARA!
YOU DOPEY LITTLE KID!
YOU *REALLY* THOUGHT THAT...?
THERE'S NO WAY *THAT* COULD HAVE HAPPENED.
AFTER *ALL*...

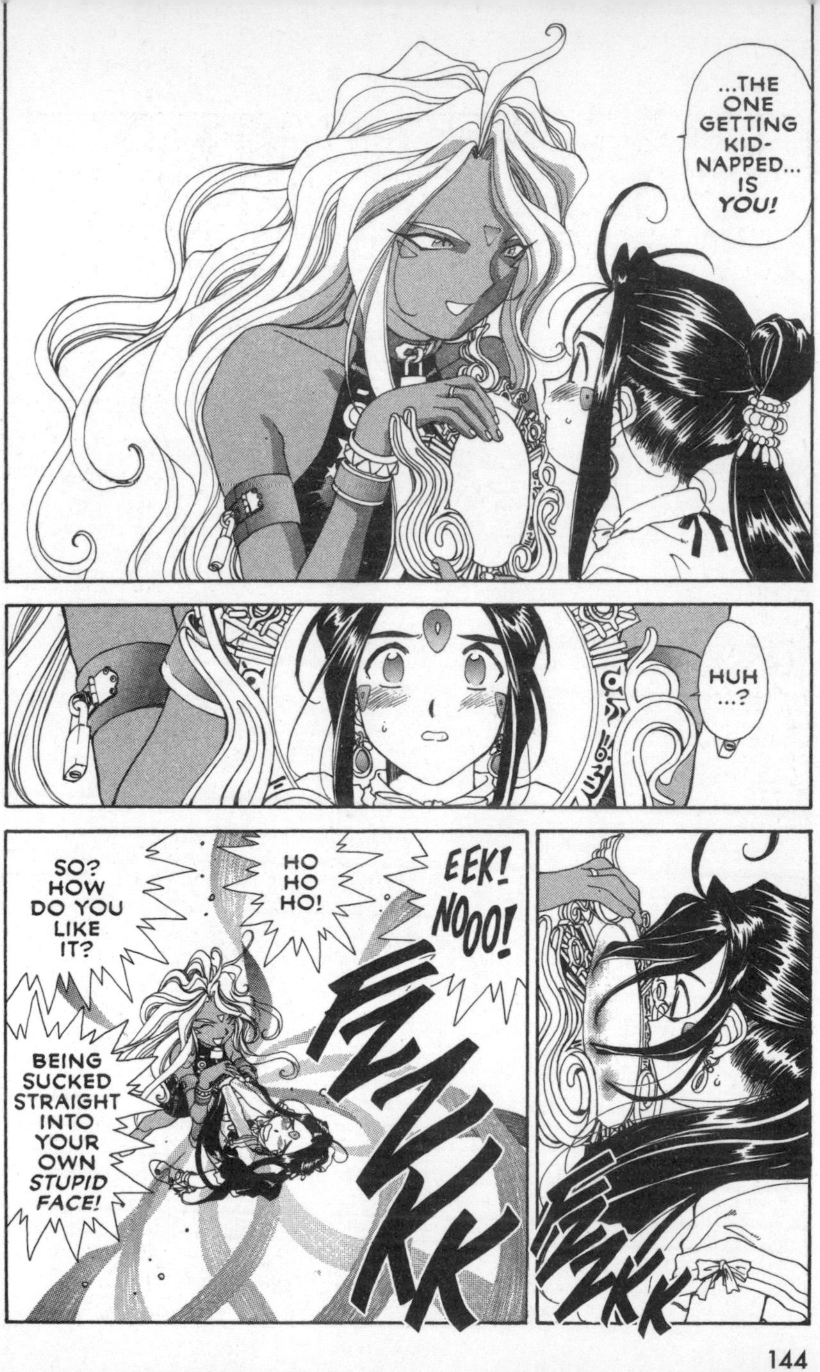
...THE ONE GETTING KID-NAPPED... IS YOU!
HUH ...?
EEK! NOOO!
HO HO HO!
SO? HOW DO YOU LIKE IT?
BEING SUCKED STRAIGHT INTO YOUR OWN STUPID FACE!

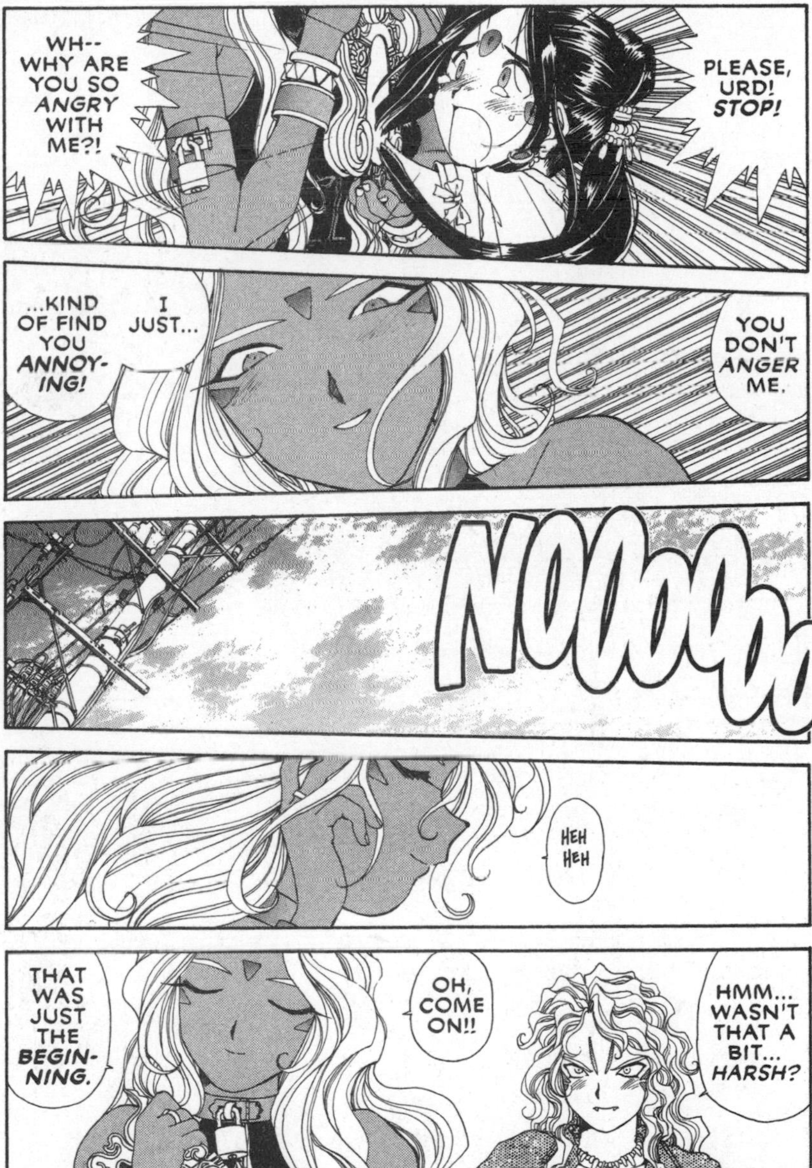
PLEASE, URD! STOP!
WH-- WHY ARE YOU SO ANGRY WITH ME?!
YOU DON'T ANGER ME.
I JUST...
...KIND OF FIND YOU ANNOYING!
NOOOOOO
HEH HEH
HMM... WASN'T THAT A BIT... HARSH?
OH, COME ON!!
THAT WAS JUST THE BEGINNING.

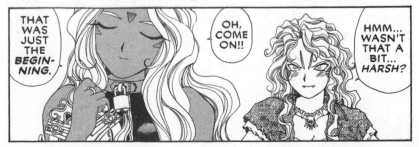

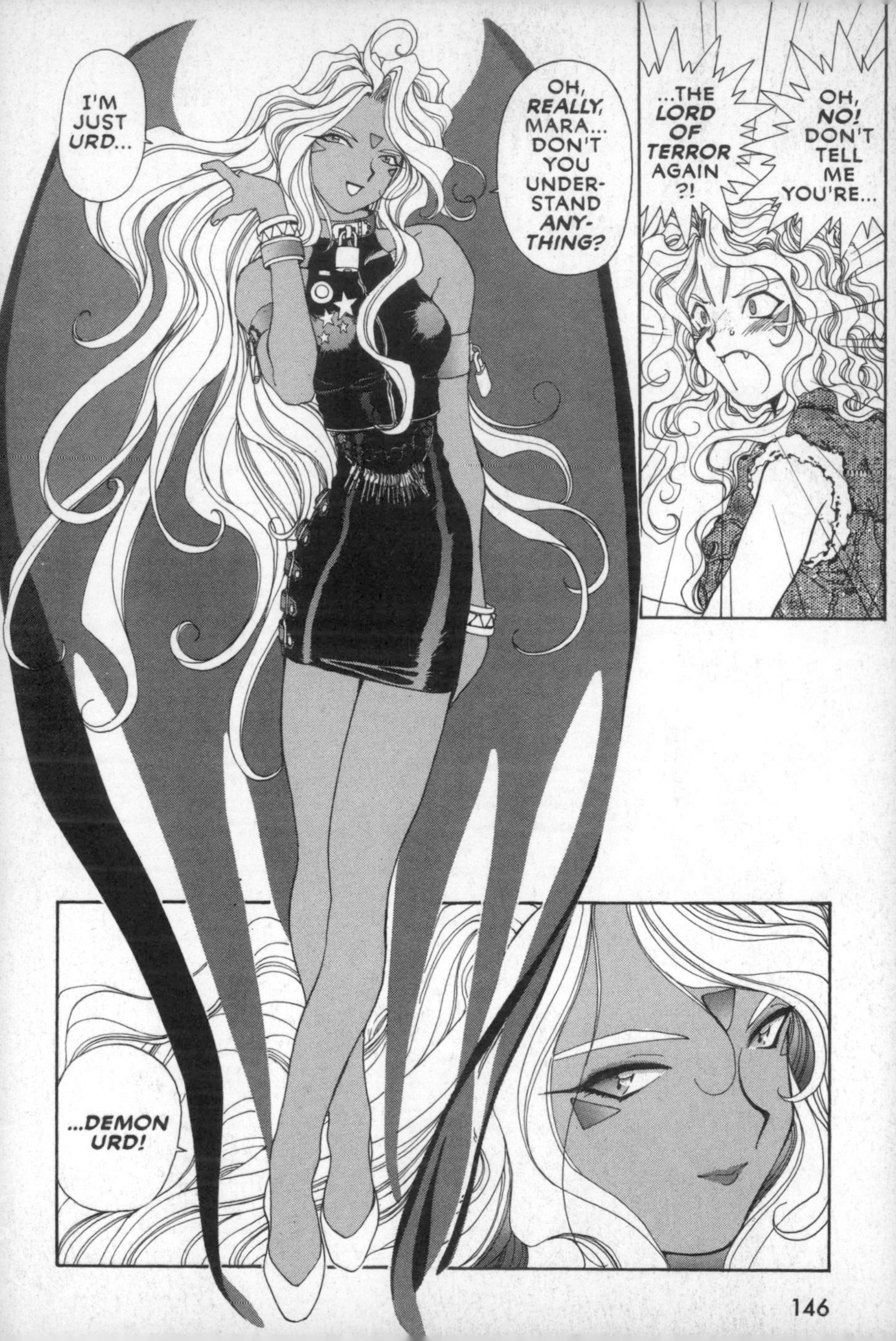
OH, NO! DON'T TELL ME YOU'RE...
...THE LORD OF TERROR AGAIN ?!
OH, REALLY, MARA... DON'T YOU UNDER-STAND ANY-THING?
I'M JUST URD...
...DEMON URD!

CHAPTER 62

Skuld Strikes Back!

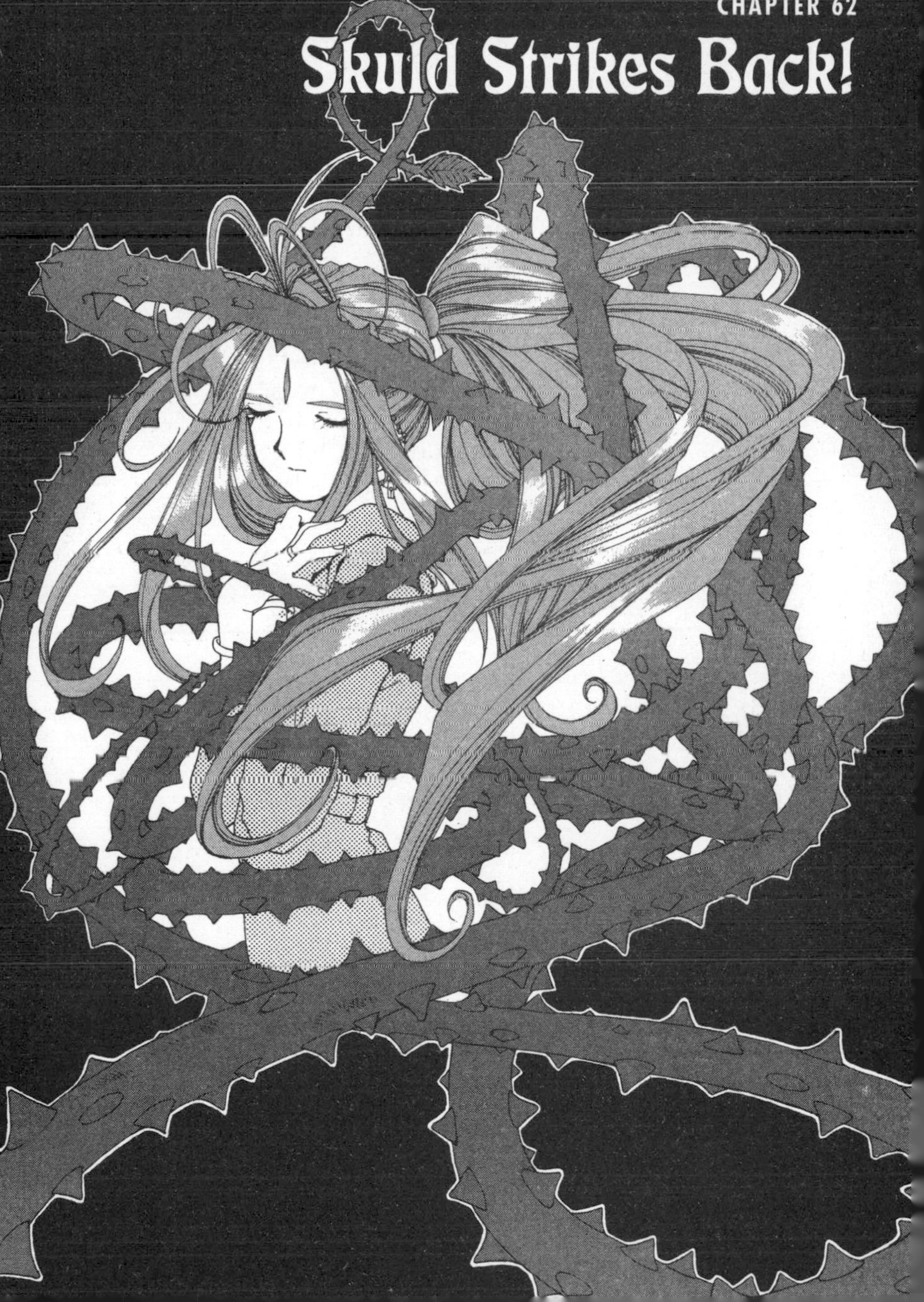

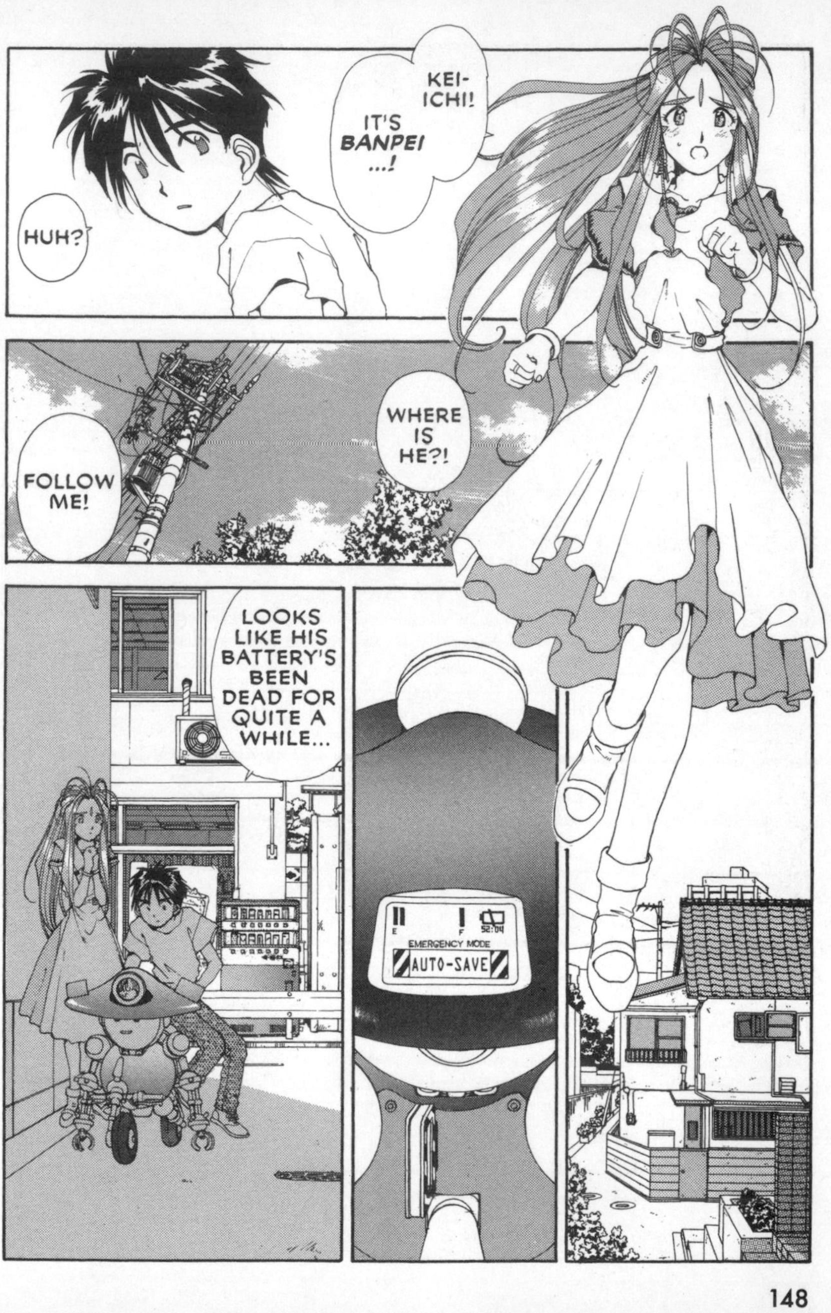
KEI-ICHI!
IT'S BANPEI ...!
HUH?
WHERE IS HE?!
FOLLOW ME!
E
F
52:04
EMERGENCY MODE
AUTO-SAVE
LOOKS LIKE HIS BATTERY'S BEEN DEAD FOR QUITE A WHILE...

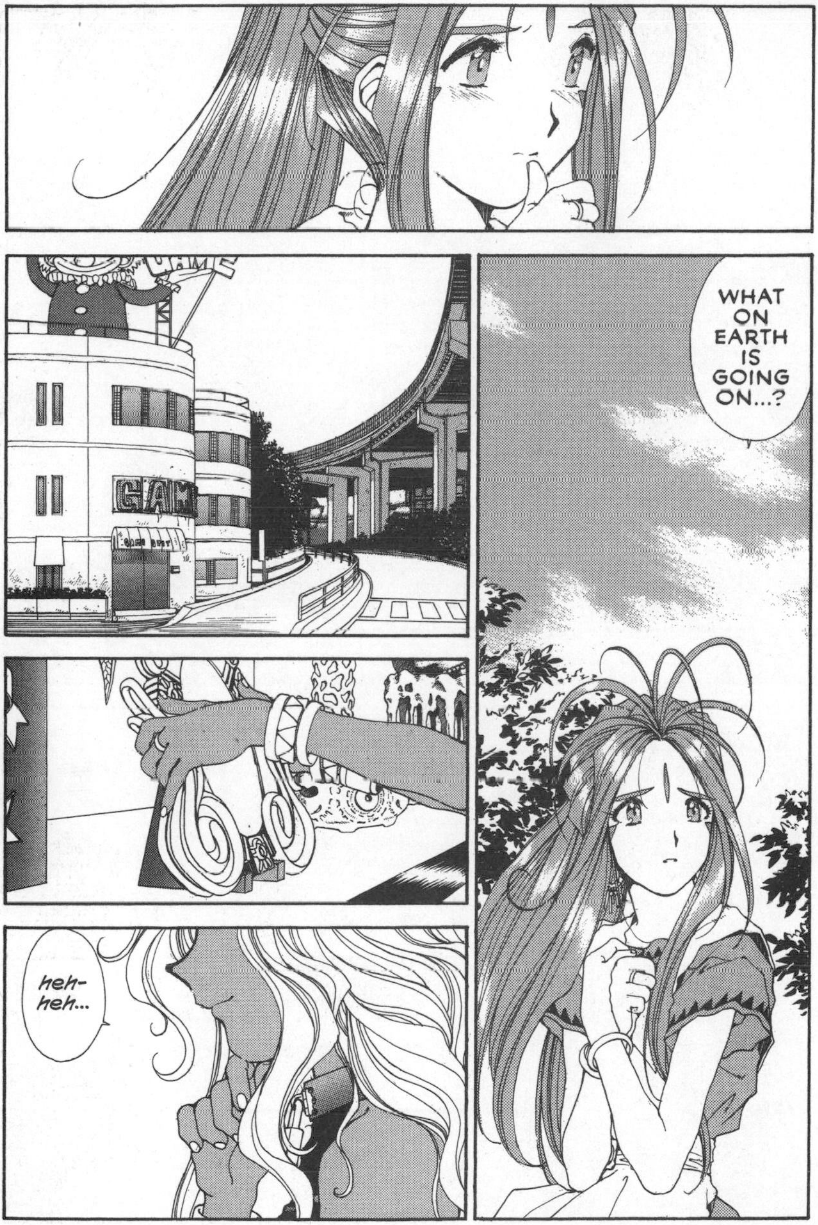
WHAT ON EARTH IS GOING ON...?
heh-heh...

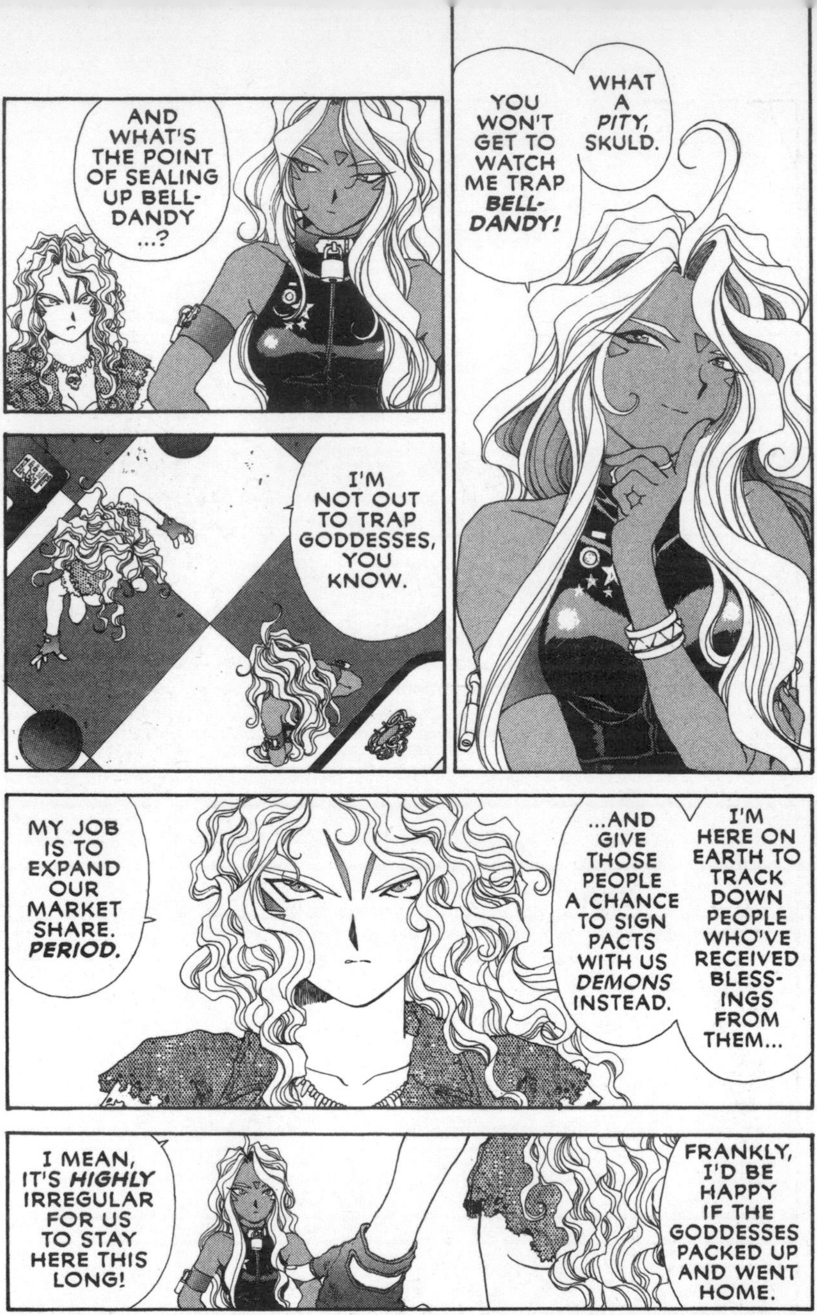
WHAT A PITY, SKULD.
YOU WON'T GET TO WATCH ME TRAP BELL-DANDY!
AND WHAT'S THE POINT OF SEALING UP BELL-DANDY ...?
I'M NOT OUT TO TRAP GODDESSES, YOU KNOW.
I'M HERE ON EARTH TO TRACK DOWN PEOPLE WHO'VE RECEIVED BLESS-INGS FROM THEM...
...AND GIVE THOSE PEOPLE A CHANCE TO SIGN PACTS WITH US DEMONS INSTEAD.
MY JOB IS TO EXPAND OUR MARKET SHARE. PERIOD.
FRANKLY, I'D BE HAPPY IF THE GODDESSES PACKED UP AND WENT HOME.
I MEAN, IT'S HIGHLY IRREGULAR FOR US TO STAY HERE THIS LONG!

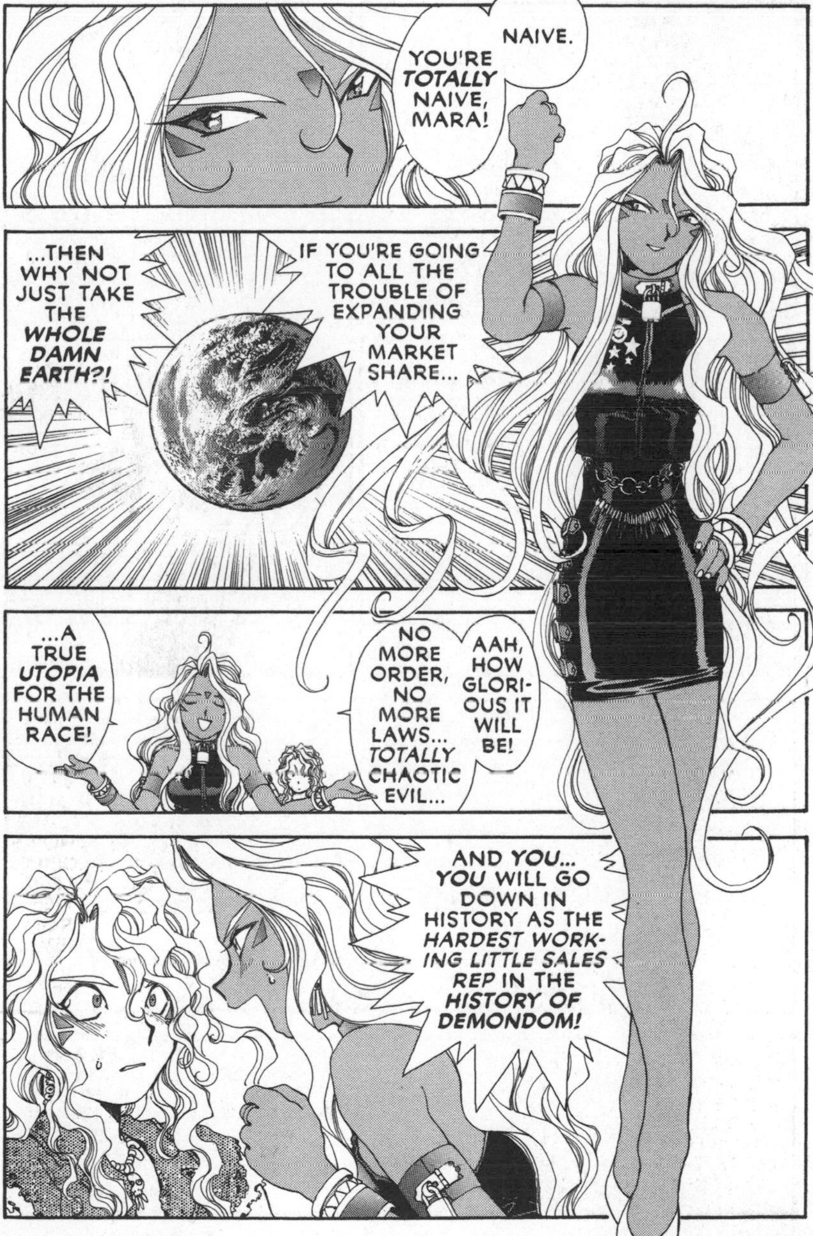

NAIVE.
YOU'RE TOTALLY NAIVE, MARA!
IF YOU'RE GOING TO ALL THE TROUBLE OF EXPANDING YOUR MARKET SHARE...
...THEN WHY NOT JUST TAKE THE WHOLE DAMN EARTH?!
AAH, HOW GLORI-OUS IT WILL BE!
NO MORE ORDER, NO MORE LAWS... TOTALLY CHAOTIC EVIL...
...A TRUE UTOPIA FOR THE HUMAN RACE!
AND YOU... YOU WILL GO DOWN IN HISTORY AS THE HARDEST WORK-ING LITTLE SALES REP IN THE HISTORY OF DEMONDOM!

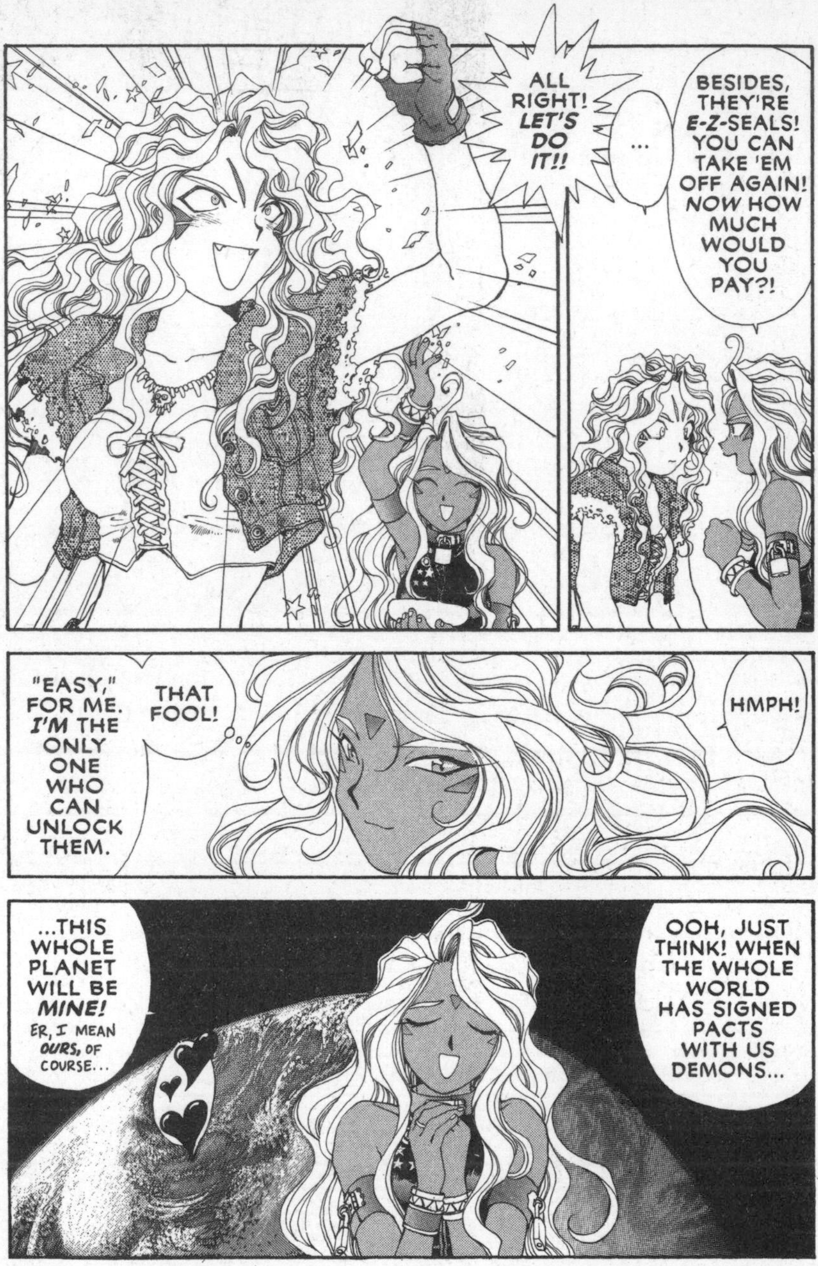
BESIDES, THEY'RE E-Z-SEALS! YOU CAN TAKE 'EM OFF AGAIN! NOW HOW MUCH WOULD YOU PAY?!
...
ALL RIGHT! LET'S DO IT!!
HMPH!
THAT FOOL!
"EASY," FOR ME. I'M THE ONLY ONE WHO CAN UNLOCK THEM.
OOH, JUST THINK! WHEN THE WHOLE WORLD HAS SIGNED PACTS WITH US DEMONS...
...THIS WHOLE PLANET WILL BE MINE!
ER, I MEAN OURS, OF COURSE...

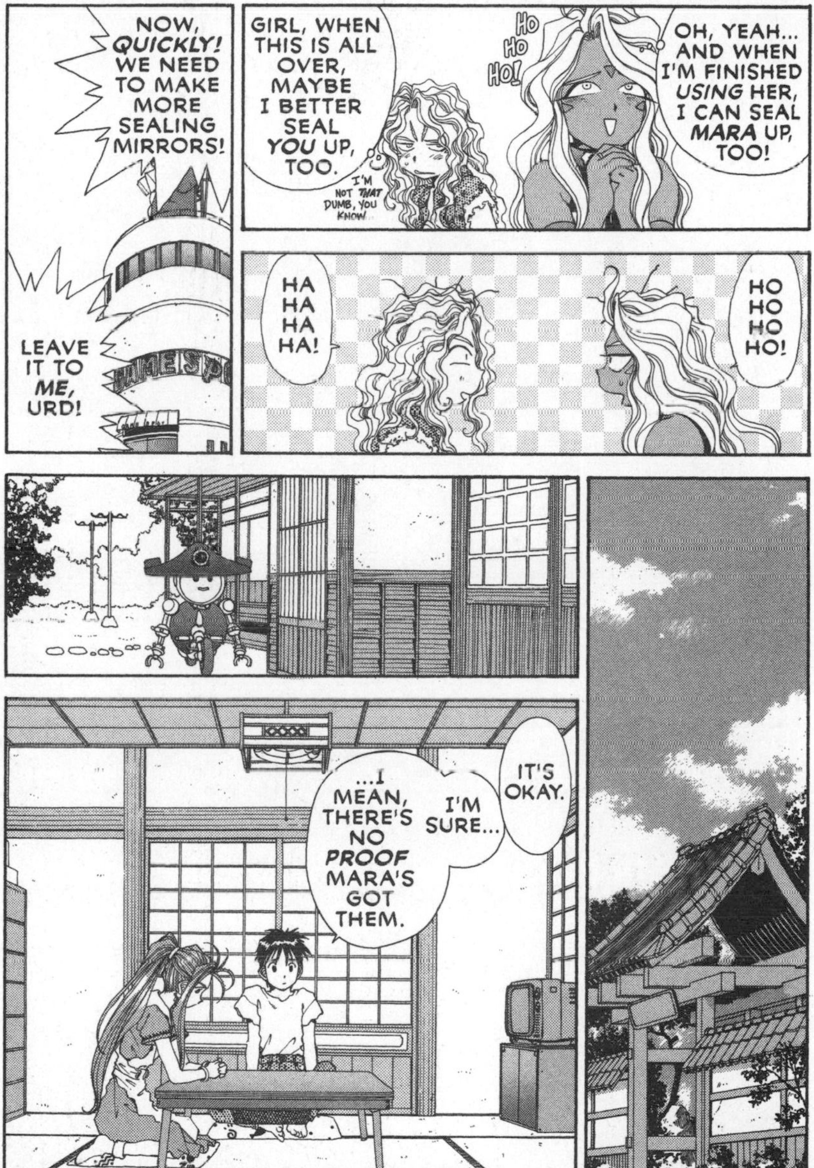
OH, YEAH... AND WHEN I'M FINISHED USING HER, I CAN SEAL MARA UP, TOO!
HO HO HO!
GIRL, WHEN THIS IS ALL OVER, MAYBE I BETTER SEAL YOU UP, TOO.
I'M NOT THAT DUMB, YOU KNOW.
HO HO HO HO!
HA HA HA HA!
NOW, QUICKLY! WE NEED TO MAKE MORE SEALING MIRRORS!
LEAVE IT TO ME, URD!
IT'S OKAY.
I'M SURE...
...I MEAN, THERE'S NO PROOF MARA'S GOT THEM.

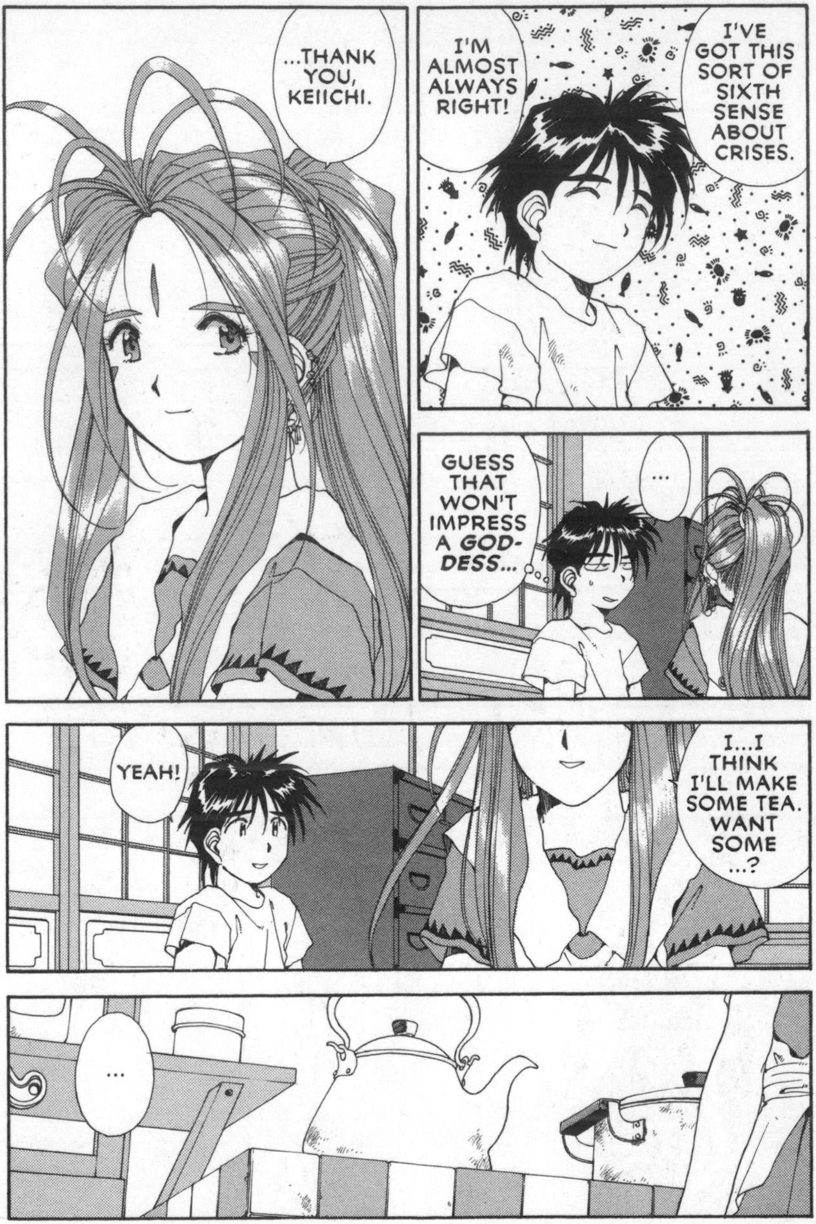
I'VE GOT THIS SORT OF SIXTH SENSE ABOUT CRISES.
I'M ALMOST ALWAYS RIGHT!
...
GUESS THAT WON'T IMPRESS A *GODDESS*...
...THANK YOU, KEIICHI.
I...I THINK I'LL MAKE SOME TEA. WANT SOME ...?
YEAH!
...

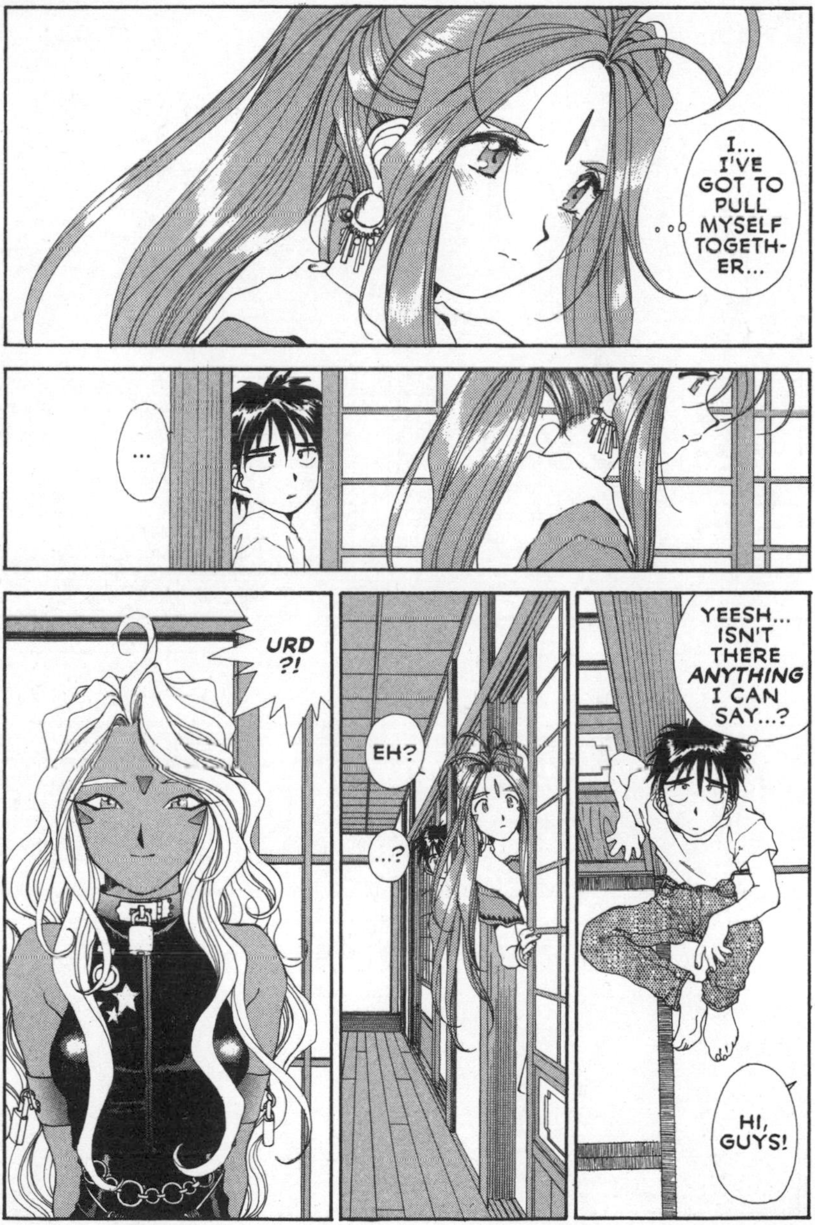
I... I'VE GOT TO PULL MYSELF TOGETH-ER...
...
YEESH... ISN'T THERE *ANYTHING* I CAN SAY...?
HI, GUYS!
EH?
...?
URD ?!

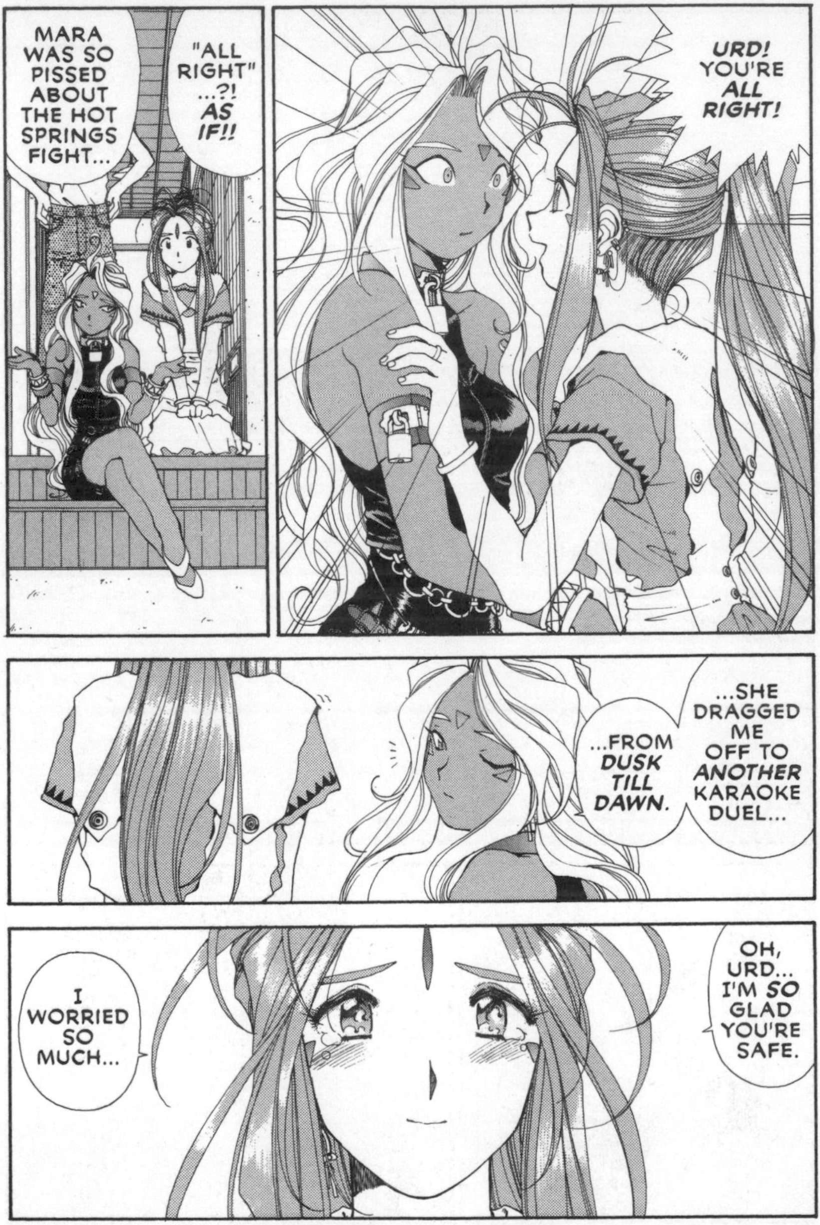
URD! YOU'RE ALL RIGHT!
"ALL RIGHT" ...?! AS IF!!
MARA WAS SO PISSED ABOUT THE HOT SPRINGS FIGHT...
...SHE DRAGGED ME OFF TO ANOTHER KARAOKE DUEL...
...FROM DUSK TILL DAWN.
OH, URD... I'M SO GLAD YOU'RE SAFE.
I WORRIED SO MUCH...

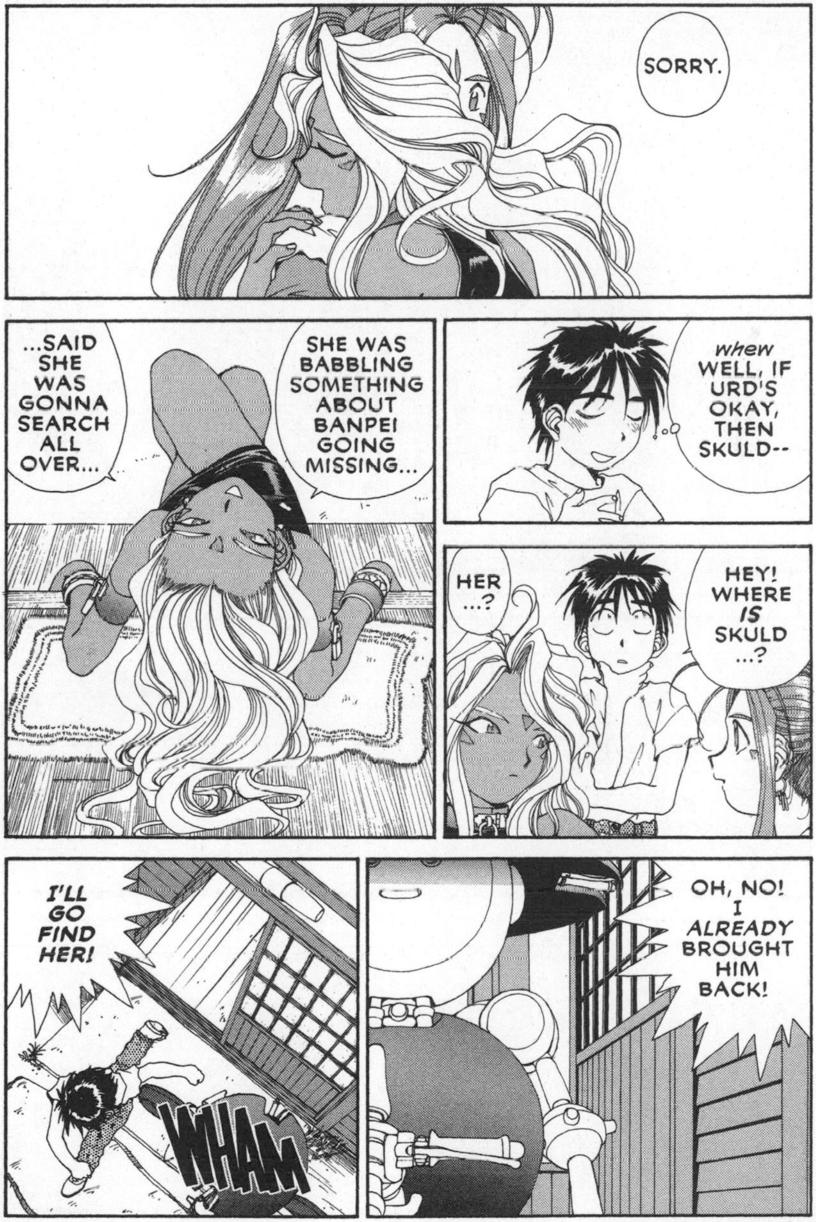
SORRY.
whew WELL, IF URD'S OKAY, THEN SKULD--
HEY! WHERE IS SKULD ...?
HER ...?
SHE WAS BABBLING SOMETHING ABOUT BANPEI GOING MISSING...
...SAID SHE WAS GONNA SEARCH ALL OVER...
OH, NO! I ALREADY BROUGHT HIM BACK!
I'LL GO FIND HER!
WHAM

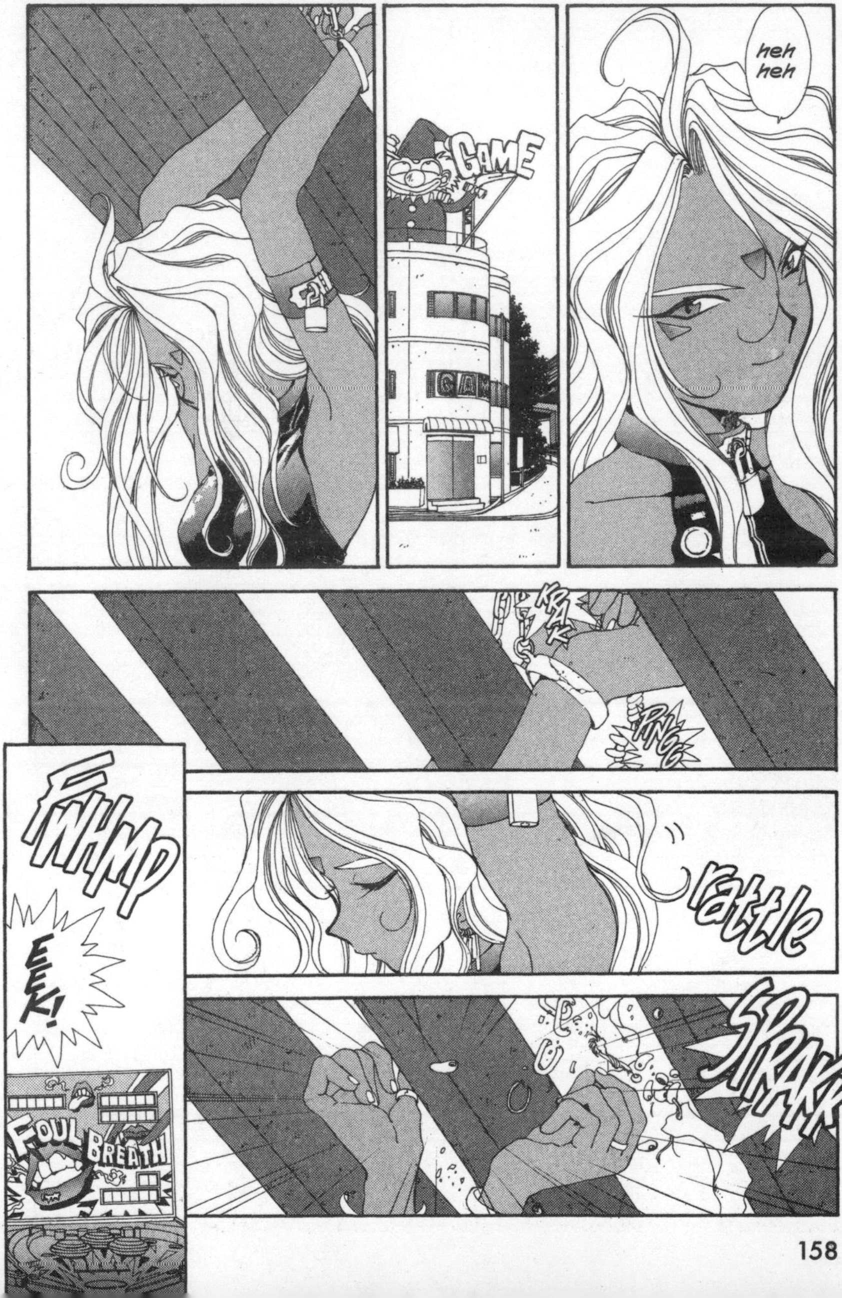
heh heh
GAME
KRAK
PINGG
rattle
SPRAKK
FWHMP
EEEK!
FOUL BREATH

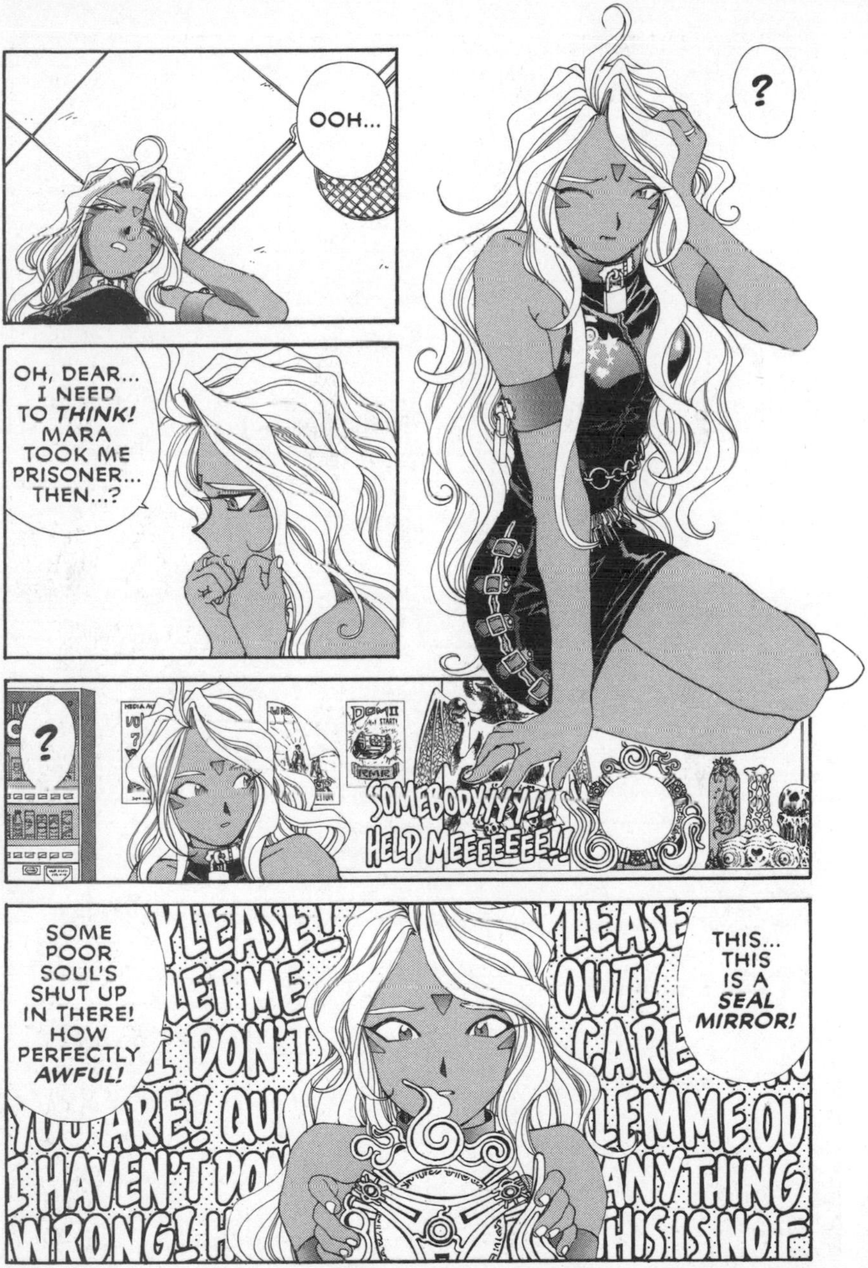
?
OOH...
OH, DEAR... I NEED TO *THINK!* MARA TOOK ME PRISONER... THEN...?
SOMEBODYYYY!! HELP MEEEEEE!!
?
THIS... THIS IS A *SEAL MIRROR!*
PLEASE
OUT!
CARE
LEMME OU
ANYTHING
THIS IS NO F
PLEASE!
LET ME
I DON'T
YOU ARE! QUI
I HAVEN'T DON
WRONG! H
SOME POOR SOUL'S SHUT UP IN THERE! HOW PERFECTLY *AWFUL!*

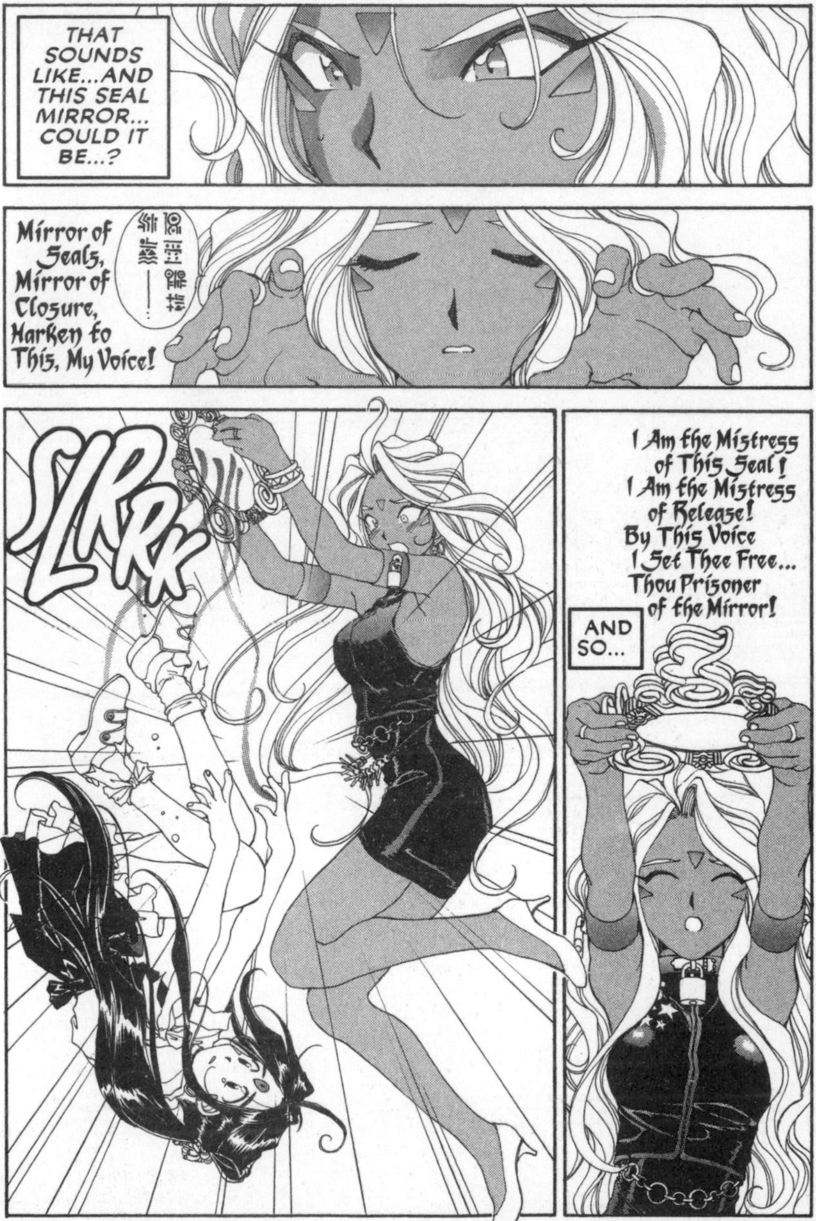
THAT SOUNDS LIKE...AND THIS SEAL MIRROR... COULD IT BE...?
Mirror of Seals, Mirror of Closure, Harken to This, My Voice!
I Am the Mistress of This Seal! I Am the Mistress of Release! By This Voice I Set Thee Free... Thou Prisoner of the Mirror!
AND SO...
SLRRK

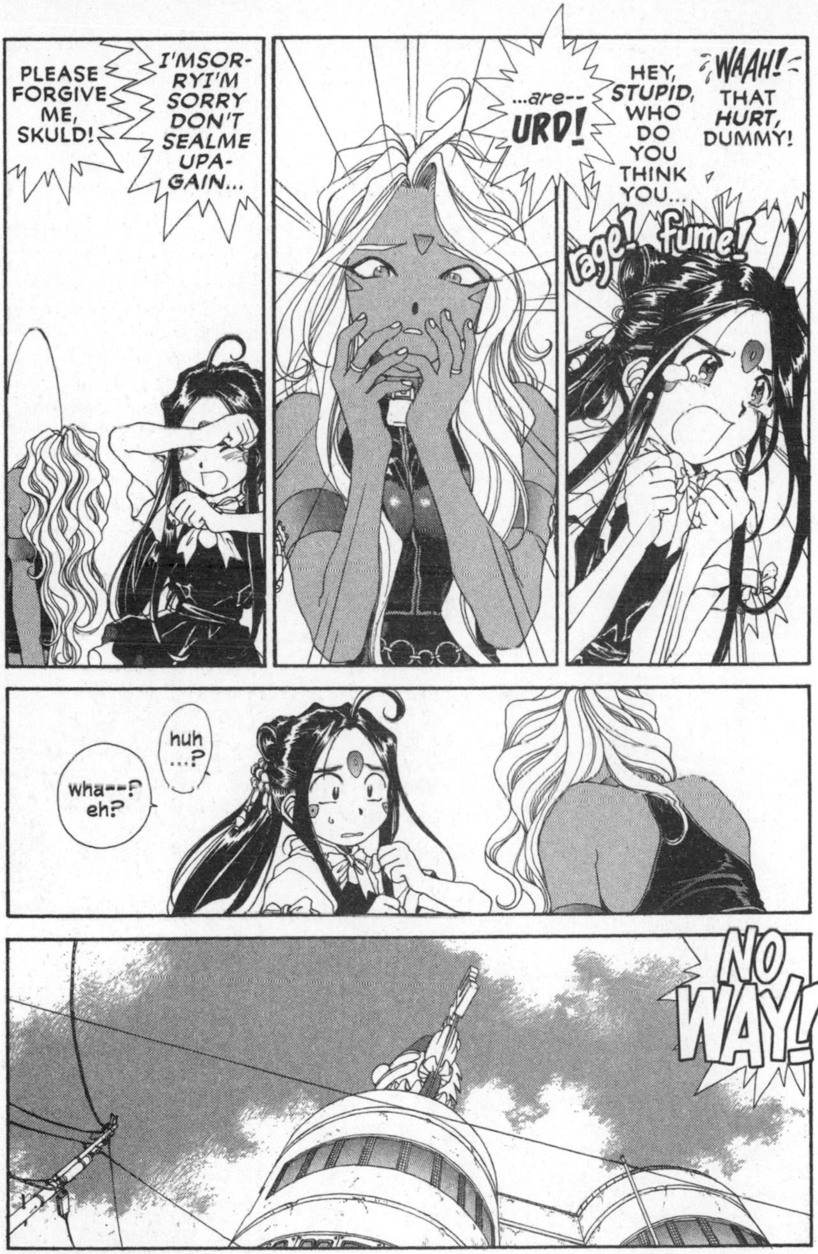
WAAH! THAT HURT, DUMMY!
HEY, STUPID, WHO DO YOU THINK YOU...
rage! fume!
...are-- URD!
I'MSORRYI'M SORRY DON'T SEALME UPAGAIN...
PLEASE FORGIVE ME, SKULD!
huh ...?
wha--? eh?
NO WAY!

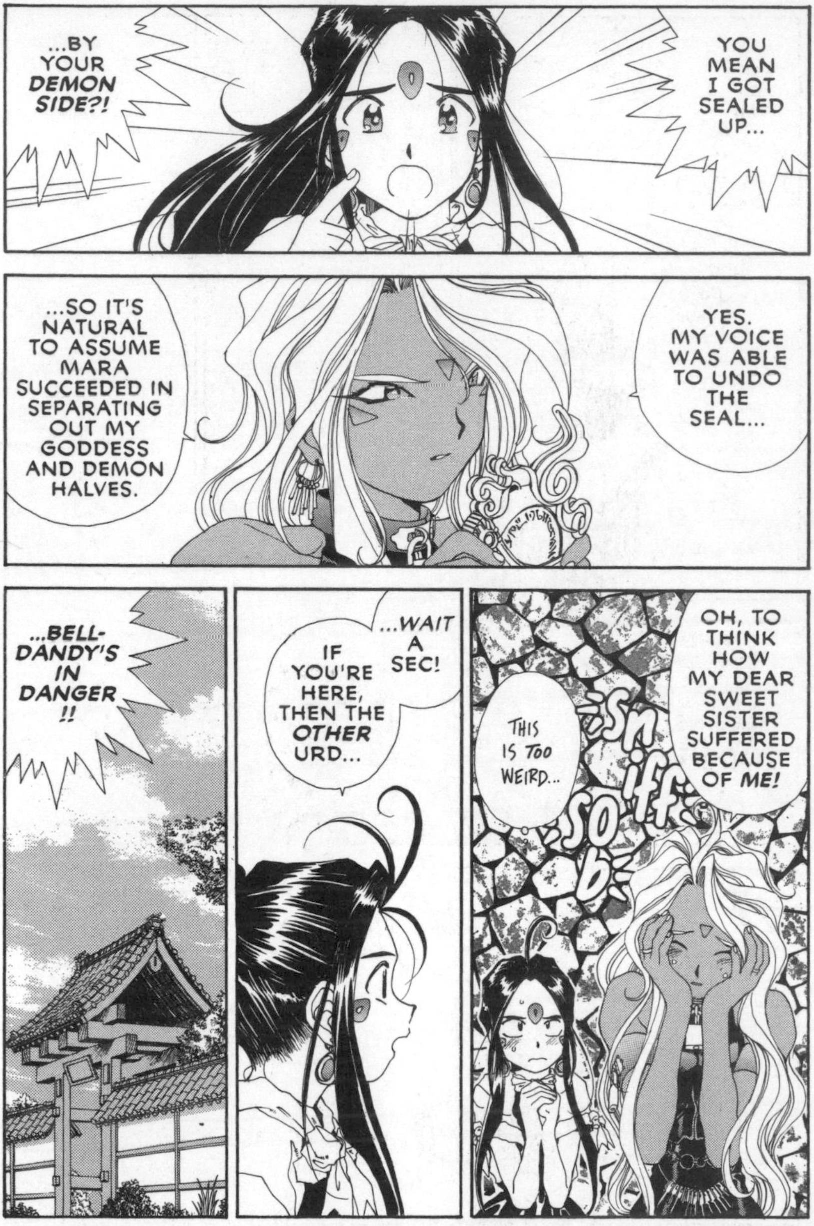
YOU MEAN I GOT SEALED UP...
...BY YOUR DEMON SIDE?!
YES. MY VOICE WAS ABLE TO UNDO THE SEAL...
...SO IT'S NATURAL TO ASSUME MARA SUCCEEDED IN SEPARATING OUT MY GODDESS AND DEMON HALVES.
OH, TO THINK HOW MY DEAR SWEET SISTER SUFFERED BECAUSE OF ME!
SNIFF
SOB
THIS IS TOO WEIRD...
...WAIT A SEC!
IF YOU'RE HERE, THEN THE OTHER URD...
...BELL-DANDY'S IN DANGER!!

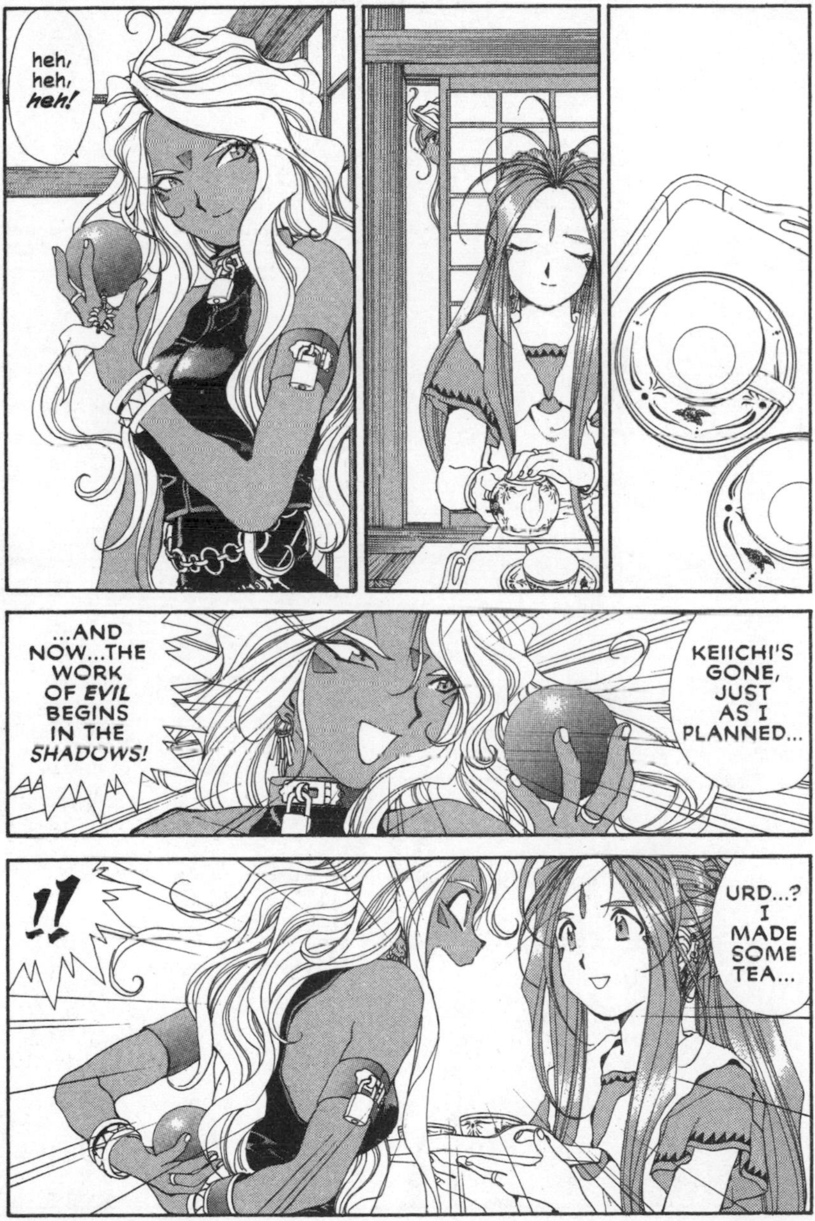
heh, heh, *heh!*
KEIICHI'S GONE, JUST AS I PLANNED...
...AND NOW...THE WORK OF *EVIL* BEGINS IN THE *SHADOWS!*
URD...? I MADE SOME TEA...
!!

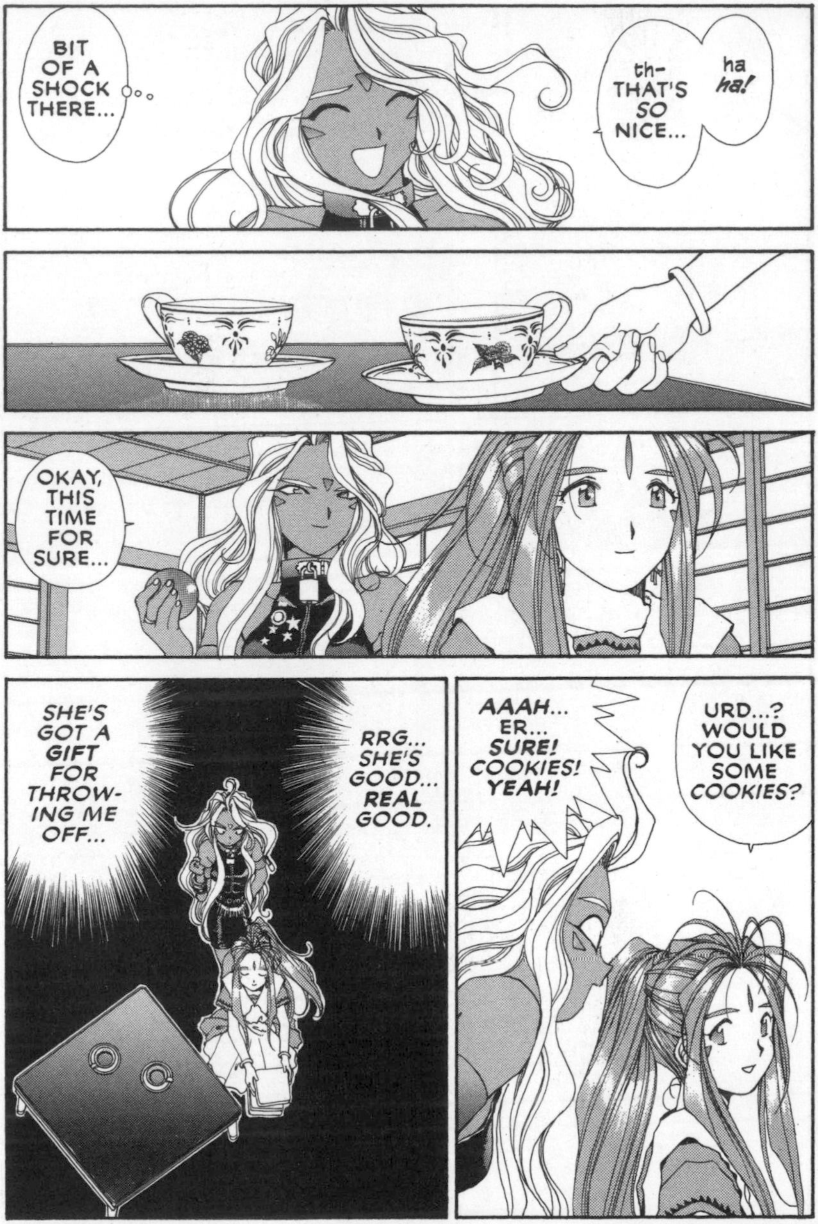
ha ha!
th-THAT'S SO NICE...
BIT OF A SHOCK THERE...
OKAY, THIS TIME FOR SURE...
URD...? WOULD YOU LIKE SOME COOKIES?
AAAH... ER... SURE! COOKIES! YEAH!
RRG... SHE'S GOOD... REAL GOOD.
SHE'S GOT A GIFT FOR THROWING ME OFF...

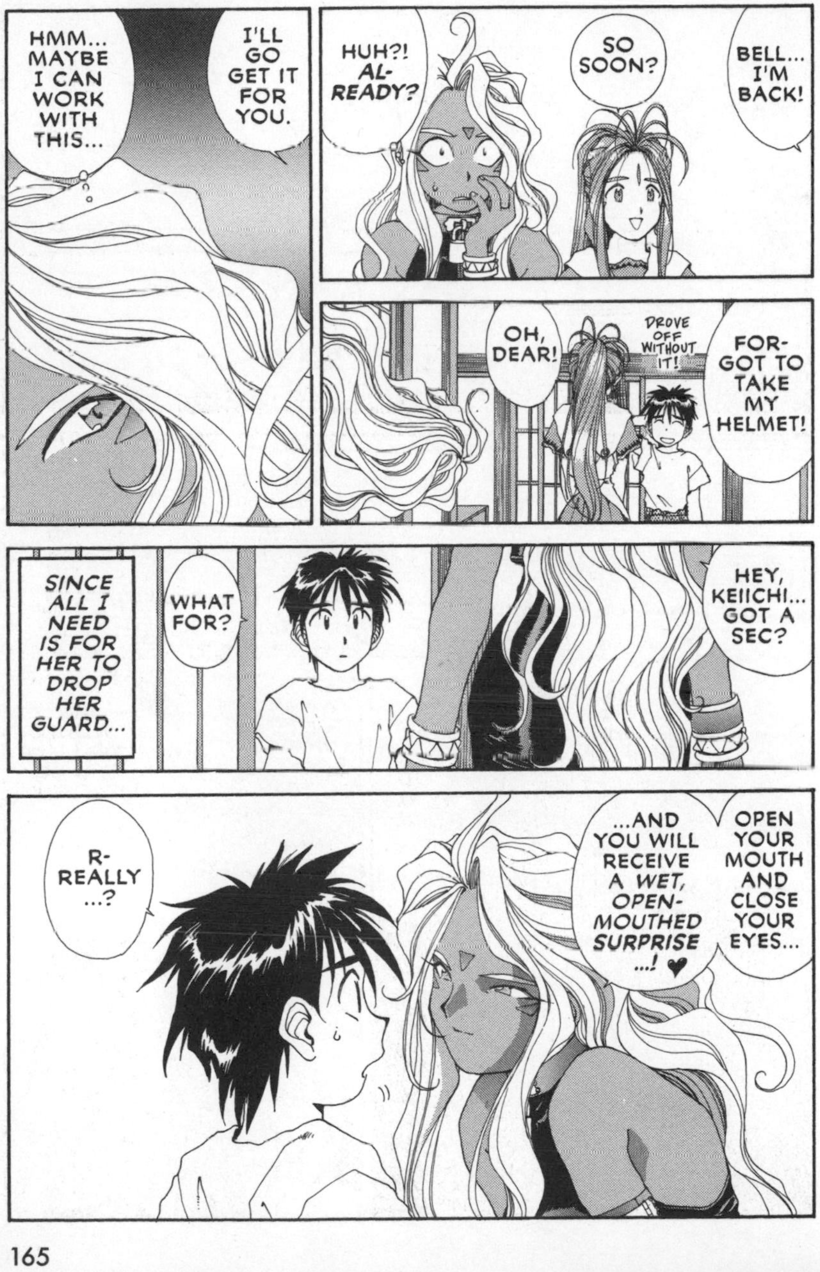
BELL... I'M BACK!
SO SOON?
HUH?! AL-READY?
FOR-GOT TO TAKE MY HELMET!
DROVE OFF WITHOUT IT!
OH, DEAR!
I'LL GO GET IT FOR YOU.
HMM... MAYBE I CAN WORK WITH THIS...
HEY, KEIICHI... GOT A SEC?
WHAT FOR?
SINCE ALL I NEED IS FOR HER TO DROP HER GUARD...
OPEN YOUR MOUTH AND CLOSE YOUR EYES...
...AND YOU WILL RECEIVE A WET, OPEN-MOUTHED SURPRISE ...! ♥
R-REALLY ...?

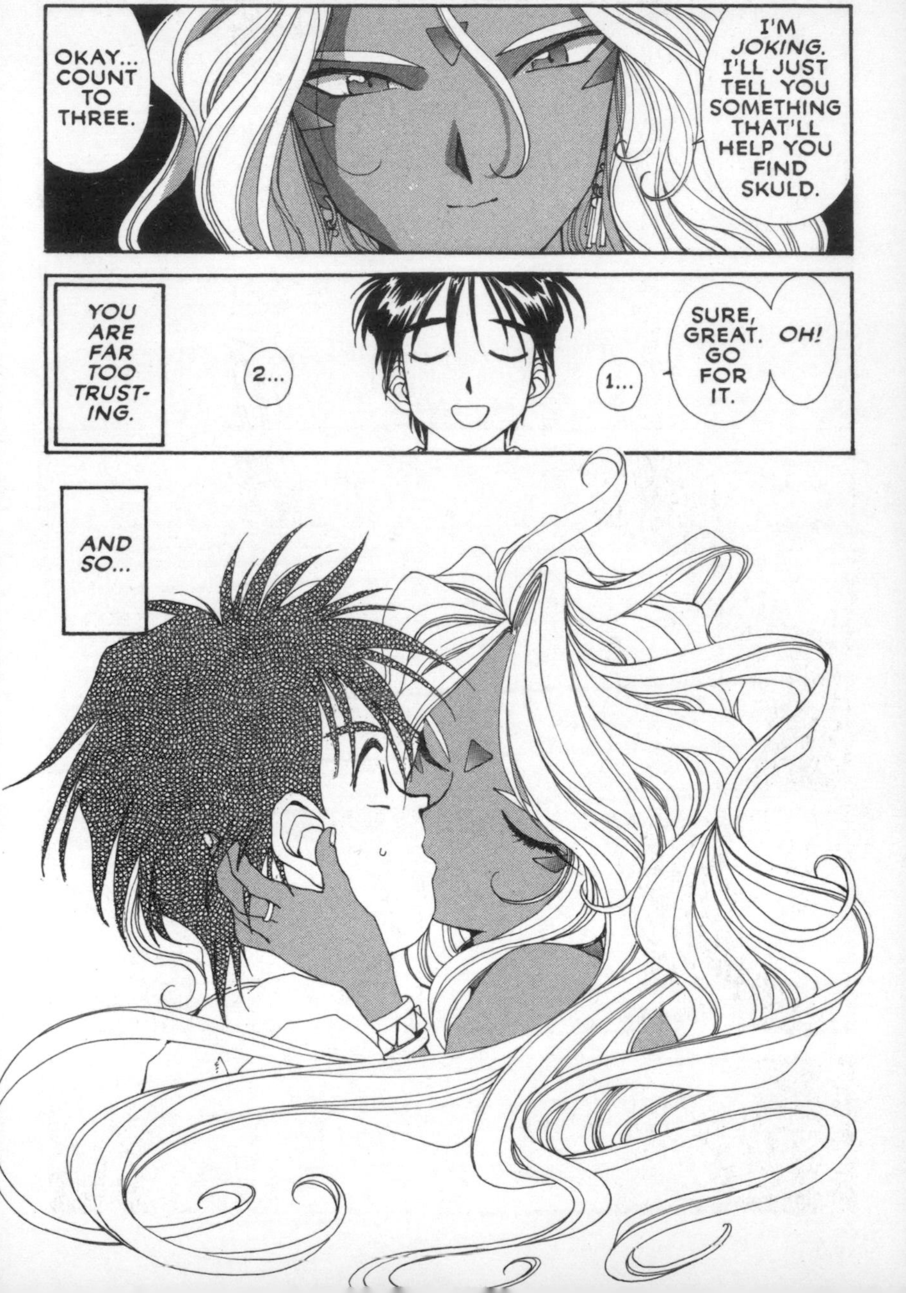
I'M *JOKING.* I'LL JUST TELL YOU SOMETHING THAT'LL HELP YOU FIND SKULD.
OKAY... COUNT TO THREE.
SURE, GREAT. GO FOR IT.
OH!
1...
2...
YOU ARE FAR TOO TRUST-ING.
AND SO...

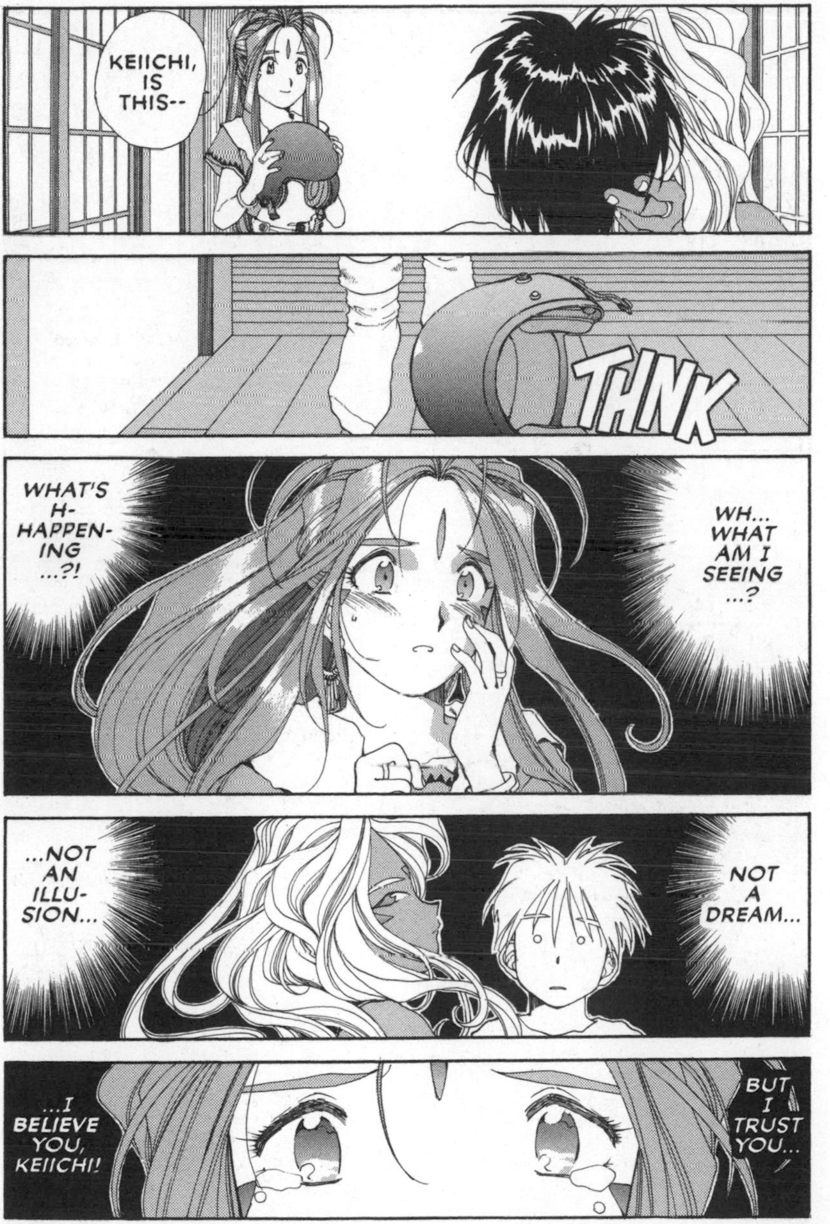
KEIICHI, IS THIS--
THNK
WH... WHAT AM I SEEING ...?
WHAT'S H-HAPPEN-ING ...?!
NOT A DREAM...
...NOT AN ILLU-SION...
BUT I TRUST YOU...
...I BELIEVE YOU, KEIICHI!

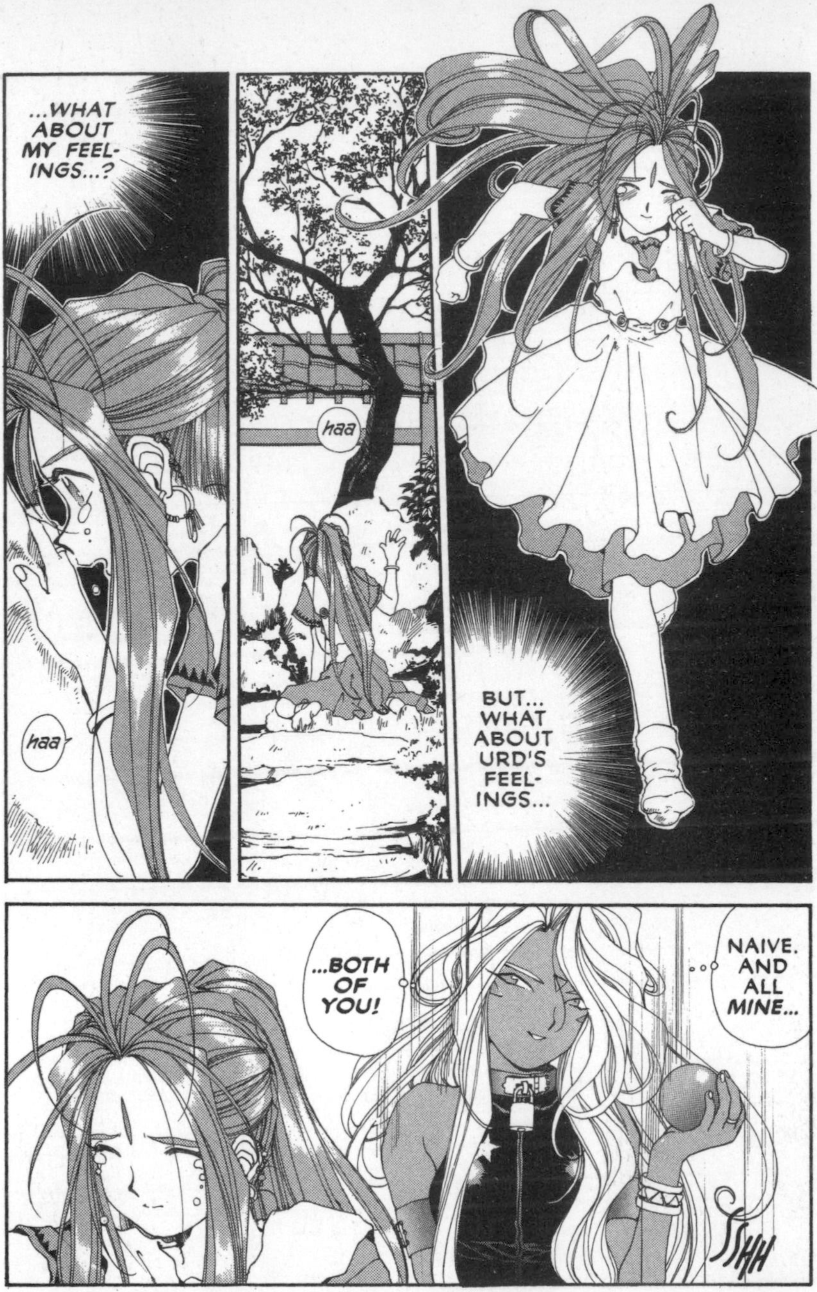
BUT... WHAT ABOUT URD'S FEEL-INGS...
haa
...WHAT ABOUT MY FEEL-INGS...?
haa
NAIVE. AND ALL MINE...
...BOTH OF YOU!
SSHH

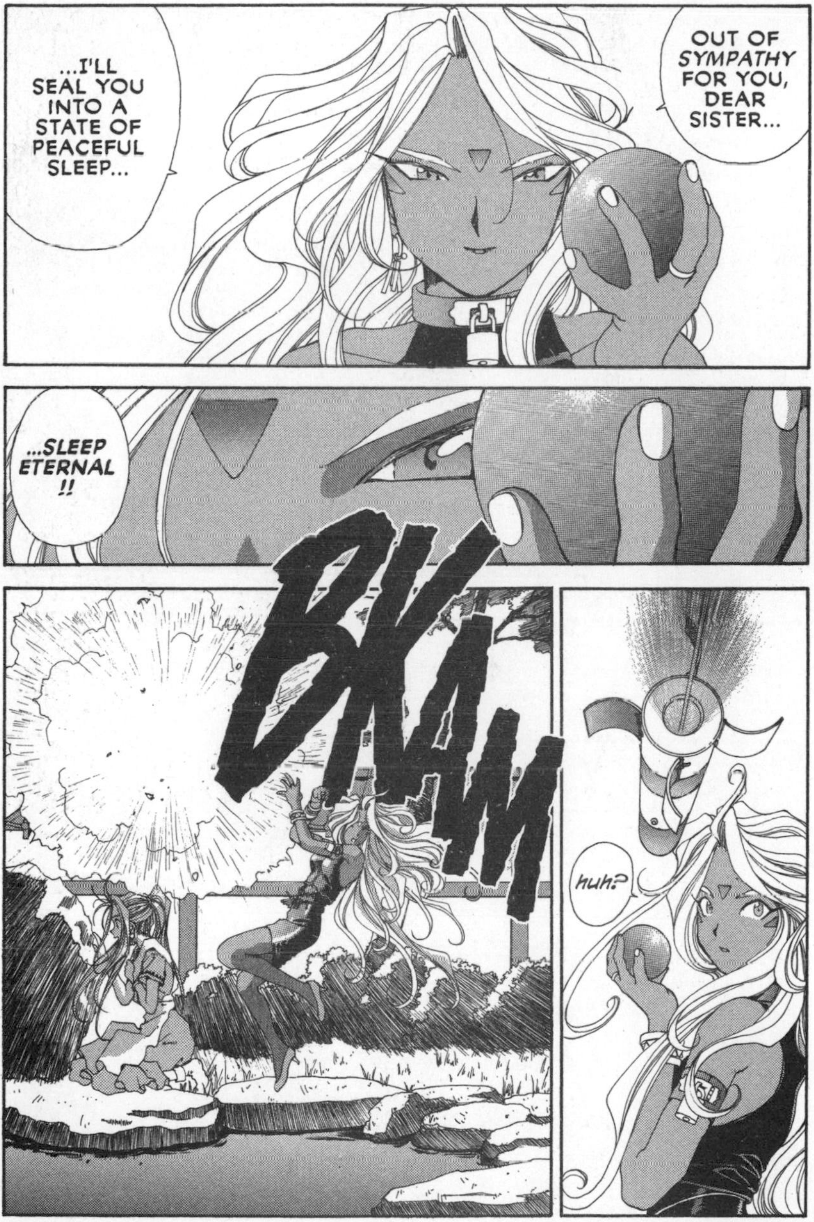
OUT OF *SYMPATHY* FOR YOU, DEAR SISTER...
...I'LL SEAL YOU INTO A STATE OF PEACEFUL SLEEP...
...SLEEP ETERNAL !!
huh?

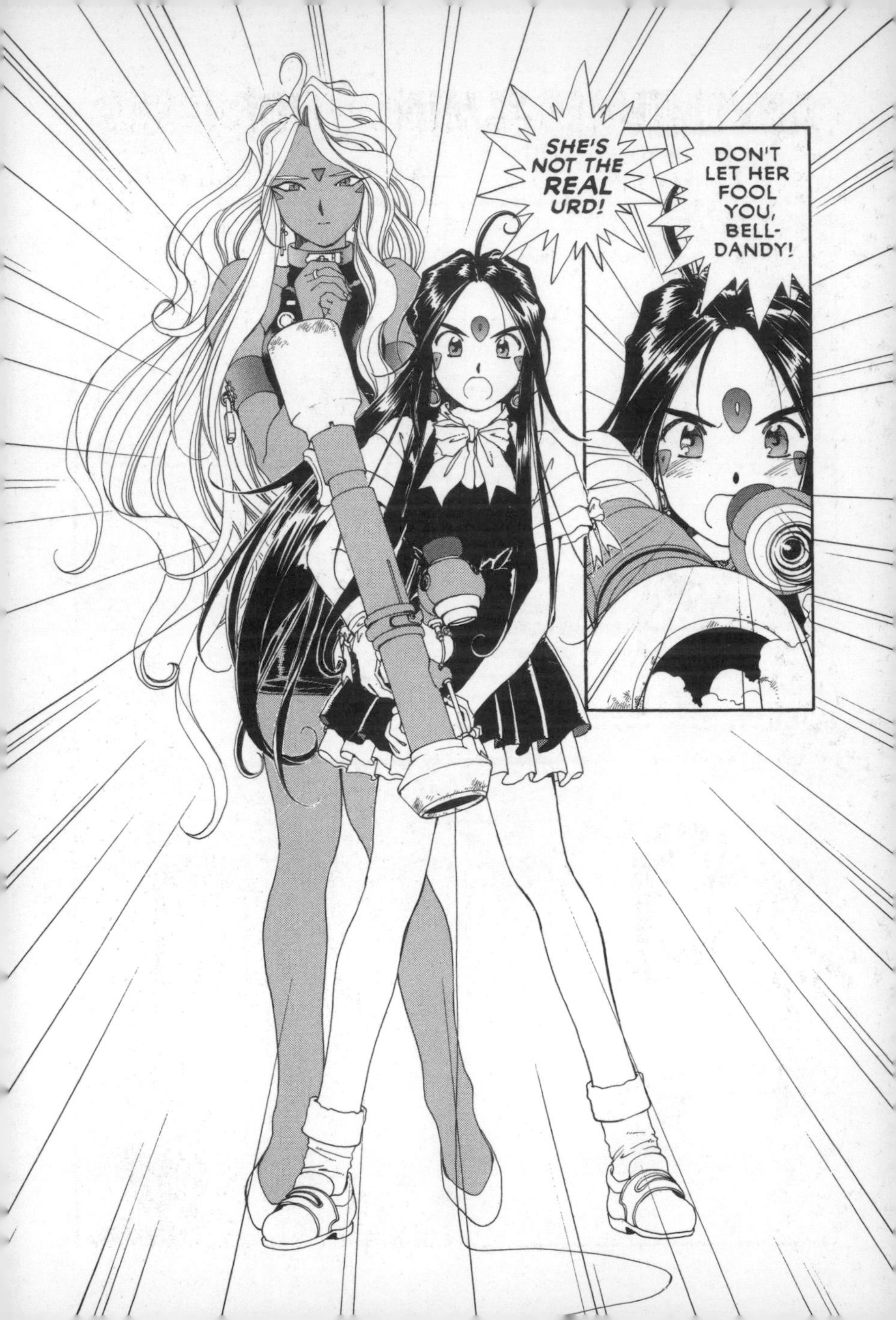
DON'T LET HER FOOL YOU, BELL-DANDY!
SHE'S NOT THE REAL URD!

ADVENTURES OF THE MINI-GODDESSES

◆ FLY FORTH, YOUNG SPIRIT! ◆

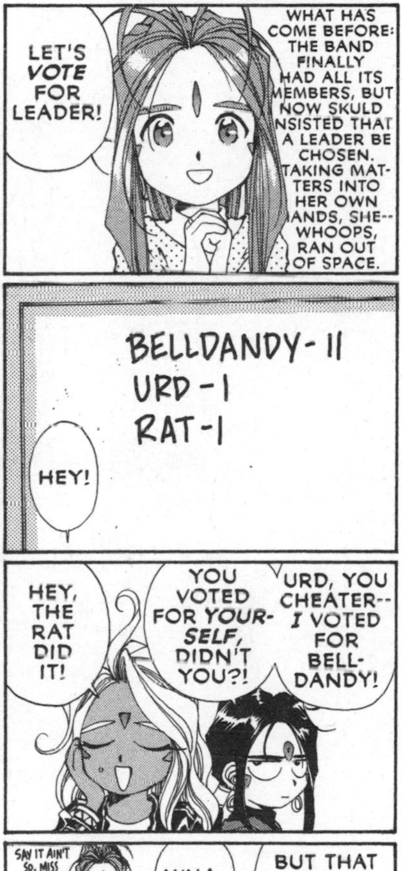
WHAT HAS COME BEFORE: THE BAND FINALLY HAD ALL ITS MEMBERS, BUT NOW SKULD INSISTED THAT A LEADER BE CHOSEN. TAKING MATTERS INTO HER OWN HANDS, SHE-- WHOOPS, RAN OUT OF SPACE.
LET'S *VOTE* FOR LEADER!
BELLDANDY - 11
URD - 1
RAT - 1
HEY!
URD, YOU CHEATER-- *I* VOTED FOR BELLDANDY!
YOU VOTED FOR *YOURSELF*, DIDN'T YOU?!
HEY, THE RAT DID IT!
BUT THAT MUST MEAN... *BELLDANDY* VOTED FOR HERSELF!
WHA--?!
SAY IT AIN'T SO, MISS BELLDANDY!

FLY FORTH, YOUNG SPIRIT!
◆ (REVISITED) ◆

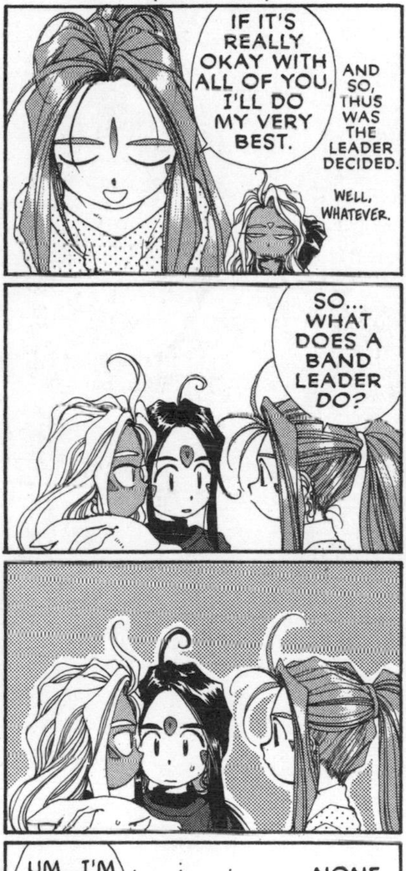
IF IT'S REALLY OKAY WITH ALL OF YOU, I'LL DO MY VERY BEST.
AND SO, THUS WAS THE LEADER DECIDED.
WELL, WHATEVER.
SO... WHAT DOES A BAND LEADER *DO?*
UM...I'M SURE IT'S NOT IMPORTANT!
NONE OF THEM REALLY HAD ANY IDEA.

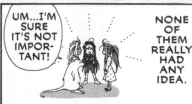

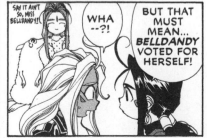

ADVENTURES OF THE MINI-GODDESSES

◆SO YOU WANT TO KNOW MY NAME?! THEN I'LL TELL YOU!◆

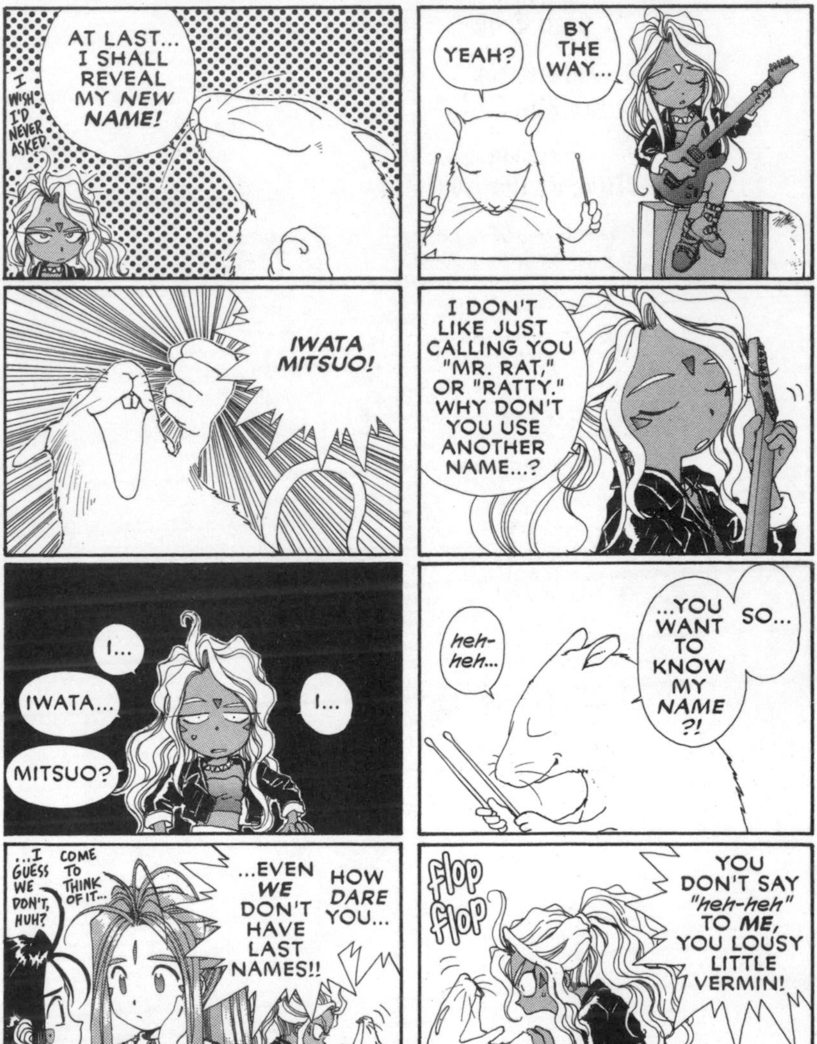

BY THE WAY...
YEAH?
I DON'T LIKE JUST CALLING YOU "MR. RAT," OR "RATTY." WHY DON'T YOU USE ANOTHER NAME...?
SO...
...YOU WANT TO KNOW MY NAME ?!
heh-heh...
YOU DON'T SAY "heh-heh" TO ME, YOU LOUSY LITTLE VERMIN!
flop flop
AT LAST... I SHALL REVEAL MY NEW NAME!
I WISH I'D NEVER ASKED.
IWATA MITSUO!
I...
I...
IWATA...
MITSUO?
HOW DARE YOU...
...EVEN WE DON'T HAVE LAST NAMES!!
COME TO THINK OF IT...
...I GUESS WE DON'T, HUH?

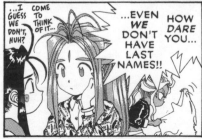

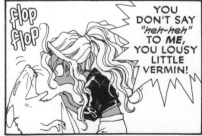

EDITOR
Carl Gustav Horn

DESIGNER
Scott Cook

ART DIRECTOR
Lia Ribacchi

PUBLISHER
Mike Richardson

English-language version
produced by Dark Horse Comics

OH MY GODDESS! Vol. 10
©2008 Kosuke Fujishima. All rights reserved. First published
in Japan in 1994 by Kodansha, Ltd., Tokyo. Publication rights for this
English edition arranged through Kodansha Ltd. All rights reserved. No
portion of this publication may be reproduced, in any form or by any
means, without the express written permission of the copyright holders.
Names, characters, places, and incidents featured in this publication are
either the product of the author's imagination or are used fictitiously. Any
resemblance to actual persons (living or dead), events, institutions, or
locales, without satiric intent, is coincidental. Dark Horse Manga™
is a trademark of Dark Horse Comics, Inc. All rights reserved.

Published by Dark Horse Manga
a division of Dark Horse Comics, Inc.
10956 SE Main Street
Milwaukie, OR 97222
www.darkhorse.com

To find a comics shop in your area,
call the Comic Shop Locator Service
toll-free at 1-888-266-4226

First edition: November 2008
ISBN 978-1-59582-190-4

1 3 5 7 9 10 8 6 4 2

Printed in Canada

letters to the
ENCHANTRESS

10956 SE Main Street, Milwaukie, Oregon 97222
omg@darkhorse.com • www.darkhorse.com

NOTE: Full addresses and e-mail addresses will not be printed, unless you ask! All fan artwork, letters, and e-mails submitted become the property of Dark Horse Comics.

We have two pieces of *Oh My Goddess!* fan art this time from Christina in Rio Linda, CA. I'm sorry I wasn't able to let you know we received it by e-mail, but it bounced. At least, I *think* I got the address right; it had a "Gaara" in it, which would have thrown me, except, fortunately, *OMG!* English-edition designer Scott Cook is a self-described Narutard. I remember the old days of ninja, the way they were in *Lone Wolf and Cub*, when they *didn't* want to be seen, and hence didn't dress like they were picking up trash by the side of the highway, with bright orange vests and safety reflectors on their foreheads. But our two different generations come together on *Gurren Lagann*, which we both think is great. FUN FACT: The producer of the English dub seen on the Sci-Fi Channel is also the translator of Dark Horse's *The Kurosagi Corpse Delivery Service!*

—CGH

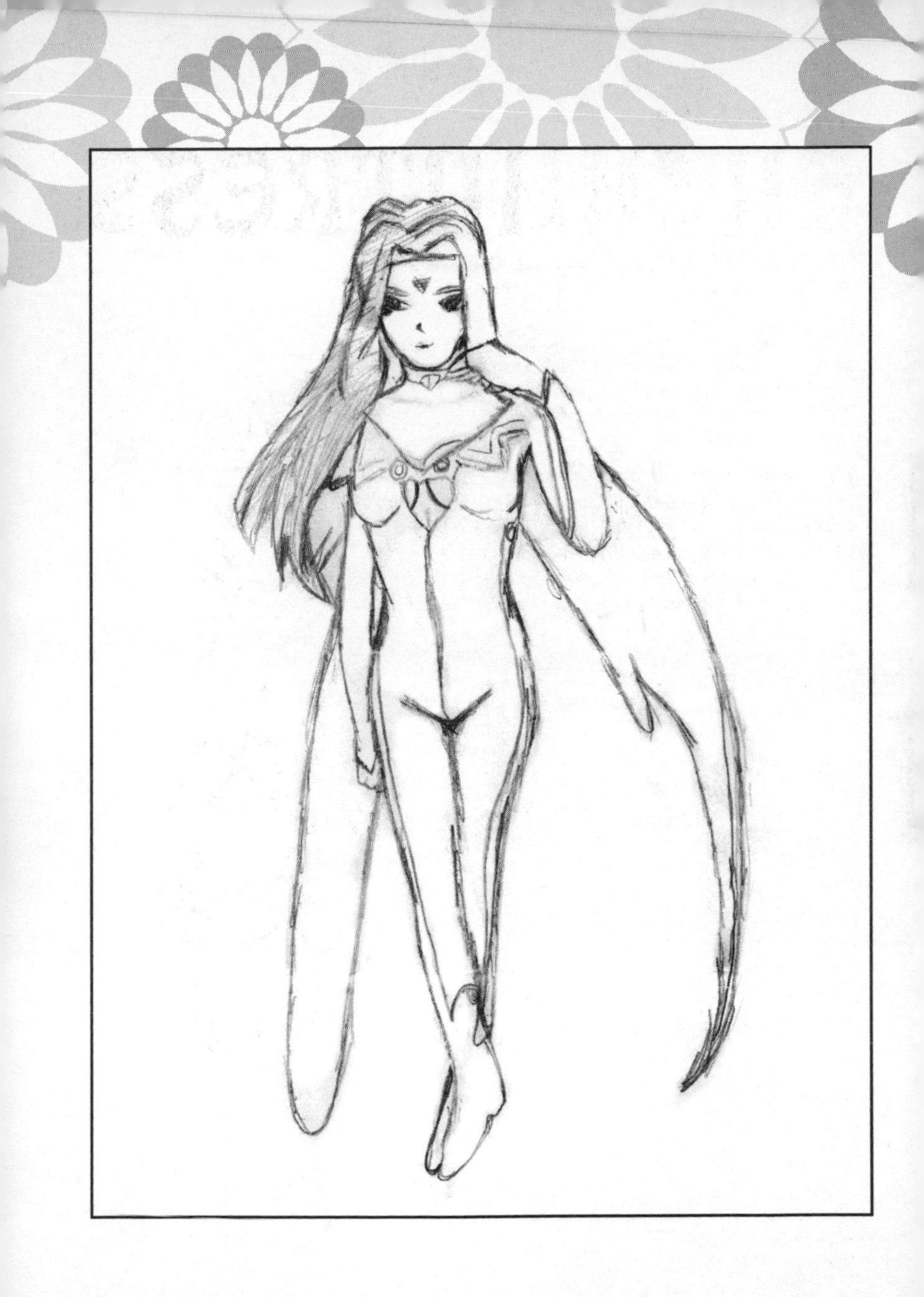

Creator Kosuke Fujishima in 1994!

His message to fans in the original Japanese *Oh My Goddess!* Vol. 10:

Dear Sir or Madam,

Hello, everyone, how are you? It's me, Fujishima. Last time, I spoke pretentiously about how I'd show you my personal helicopter, but unfortunately my chopper's in the shop right now. So instead, I'd like to introduce you to my mecha: River Horse II. Its gearhead exterior is certain to pique the interest of manly men, whereas its psychedelic color scheme is reminiscent of what future mecha will look like. It's a time paradox. It's also a killing machine*. I know you're probably thinking at this point, "whatever." But I'm telling you, whenever I drive it, I have to hold on tight.

Sincerely yours.

A reference to the Deep Purple song Urd mangles on page 112. In fact, the Japanese version of the lyrics **does say "atsui (hot) machine" rather than "killing machine."—ed.*

AN ALL-NEW NOVEL BASED ON THE HIT MANGA AND ANIME!

OH MY GODDESS!
— F I R S T   E N D —

WRITTEN BY
YUMI TOHMA

WITH ILLUSTRATIONS BY
KOSUKE FUJISHIMA and HIDENORI MATSUBARA

Keiichi Morisato was a typical college student—a failure with women, he was struggling to get through his classes and in general living a pretty nondescript life. That is, until he dialed a wrong number and accidentally summoned the goddess Belldandy. Not believing Belldandy was a goddess and that she could grant his every wish, Keiichi wished for her to stay with him forever. As they say, be careful what you wish for! Now bound to Earth and at Keiichi's side for life, the lives of this goddess and human will never be the same again!

ISBN 978-1-59582-137-9 | $14.95

DARK HORSE BOOKS

darkhorse.com

AVAILABLE AT YOUR LOCAL COMICS SHOP OR BOOKSTORE
To find a comics shop in your area, call 1.888.266.4226. For more information or to order direct: •On the web: darkhorse.com •E-mail: mailorder@darkhorse.com •Phone: 1.800.862.0052 Mon.–Fri. 9 AM to 5 PM Pacific Time.

Oh My Goddess!: First End © 2006, 2007 Yumi Tohma/Kosuke Fujishima. All rights reserved. First published in Japan in 2006 by Kodansha Ltd., Tokyo. Publication for this English edition arranged through Kodansha Ltd. Dark Horse Books® and the Dark Horse logo are registered trademarks of Dark Horse Comics, Inc. All rights reserved. (BL7056)

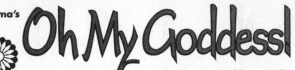

Kosuke Fujishima's

Oh My Goddess!

Can't wait on the Goddesses? Change directions!

Just gotten into the new unflopped editions of *Oh My Goddess!*, and found you can't wait to see what happens next? Have no fear! The first **20 volumes** of *Oh My Goddess!* are available ***right now*** in Western-style editions! Released between 1994 and 2005, our *OMG!* Western-style volumes feature premium paper, and pages 40% larger than those of the unflopped editions! If you've already got some of the unflopped volumes and want to know which Western-style ones to get to catch up, check out http://www.darkhorse.com/Zones/Manga for a complete breakdown of how the editions compare!

Vol. 1: Wrong Number
ISBN 1-56971-669-2 / $13.95

Vol. 2: Leader of the Pack
ISBN 1-56971-764-8 / $13.95

Vol. 3: Final Exam
ISBN 1-56971-765-6 / $13.95

Vol. 4: Love Potion No. 9
ISBN 1-56971-252-2 / $14.95

Vol. 5: Sympathy for the Devil
ISBN 1-56971-329-4 / $13.95

Vol. 6: Terrible Master Urd
ISBN 1-56971-369-3 / $14.95

Vol. 7: The Queen of Vengeance
ISBN 1-56971-431-2 / $13.95

Vol. 8: Mara Strikes Back!
ISBN 1-56971-449-5 / $14.95

Vol. 9: Ninja Master
ISBN 1-56971-474-6 / $13.95

Vol. 10: Miss Keiichi
ISBN 1-56971-522-X / $16.95

Vol. 11: The Devil in Miss Urd
ISBN 1-56971-540-8 / $14.95

Vol. 12: The Fourth Goddess
ISBN 1-56971-551-3 / $18.95

Vol. 13: Childhood's End
ISBN 1-56971-685-4/ $15.95

Vol. 14: Queen Sayoko
ISBN 1-56971-766-4 / $16.95

Vol. 15: Hand in Hand
ISBN 1-56971-921-7 / $17.95

Vol. 16: Mystery Child
ISBN 1-56971-950-0 / $18.95

Vol. 17: Traveler
ISBN 1-56971-986-1 / $17.95

Vol. 18: The Phantom Racer
ISBN 1-59307-217-1 / $17.95

Vol. 19/20: Sora Unchained
ISBN 1-59307-316-X / $18.95

Adventures of the Mini-Goddesses
ISBN 1-56971-421-5 / $9.95

AVAILABLE AT YOUR LOCAL COMICS SHOP OR BOOKSTORE
*To find a comics shop in your area, call 1-888-266-4226

For more information or to order direct:
•On the web: darkhorse.com
•E-mail: mailorder@darkhorse.com
•Phone: 1-800-862-0052 Mon.-Fri. 9 A.M. to 5 P.M. Pacific Time.

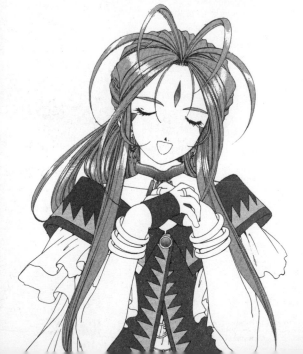

DARK HORSE MANGA

【トランスルーセント】
translucent

Can you see right through her?

By Kazuhiro Okamoto

Shizuka is an introverted girl dealing with schoolwork, boys, and a medical condition that has begun to turn her invisible! She finds support with Mamoru, a boy who is falling for Shizuka despite her condition, and with Keiko, a woman who suffers from the same illness and has finally turned *completely* invisible! *Translucent's* exploration of what people see, what people think they see, and what people wish to see in themselves, and others, makes for an emotionally sensitive manga peppered with moments of surprising humor, heartbreak, and drama.

VOLUME 1
ISBN 978-1-59307-647-4

VOLUME 2
ISBN 978-1-59307-677-1

VOLUME 3
ISBN 978-1-59307-679-5

VOLUME 4
ISBN 978-1-59582-218-5

$9.95 Each!

Previews for *TRANSLUCENT* and other DARK HORSE MANGA titles can be found at darkhorse.com!

DARK HORSE MANGA

REVISED EDITIONS!

Kenichi Sonoda's original *Gunsmith Cats* stories are back, revised and repackaged as deluxe omnibus editions!

Rally Vincent and Minnie-May Hopkins are experts in their respective fields of marksmanship and explosives, but they're so cute you'd never know! Neither would the perps unlucky enough to be hunted by these two bounty-hunting girls on the dangerous streets of Chicago.

Presented for the first time in their authentic Japanese format, these giant-sized volumes are action-packed, unretouched, unflopped, and sure to please.

VOLUME 1
ISBN 978-1-59307-748-8

VOLUME 2
ISBN 978-1-59307-768-6

VOLUME 3
ISBN 978-1-59307-818-8

VOLUME 4
ISBN 978-1-59307-862-1

$16.95 each!

AVAILABLE AT YOUR LOCAL COMICS SHOP OR BOOKSTORE!

To find a comics shop in your area, call 1-888-266-4226. For more information or to order direct visit darkhorse.com or call 1-800-862-0052 Mon.–Fri. 9 AM to 5 PM Pacific Time. *Prices and availability subject to change without notice.

DARK HORSE MANGA